ULTIMATE SPIDER-MAN

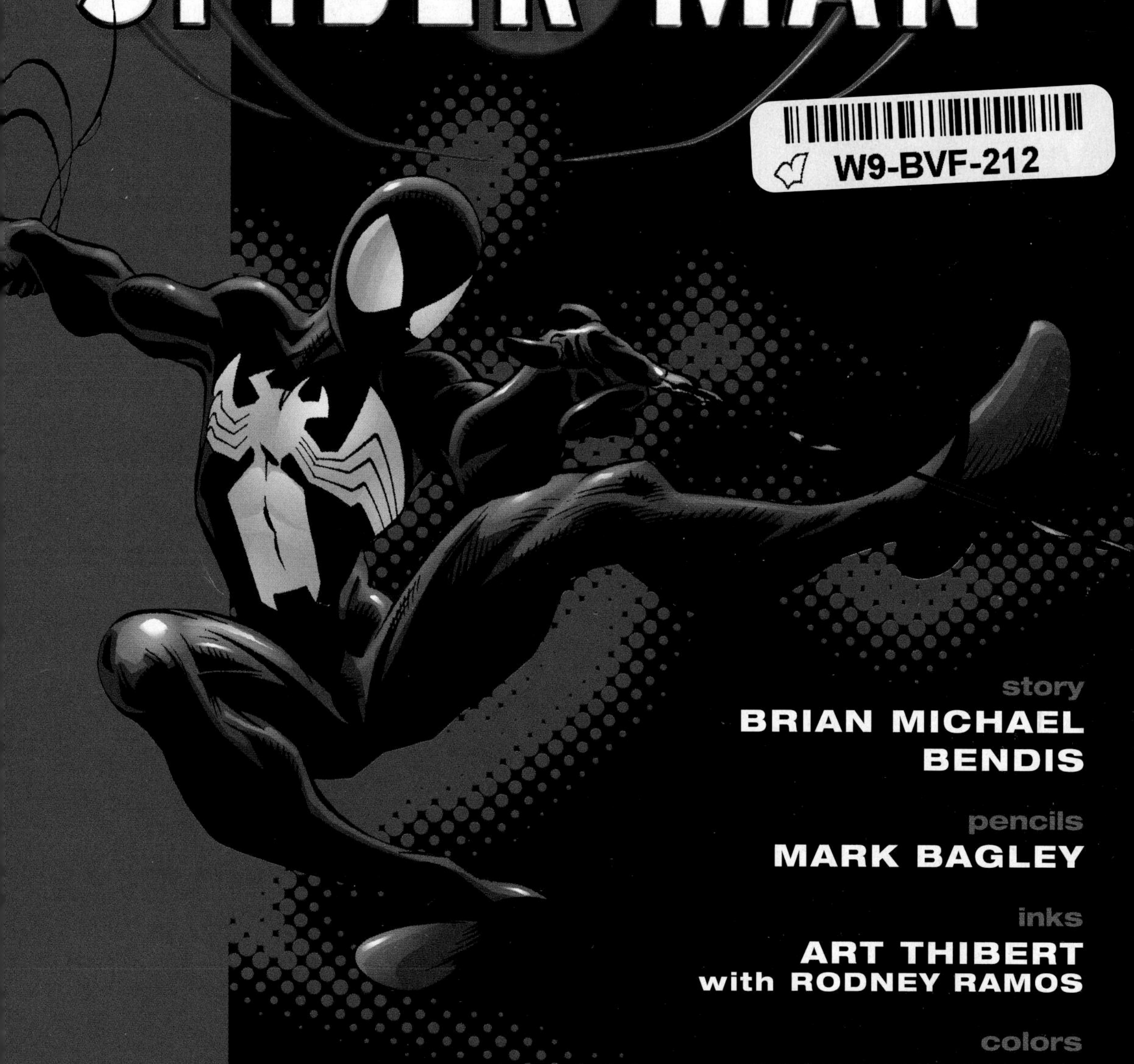

story
BRIAN MICHAEL BENDIS

pencils
MARK BAGLEY

inks
ART THIBERT
with RODNEY RAMOS

colors
TRANSPARENCY DIGITAL

letters
CHRIS ELIOPOULOS

VENOM

VENOM

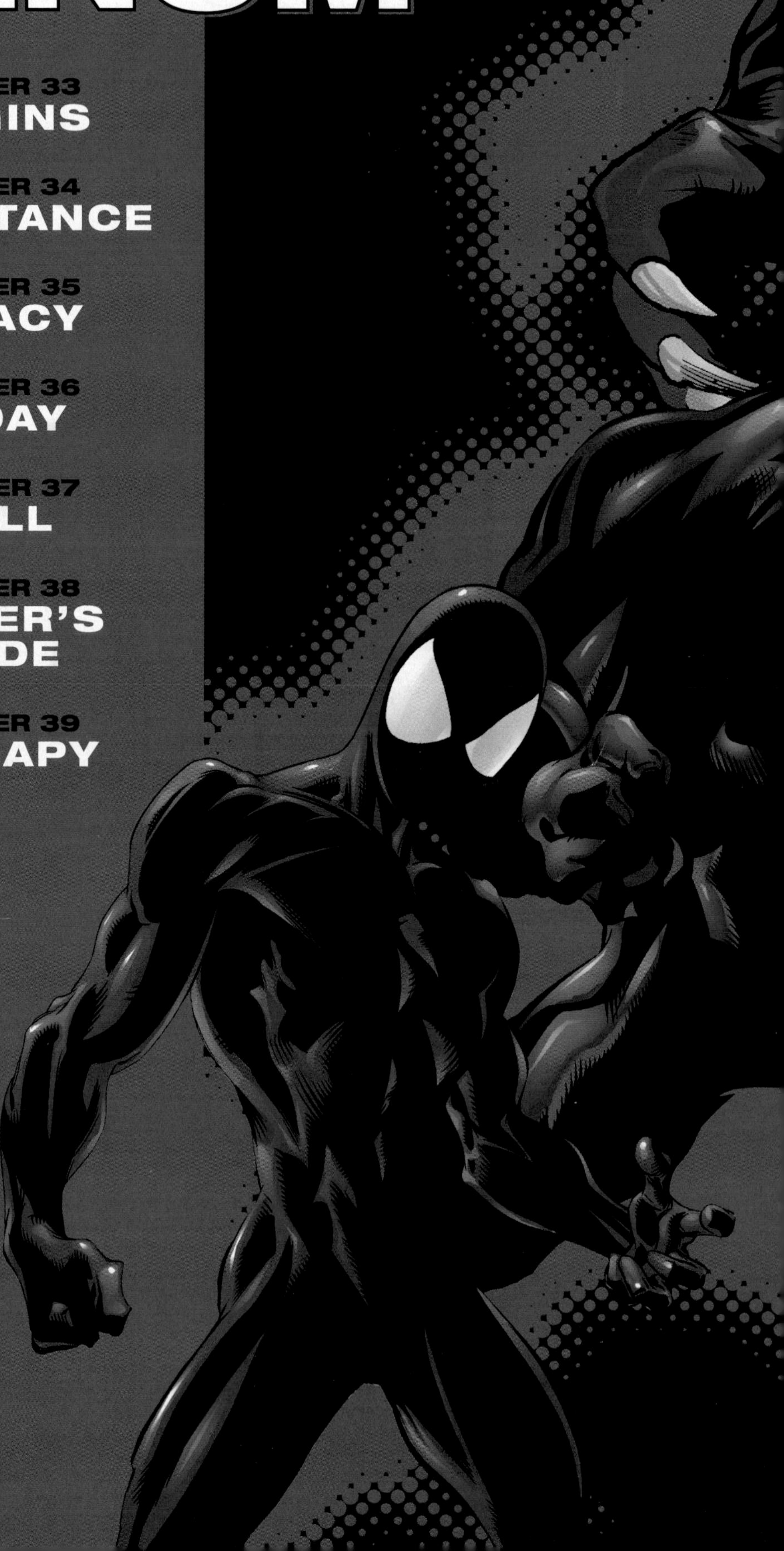

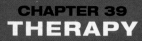

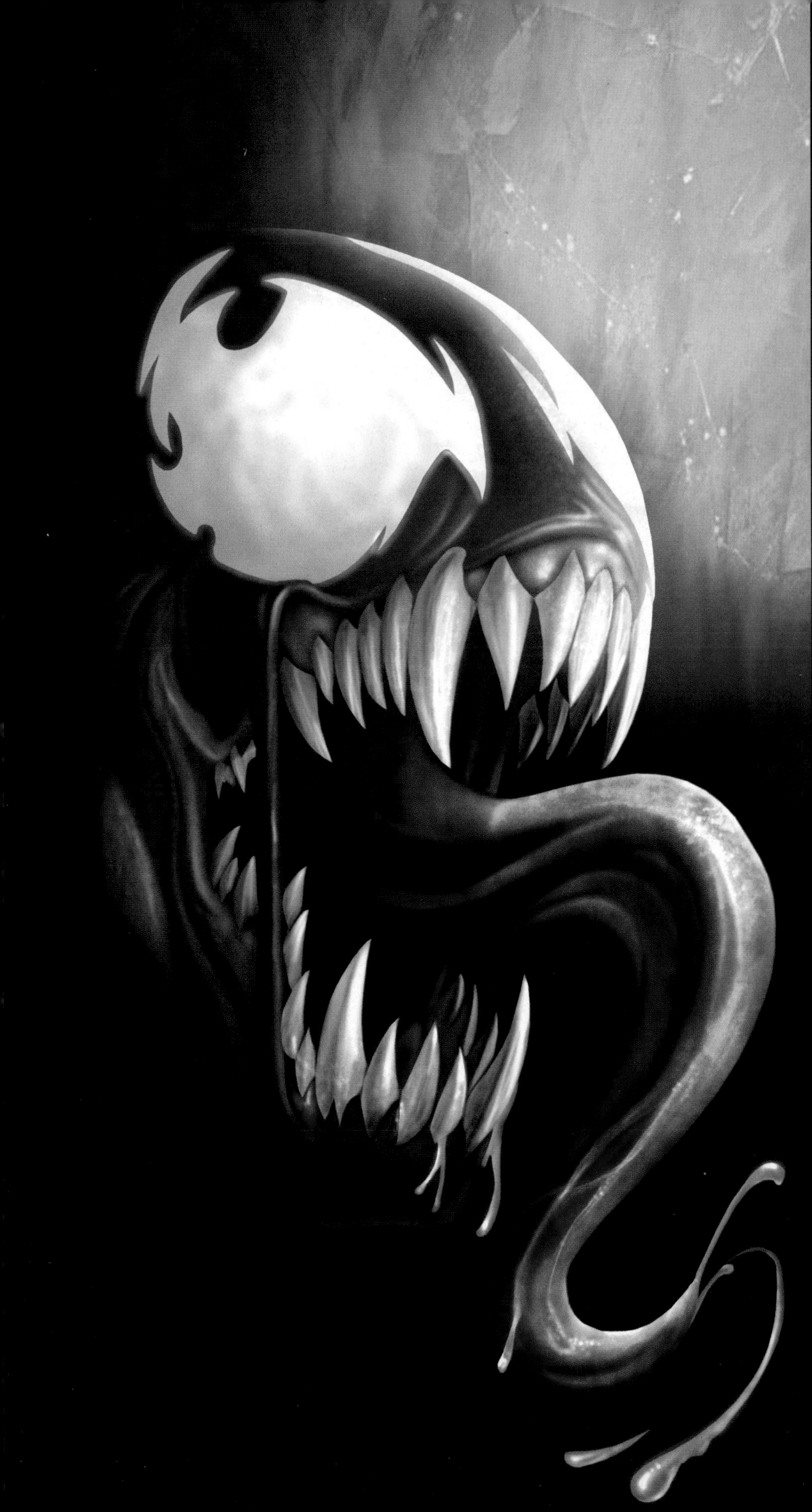

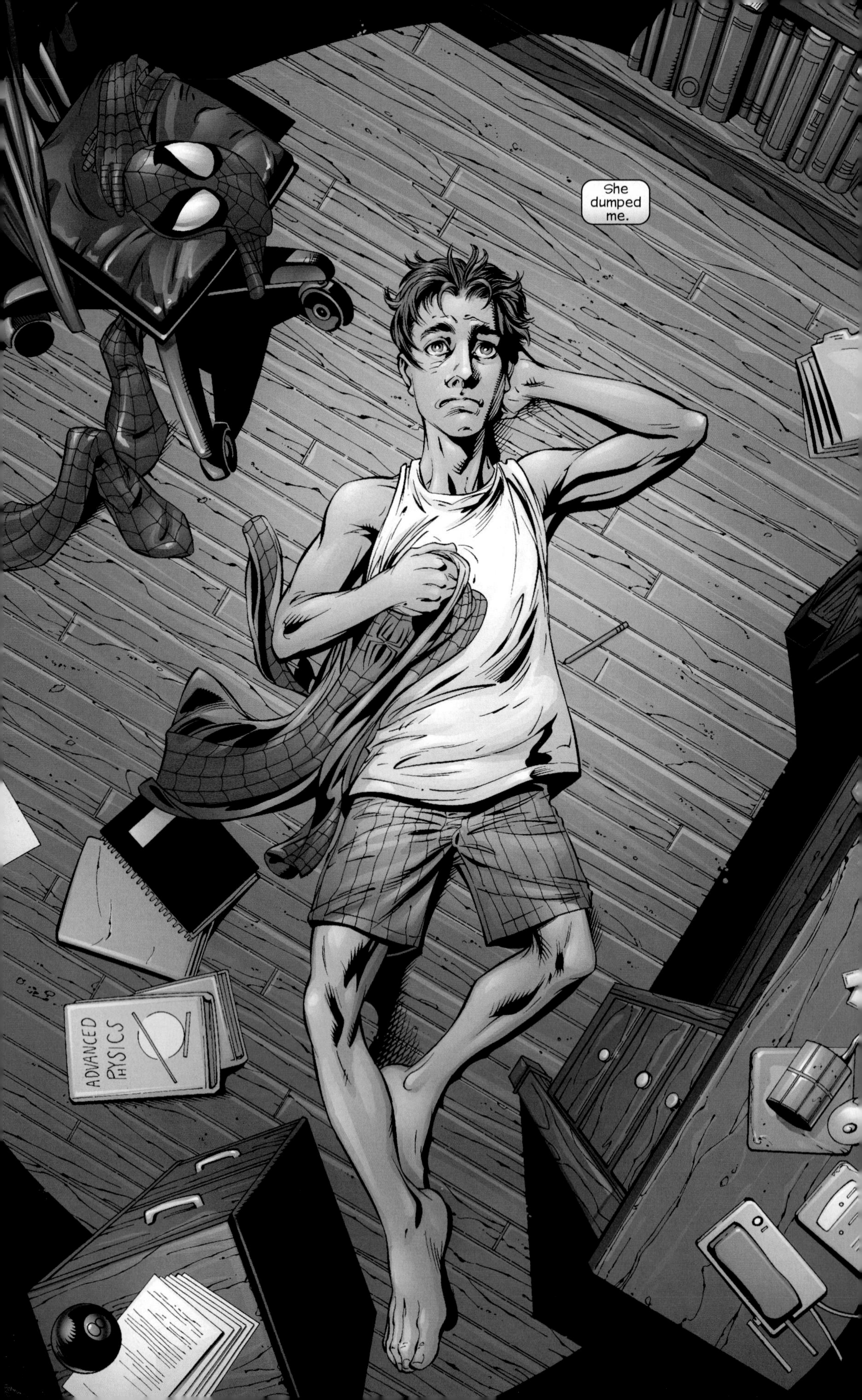

She dumped me.
ADVANCED

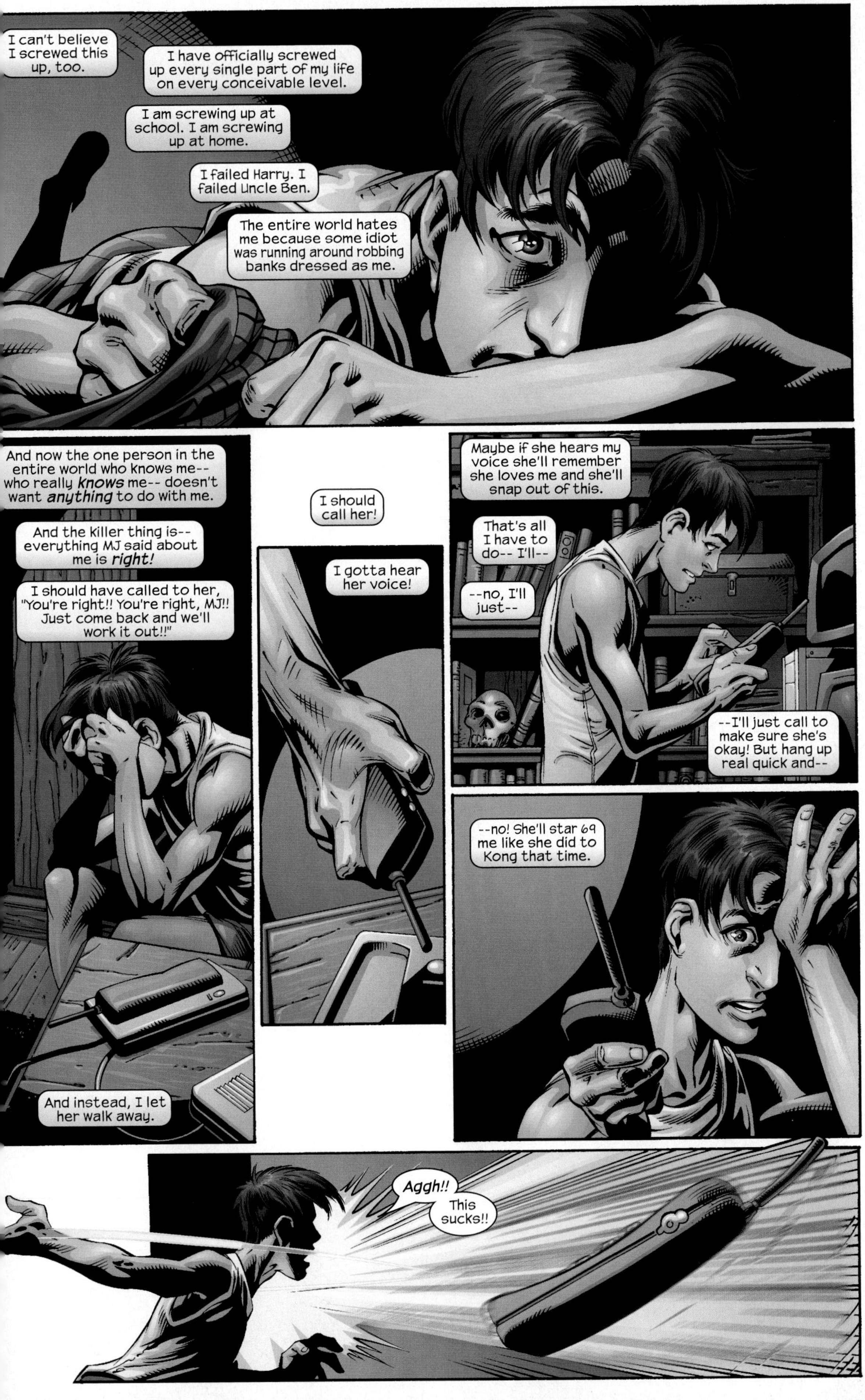
I can't believe I screwed this up, too.
I have officially screwed up every single part of my life on every conceivable level.
I am screwing up at school. I am screwing up at home.
I failed Harry. I failed Uncle Ben.
The entire world hates me because some idiot was running around robbing banks dressed as me.
And now the one person in the entire world who knows me-- who really *knows* me-- doesn't want *anything* to do with me.
And the killer thing is-- everything MJ said about me is *right!*
I should have called to her, "You're right!! You're right, MJ!! Just come back and we'll work it out!!"
And instead, I let her walk away.
I should call her!
I gotta hear her voice!
Maybe if she hears my voice she'll remember she loves me and she'll snap out of this.
That's all I have to do-- I'll--
--no, I'll just--
--I'll just call to make sure she's okay! But hang up real quick and--
--no! She'll star 69 me like she did to Kong that time.
Aggh!!
This sucks!!

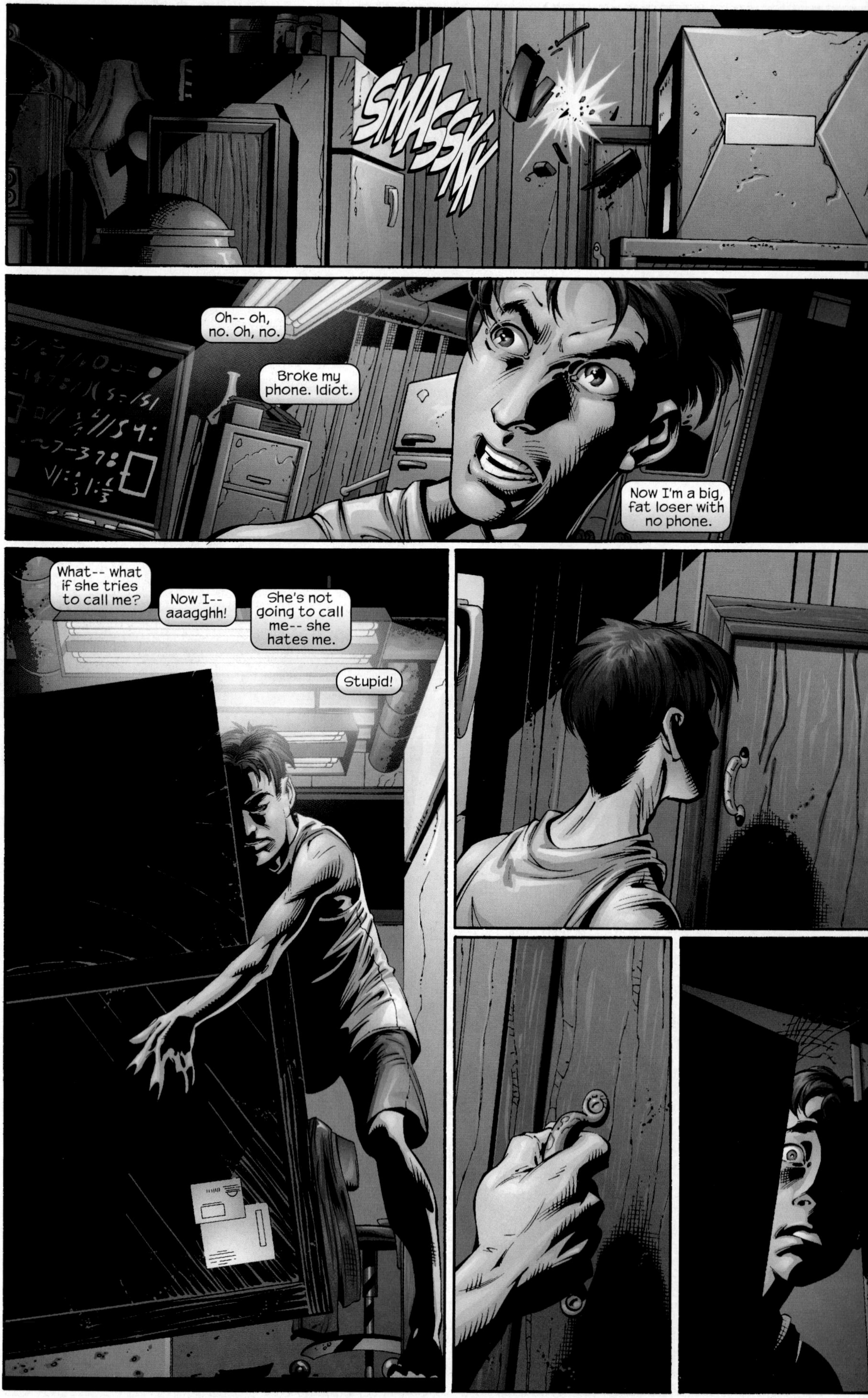
SMASSKK
Oh-- oh, no. Oh, no.
Broke my phone. Idiot.
Now I'm a big, fat loser with no phone.
What-- what if she tries to call me?
Now I-- aaagghh!
She's not going to call me-- she hates me.
Stupid!

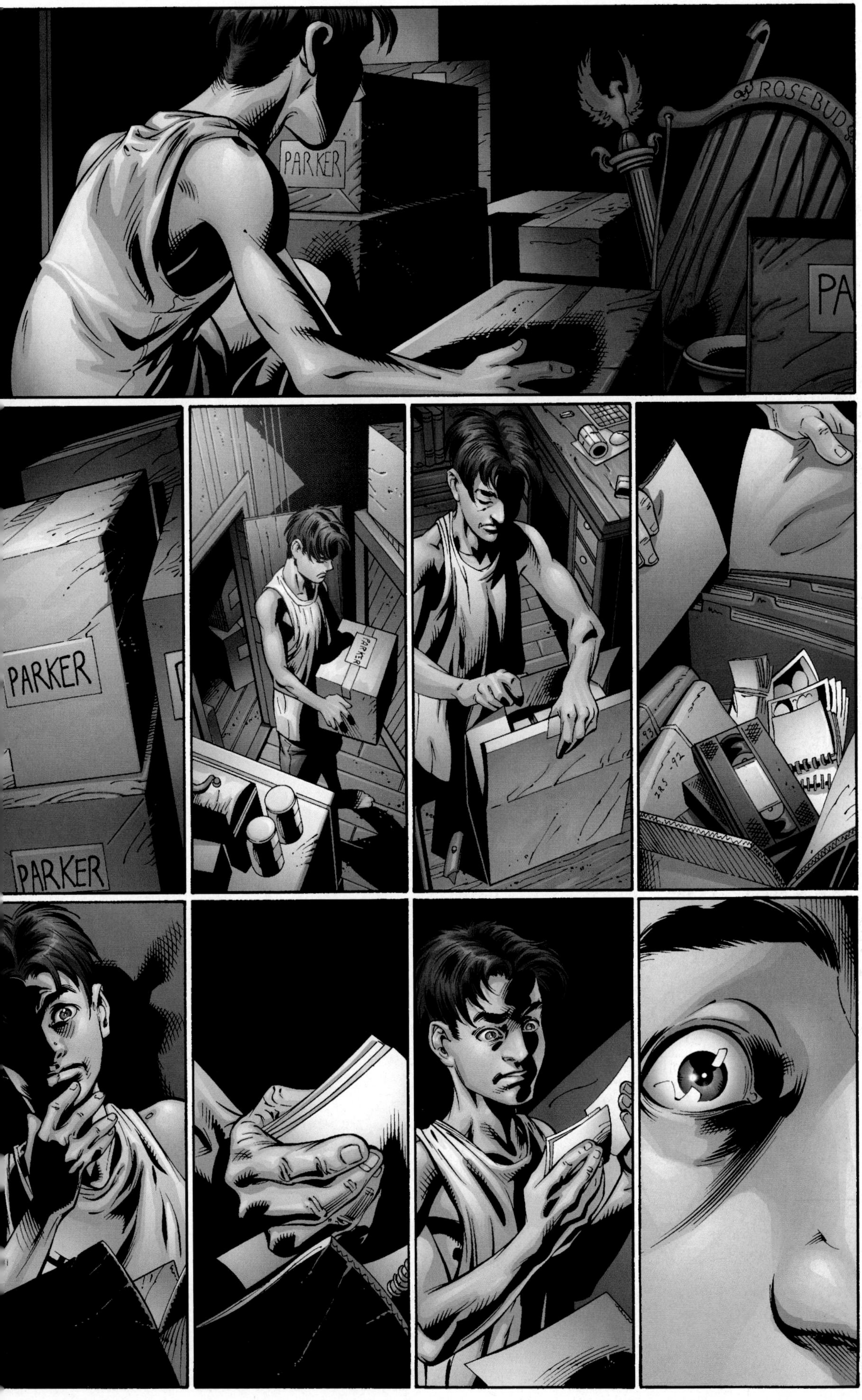
ROSEBUD
PARKER
PA
PARKER
PARKER
PARKER
PARKER

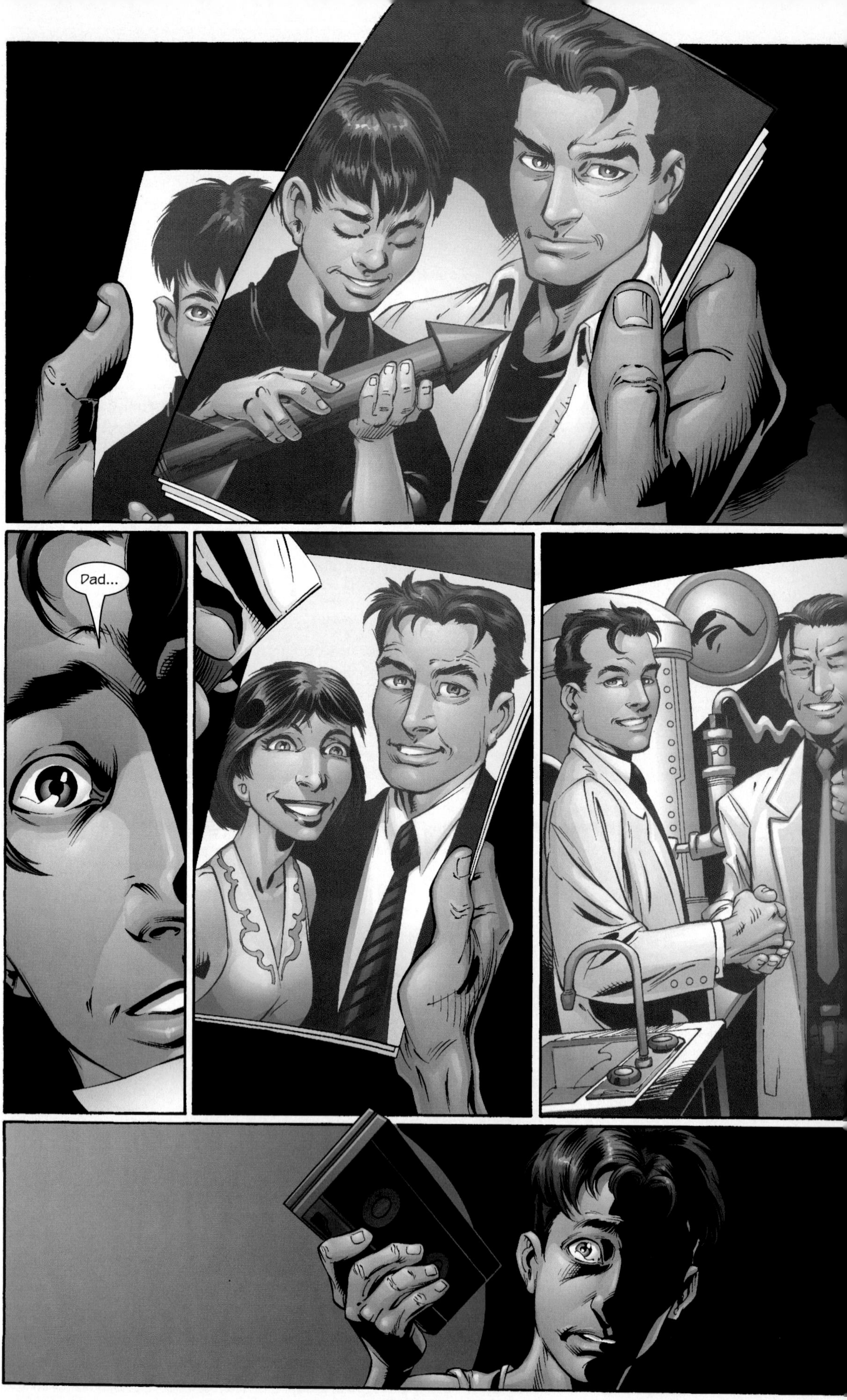
Dad...

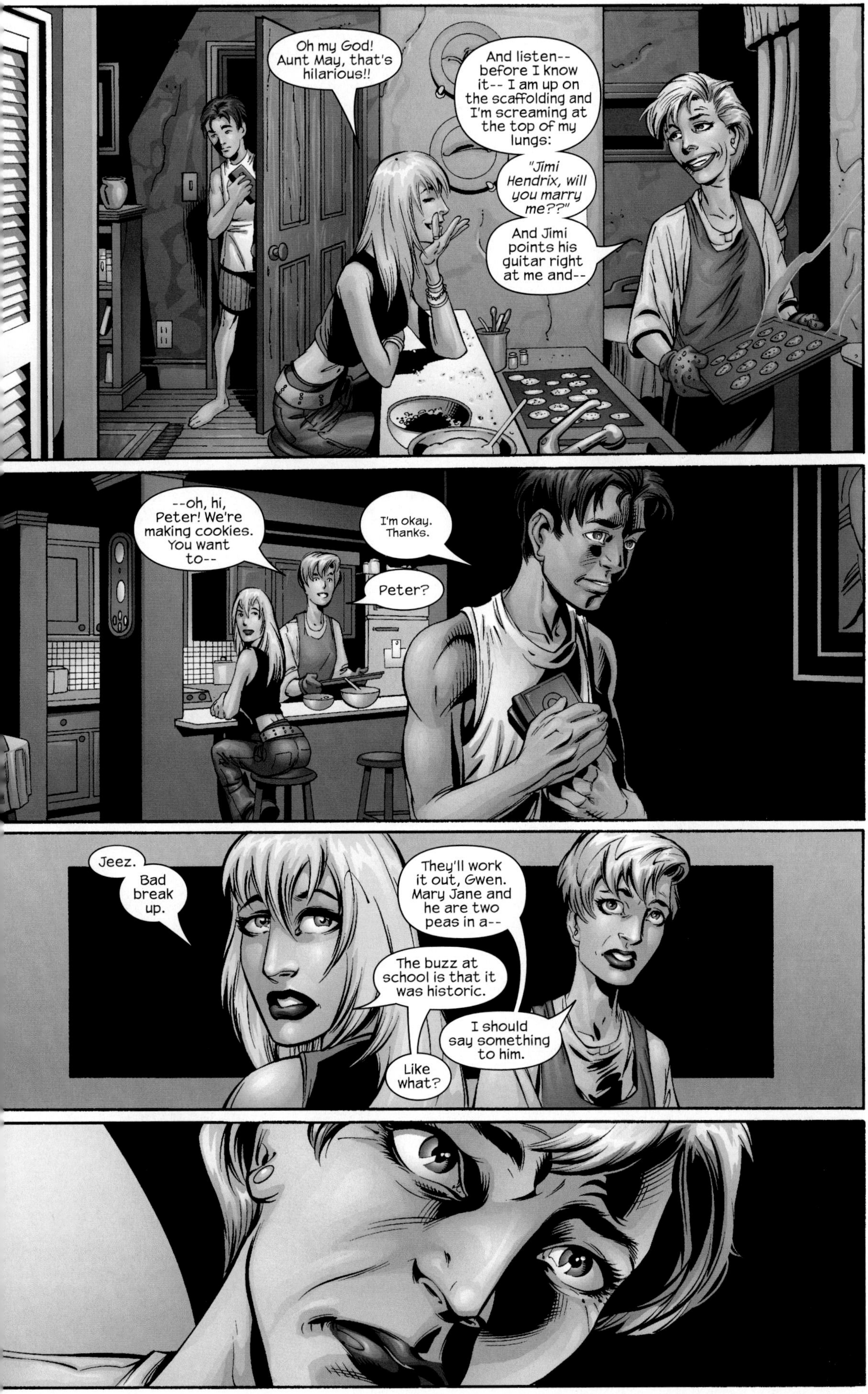
Oh my God! Aunt May, that's hilarious!!
And listen-- before I know it-- I am up on the scaffolding and I'm screaming at the top of my lungs:
"Jimi Hendrix, will you marry me??"
And Jimi points his guitar right at me and--
--oh, hi, Peter! We're making cookies. You want to--
I'm okay. Thanks.
Peter?
Jeez. Bad break up.
They'll work it out, Gwen. Mary Jane and he are two peas in a--
The buzz at school is that it was historic.
I should say something to him.
Like what?

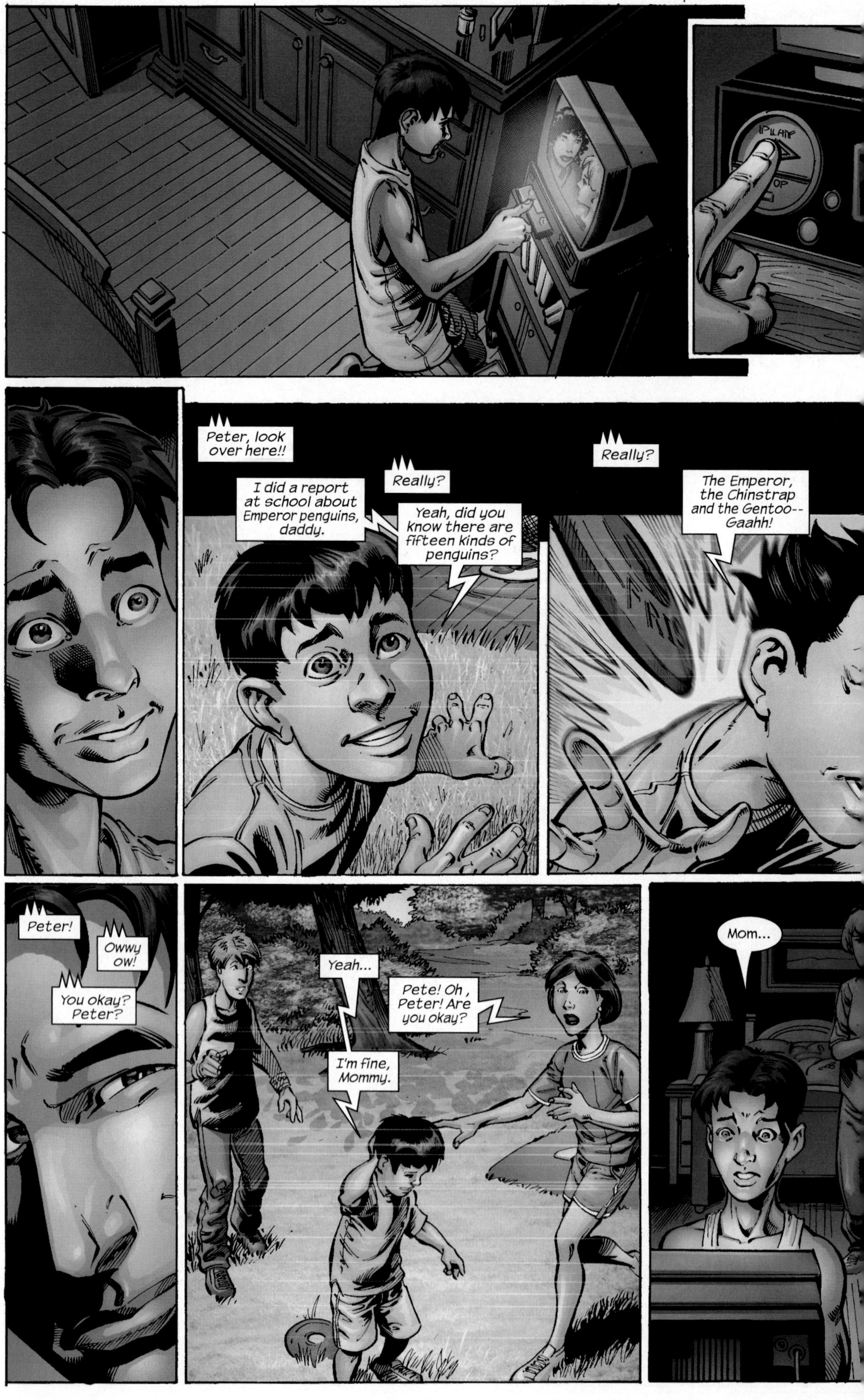

PLAY
Peter, look over here!!
I did a report at school about Emperor penguins, daddy.
Really?
Yeah, did you know there are fifteen kinds of penguins?
Really?
The Emperor, the Chinstrap and the Gentoo-- Gaahh!
Peter!
Owwy ow!
You okay? Peter?
Yeah...
Pete! Oh, Peter! Are you okay?
I'm fine, Mommy.
Mom...

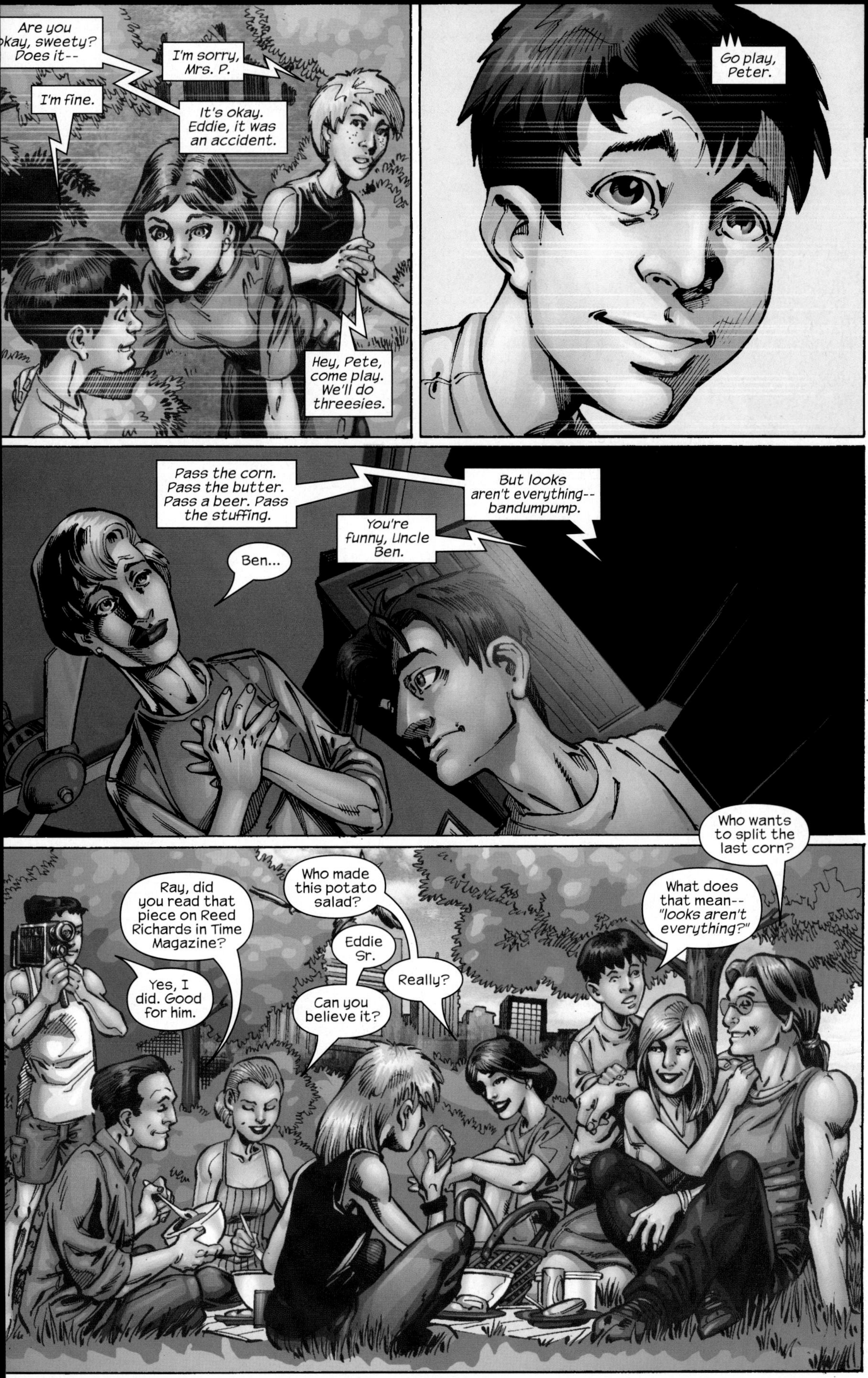
Are you okay, sweety? Does it--
I'm sorry, Mrs. P.
I'm fine.
It's okay. Eddie, it was an accident.
Hey, Pete, come play. We'll do threesies.
Go play, Peter.
Pass the corn. Pass the butter. Pass a beer. Pass the stuffing.
But looks aren't everything-- bandumpump.
You're funny, Uncle Ben.
Ben...
Ray, did you read that piece on Reed Richards in Time Magazine?
Yes, I did. Good for him.
Who made this potato salad?
Eddie Sr.
Really?
Can you believe it?
Who wants to split the last corn?
What does that mean-- "looks aren't everything?"

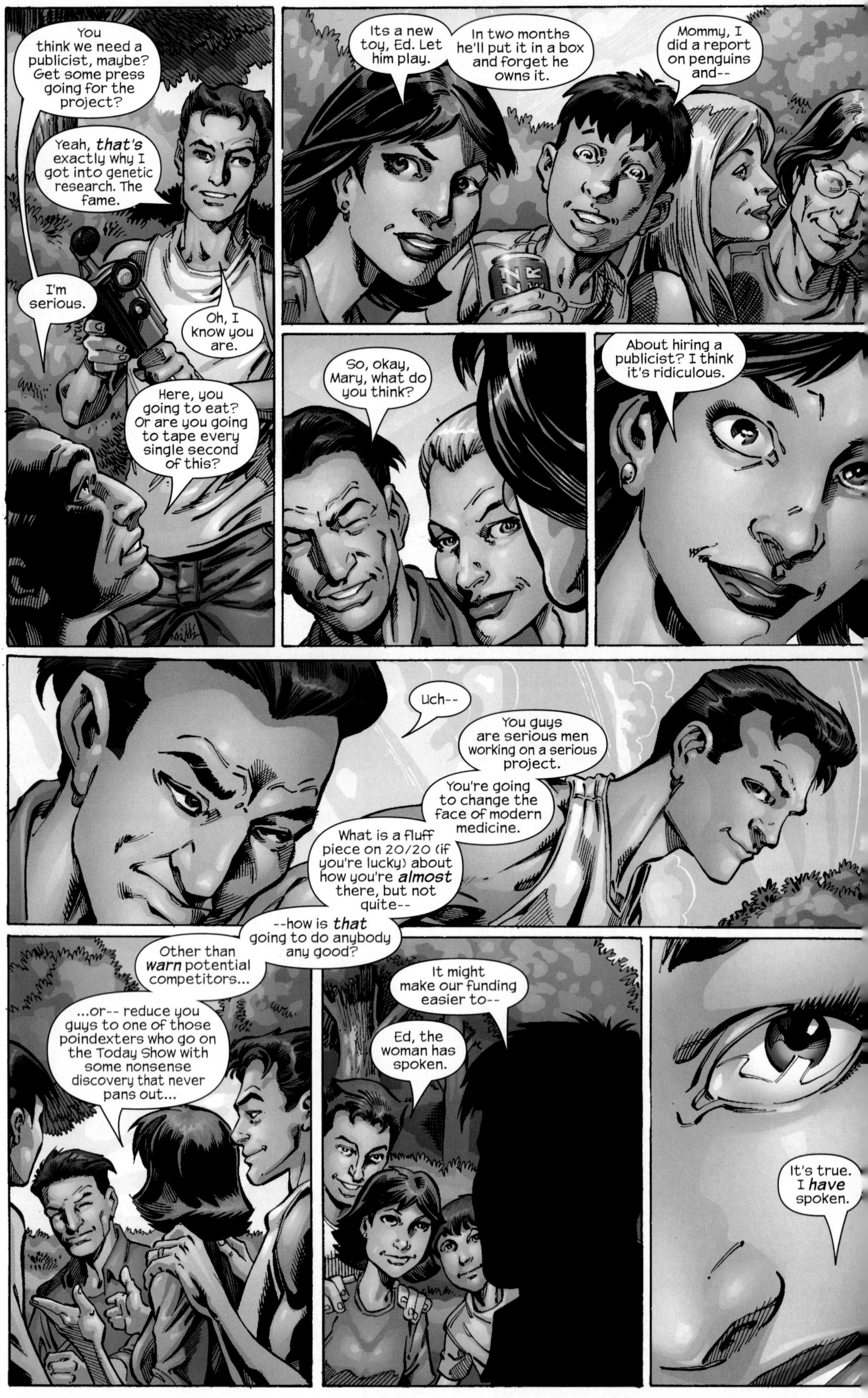
You think we need a publicist, maybe? Get some press going for the project?
Yeah, *that's* exactly why I got into genetic research. The fame.
I'm serious.
Oh, I know you are.
Here, you going to eat? Or are you going to tape every single second of this?
Its a new toy, Ed. Let him play.
In two months he'll put it in a box and forget he owns it.
Mommy, I did a report on penguins and--
So, okay, Mary, what do you think?
About hiring a publicist? I think it's ridiculous.
Uch--
You guys are serious men working on a serious project.
You're going to change the face of modern medicine.
What is a fluff piece on 20/20 (if you're lucky) about how you're *almost* there, but not quite--
--how is *that* going to do anybody any good?
Other than *warn* potential competitors...
...or-- reduce you guys to one of those poindexters who go on the Today Show with some nonsense discovery that never pans out...
It might make our funding easier to--
Ed, the woman has spoken.
It's true. I *have* spoken.

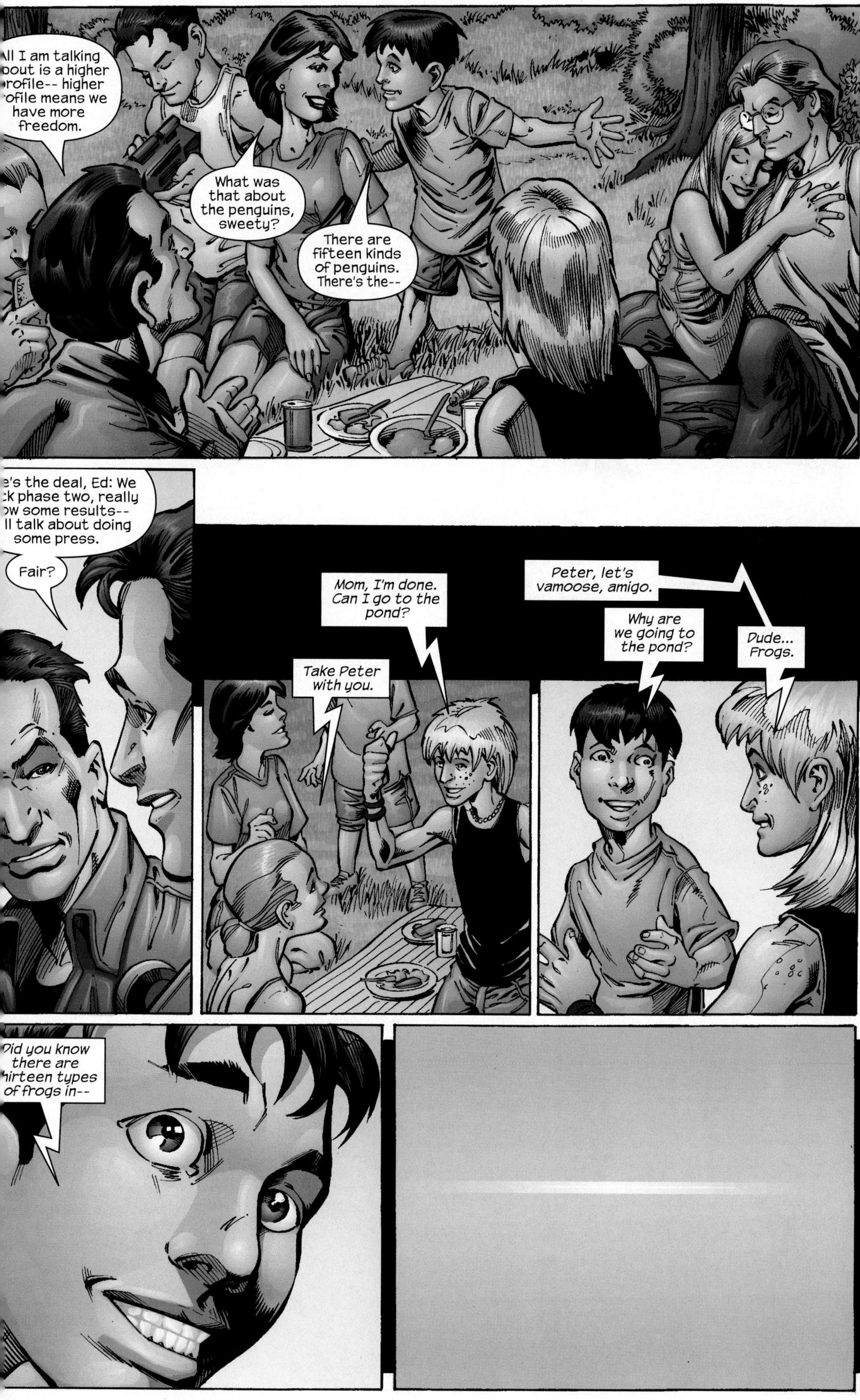
ll I am talking bout is a higher rofile-- higher rofile means we have more freedom.
What was that about the penguins, sweety?
There are fifteen kinds of penguins. There's the--
e's the deal, Ed: We ck phase two, really ow some results-- ll talk about doing some press.
Fair?
Mom, I'm done. Can I go to the pond?
Take Peter with you.
Peter, let's vamoose, amigo.
Why are we going to the pond?
Dude... Frogs.
id you know there are hirteen types of frogs in--

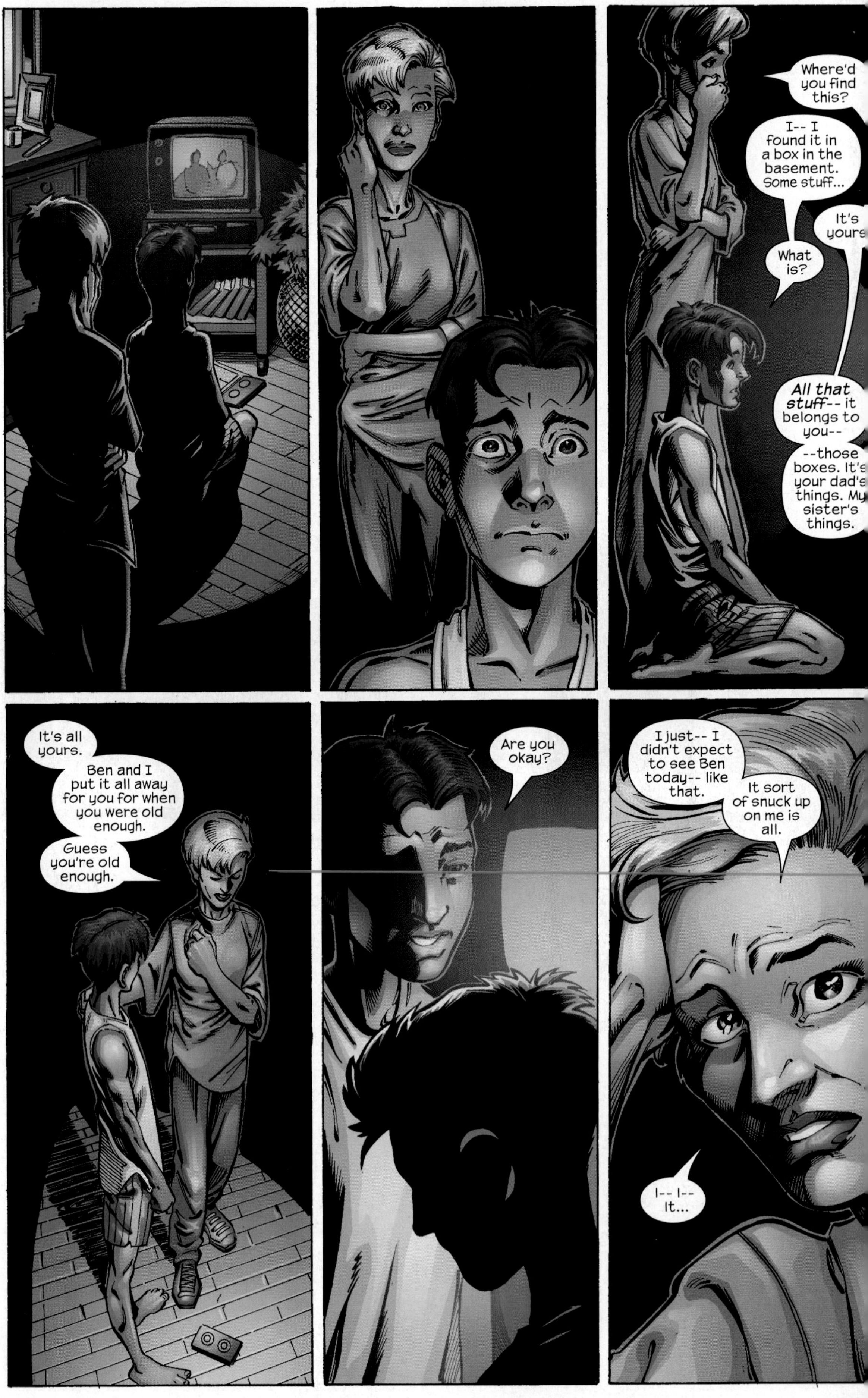
Where'd you find this?
I-- I found it in a box in the basement. Some stuff...
What is?
It's yours
All that stuff-- it belongs to you--
--those boxes. It's your dad's things. My sister's things.
It's all yours.
Ben and I put it all away for you for when you were old enough.
Guess you're old enough.
Are you okay?
I just-- I didn't expect to see Ben today-- like that.
It sort of snuck up on me is all.
I-- I-- It...

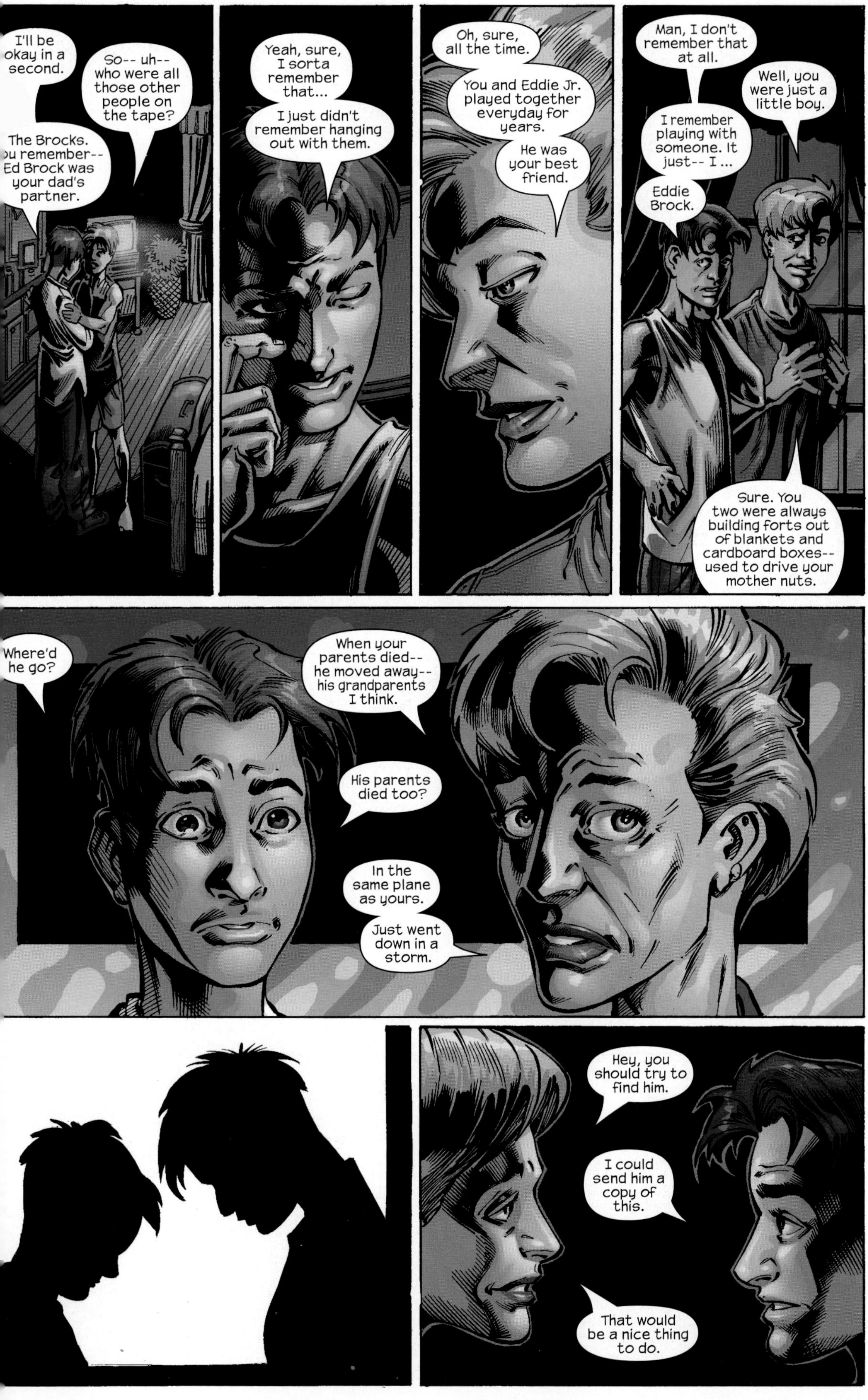
I'll be okay in a second.
So-- uh-- who were all those other people on the tape?
The Brocks. ...u remember-- Ed Brock was your dad's partner.
Yeah, sure, I sorta remember that...
I just didn't remember hanging out with them.
Oh, sure, all the time.
You and Eddie Jr. played together everyday for years.
He was your best friend.
Man, I don't remember that at all.
I remember playing with someone. It just-- I ...
Eddie Brock.
Well, you were just a little boy.
Sure. You two were always building forts out of blankets and cardboard boxes-- used to drive your mother nuts.
Where'd he go?
When your parents died-- he moved away-- his grandparents I think.
His parents died too?
In the same plane as yours.
Just went down in a storm.
Hey, you should try to find him.
I could send him a copy of this.
That would be a nice thing to do.

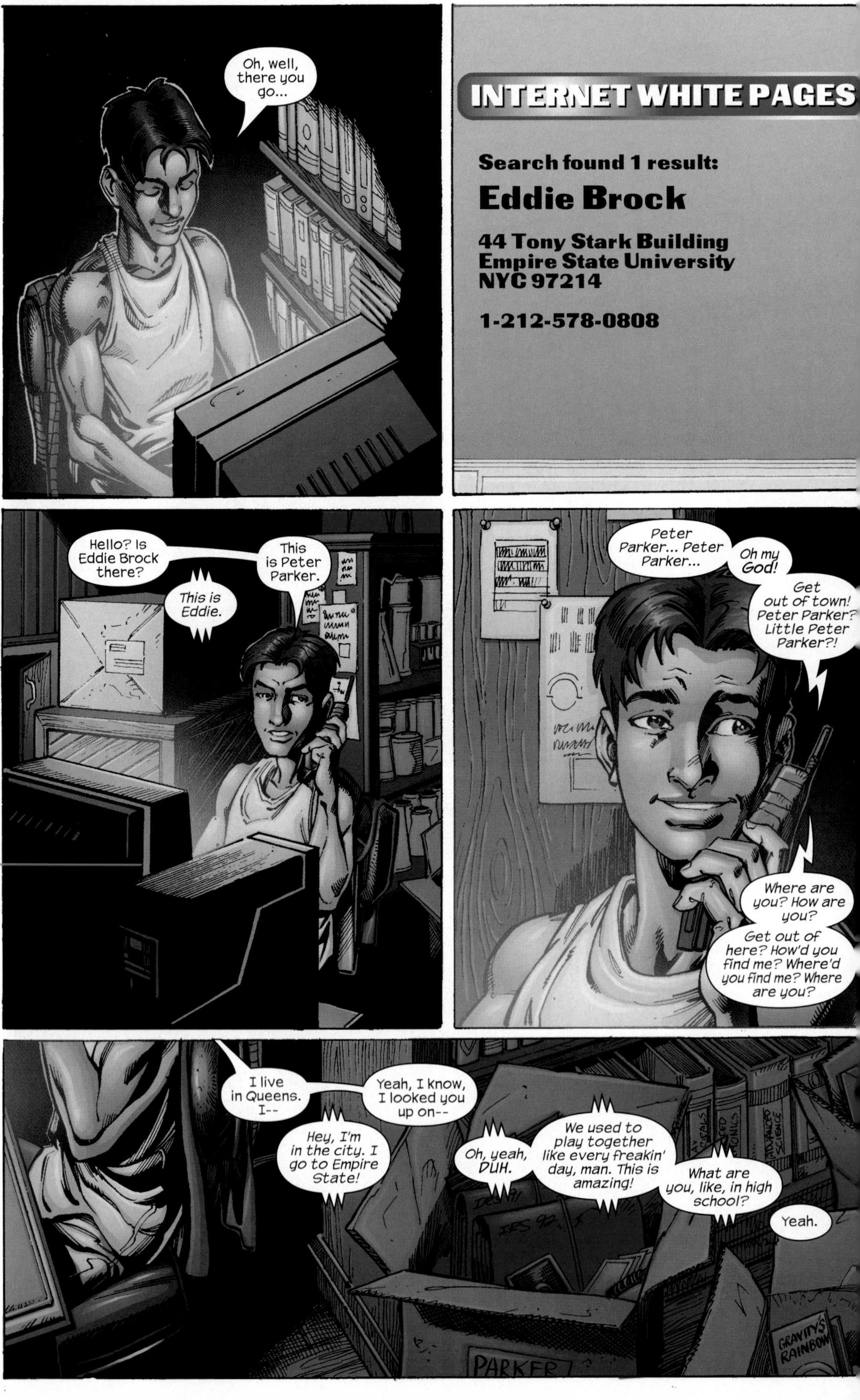
Oh, well, there you go...
INTERNET WHITE PAGES
Search found 1 result:
Eddie Brock
44 Tony Stark Building
Empire State University
NYC 97214
1-212-578-0808
Hello? Is Eddie Brock there?
This is Peter Parker.
This is Eddie.
Peter Parker... Peter Parker...
Oh my God!
Get out of town! Peter Parker? Little Peter Parker?!
Where are you? How are you?
Get out of here? How'd you find me? Where'd you find me? Where are you?
I live in Queens. I--
Yeah, I know, I looked you up on--
Hey, I'm in the city. I go to Empire State!
Oh, yeah, DUH.
We used to play together like every freakin' day, man. This is amazing!
What are you, like, in high school?
Yeah.
ADVANCED SCIENCE
GRAVITY'S RAINBOW
PARKER

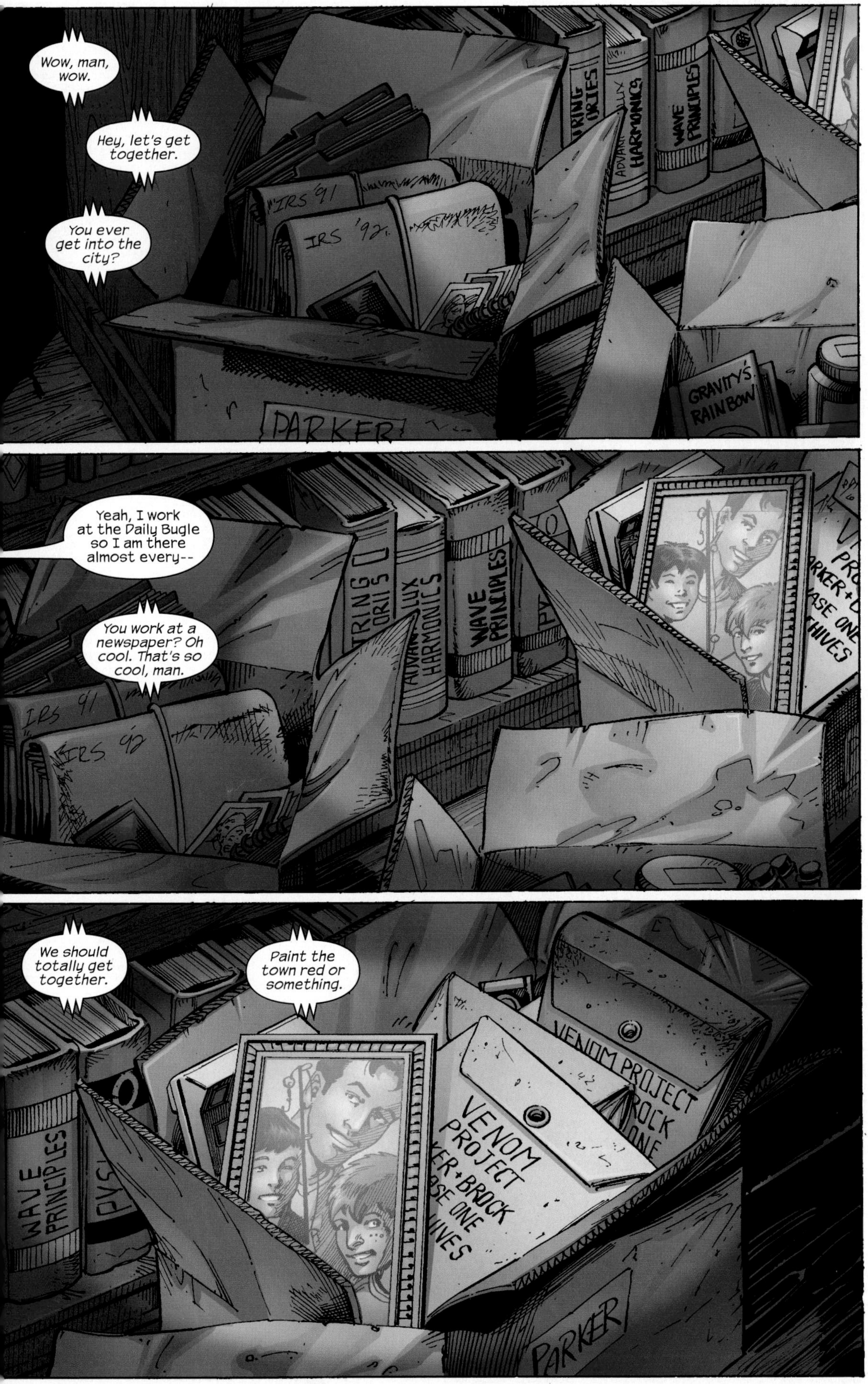
Wow, man, wow.
Hey, let's get together.
You ever get into the city?
IRS '91
IRS '92
HARMONICS
WAVE PRINCIPLES
GRAVITY'S RAINBOW
PARKER
Yeah, I work at the Daily Bugle so I am there almost every--
You work at a newspaper? Oh cool. That's so cool, man.
WAVE PRINCIPLES
We should totally get together.
Paint the town red or something.
WAVE PRINCIPLES
VENOM PROJECT
VENOM PROJECT
PARKER

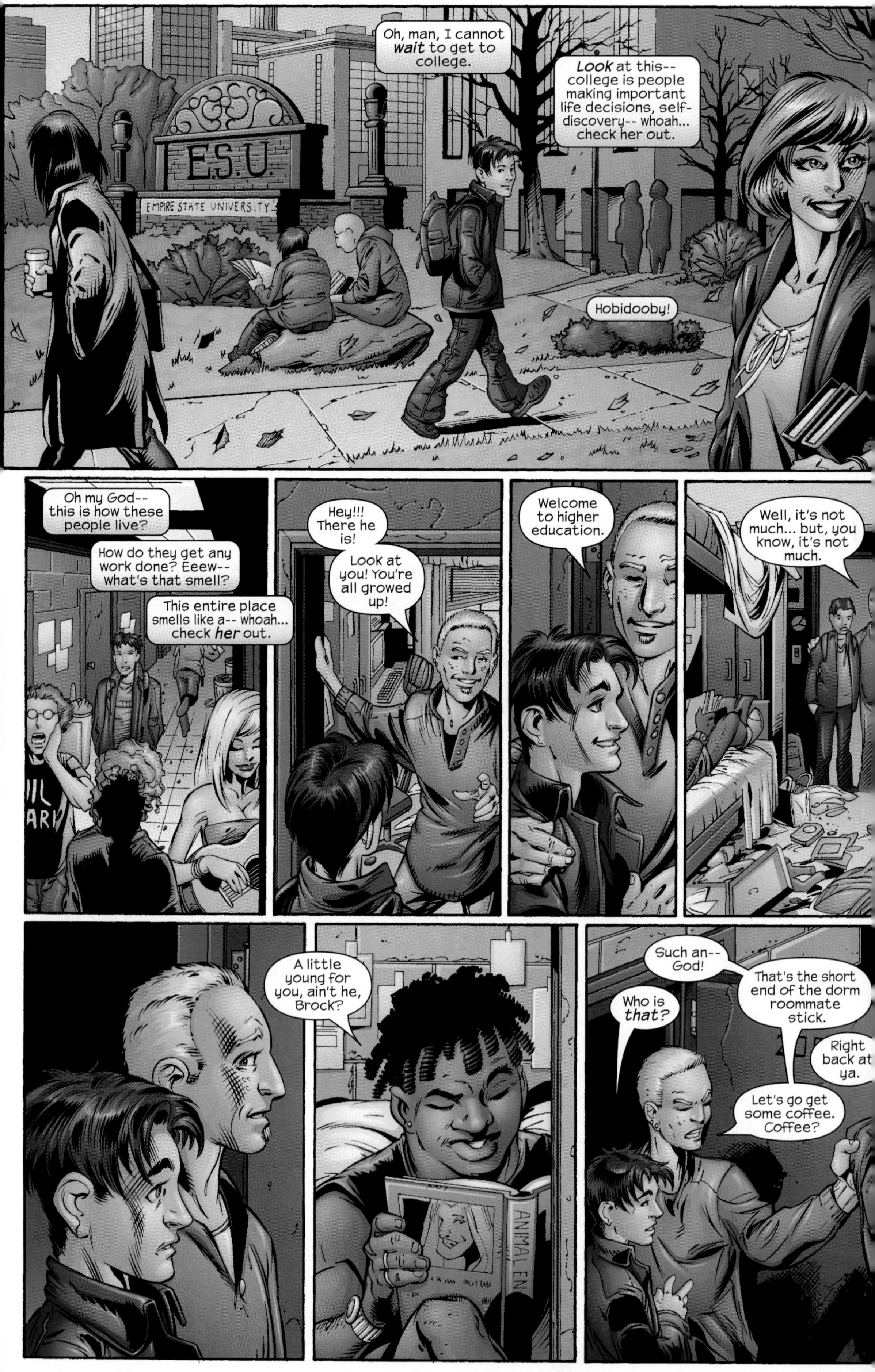
Oh, man, I cannot *wait* to get to college.
Look at this-- college is people making important life decisions, self-discovery-- whoah... check her out.
E.S.U.
EMPIRE STATE UNIVERSITY
Hobidooby!
Oh my God-- this is how these people live?
How do they get any work done? Eeew-- what's that smell?
This entire place smells like a-- whoah... check *her* out.
Hey!!! There he is!
Look at you! You're all growed up!
Welcome to higher education.
Well, it's not much... but, you know, it's not much.
A little young for you, ain't he, Brock?
ANIMAL EN
Such an-- God!
Who is *that*?
That's the short end of the dorm roommate stick.
Right back at ya.
Let's go get some coffee. Coffee?

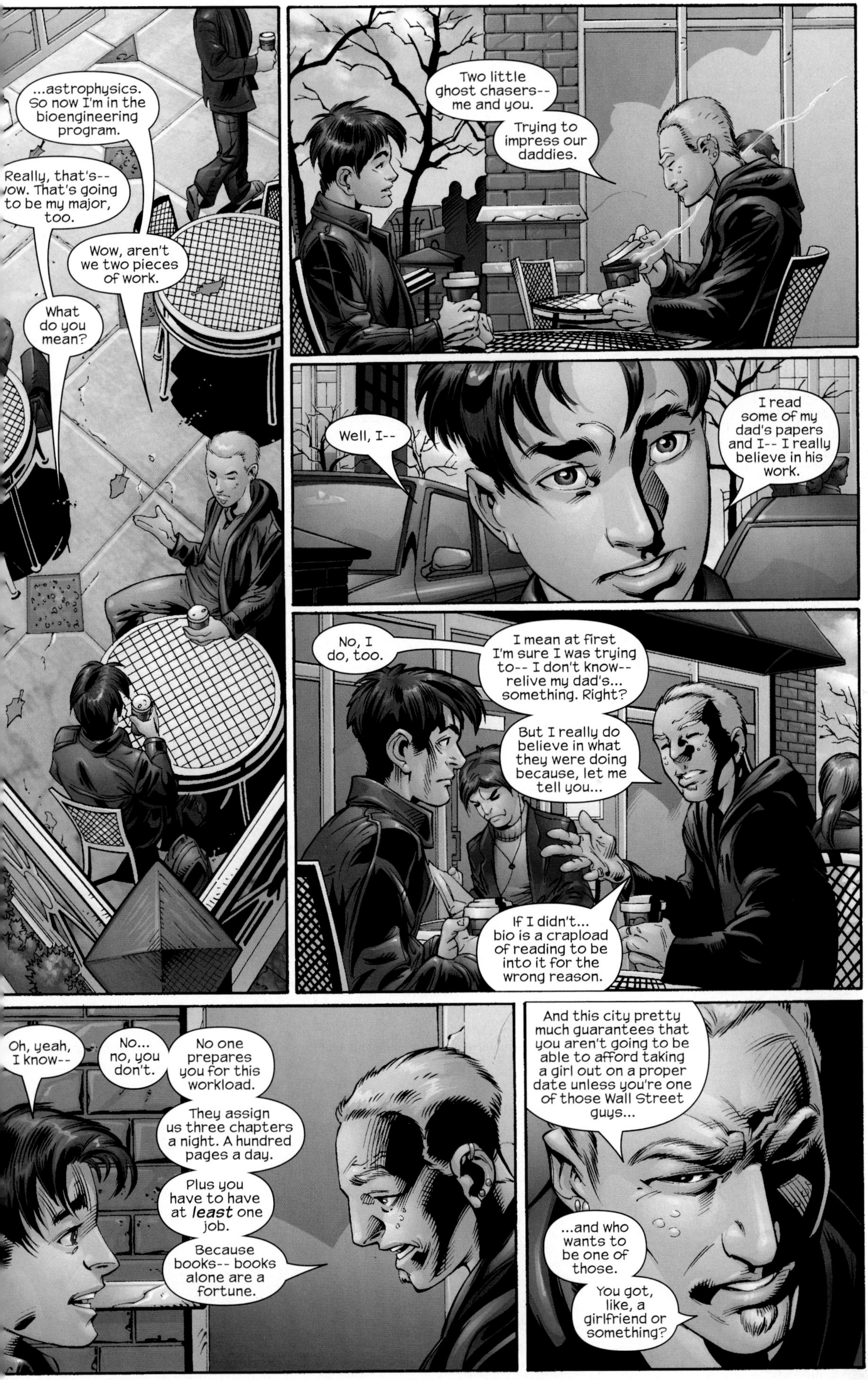

...astrophysics. So now I'm in the bioengineering program.
Really, that's-- wow. That's going to be my major, too.
Wow, aren't we two pieces of work.
What do you mean?
Two little ghost chasers-- me and you.
Trying to impress our daddies.
Well, I--
I read some of my dad's papers and I-- I really believe in his work.
No, I do, too.
I mean at first I'm sure I was trying to-- I don't know-- relive my dad's... something. Right?
But I really do believe in what they were doing because, let me tell you...
If I didn't... bio is a crapload of reading to be into it for the wrong reason.
Oh, yeah, I know--
No... no, you don't.
No one prepares you for this workload.
They assign us three chapters a night. A hundred pages a day.
Plus you have to have at *least* one job.
Because books-- books alone are a fortune.
And this city pretty much guarantees that you aren't going to be able to afford taking a girl out on a proper date unless you're one of those Wall Street guys...
...and who wants to be one of those.
You got, like, a girlfriend or something?

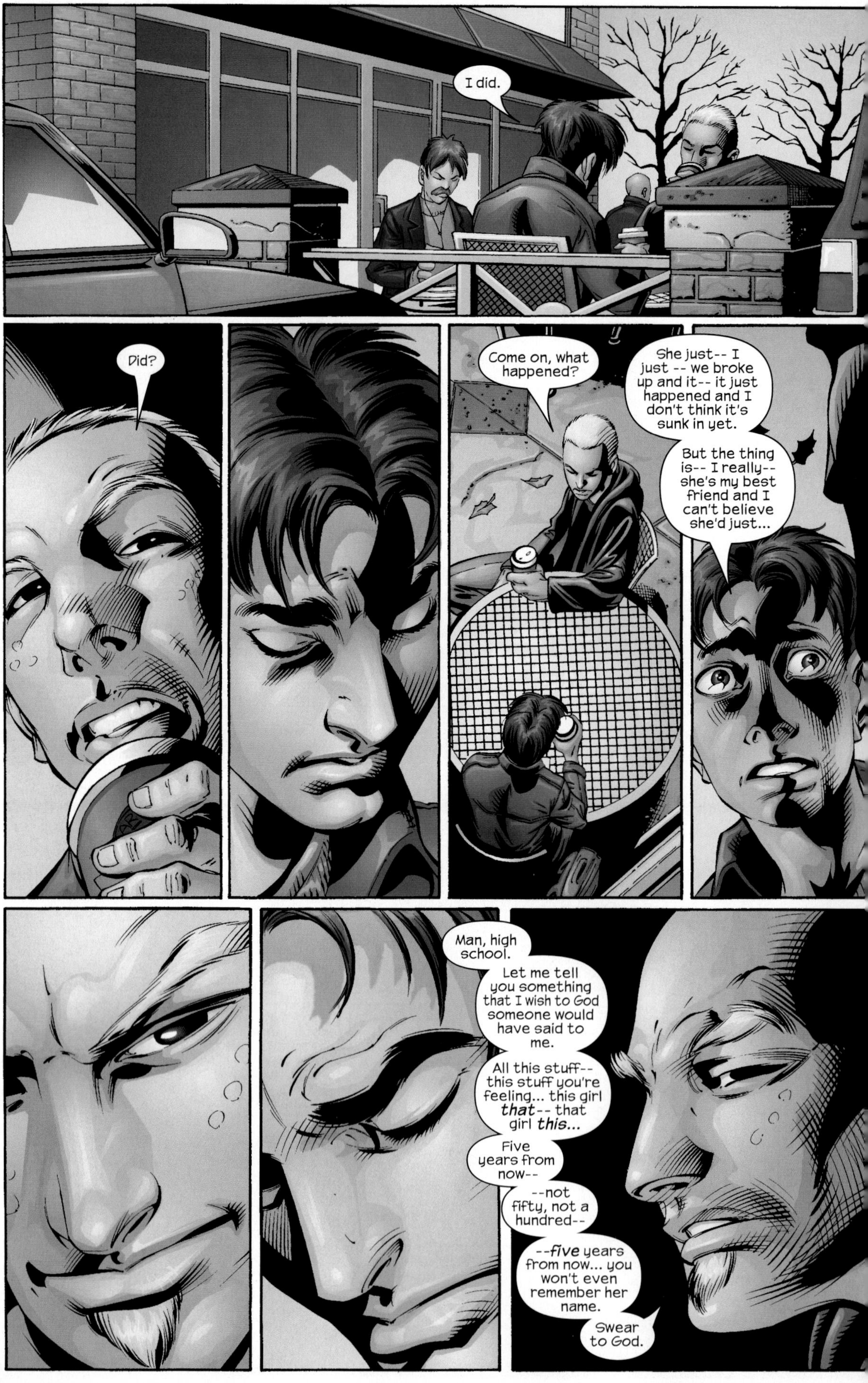
I did.
Did?
Come on, what happened?
She just-- I just -- we broke up and it-- it just happened and I don't think it's sunk in yet.
But the thing is-- I really-- she's my best friend and I can't believe she'd just...
Man, high school.
Let me tell you something that I wish to God someone would have said to me.
All this stuff-- this stuff you're feeling... this girl *that*-- that girl *this*...
Five years from now--
--not fifty, not a hundred--
--*five* years from now... you won't even remember her name.
Swear to God.

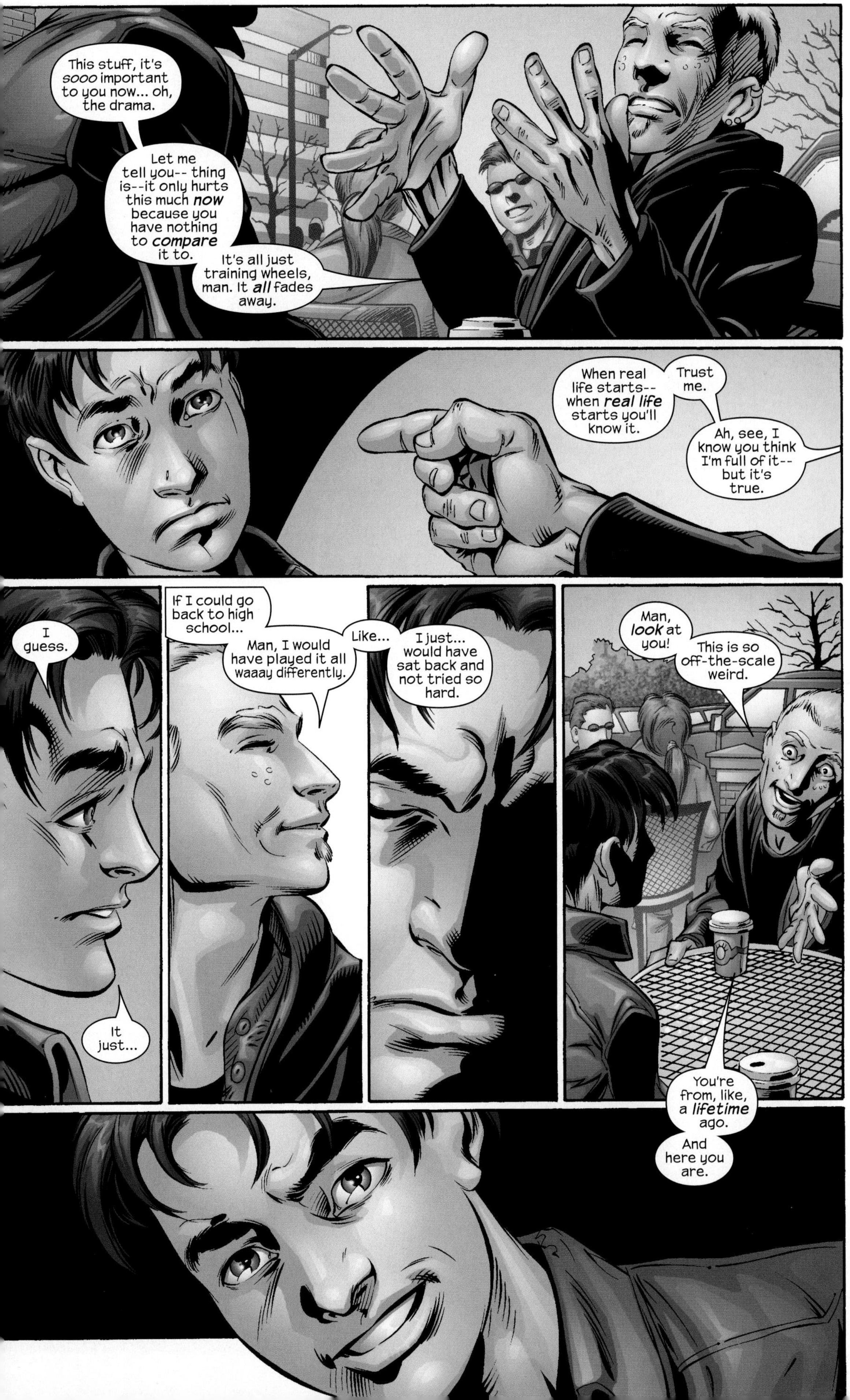
This stuff, it's *sooo* important to you now... oh, the drama.
Let me tell you-- thing is--it only hurts this much **now** because you have nothing to **compare** it to.
It's all just training wheels, man. It **all** fades away.
When real life starts-- when **real life** starts you'll know it.
Trust me.
Ah, see, I know you think I'm full of it-- but it's true.
I guess.
It just...
If I could go back to high school...
Man, I would have played it all waaay differently.
Like...
I just... would have sat back and not tried so hard.
Man, **look** at you!
This is so off-the-scale weird.
You're from, like, a **lifetime** ago.
And here you are.

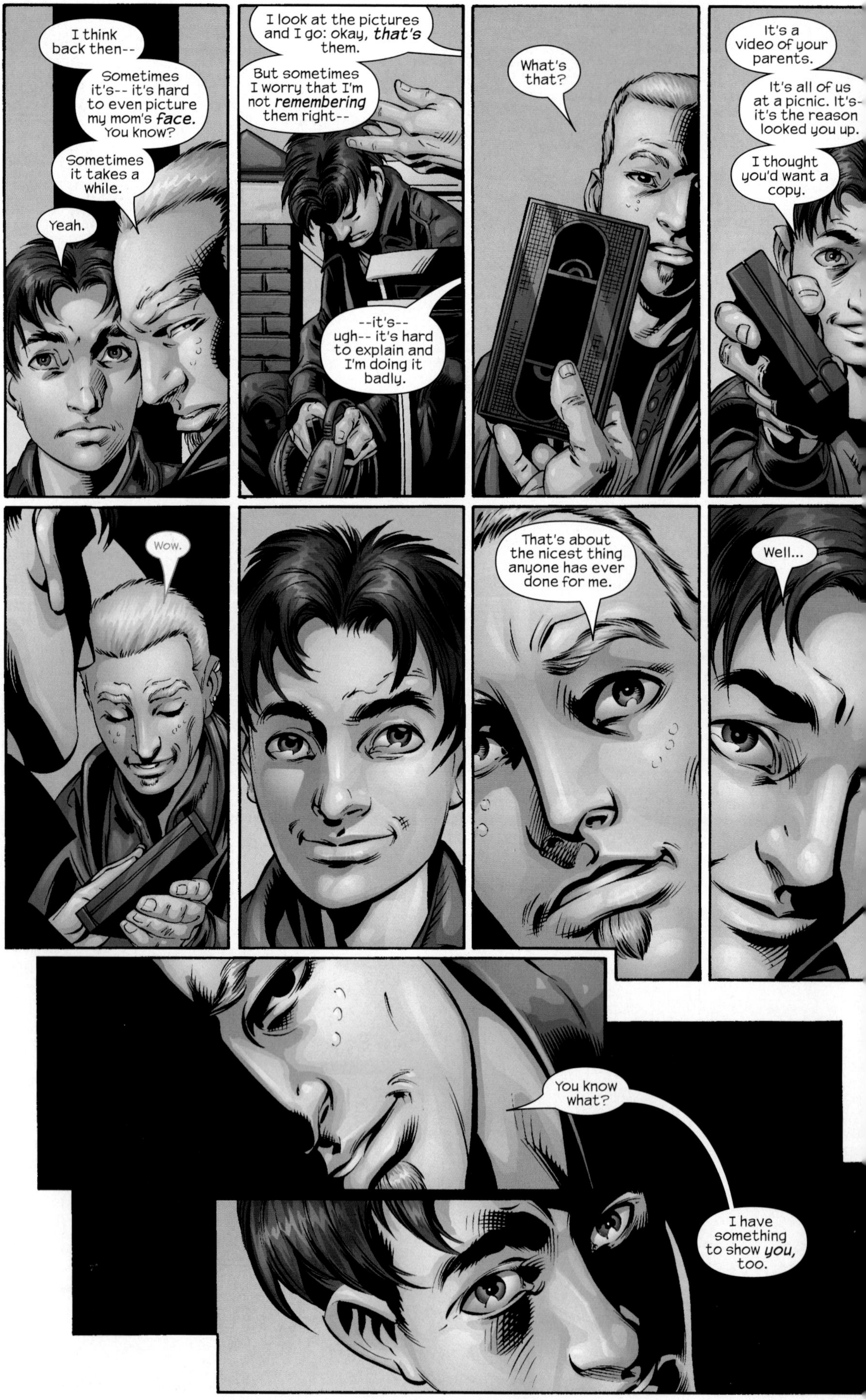
I think back then--
Sometimes it's-- it's hard to even picture my mom's *face.* You know?
Sometimes it takes a while.
Yeah.
I look at the pictures and I go: okay, *that's* them.
But sometimes I worry that I'm not *remembering* them right--
--it's-- ugh-- it's hard to explain and I'm doing it badly.
What's that?
It's a video of your parents.
It's all of us at a picnic. It's- it's the reason looked you up.
I thought you'd want a copy.
Wow.
That's about the nicest thing anyone has ever done for me.
Well...
You know what?
I have something to show *you,* too.

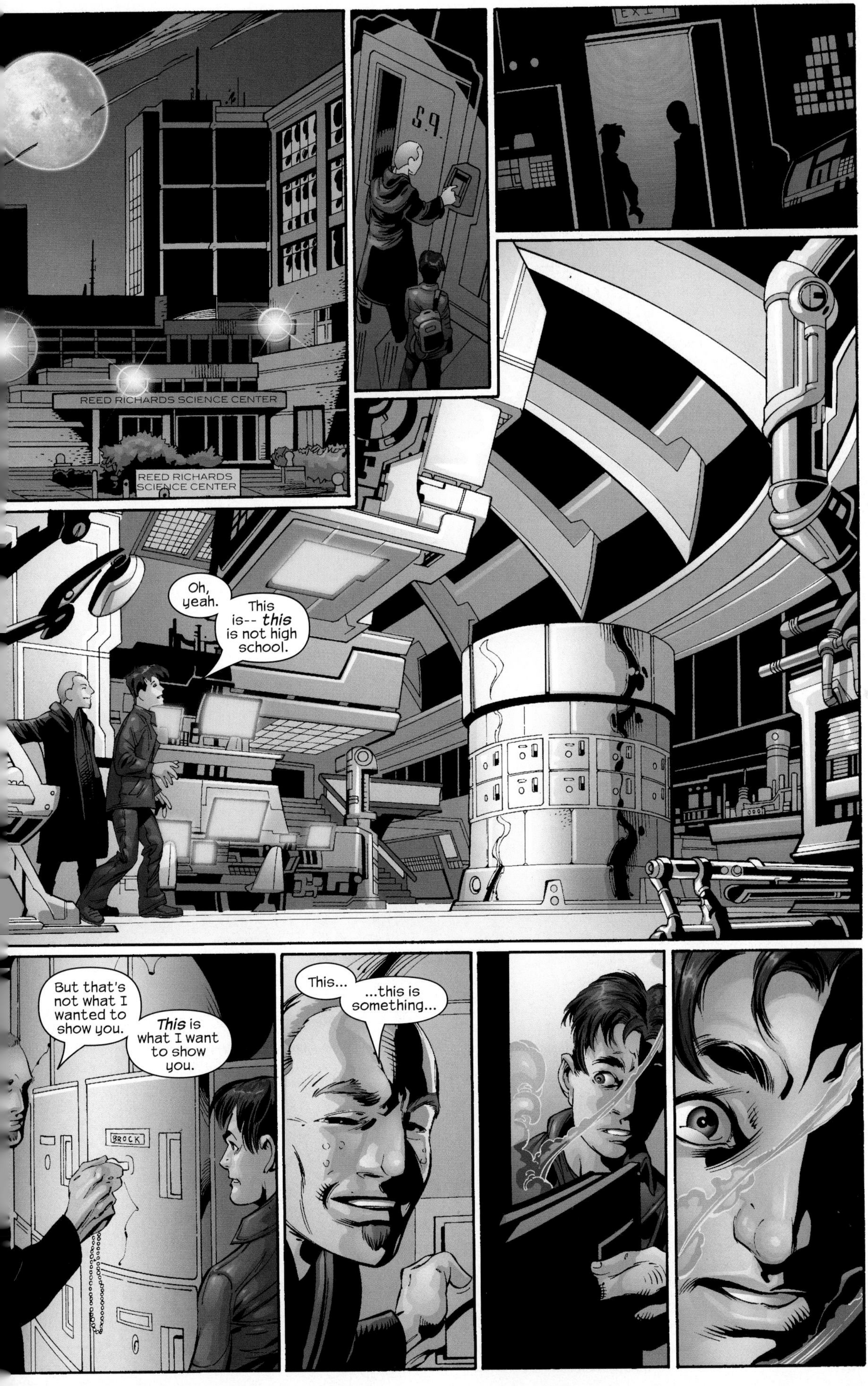
REED RICHARDS SCIENCE CENTER
REED RICHARDS SCIENCE CENTER
S.9.
EXIT
Oh, yeah.
This is-- *this* is not high school.
But that's not what I wanted to show you.
This is what I want to show you.
BROCK
This...
...this is something...

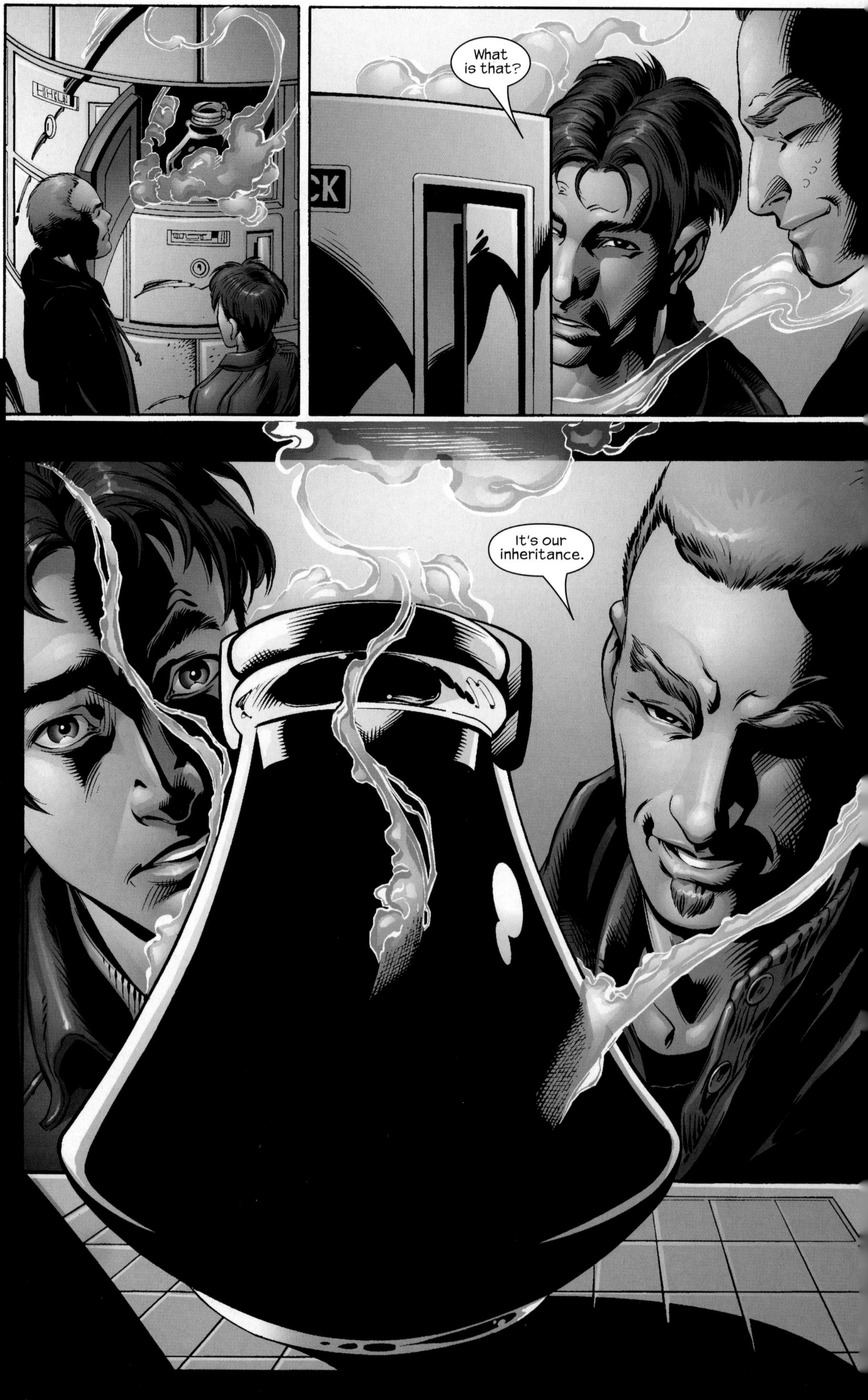
What is that?
It's our inheritance.

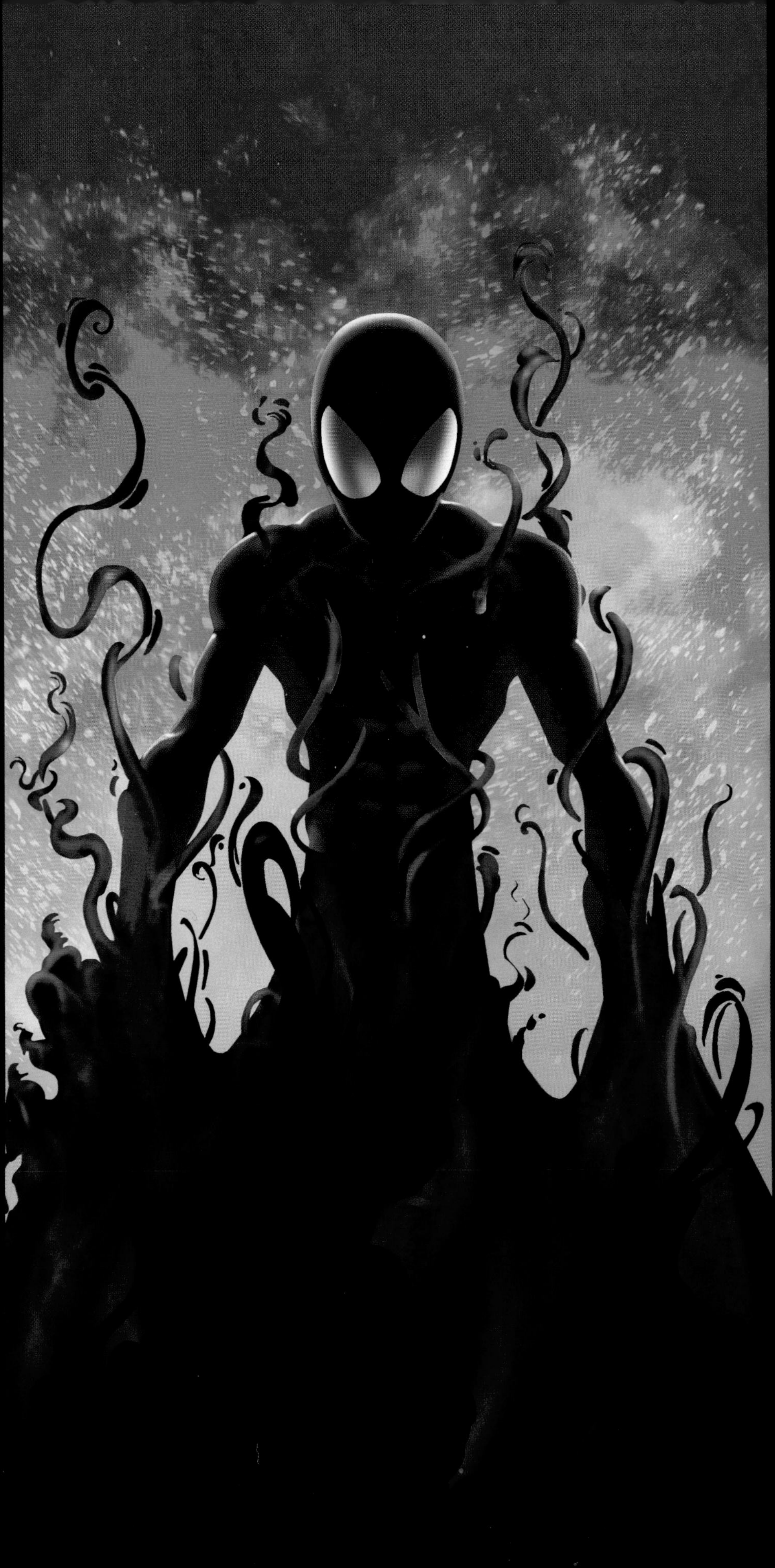

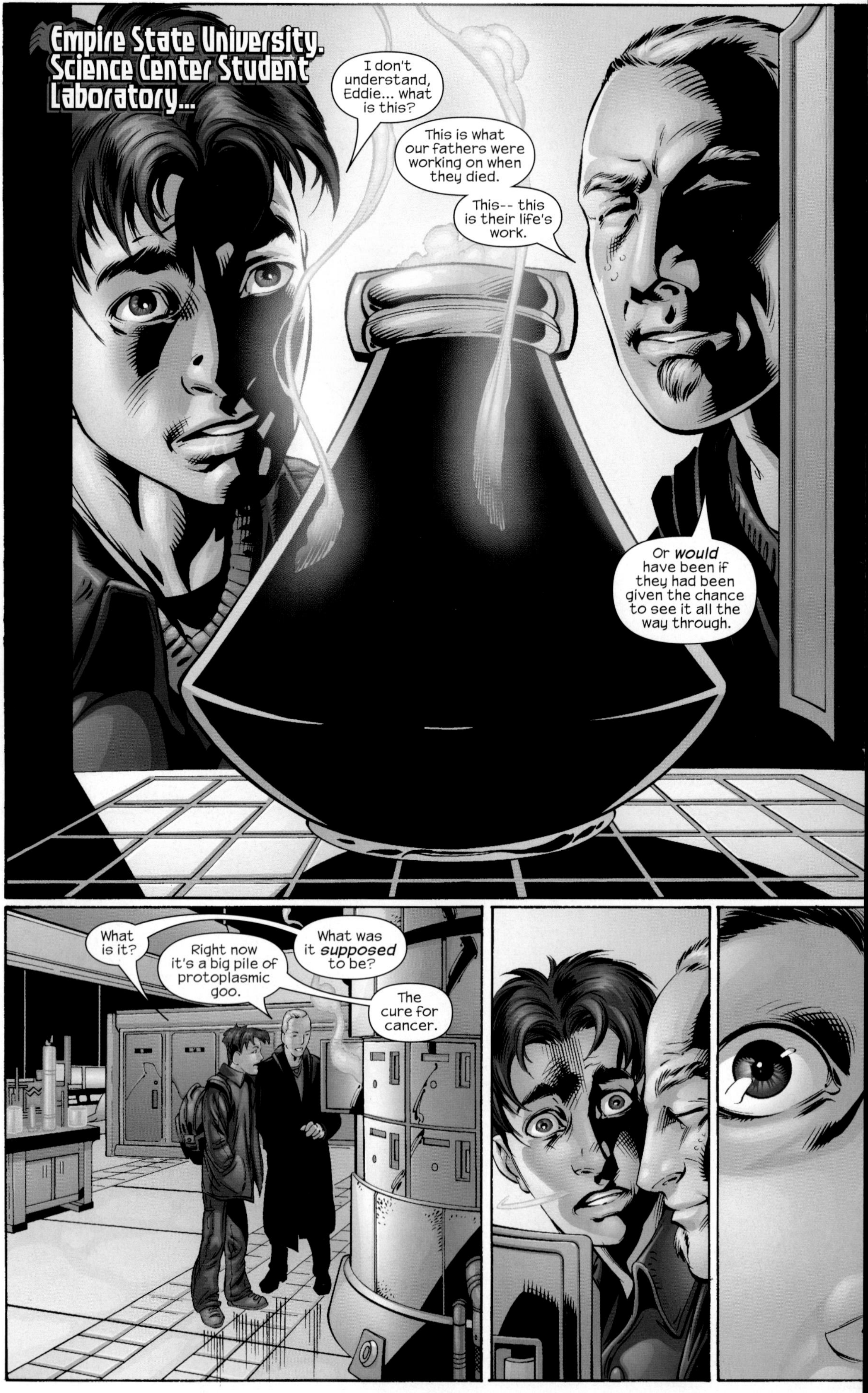
Empire State University. Science Center Student Laboratory...
I don't understand, Eddie... what is this?
This is what our fathers were working on when they died.
This-- this is their life's work.
Or *would* have been if they had been given the chance to see it all the way through.
What is it?
Right now it's a big pile of protoplasmic goo.
What was it *supposed* to be?
The cure for cancer.

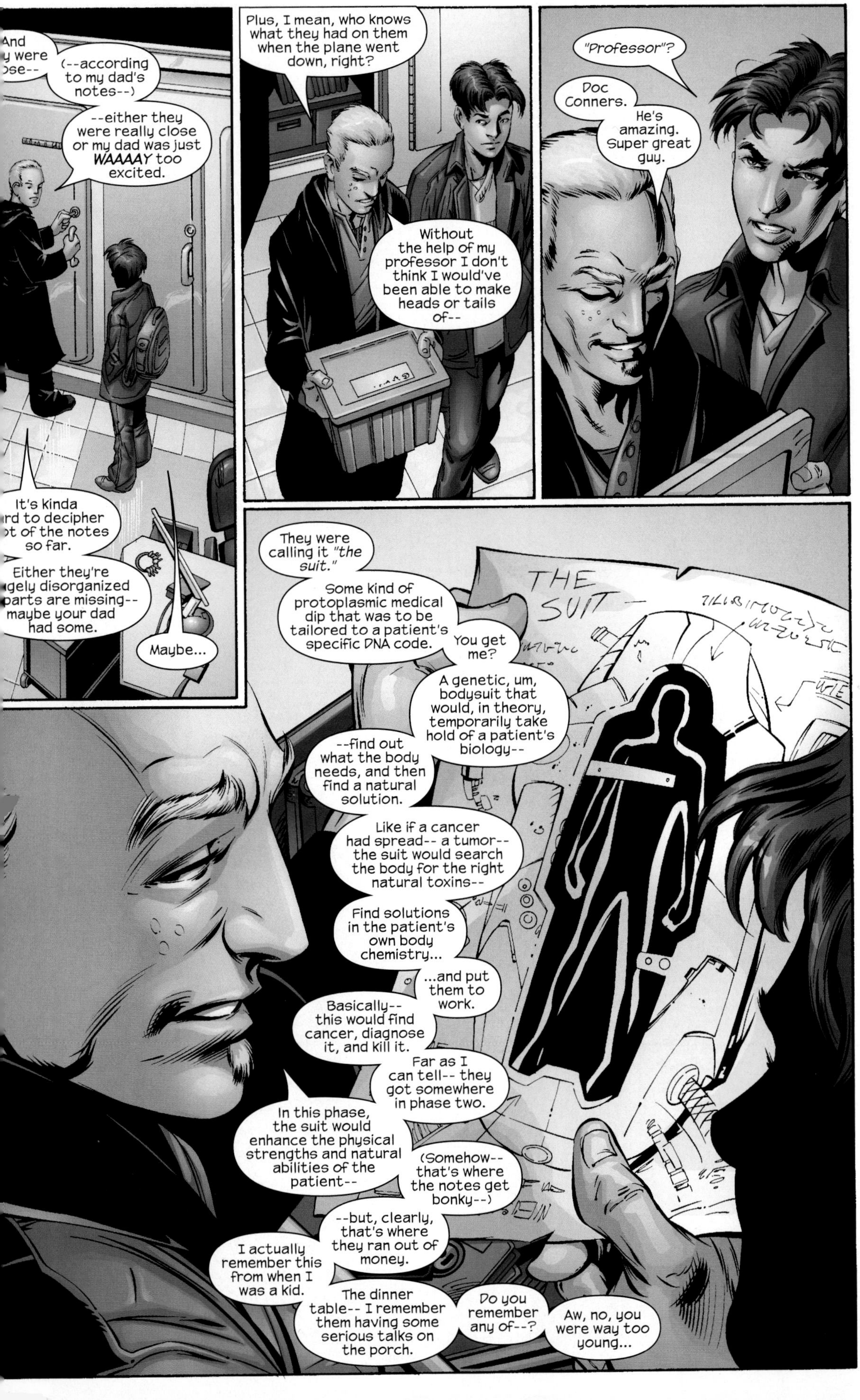

And
y were
ose--
(--according to my dad's notes--)
--either they were really close or my dad was just WAAAAY too excited.
Plus, I mean, who knows what they had on them when the plane went down, right?
Without the help of my professor I don't think I would've been able to make heads or tails of--
"Professor"?
Doc Conners.
He's amazing. Super great guy.
It's kinda
rd to decipher
ot of the notes
so far.
Either they're
gely disorganized
parts are missing--
maybe your dad
had some.
Maybe...
They were calling it "the suit."
Some kind of protoplasmic medical dip that was to be tailored to a patient's specific DNA code.
You get me?
A genetic, um, bodysuit that would, in theory, temporarily take hold of a patient's biology--
--find out what the body needs, and then find a natural solution.
Like if a cancer had spread-- a tumor-- the suit would search the body for the right natural toxins--
Find solutions in the patient's own body chemistry...
...and put them to work.
Basically-- this would find cancer, diagnose it, and kill it.
Far as I can tell-- they got somewhere in phase two.
In this phase, the suit would enhance the physical strengths and natural abilities of the patient--
(Somehow-- that's where the notes get bonky--)
--but, clearly, that's where they ran out of money.
I actually remember this from when I was a kid.
The dinner table-- I remember them having some serious talks on the porch.
Do you remember any of--?
Aw, no, you were way too young...
THE SUIT

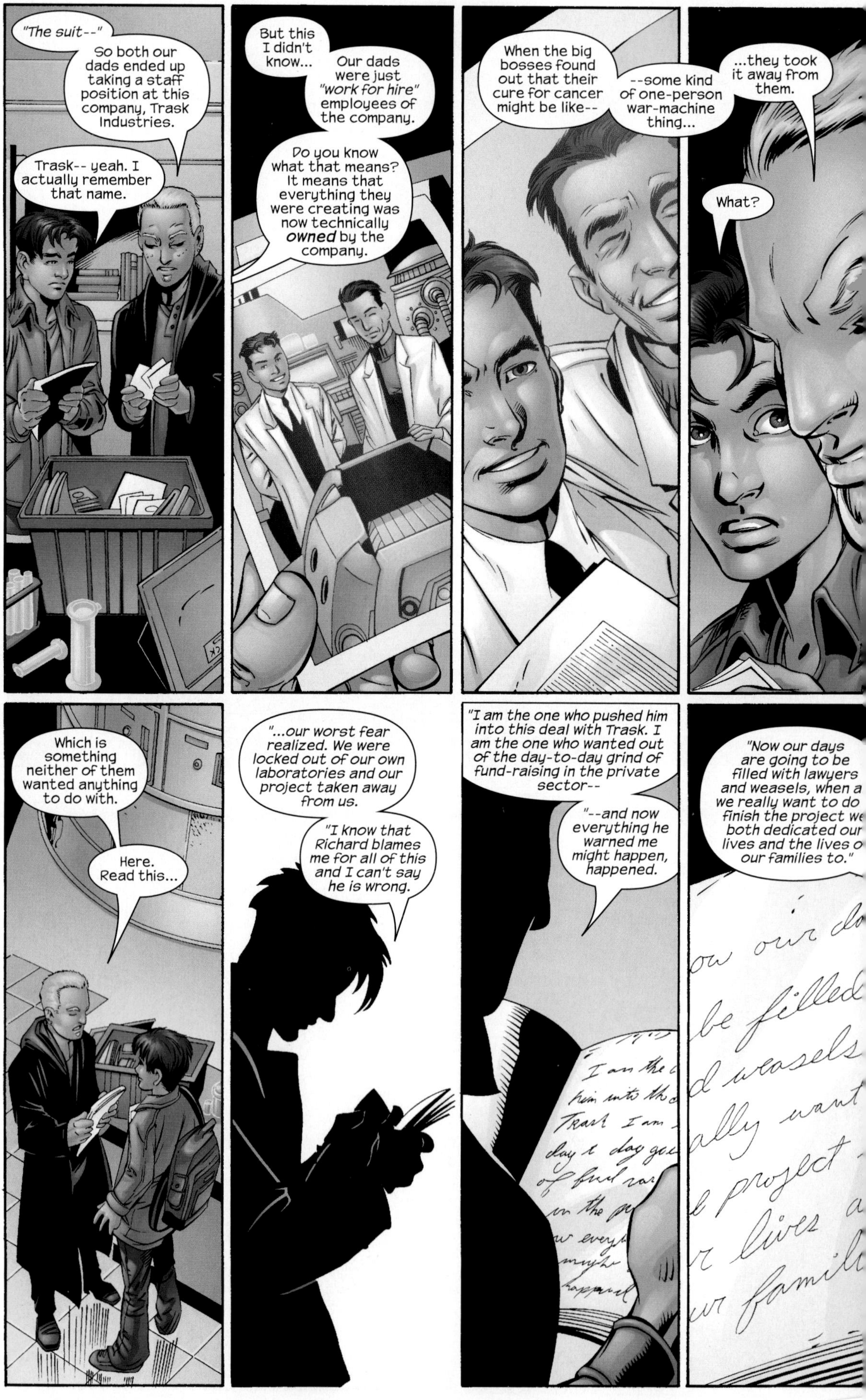
"The suit--"
So both our dads ended up taking a staff position at this company, Trask Industries.
Trask-- yeah. I actually remember that name.
But this I didn't know...
Our dads were just "work for hire" employees of the company.
Do you know what that means? It means that everything they were creating was now technically **owned** by the company.
When the big bosses found out that their cure for cancer might be like--
--some kind of one-person war-machine thing...
...they took it away from them.
What?
Which is something neither of them wanted anything to do with.
Here. Read this...
"...our worst fear realized. We were locked out of our own laboratories and our project taken away from us.
"I know that Richard blames me for all of this and I can't say he is wrong.
"I am the one who pushed him into this deal with Trask. I am the one who wanted out of the day-to-day grind of fund-raising in the private sector--
"--and now everything he warned me might happen, happened.
"Now our days are going to be filled with lawyers and weasels, when a we really want to do finish the project we both dedicated our lives and the lives o our families to."

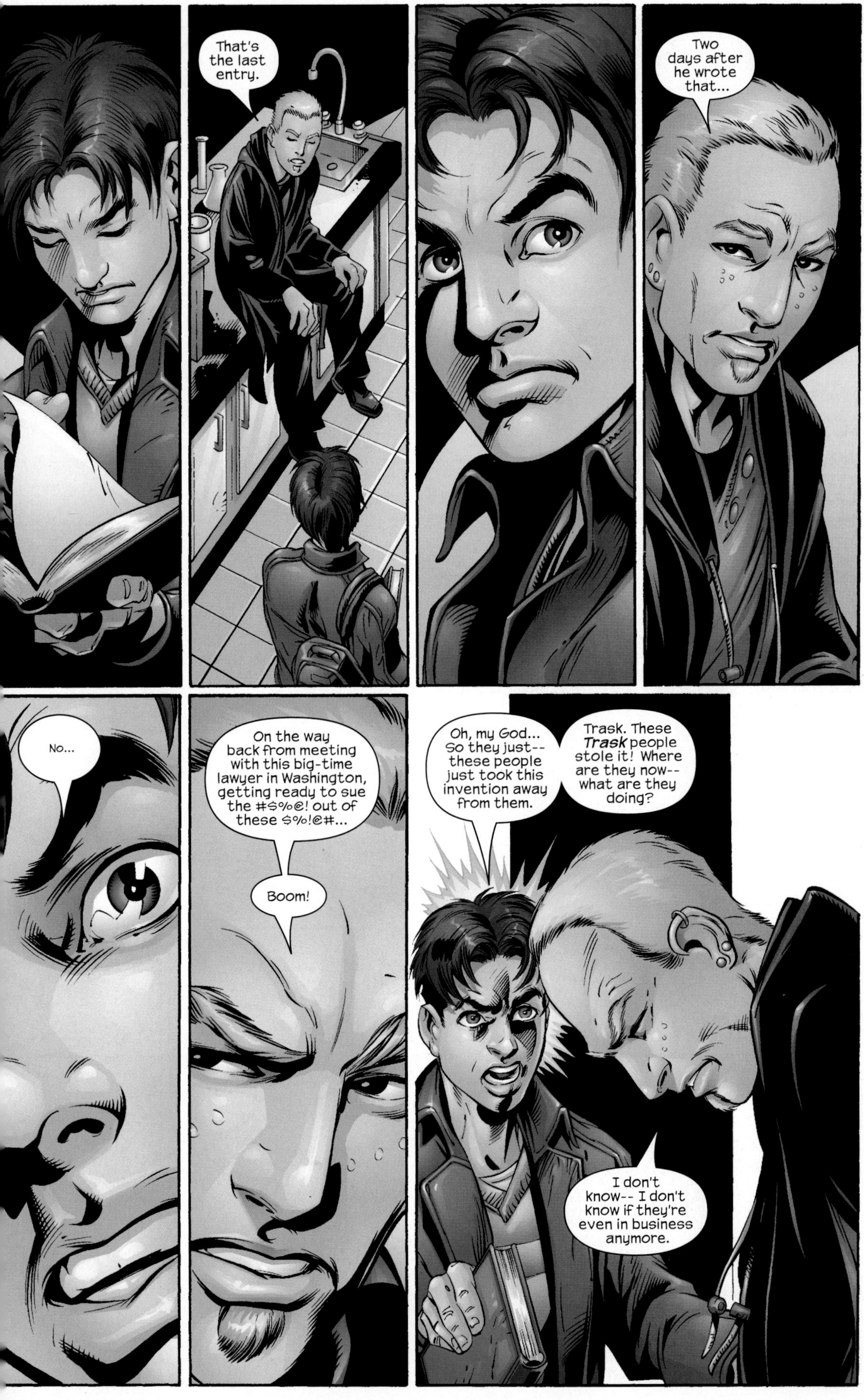
That's the last entry.
Two days after he wrote that...
No...
On the way back from meeting with this big-time lawyer in Washington, getting ready to sue the #$%@! out of these $%!@#...
Boom!
Oh, my God... So they just-- these people just took this invention away from them.
Trask. These *Trask* people stole it! Where are they now-- what are they doing?
I don't know-- I don't know if they're even in business anymore.

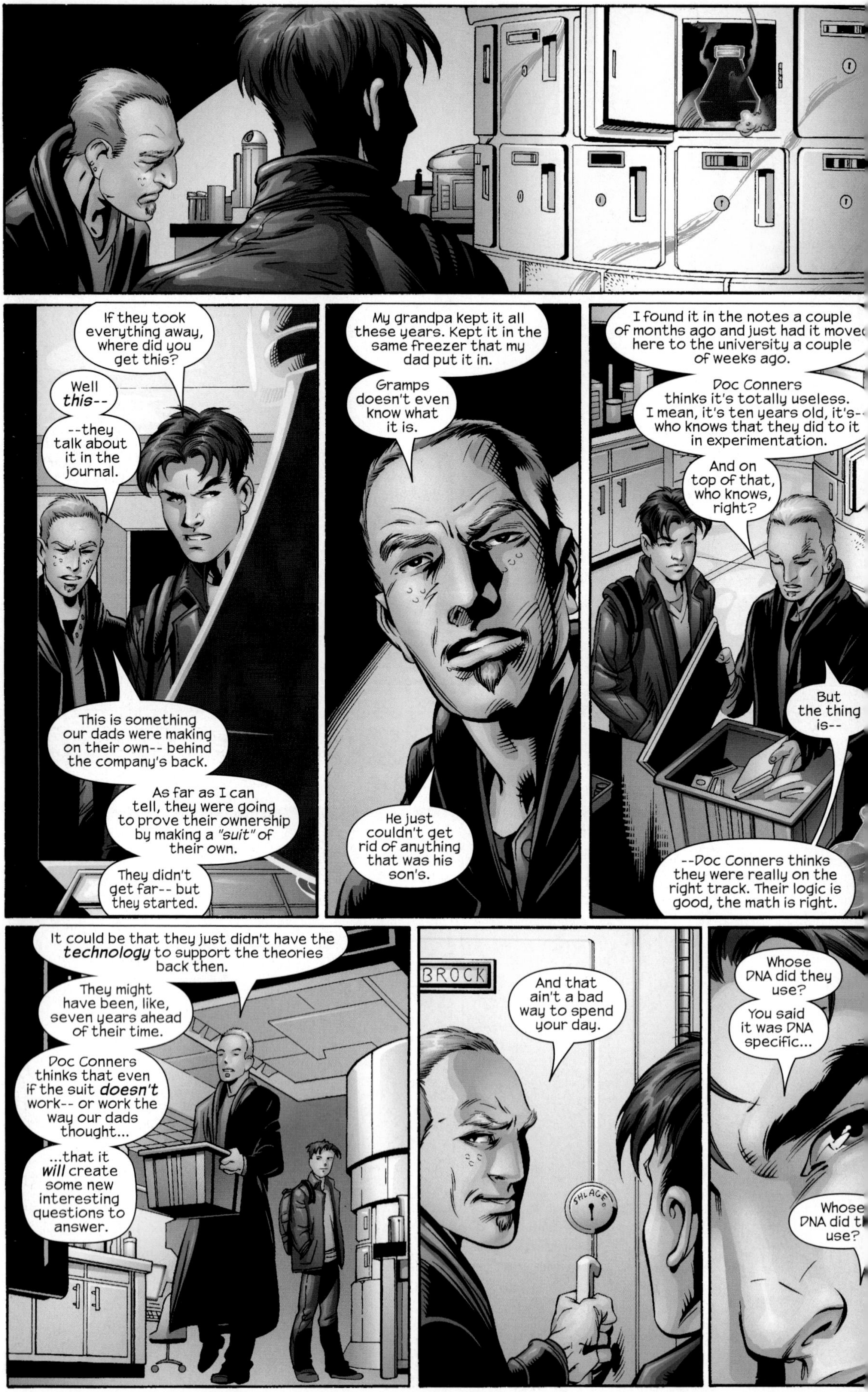

If they took everything away, where did you get this?
Well this--
--they talk about it in the journal.
This is something our dads were making on their own-- behind the company's back.
As far as I can tell, they were going to prove their ownership by making a "suit" of their own.
They didn't get far-- but they started.
My grandpa kept it all these years. Kept it in the same freezer that my dad put it in.
Gramps doesn't even know what it is.
He just couldn't get rid of anything that was his son's.
I found it in the notes a couple of months ago and just had it moved here to the university a couple of weeks ago.
Doc Conners thinks it's totally useless. I mean, it's ten years old, it's-- who knows what they did to it in experimentation.
And on top of that, who knows, right?
But the thing is--
--Doc Conners thinks they were really on the right track. Their logic is good, the math is right.
It could be that they just didn't have the technology to support the theories back then.
They might have been, like, seven years ahead of their time.
Doc Conners thinks that even if the suit doesn't work-- or work the way our dads thought...
...that it will create some new interesting questions to answer.
BROCK
And that ain't a bad way to spend your day.
SHLAGE
Whose DNA did they use?
You said it was DNA specific...
Whose DNA did they use?

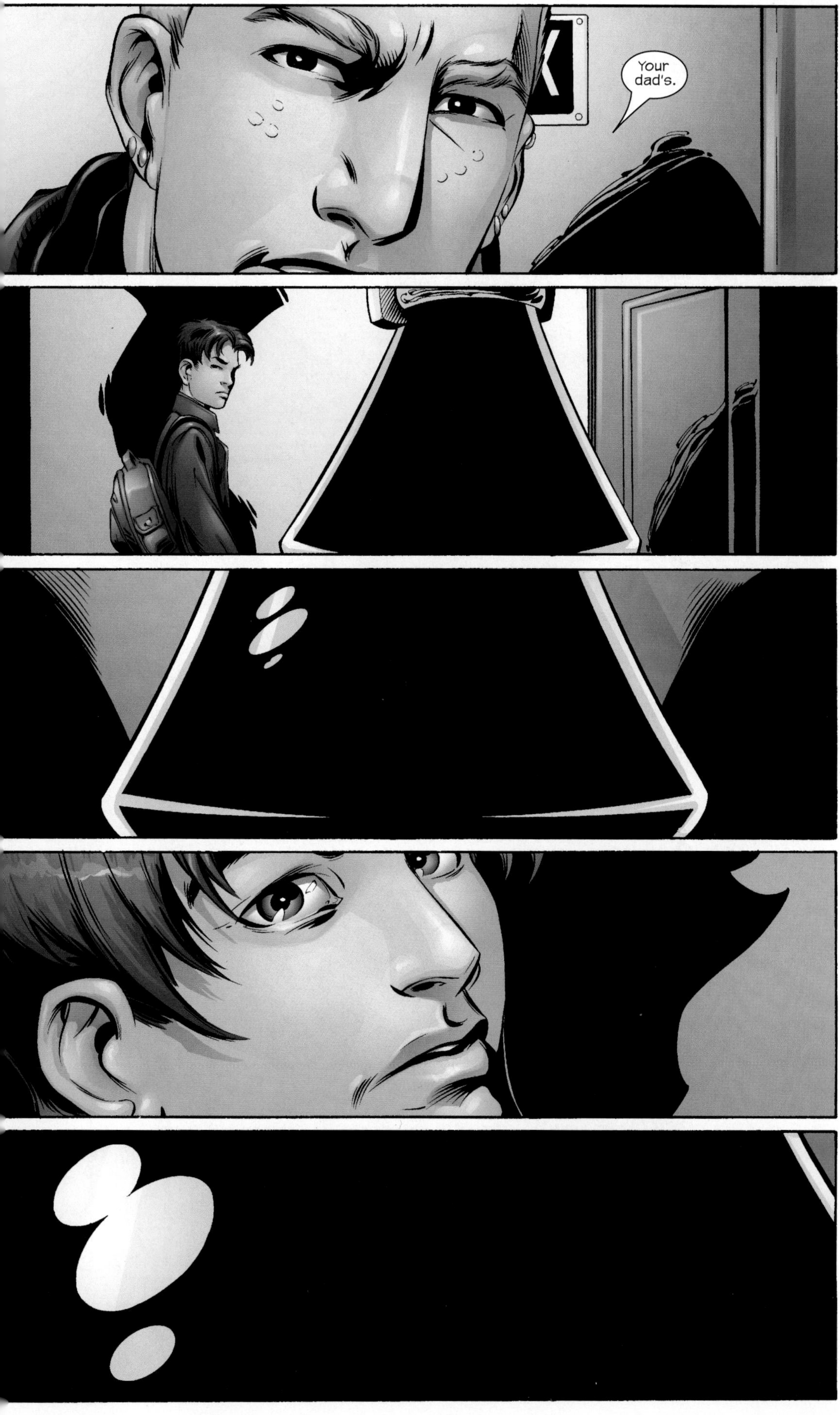
Your dad's.

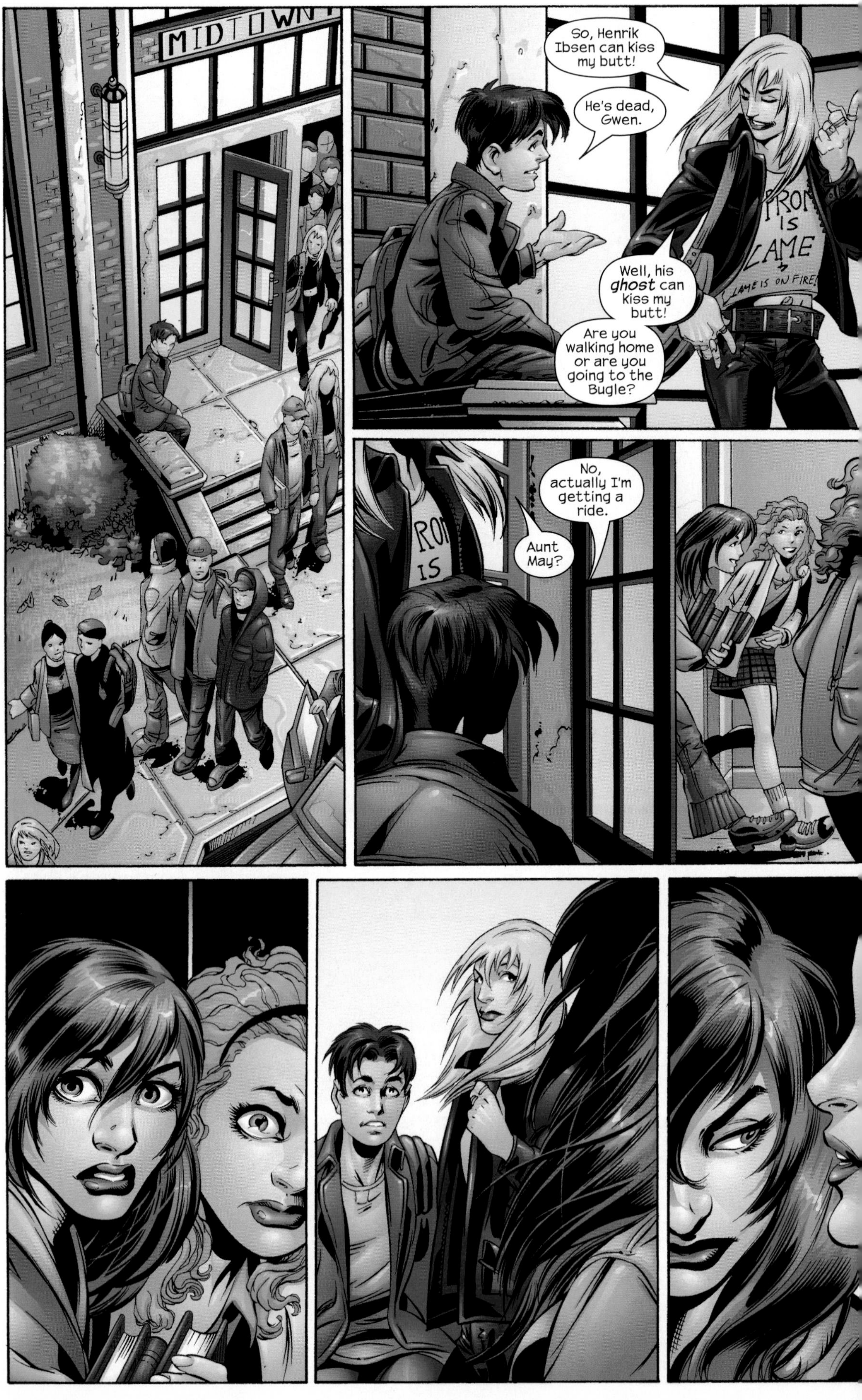
MIDTOWN
So, Henrik Ibsen can kiss my butt!
He's dead, Gwen.
Well, his *ghost* can kiss my butt!
Are you walking home or are you going to the Bugle?
Aunt May?
No, actually I'm getting a ride.

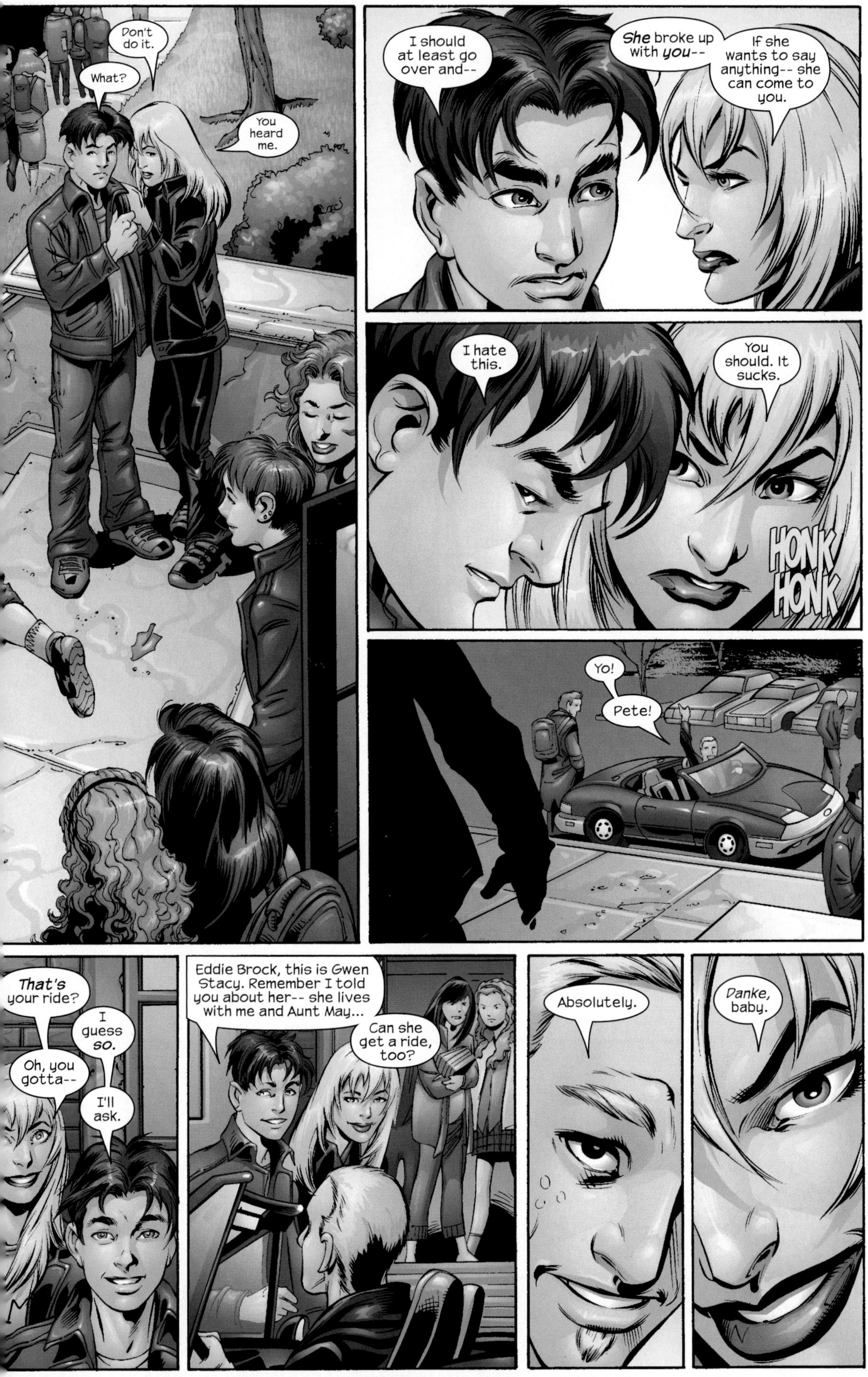
Don't do it.
What?
You heard me.
I should at least go over and--
She broke up with you--
If she wants to say anything-- she can come to you.
I hate this.
You should. It sucks.
HONK HONK
Yo!
Pete!
That's your ride?
I guess so.
Oh, you gotta--
I'll ask.
Eddie Brock, this is Gwen Stacy. Remember I told you about her-- she lives with me and Aunt May...
Can she get a ride, too?
Absolutely.
Danke, baby.

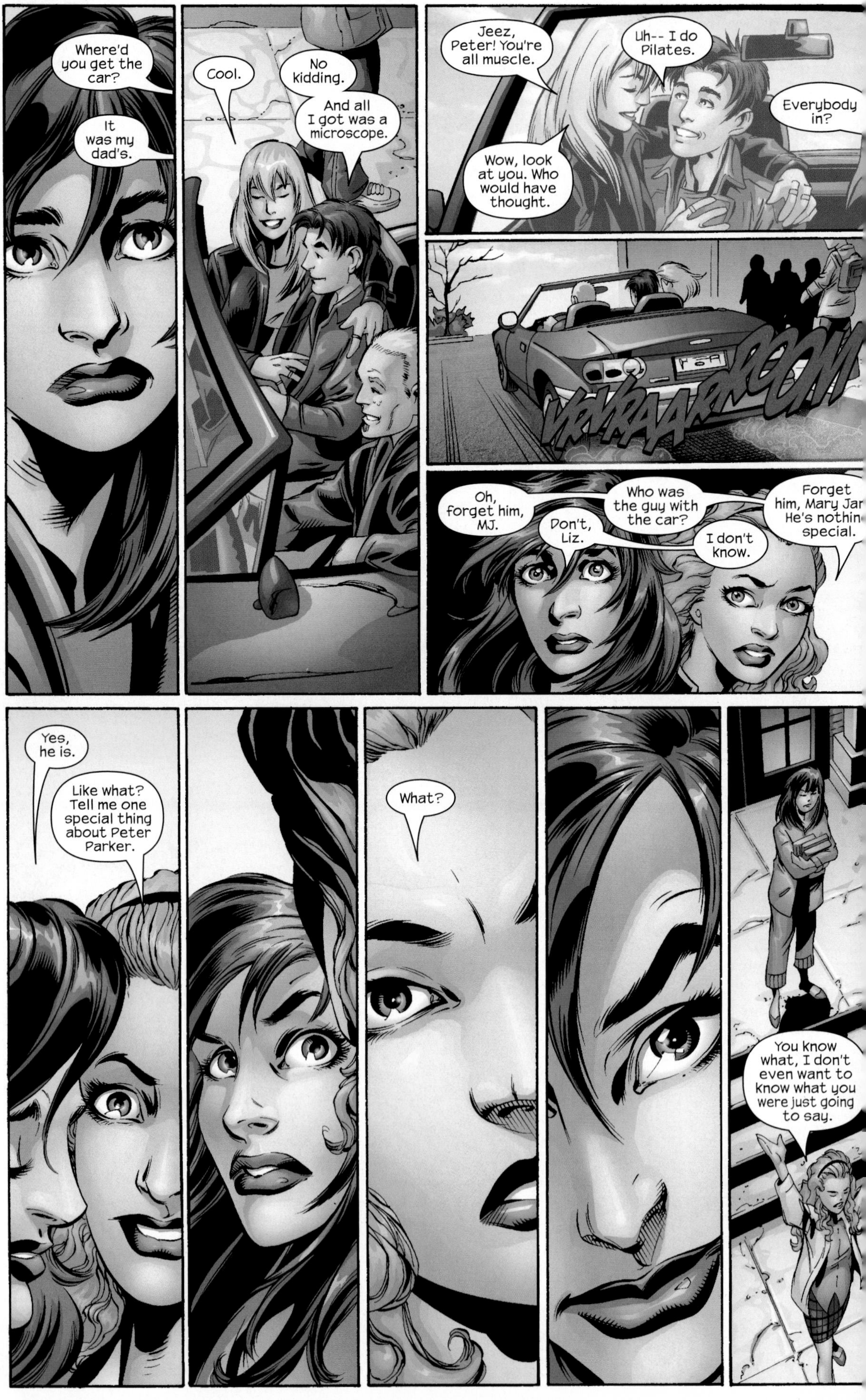
Where'd you get the car?
It was my dad's.
Cool.
No kidding.
And all I got was a microscope.
Jeez, Peter! You're all muscle.
Uh-- I do Pilates.
Wow, look at you. Who would have thought.
Everybody in?
VRVRAARROOM
Oh, forget him, MJ.
Who was the guy with the car?
Don't, Liz.
I don't know.
Forget him, Mary Jar
He's nothin
special.
Yes, he is.
Like what? Tell me one special thing about Peter Parker.
What?
You know what, I don't even want to know what you were just going to say.

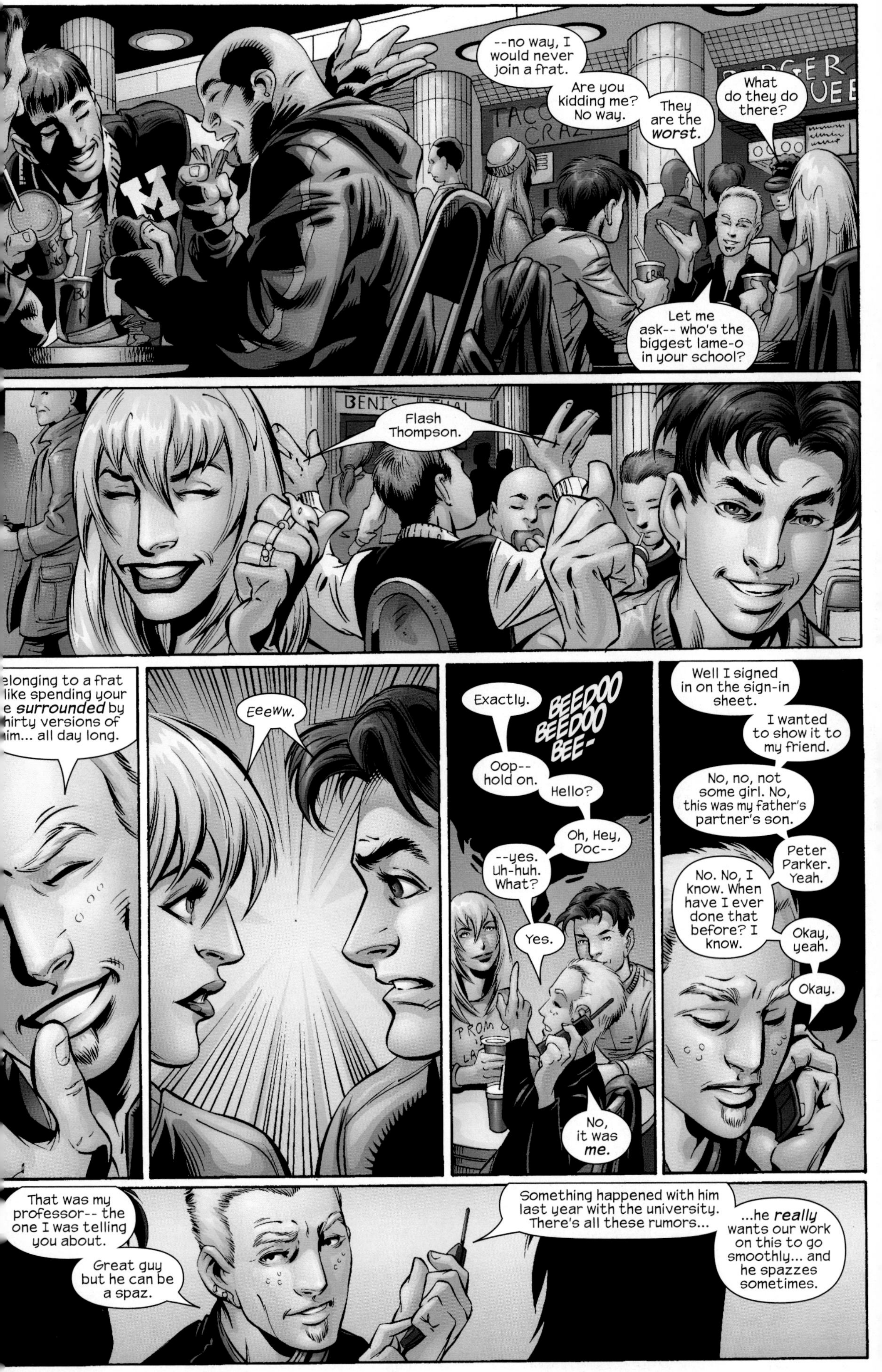
--no way, I would never join a frat.
Are you kidding me? No way.
They are the *worst.*
What do they do there?
TACO CRAZ
BURGER QUEE
Let me ask-- who's the biggest lame-o in your school?
BENI'S THAI
Flash Thompson.
elonging to a frat like spending your e *surrounded* by hirty versions of im... all day long.
EeeWw.
Exactly.
BEEDOO BEEDOO BEE-
Oop-- hold on.
Hello?
Oh, Hey, Doc--
--yes. Uh-huh. What?
Yes.
No, it was *me.*
Well I signed in on the sign-in sheet.
I wanted to show it to my friend.
No, no, not some girl. No, this was my father's partner's son.
Peter Parker. Yeah.
No. No, I know. When have I ever done that before? I know.
Okay, yeah.
Okay.
That was my professor-- the one I was telling you about.
Great guy but he can be a spaz.
Something happened with him last year with the university. There's all these rumors...
...he *really* wants our work on this to go smoothly... and he spazzes sometimes.

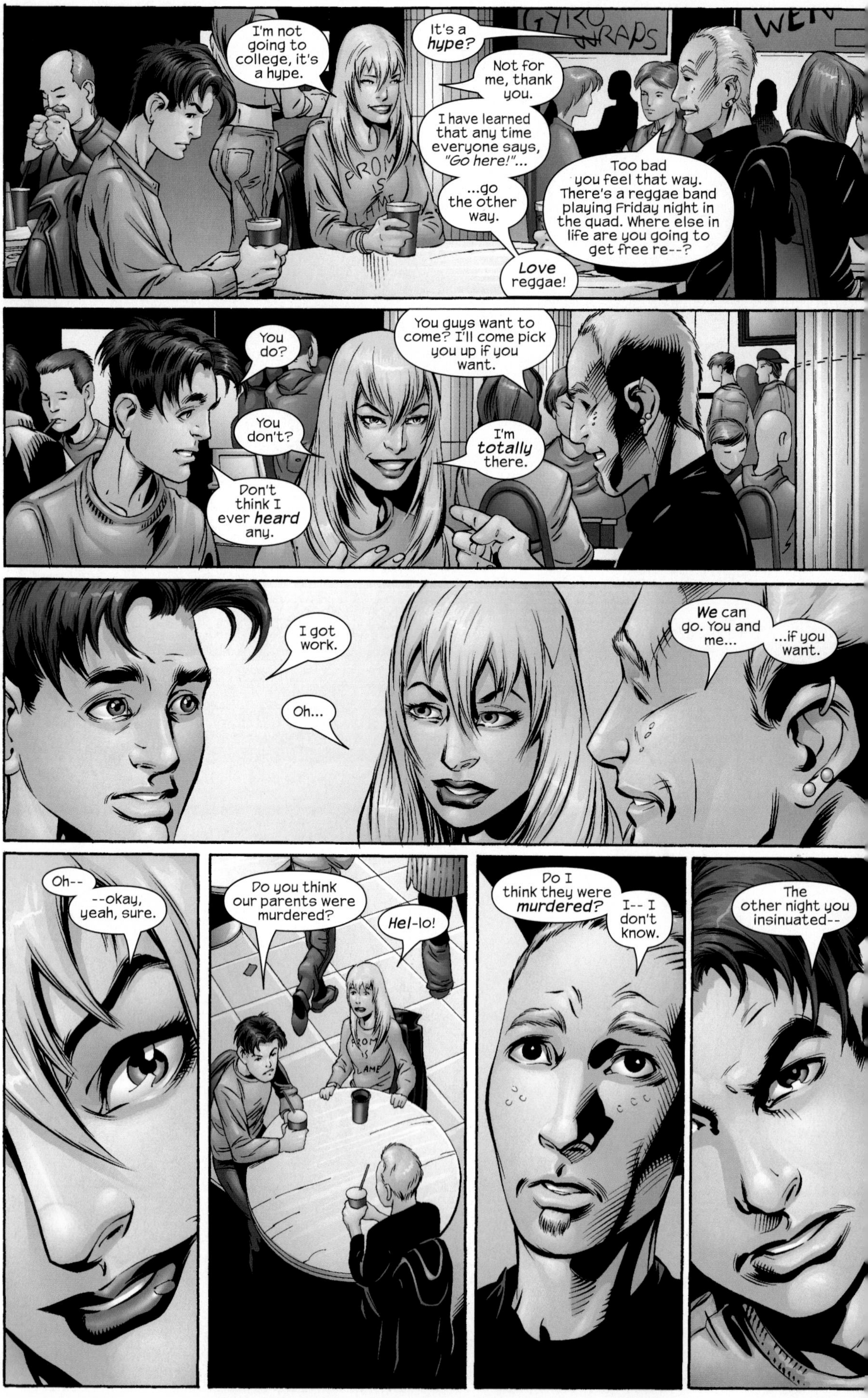
I'm not going to college, it's a hype.
It's a *hype*?
Not for me, thank you.
I have learned that any time everyone says, *"Go here!"*...
...go the other way.
Too bad you feel that way. There's a reggae band playing Friday night in the quad. Where else in life are you going to get free re--?
Love reggae!
GYRO WRAPS
You do?
You don't?
Don't think I ever *heard* any.
You guys want to come? I'll come pick you up if you want.
I'm *totally* there.
I got work.
Oh...
We can go. You and me...
...if you want.
Oh--
--okay, yeah, sure.
Do you think our parents were murdered?
Hel-lo!
Do I think they were *murdered?*
I-- I don't know.
The other night you insinuated--

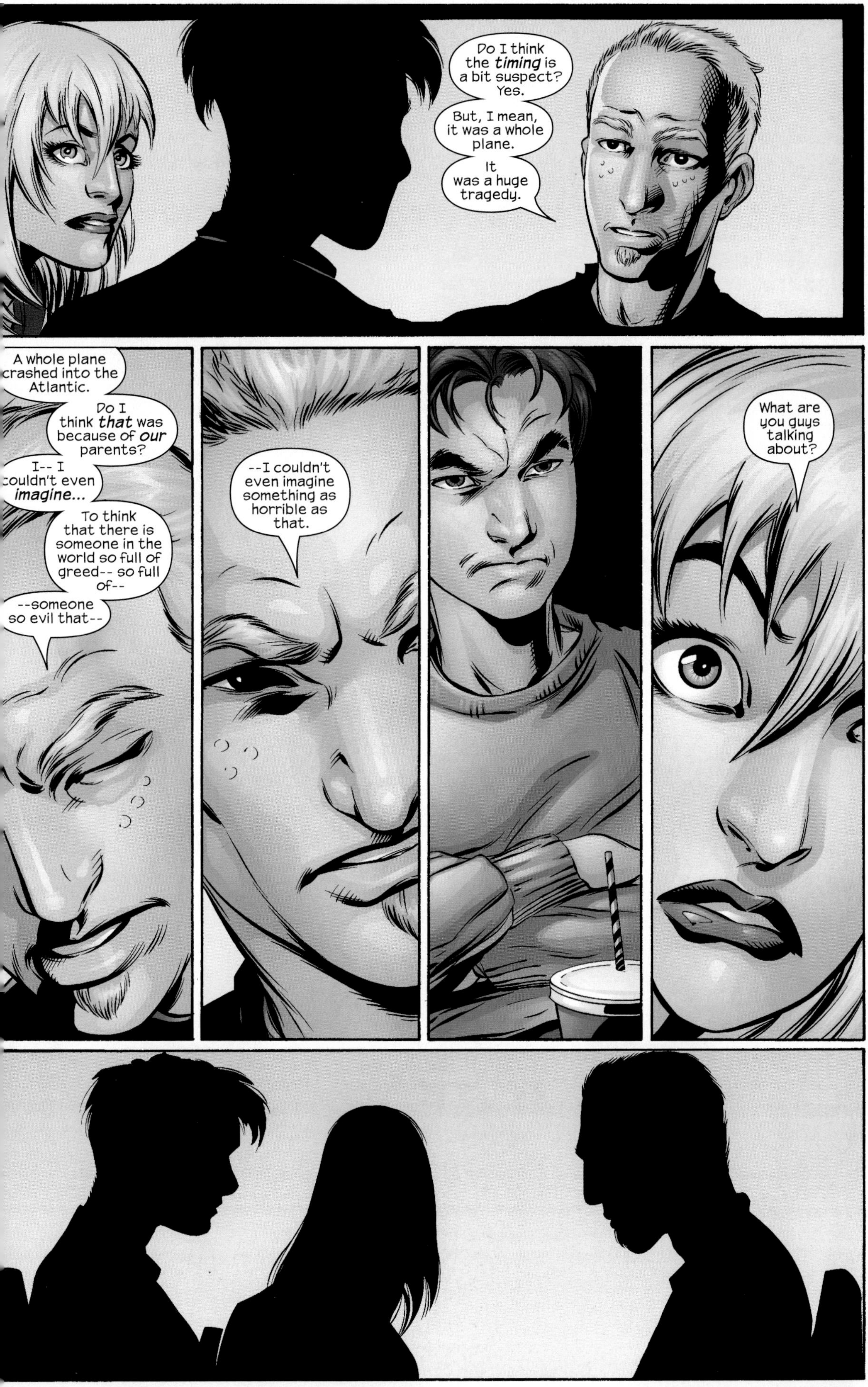
Do I think the *timing* is a bit suspect? Yes.
But, I mean, it was a whole plane.
It was a huge tragedy.
A whole plane crashed into the Atlantic.
Do I think *that* was because of *our* parents?
I-- I couldn't even *imagine...*
To think that there is someone in the world so full of greed-- so full of--
--someone so evil that--
--I couldn't even imagine something as horrible as that.
What are you guys talking about?

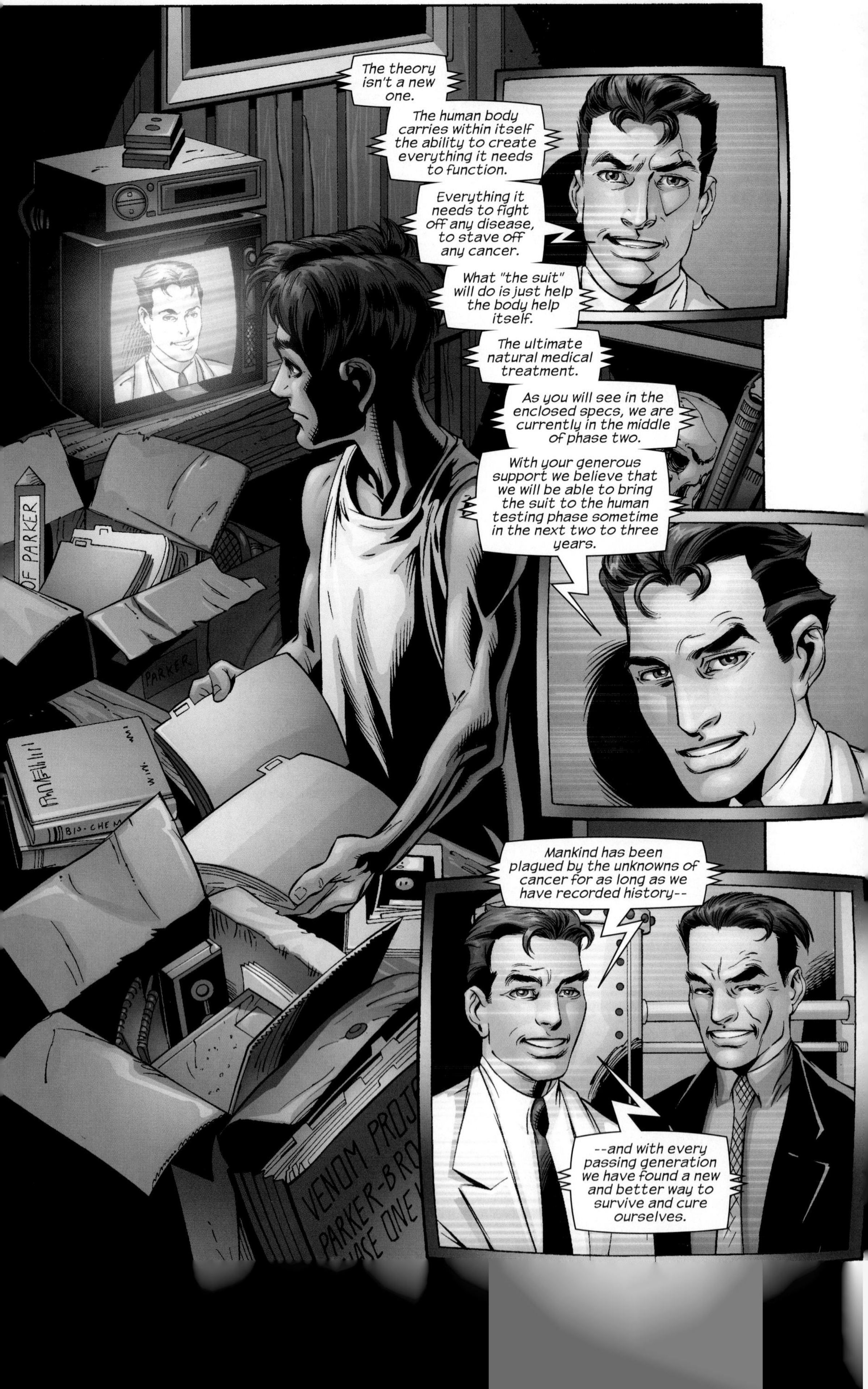
The theory isn't a new one.
The human body carries within itself the ability to create everything it needs to function.
Everything it needs to fight off any disease, to stave off any cancer.
What "the suit" will do is just help the body help itself.
The ultimate natural medical treatment.
As you will see in the enclosed specs, we are currently in the middle of phase two.
With your generous support we believe that we will be able to bring the suit to the human testing phase sometime in the next two to three years.
Mankind has been plagued by the unknowns of cancer for as long as we have recorded history--
--and with every passing generation we have found a new and better way to survive and cure ourselves.
PARKER

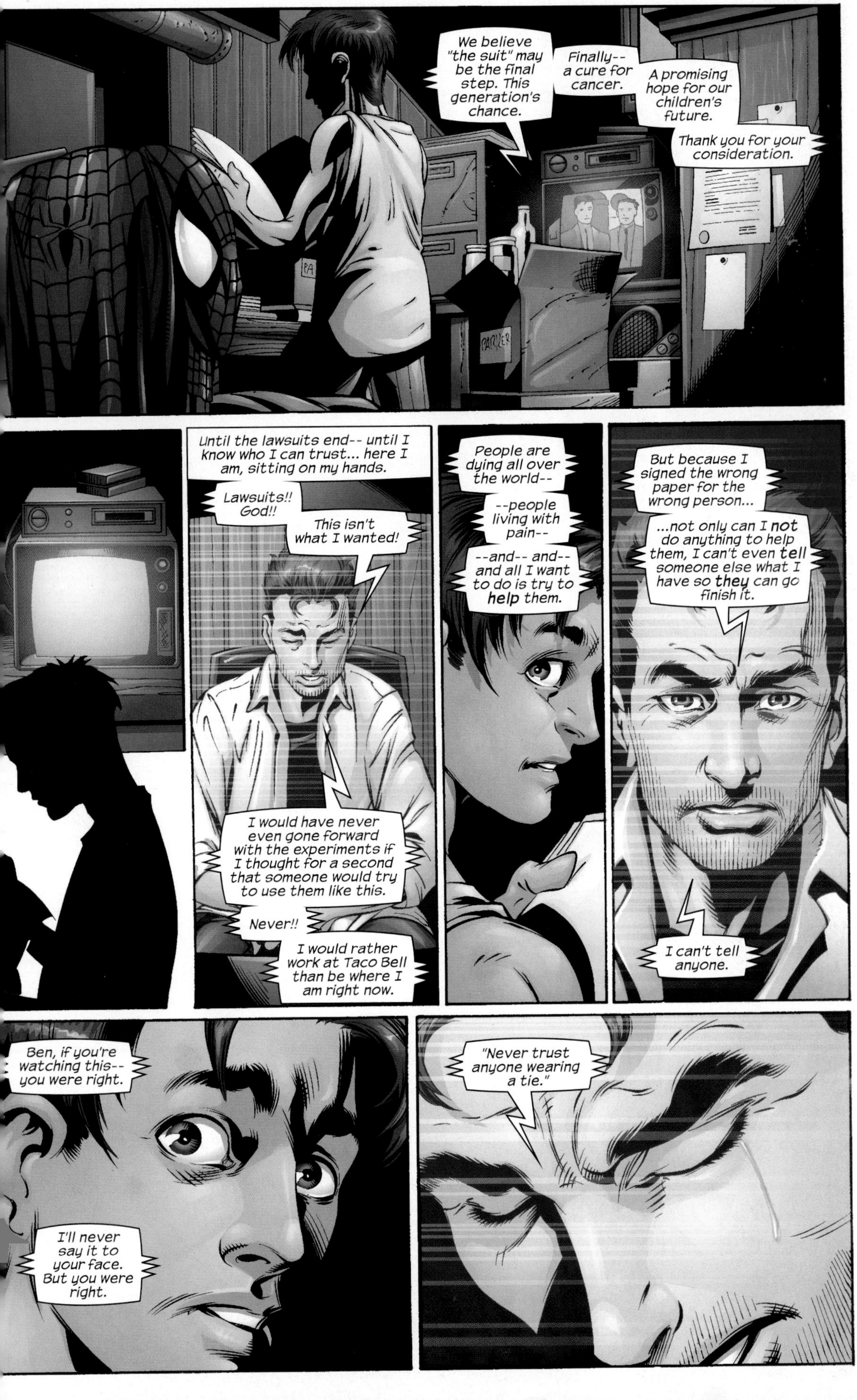

We believe "the suit" may be the final step. This generation's chance.
Finally-- a cure for cancer.
A promising hope for our children's future.
Thank you for your consideration.
Until the lawsuits end-- until I know who I can trust... here I am, sitting on my hands.
Lawsuits!! God!!
This isn't what I wanted!
I would have never even gone forward with the experiments if I thought for a second that someone would try to use them like this.
Never!!
I would rather work at Taco Bell than be where I am right now.
People are dying all over the world--
--people living with pain--
--and-- and-- and all I want to do is try to **help** them.
But because I signed the wrong paper for the wrong person...
...not only can I **not** do anything to help them, I can't even **tell** someone else what I have so **they** can go finish it.
I can't tell anyone.
Ben, if you're watching this-- you were right.
I'll never say it to your face. But you were right.
"Never trust anyone wearing a tie."

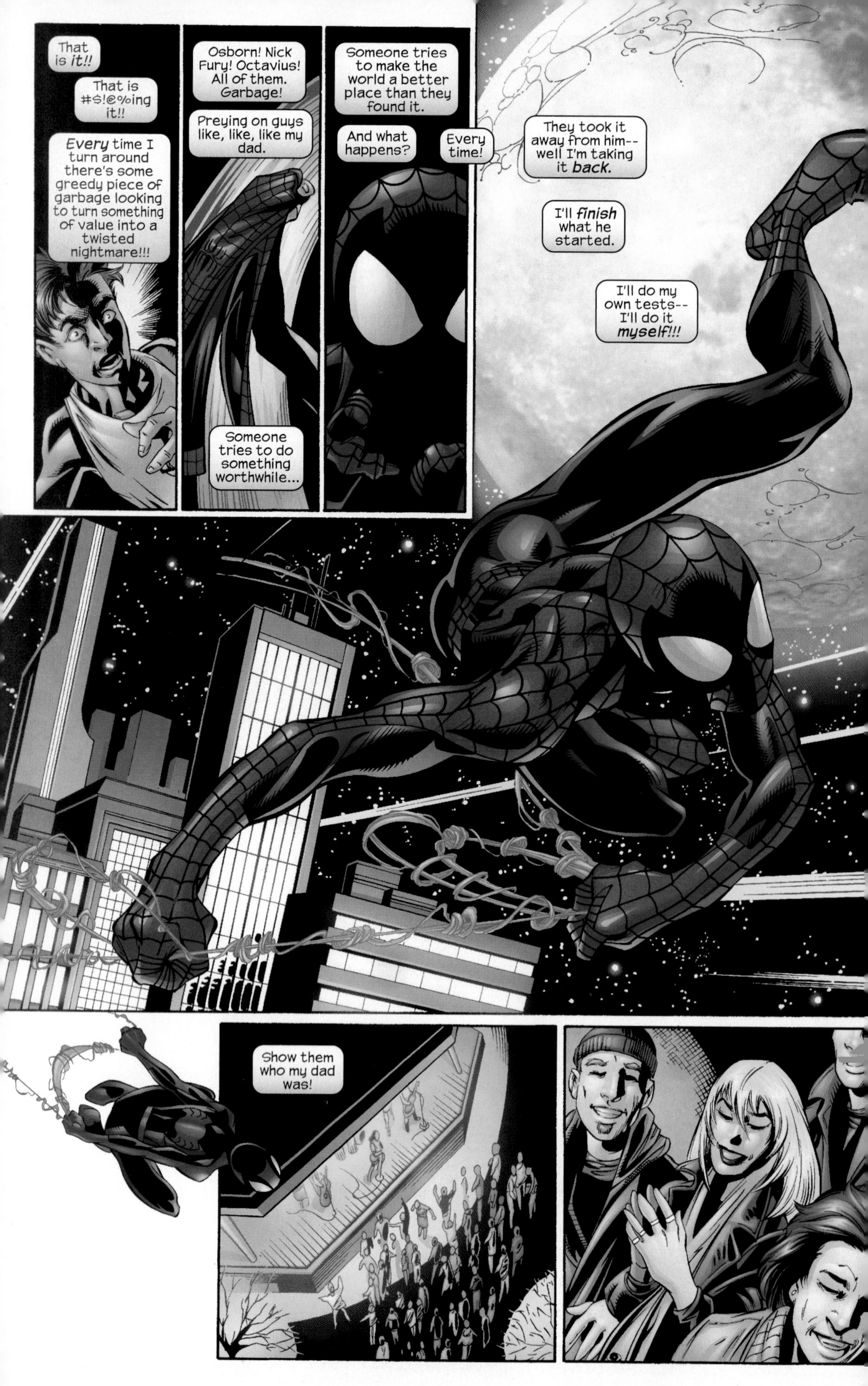
That is it!!
That is #$!@%ing it!!
Every time I turn around there's some greedy piece of garbage looking to turn something of value into a twisted nightmare!!!
Osborn! Nick Fury! Octavius! All of them. Garbage!
Preying on guys like, like, like my dad.
Someone tries to do something worthwhile...
Someone tries to make the world a better place than they found it.
And what happens?
Every time!
They took it away from him-- well I'm taking it back.
I'll finish what he started.
I'll do my own tests-- I'll do it myself!!!
Show them who my dad was!

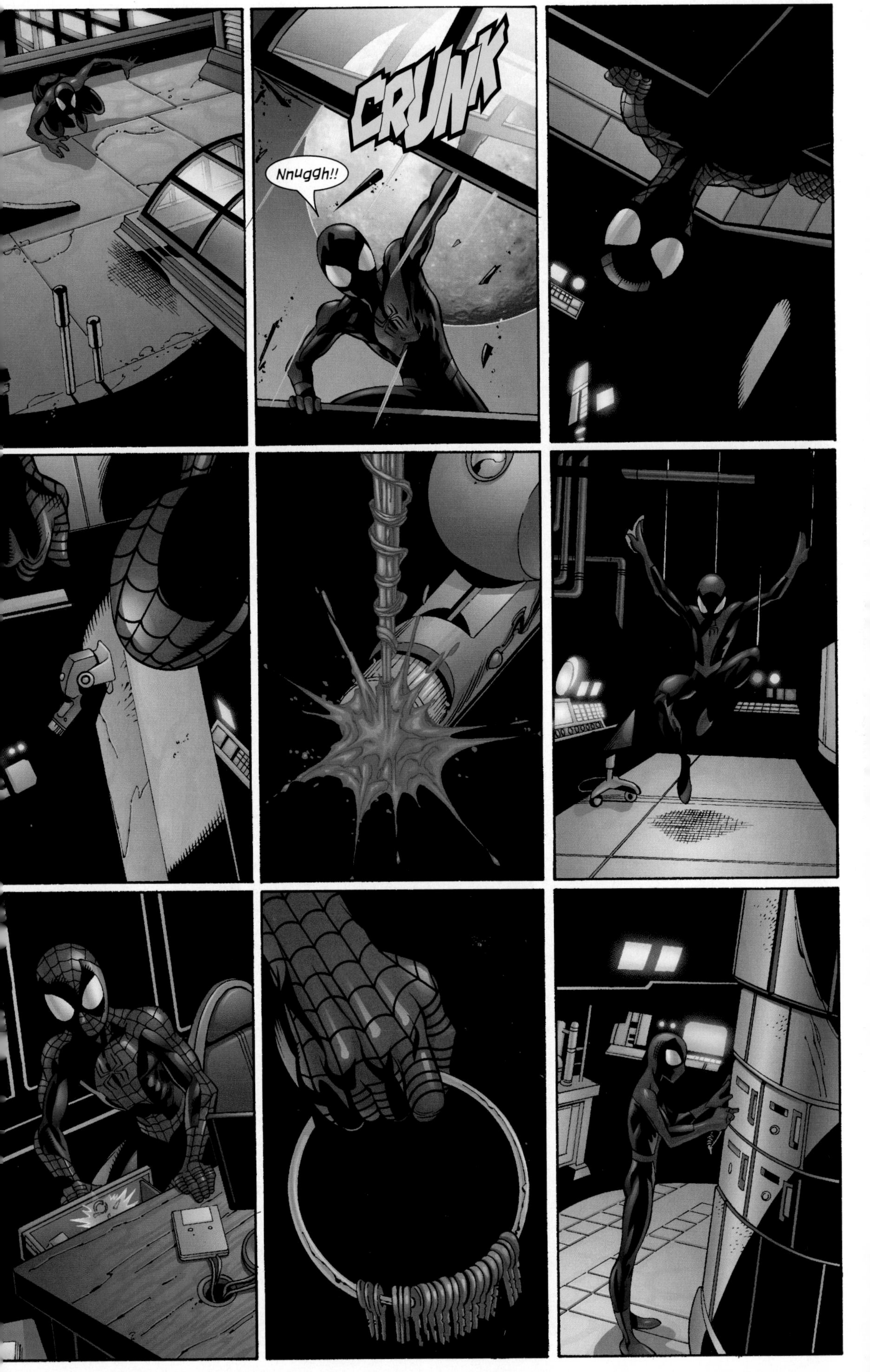
CRUNK
Nnuggh!!

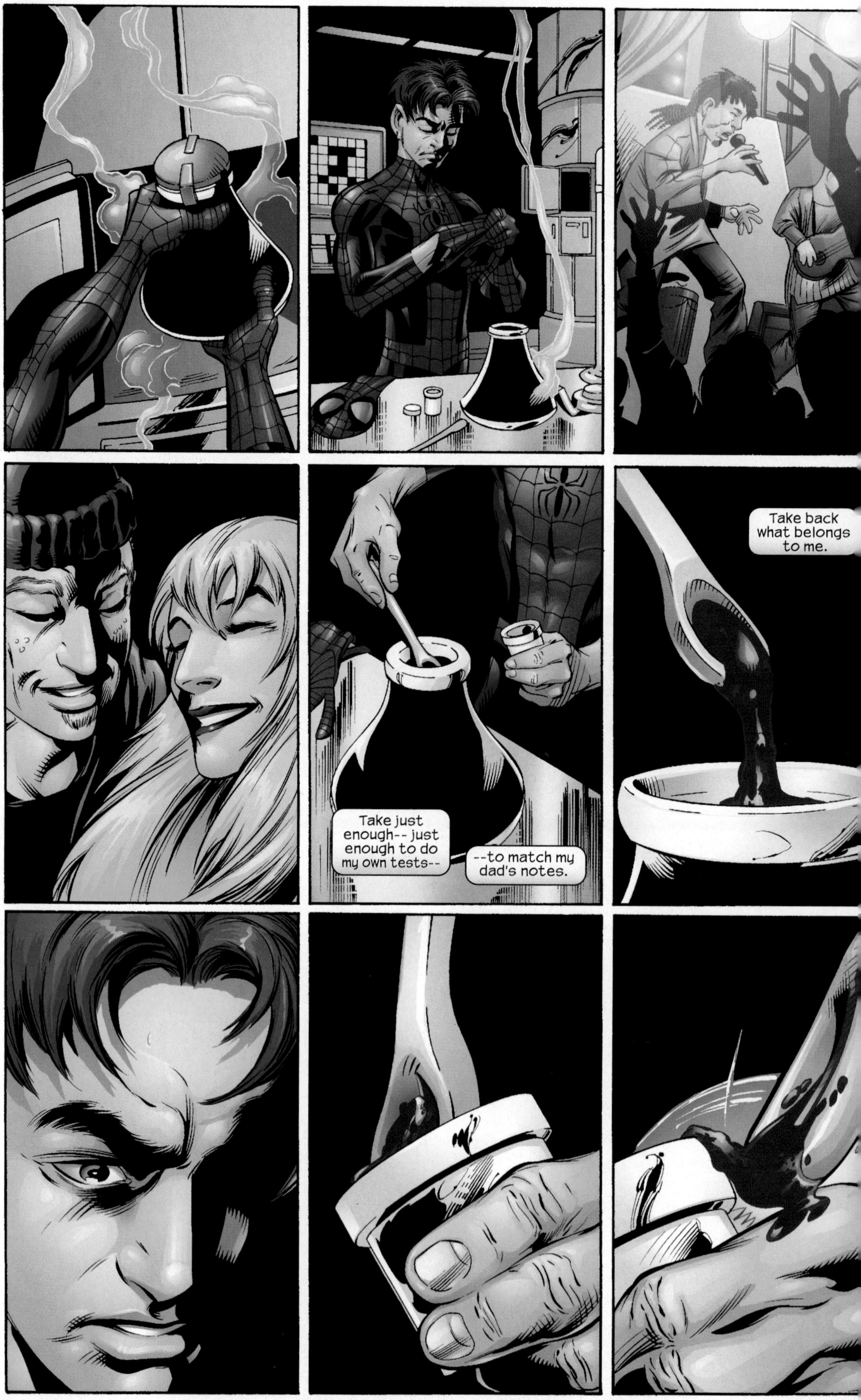
Take just enough-- just enough to do my own tests--
--to match my dad's notes.
Take back what belongs to me.

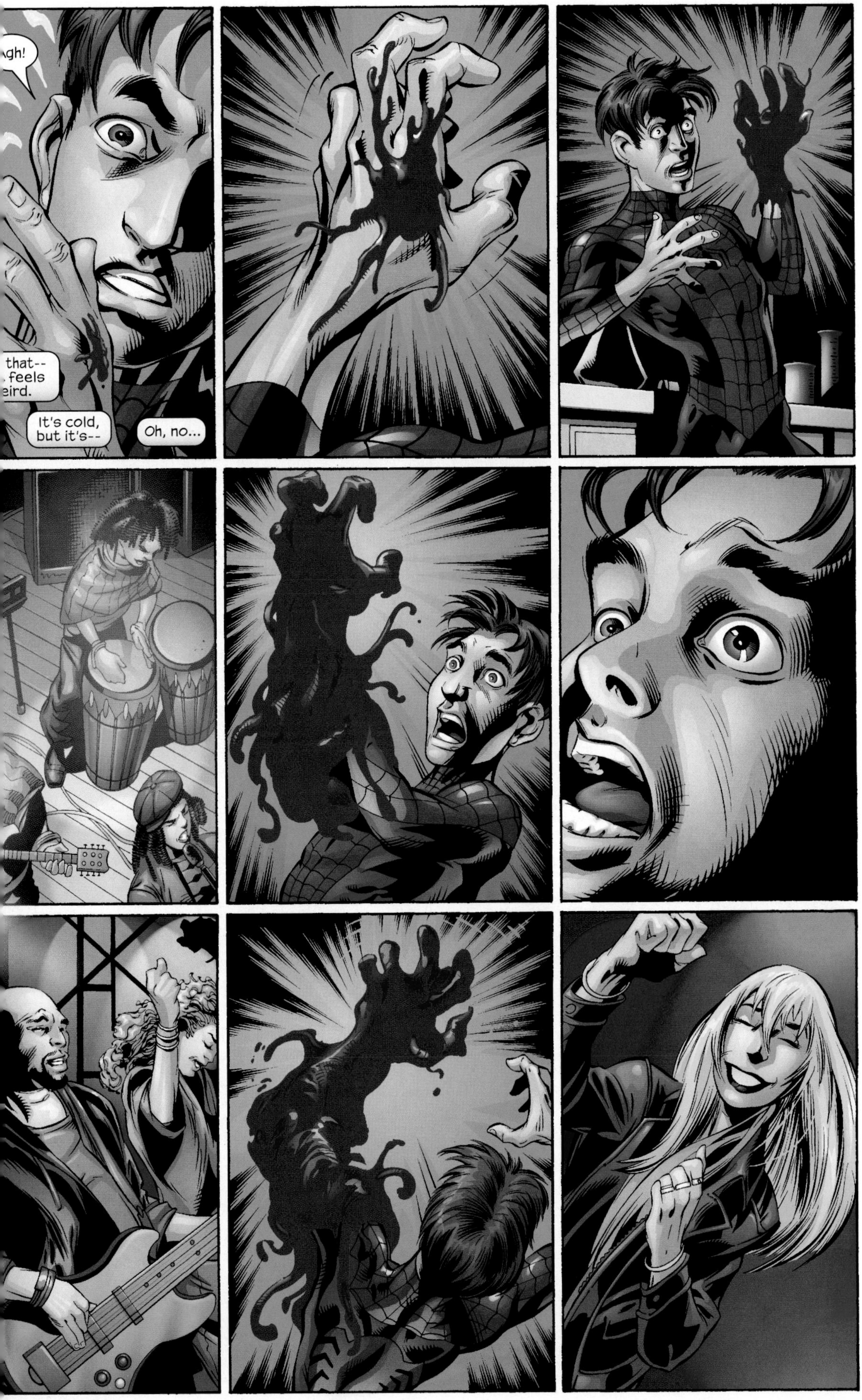

gh!
that--
feels
eird.
It's cold,
but it's--
Oh, no...

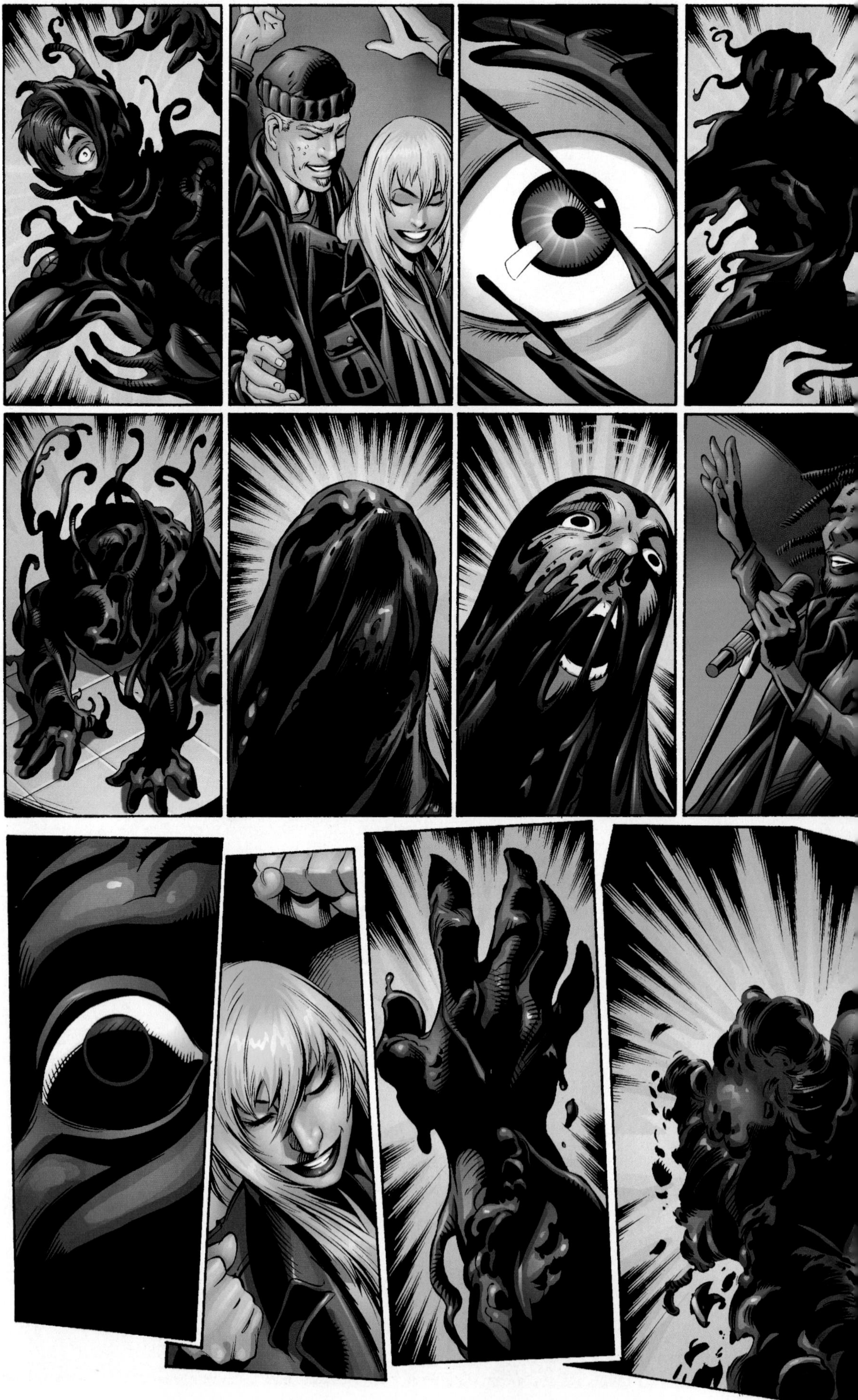

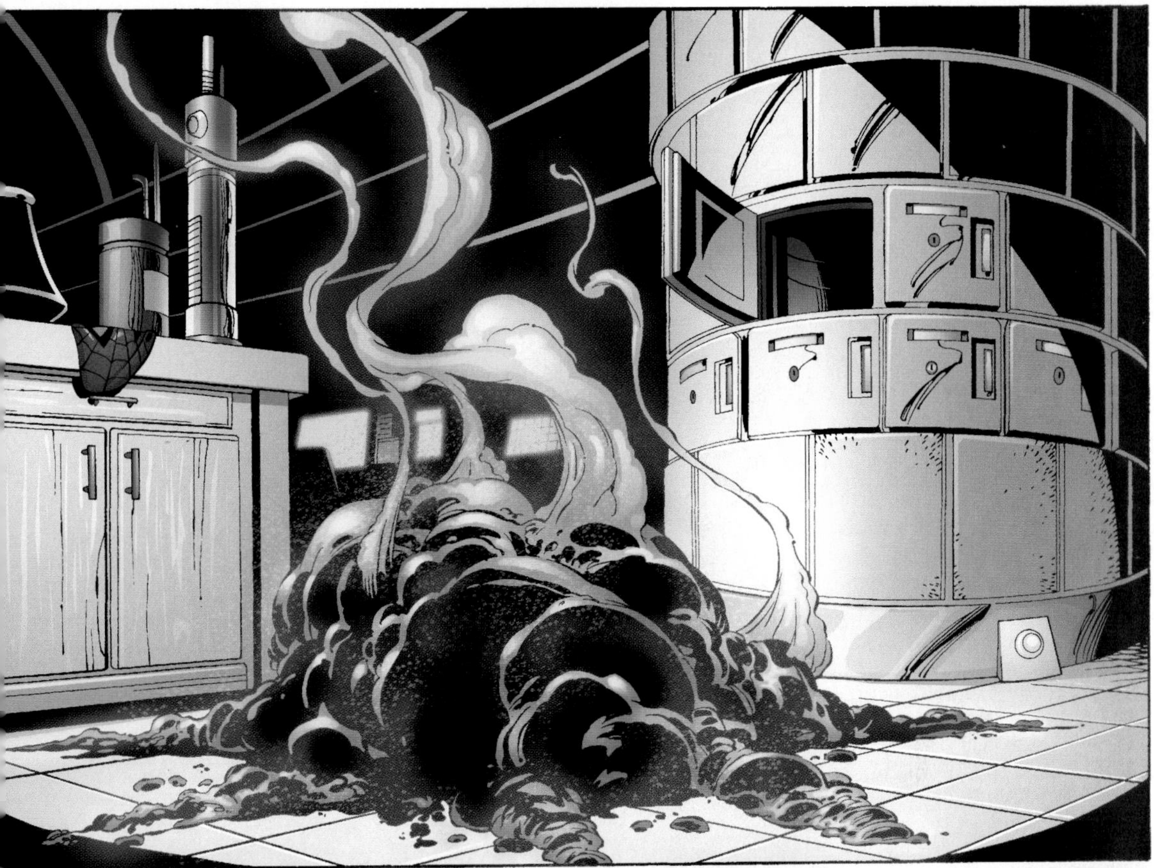

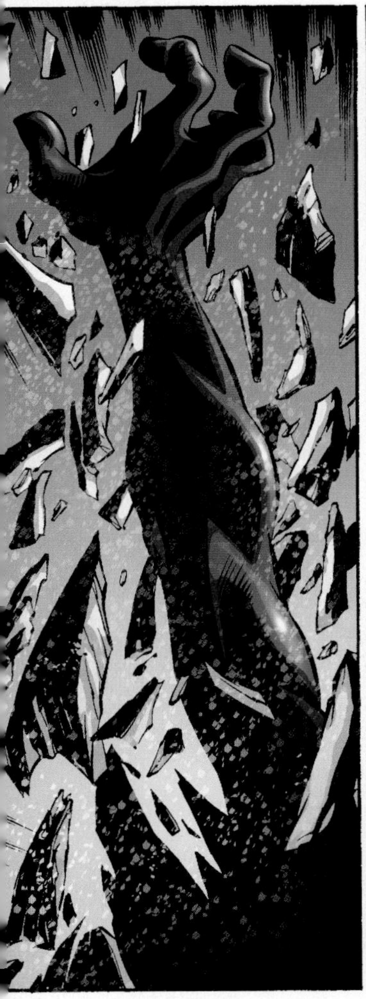

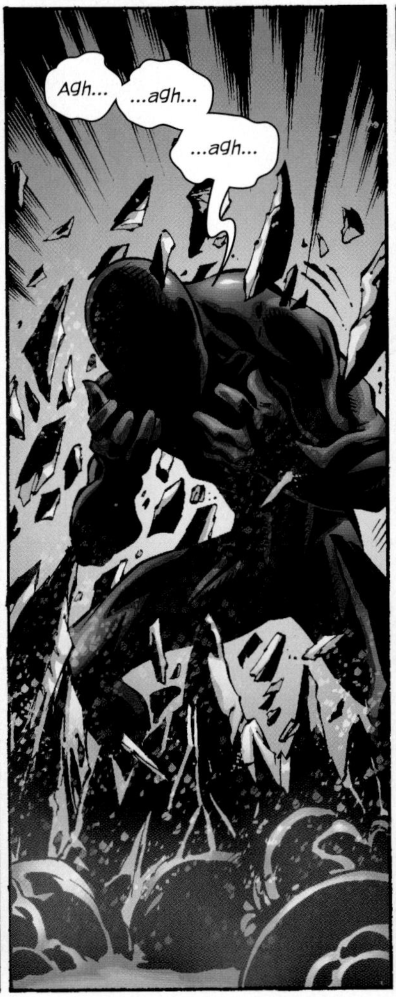
Agh...
...agh...
...agh...

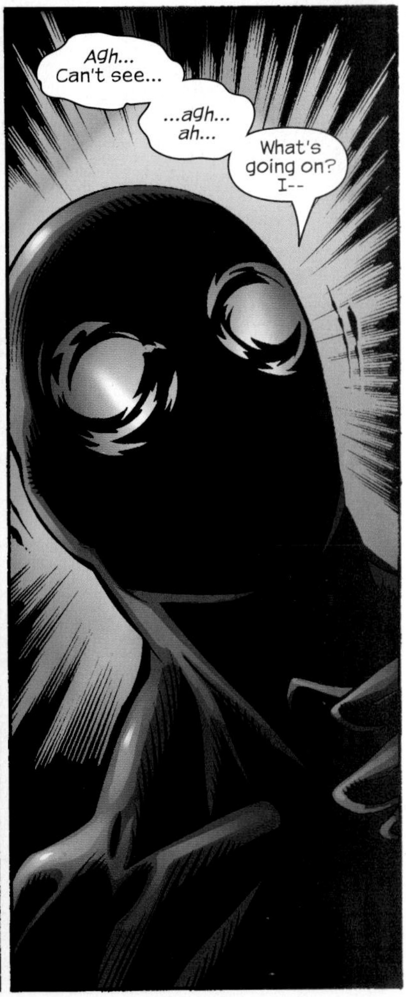
Agh... Can't see...
...agh... ah...
What's going on? I--

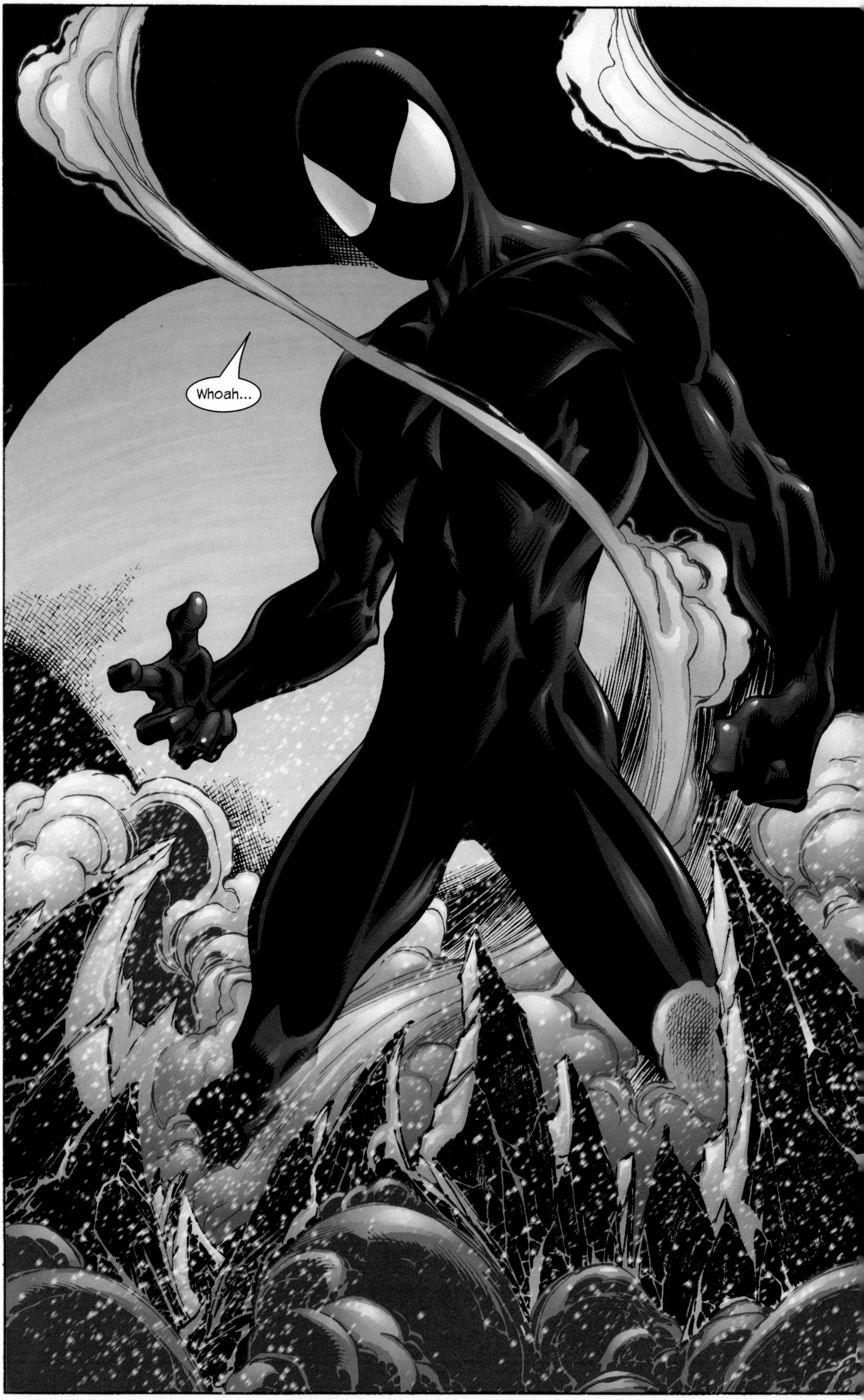
Whoah...

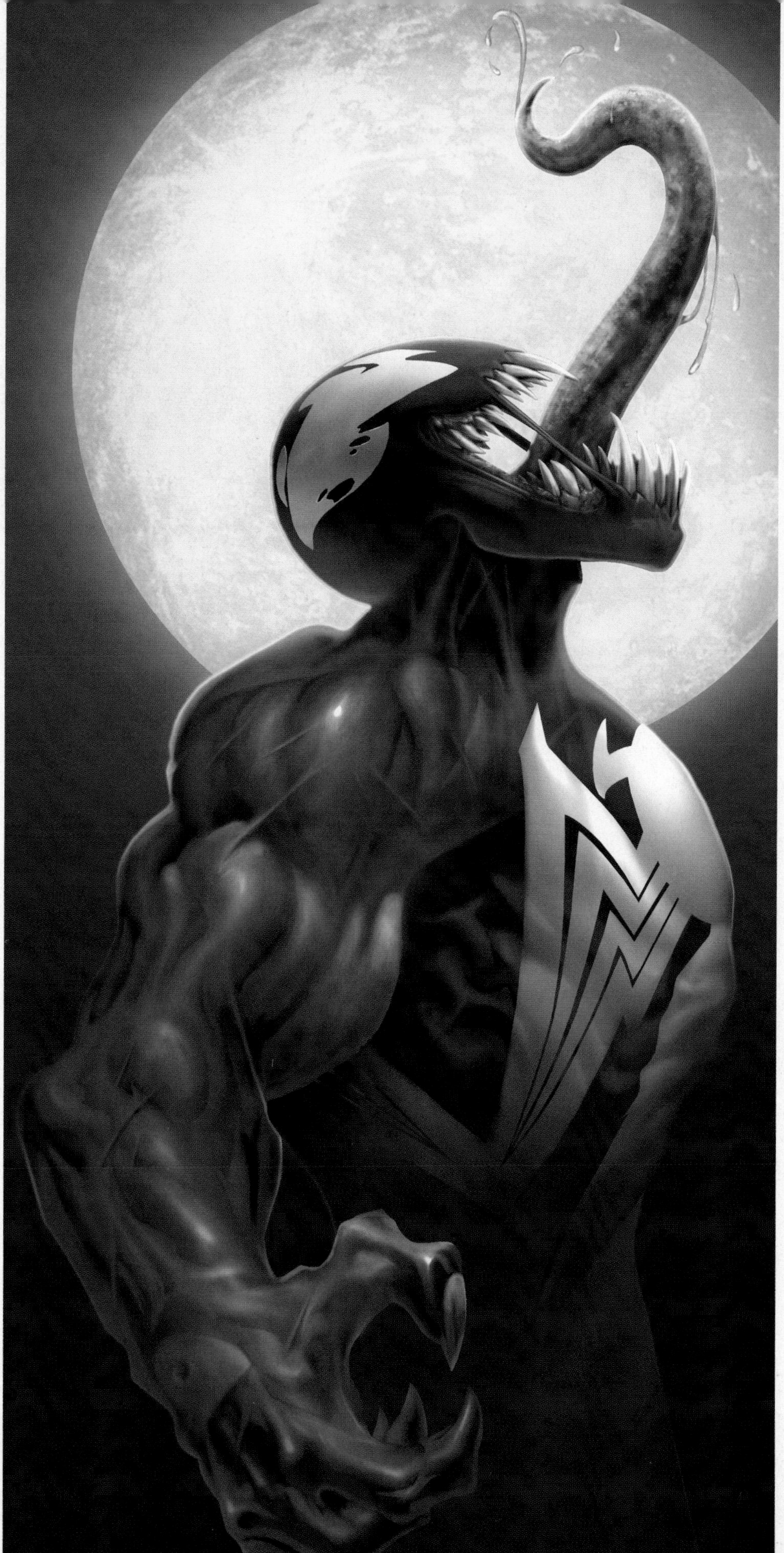

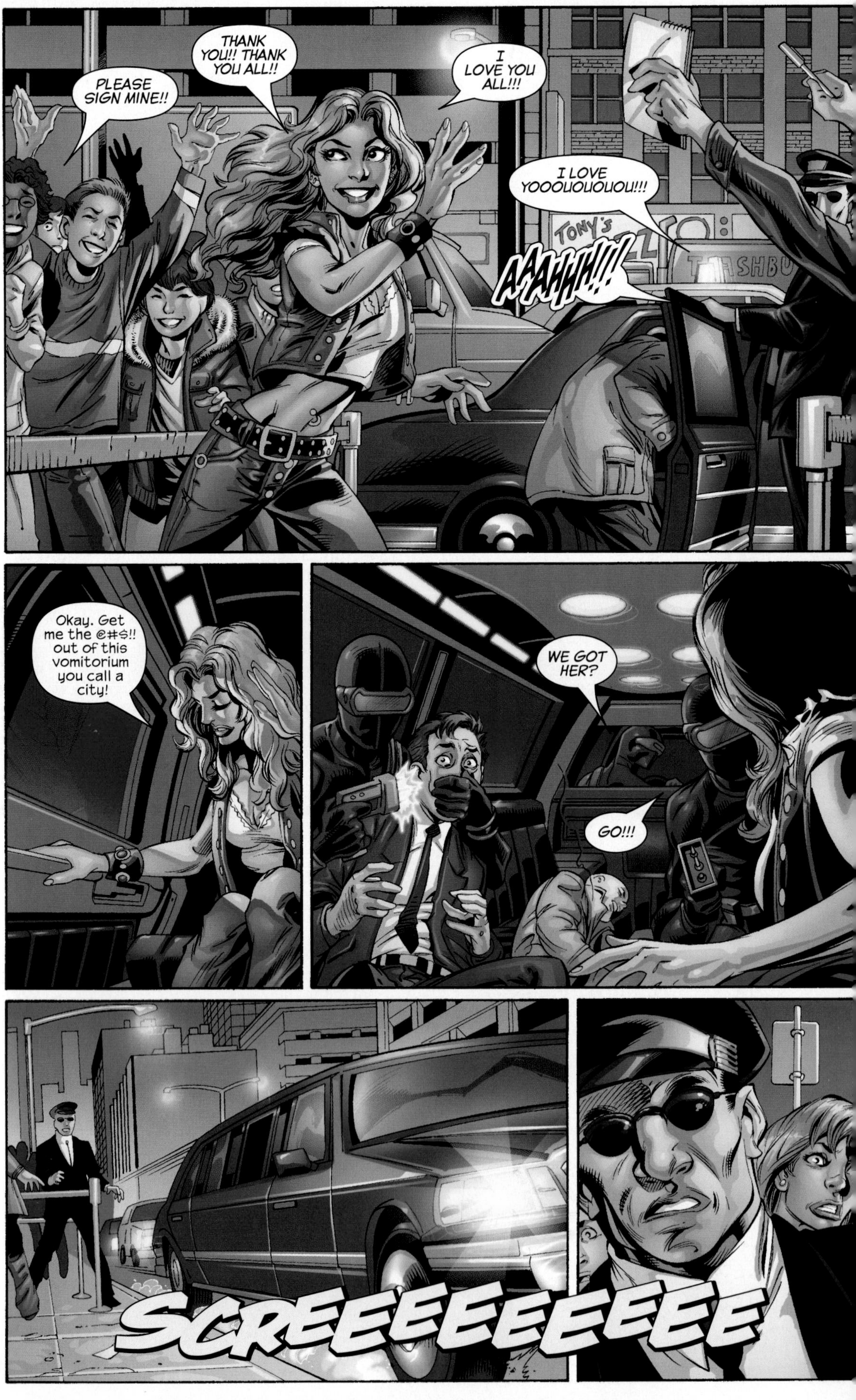
PLEASE SIGN MINE!!
THANK YOU!! THANK YOU ALL!!
I LOVE YOU ALL!!!
I LOVE YOOOUOUOUOU!!!
TONY'S
AAAHHH!!!
Okay. Get me the @#$!! out of this vomitorium you call a city!
WE GOT HER?
GO!!!
SCREEEEEEEEEE

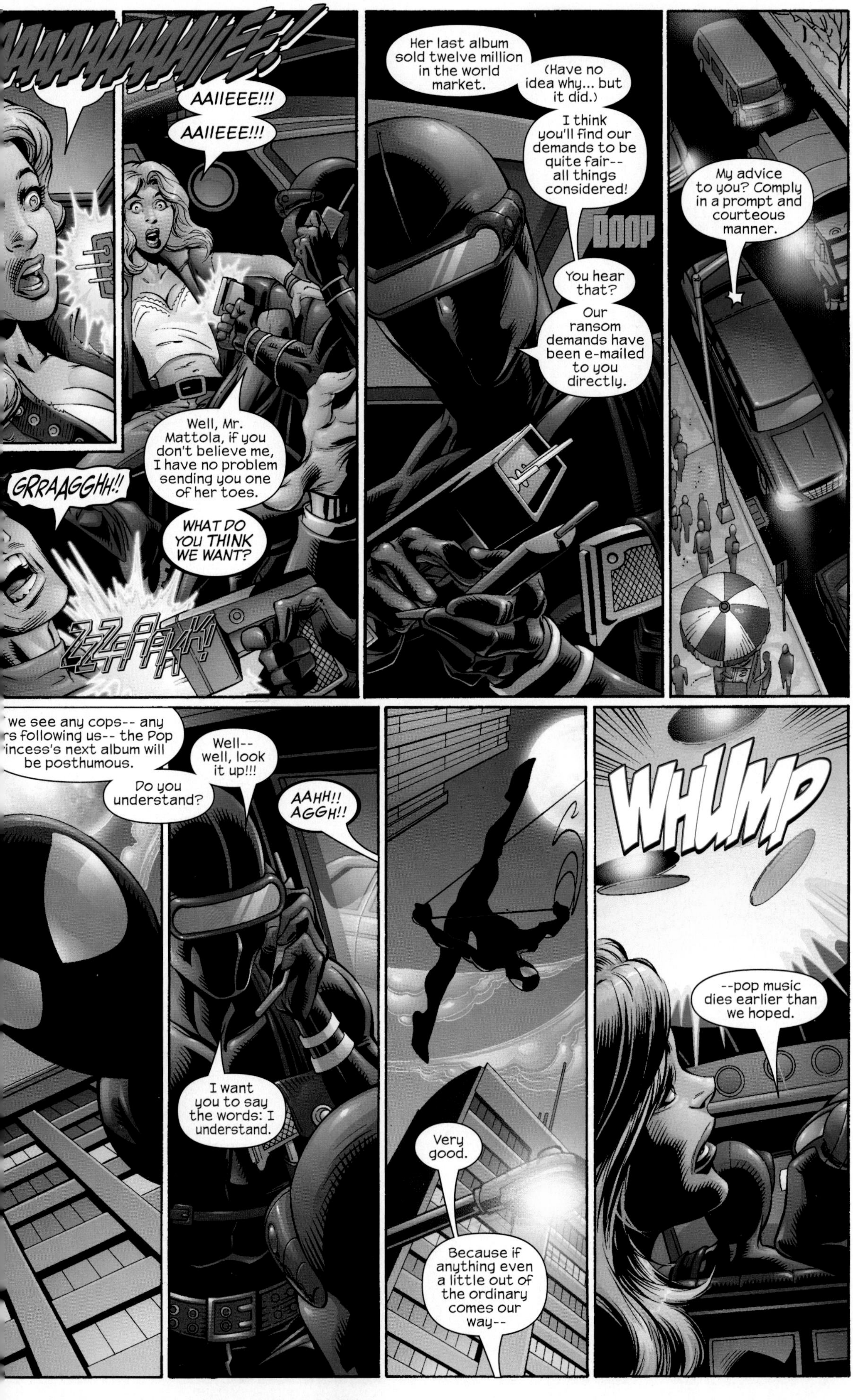
AAAAAAAAAAIIEE!!
AAIIEEE!!!
AAIIEEE!!!
Well, Mr. Mattola, if you don't believe me, I have no problem sending you one of her toes.
GRRAAGGHH!!
WHAT DO YOU THINK WE WANT?
Her last album sold twelve million in the world market.
(Have no idea why... but it did.)
I think you'll find our demands to be quite fair-- all things considered!
BOOP
You hear that?
Our ransom demands have been e-mailed to you directly.
My advice to you? Comply in a prompt and courteous manner.
we see any cops-- any
rs following us-- the Pop
rincess's next album will
be posthumous.
Do you understand?
Well-- well, look it up!!!
AAHH!! AGGH!!
I want you to say the words: I understand.
Very good.
Because if anything even a little out of the ordinary comes our way--
WHUMP
--pop music dies earlier than we hoped.

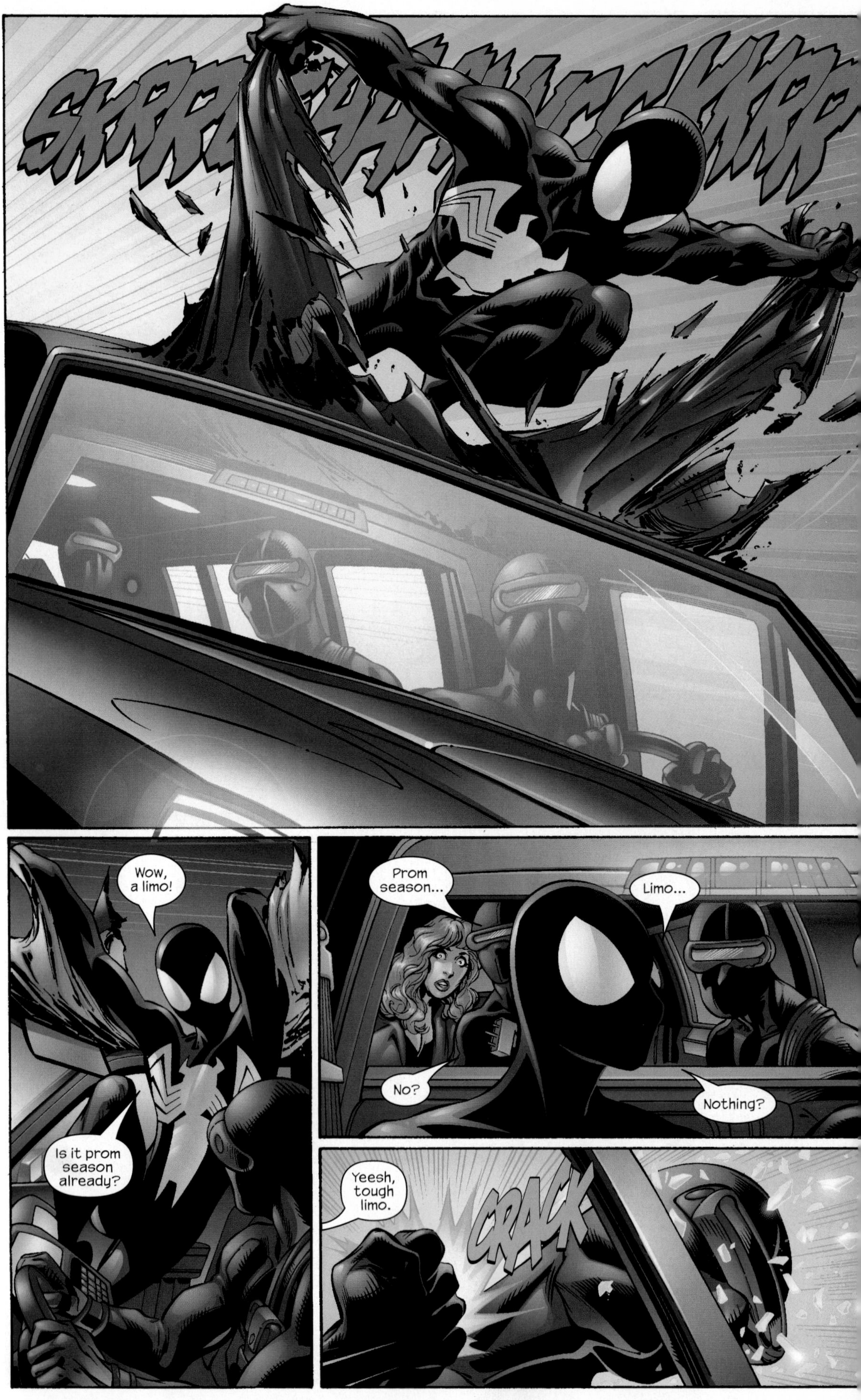
SKRRRSHHHRRRAAAACCCHHKRR
Wow, a limo!
Is it prom season already?
Prom season...
Limo...
No?
Nothing?
Yeesh, tough limo.
CRACK

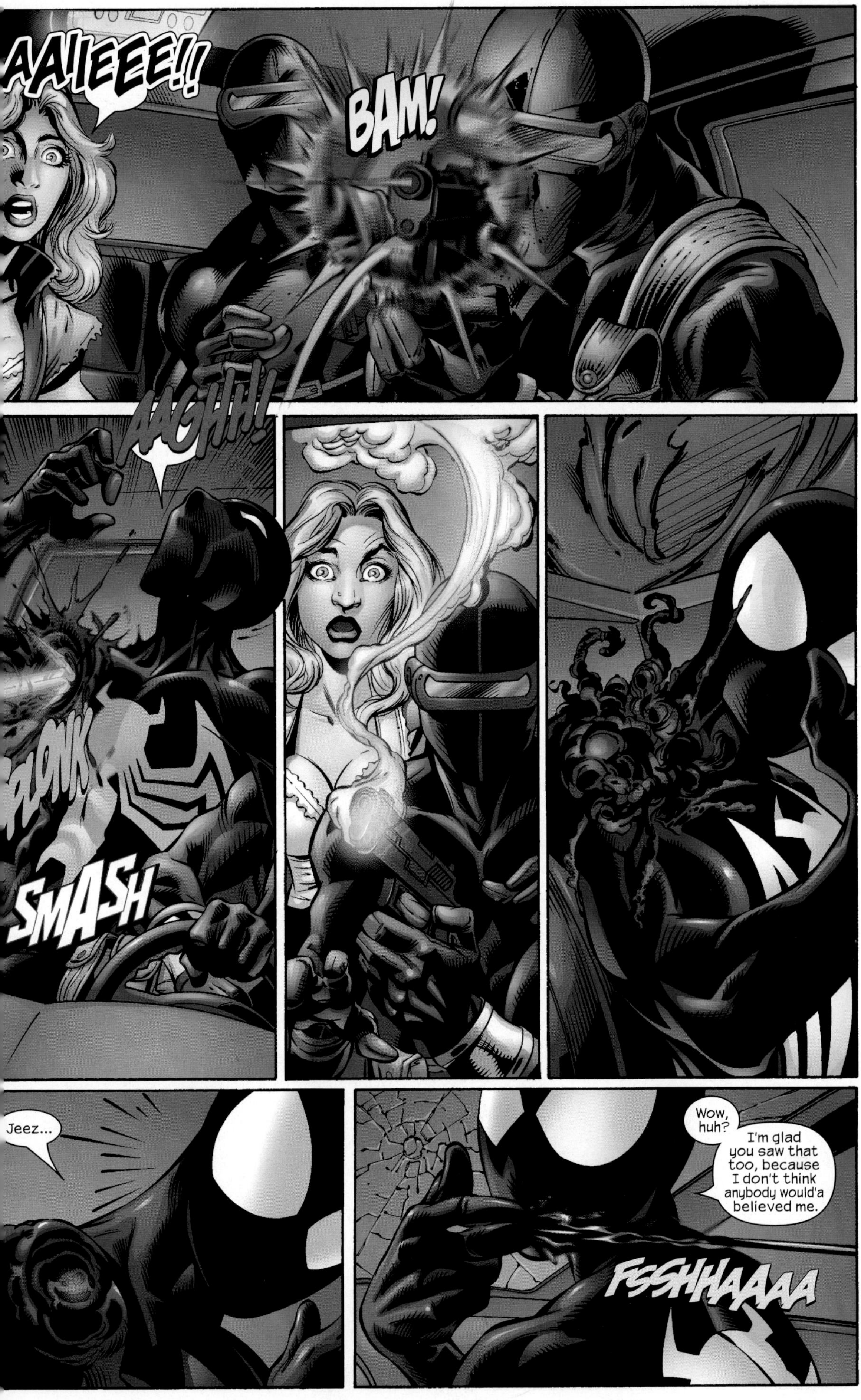
AA!IEEE!!
BAM!
AAGHH!
PLONK
SMASH
Jeez...
Wow, huh?
I'm glad you saw that too, because I don't think anybody would'a believed me.
FSSHHAAAA

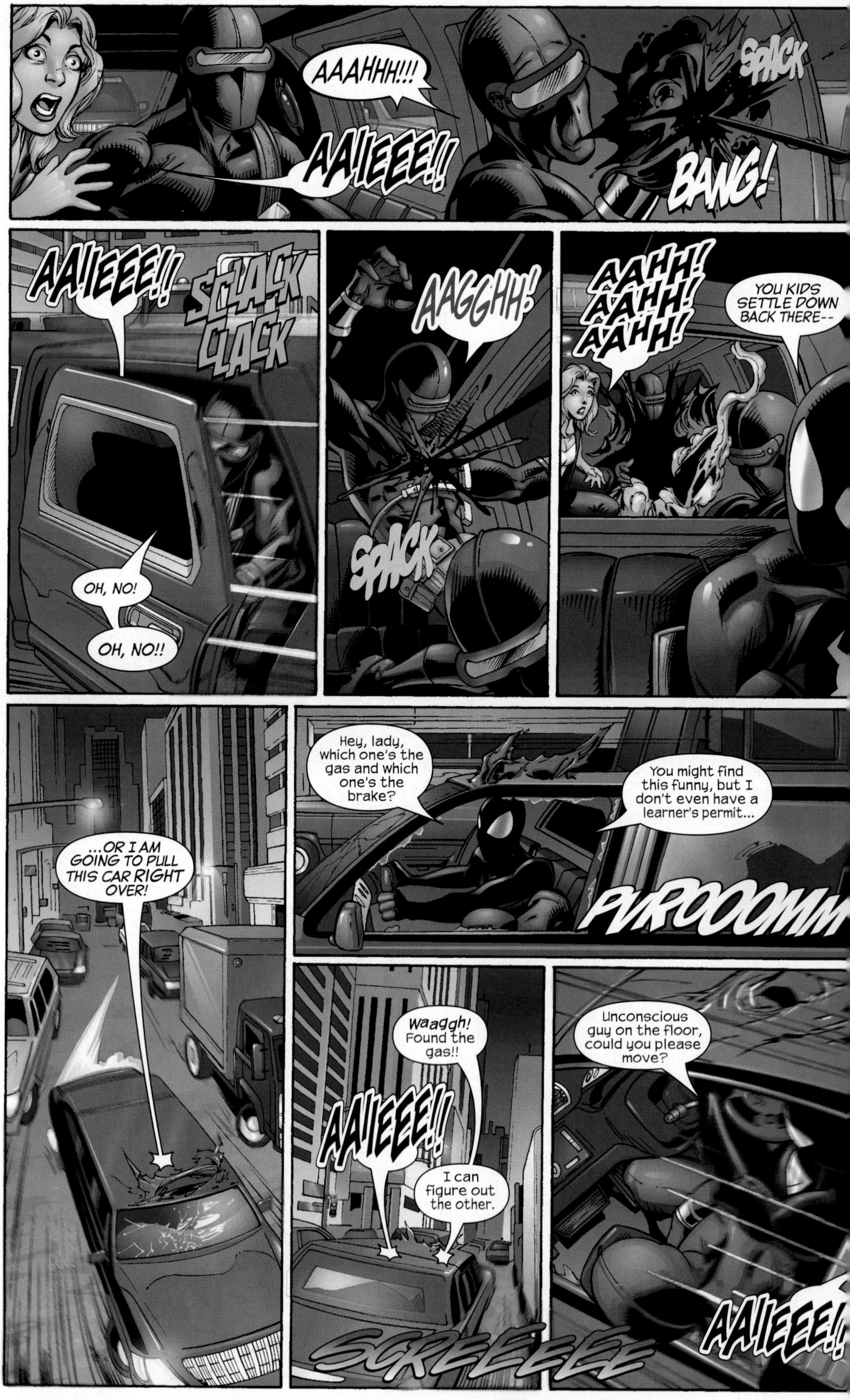
AAAHHH!!!
AA!EEE!!
SPACK
BANG!
AA!EEE!!
SCHLACK
CLACK
OH, NO!
OH, NO!!
AAGGHH!
SPACK
AAHH!
AAHH!
AAHH!
YOU KIDS SETTLE DOWN BACK THERE--
...OR I AM GOING TO PULL THIS CAR RIGHT OVER!
Hey, lady, which one's the gas and which one's the brake?
You might find this funny, but I don't even have a learner's permit...
PVROOOMM
Waaggh! Found the gas!!
AA!EEE!!
I can figure out the other.
SCREEEEEE
Unconscious guy on the floor, could you please move?
AA!EEE!!

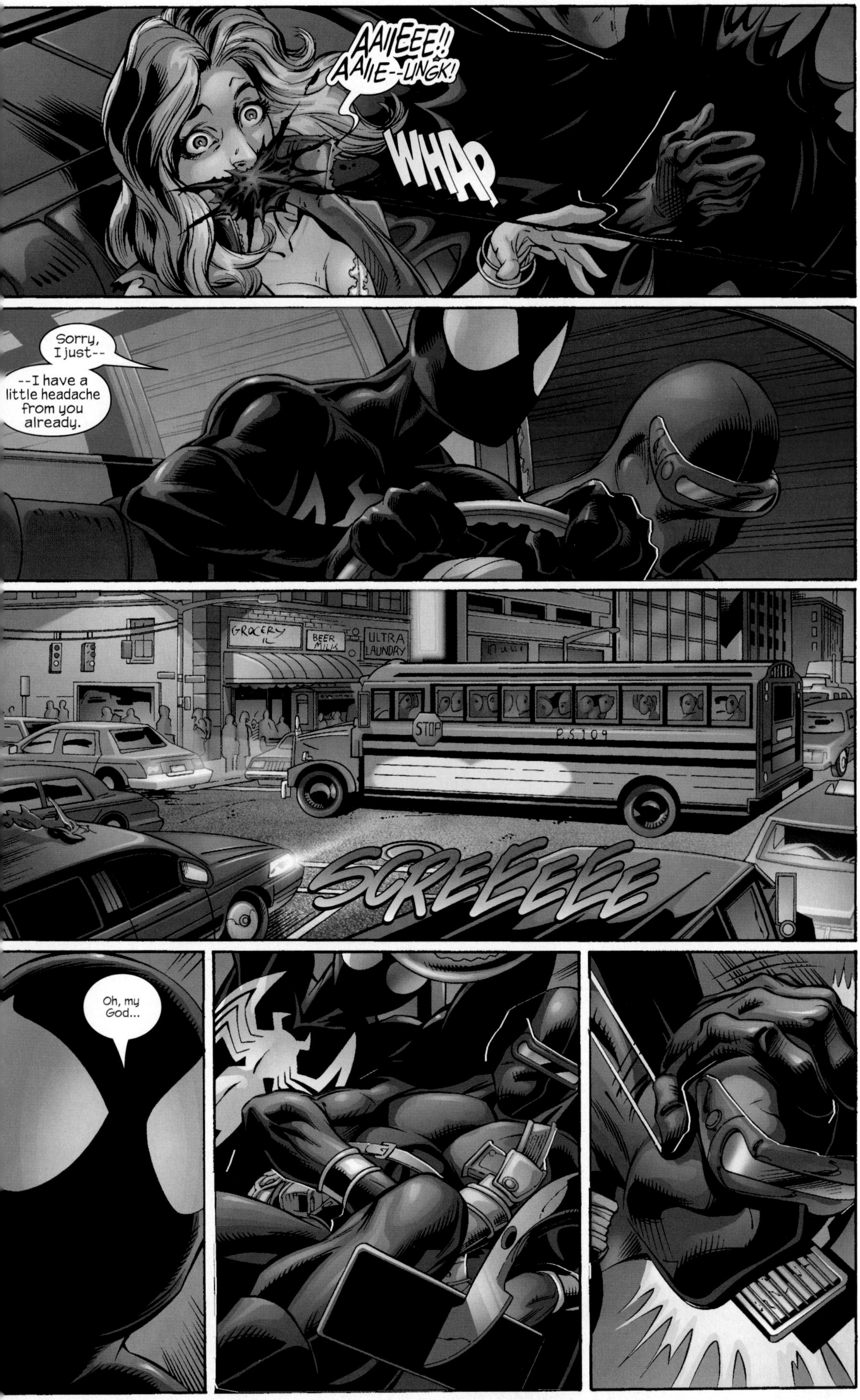
AAIIEEE!!
AAIIE--UNGK!
WHAP
Sorry, I just--
--I have a little headache from you already.
GROCERY
BEER MILK
ULTRA LAUNDRY
STOP
P.S.109
SCREEEEEE
Oh, my God...

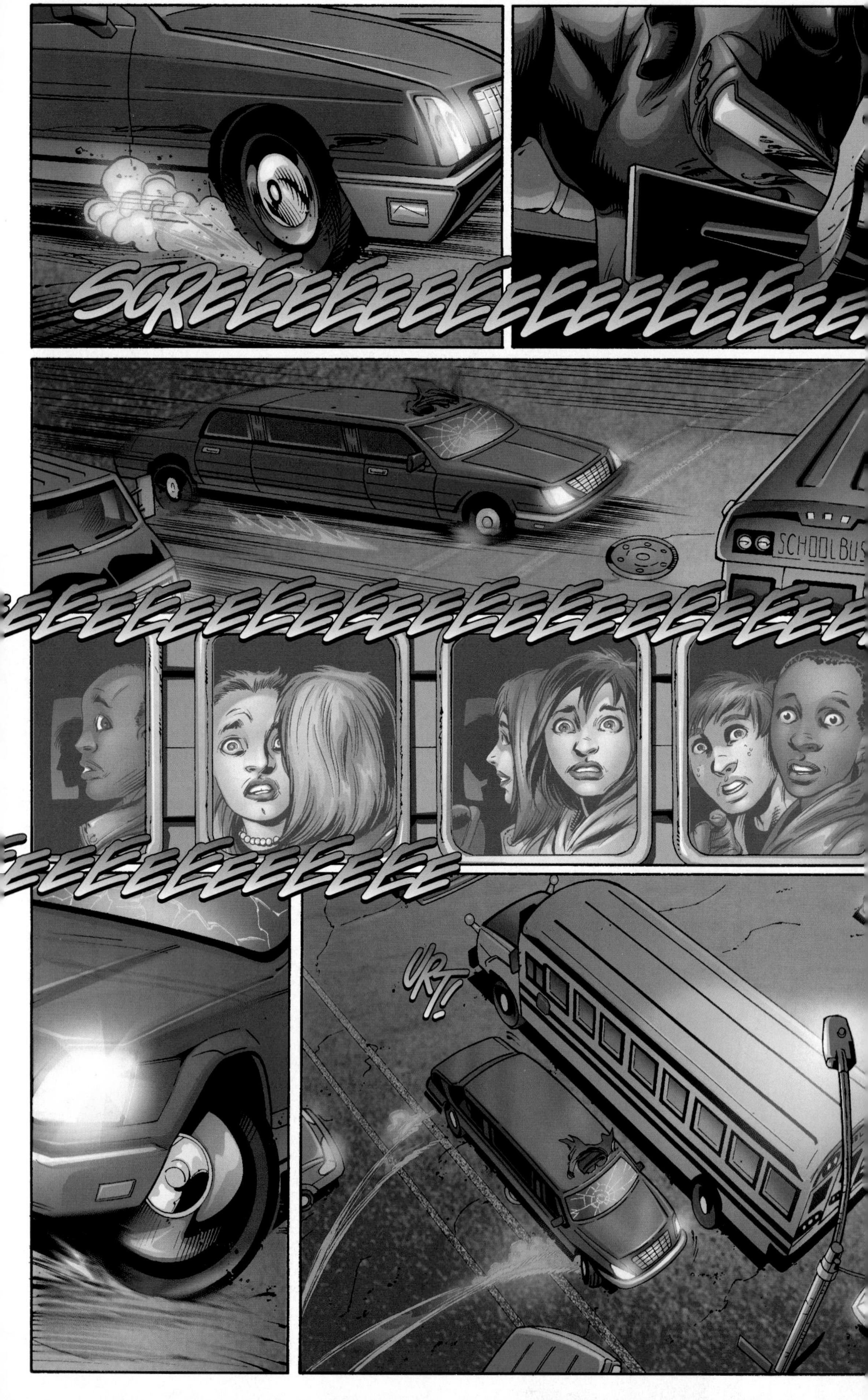
SCREEEEEEEEEEEEEEEEE
EEEEEEEEEEEEEEEEEEEEEEEE
SCHOOLBUS
EEEEEEEEEEEEE
URT!

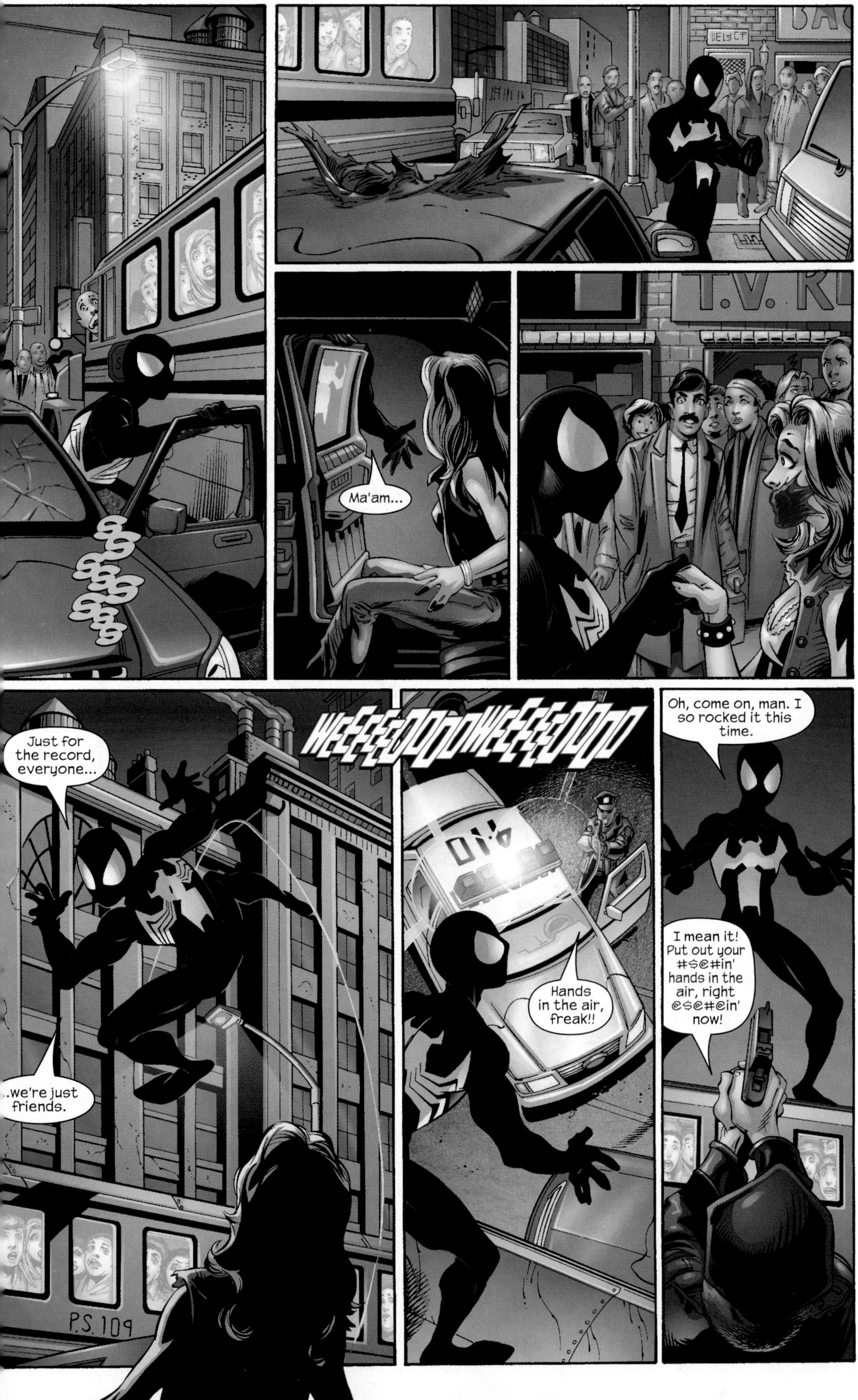
Ma'am...
Just for the record, everyone...
..we're just friends.
WEEEEOOOOWEEEEOOOO
Hands in the air, freak!!
Oh, come on, man. I so rocked it this time.
I mean it! Put out your #$@#in' hands in the air, right @$@#@in' now!
P.S. 109

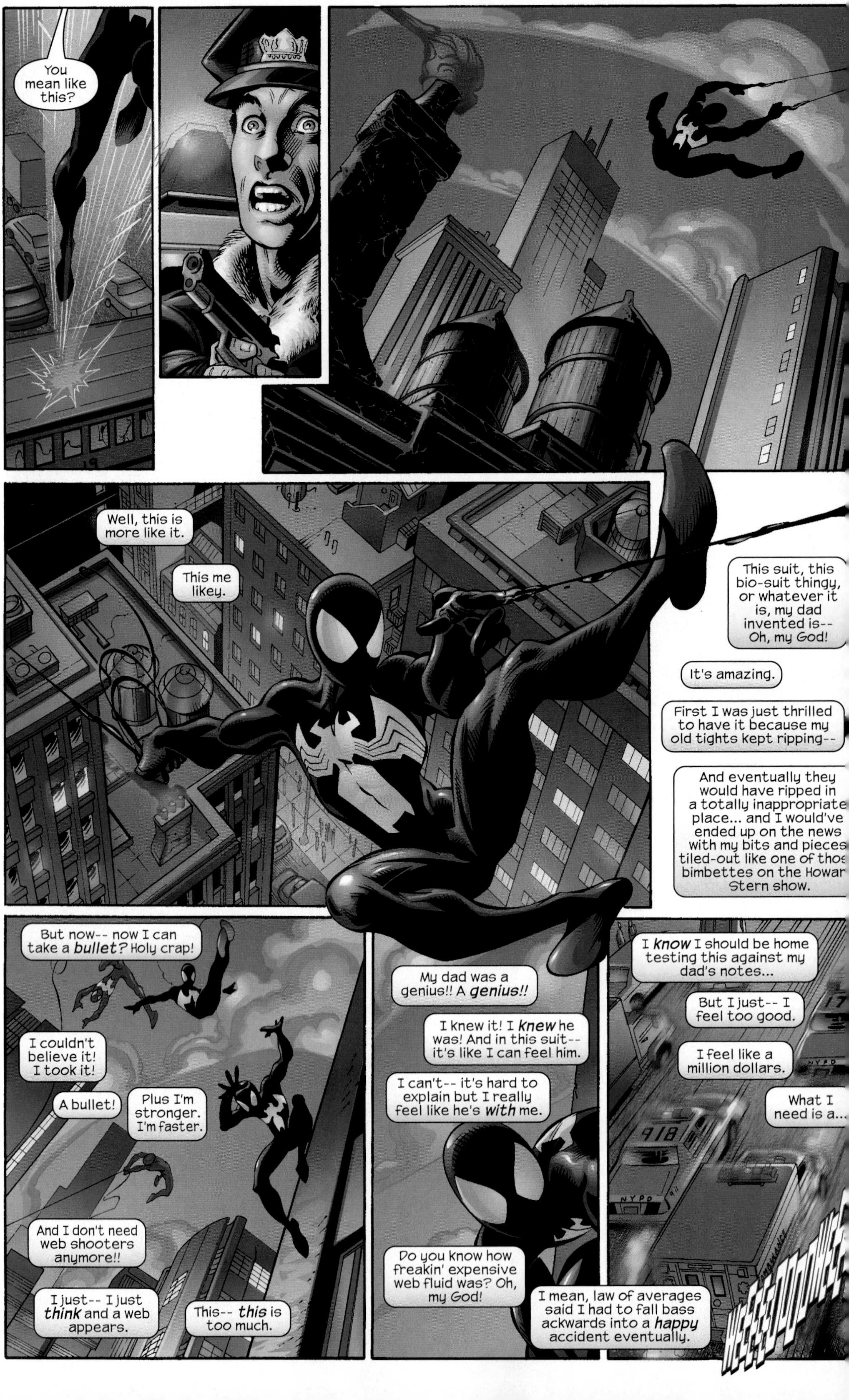

You mean like this?
Well, this is more like it.
This me likey.
This suit, this bio-suit thingy, or whatever it is, my dad invented is-- Oh, my God!
It's amazing.
First I was just thrilled to have it because my old tights kept ripping--
And eventually they would have ripped in a totally inappropriat place... and I would've ended up on the news with my bits and pieces tiled-out like one of thos bimbettes on the Howar Stern show.
But now-- now I can take a *bullet*? Holy crap!
I couldn't believe it! I took it!
A bullet!
Plus I'm stronger. I'm faster.
And I don't need web shooters anymore!!
I just-- I just *think* and a web appears.
This-- *this* is too much.
My dad was a genius!! A *genius!!*
I knew it! I *knew* he was! And in this suit-- it's like I can feel him.
I can't-- it's hard to explain but I really feel like he's *with* me.
Do you know how freakin' expensive web fluid was? Oh, my God!
I mean, law of averages said I had to fall bass ackwards into a *happy* accident eventually.
I *know* I should be home testing this against my dad's notes...
But I just-- I feel too good.
I feel like a million dollars.
What I need is a...

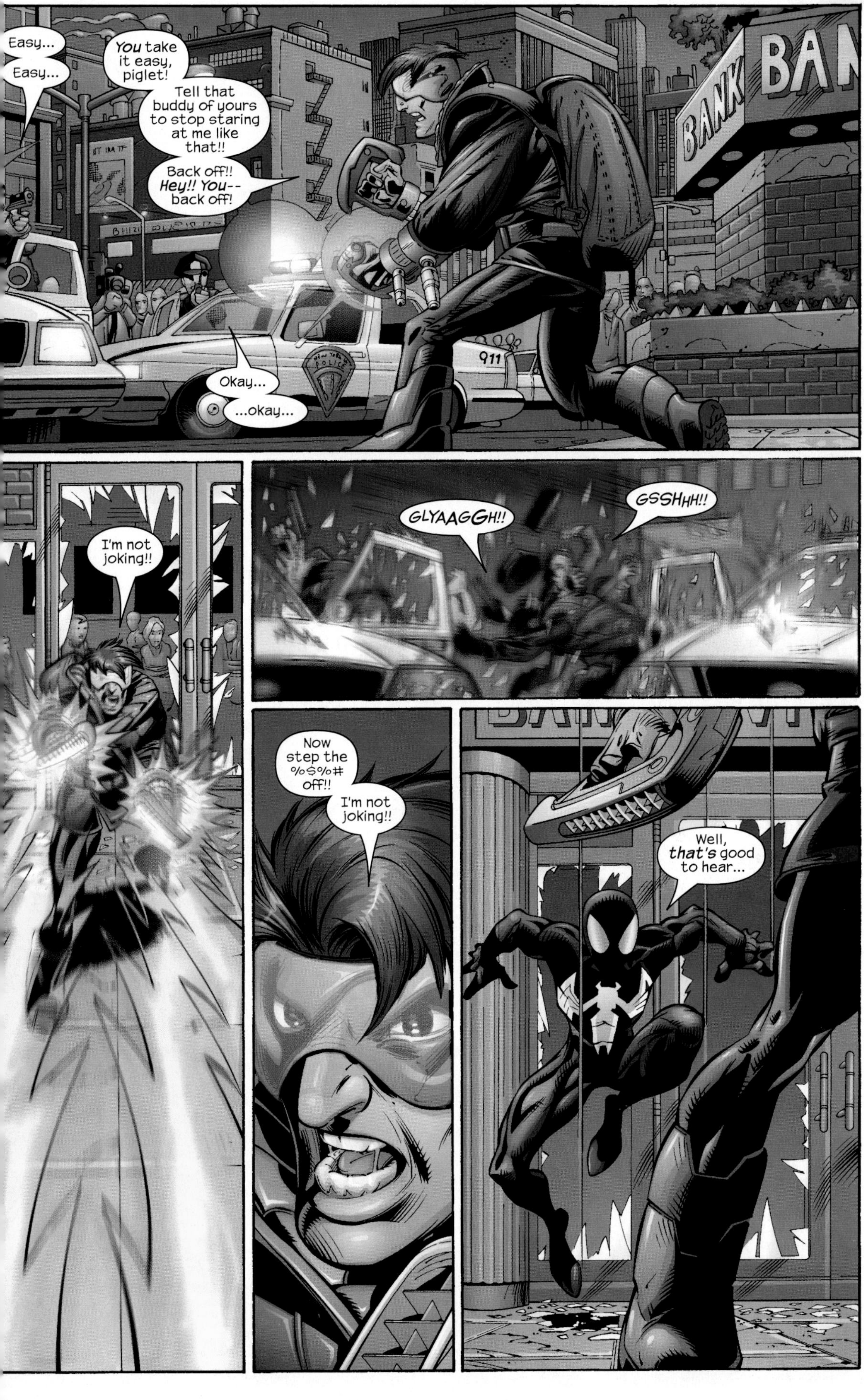

Easy...
Easy...
You take it easy, piglet!
Tell that buddy of yours to stop staring at me like that!!
Back off!! Hey!! You-- back off!
Okay...
...okay...
BANK
BAN
I'm not joking!!
GLYAAGGH!!
GSSHHH!!
Now step the %$%# off!!
I'm not joking!!
Well, that's good to hear...

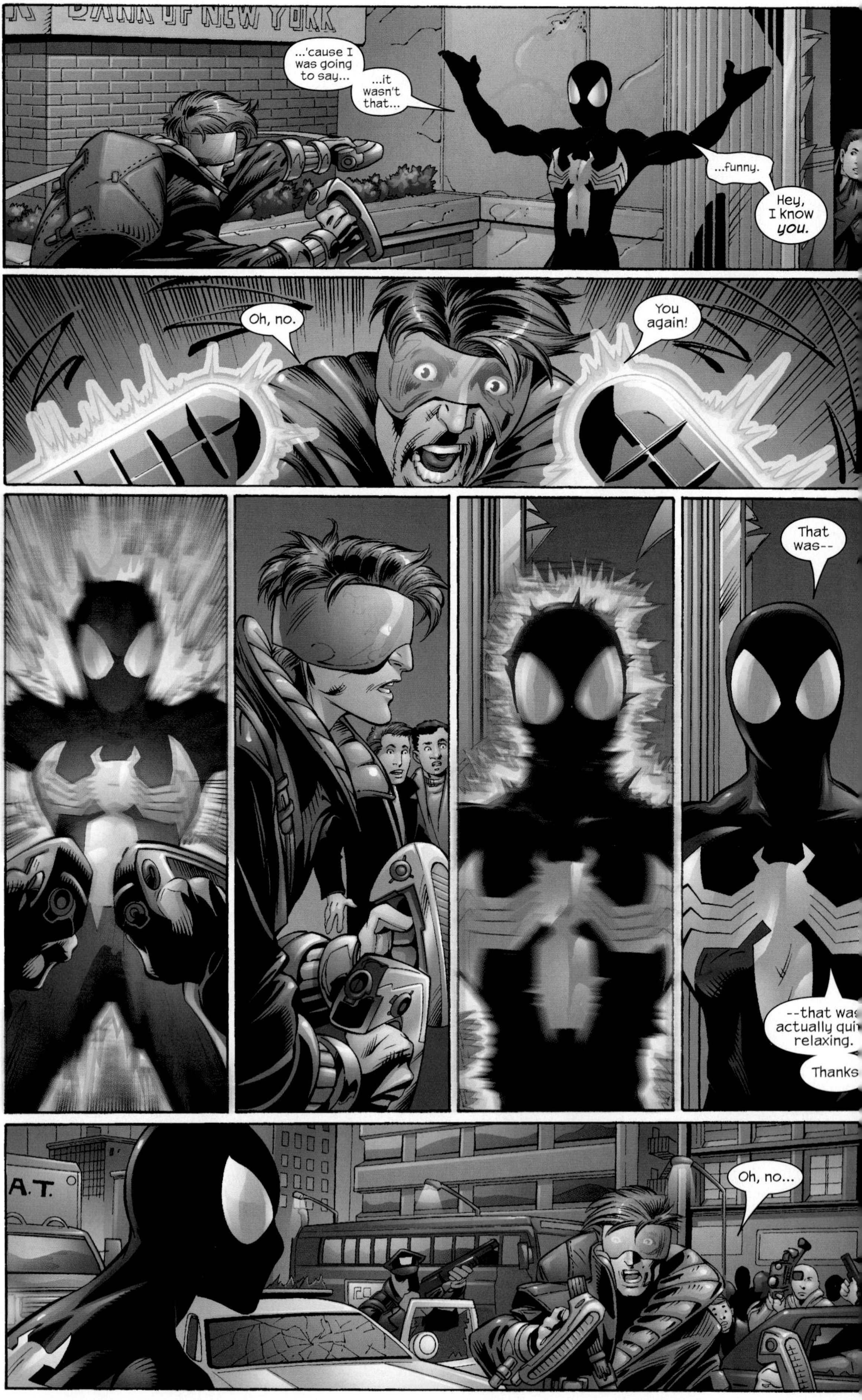
BANK OF NEW YORK
...'cause I was going to say...
...it wasn't that...
...funny.
Hey, I know you.
Oh, no.
You again!
That was--
--that was actually qui relaxing.
Thanks
A.T.
Oh, no...

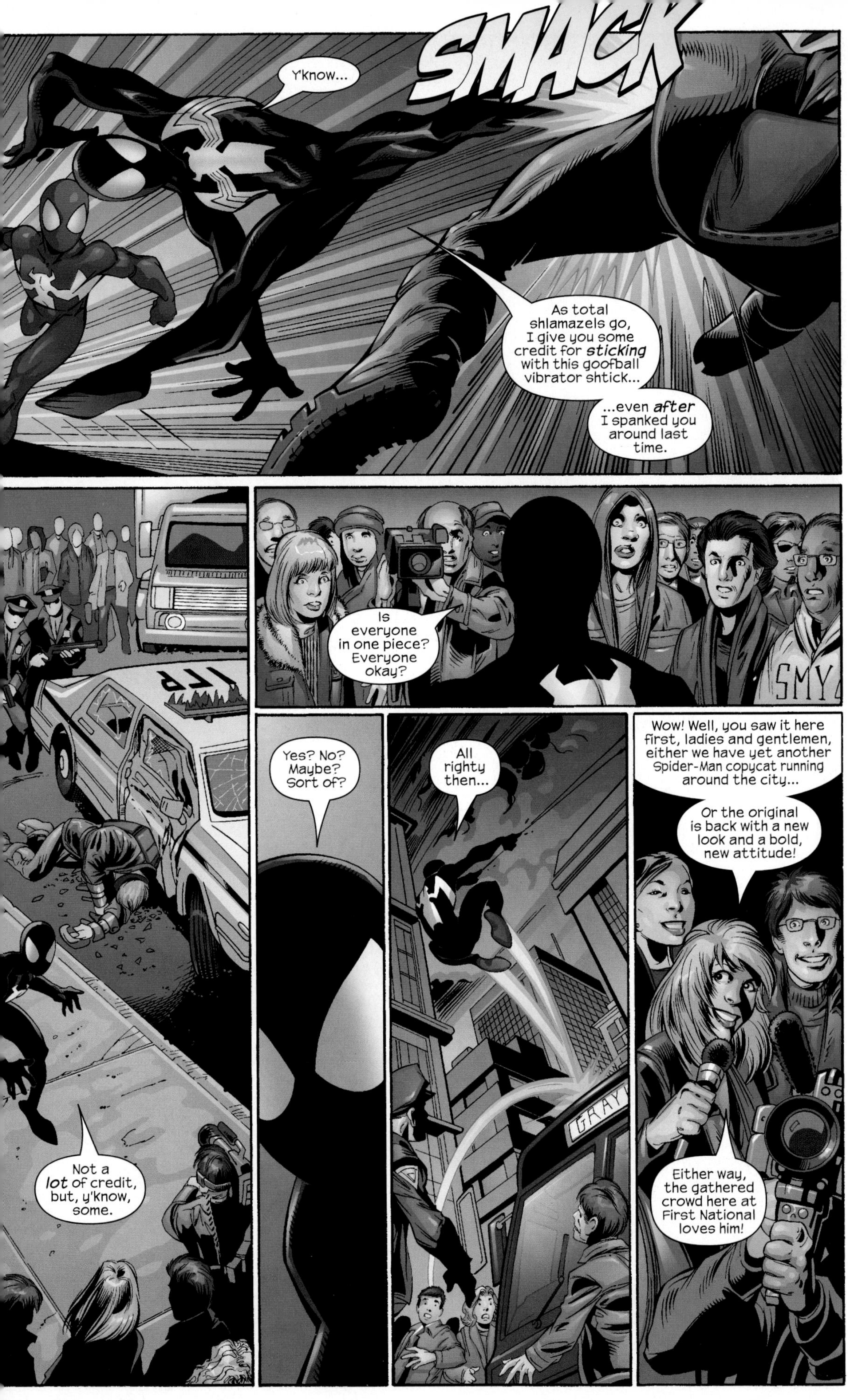
SMACK
Y'know...
As total shlamazels go, I give you some credit for *sticking* with this goofball vibrator shtick...
...even *after* I spanked you around last time.
Not a *lot* of credit, but, y'know, some.
Is everyone in one piece? Everyone okay?
Yes? No? Maybe? Sort of?
All righty then...
Wow! Well, you saw it here first, ladies and gentlemen, either we have yet another Spider-Man copycat running around the city...
Or the original is back with a new look and a bold, new attitude!
Either way, the gathered crowd here at First National loves him!

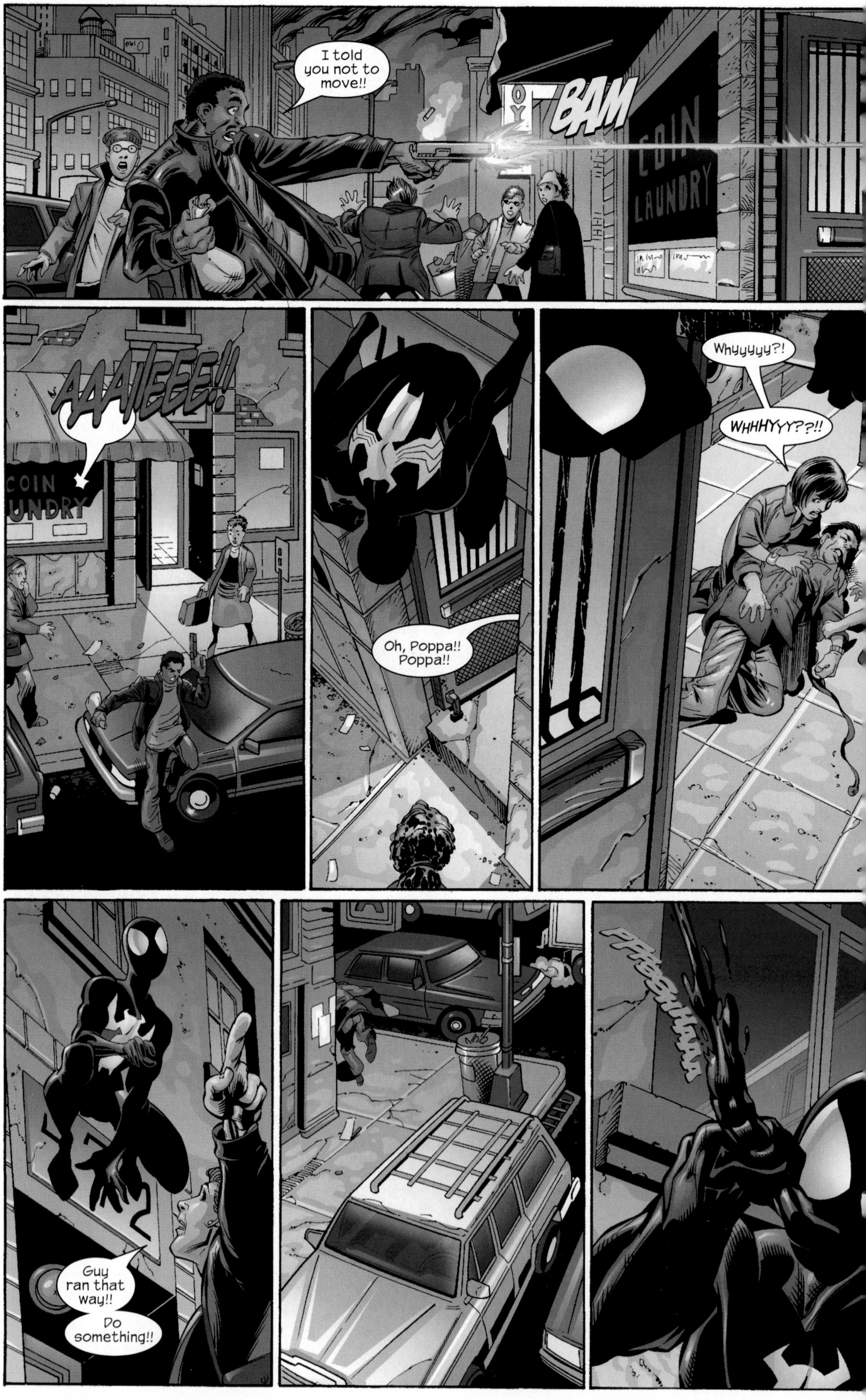
I told you not to move!!
BAM
COIN LAUNDRY
AAAIEEE!!
Oh, Poppa!! Poppa!!
Whyyyyy?!
WHHHYYY??!!
Guy ran that way!!
Do something!!

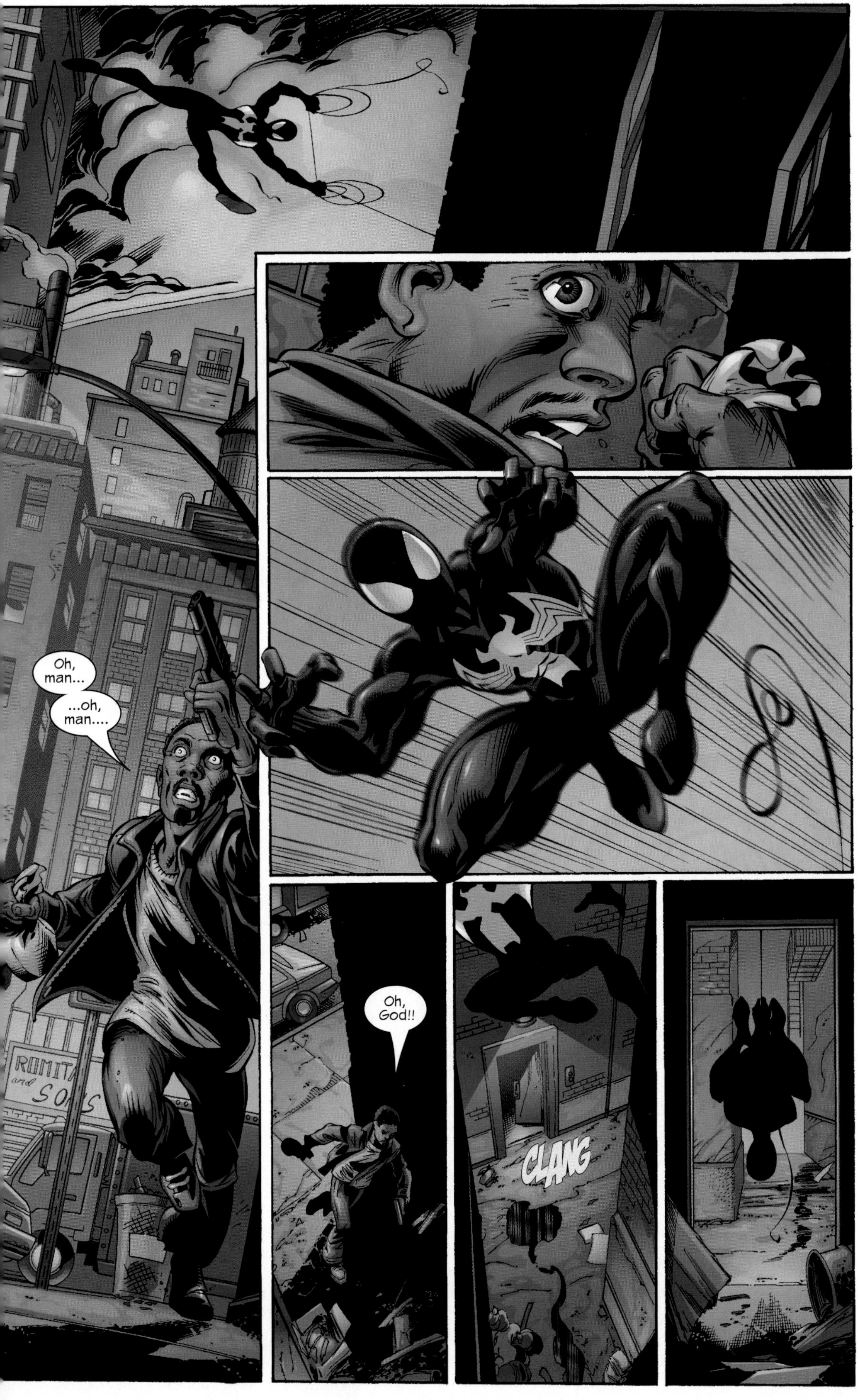

Oh, man...
...oh, man....
Oh, God!!
CLANG

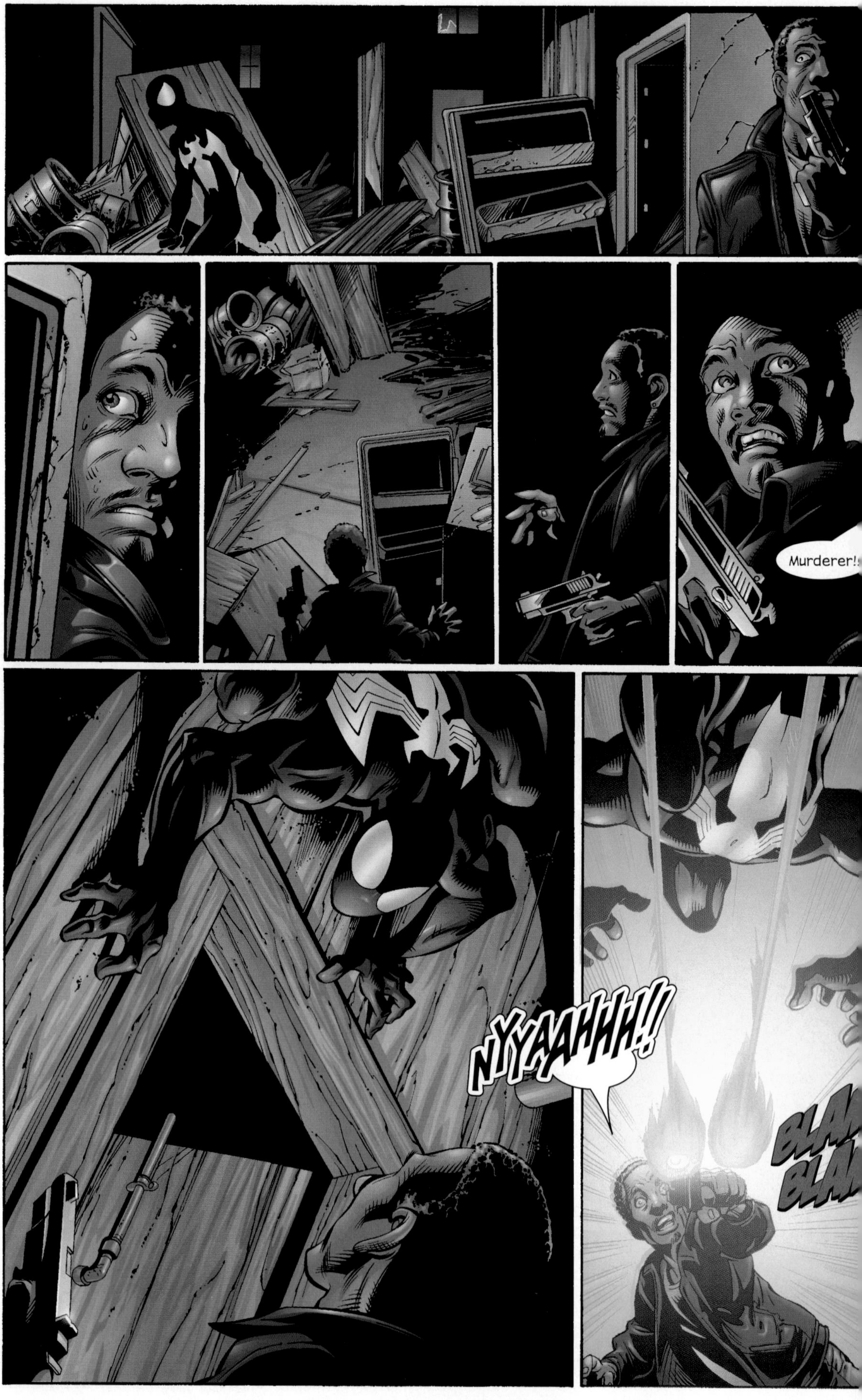
Murderer!
NYAAHHH!!
BLAM
BLAM

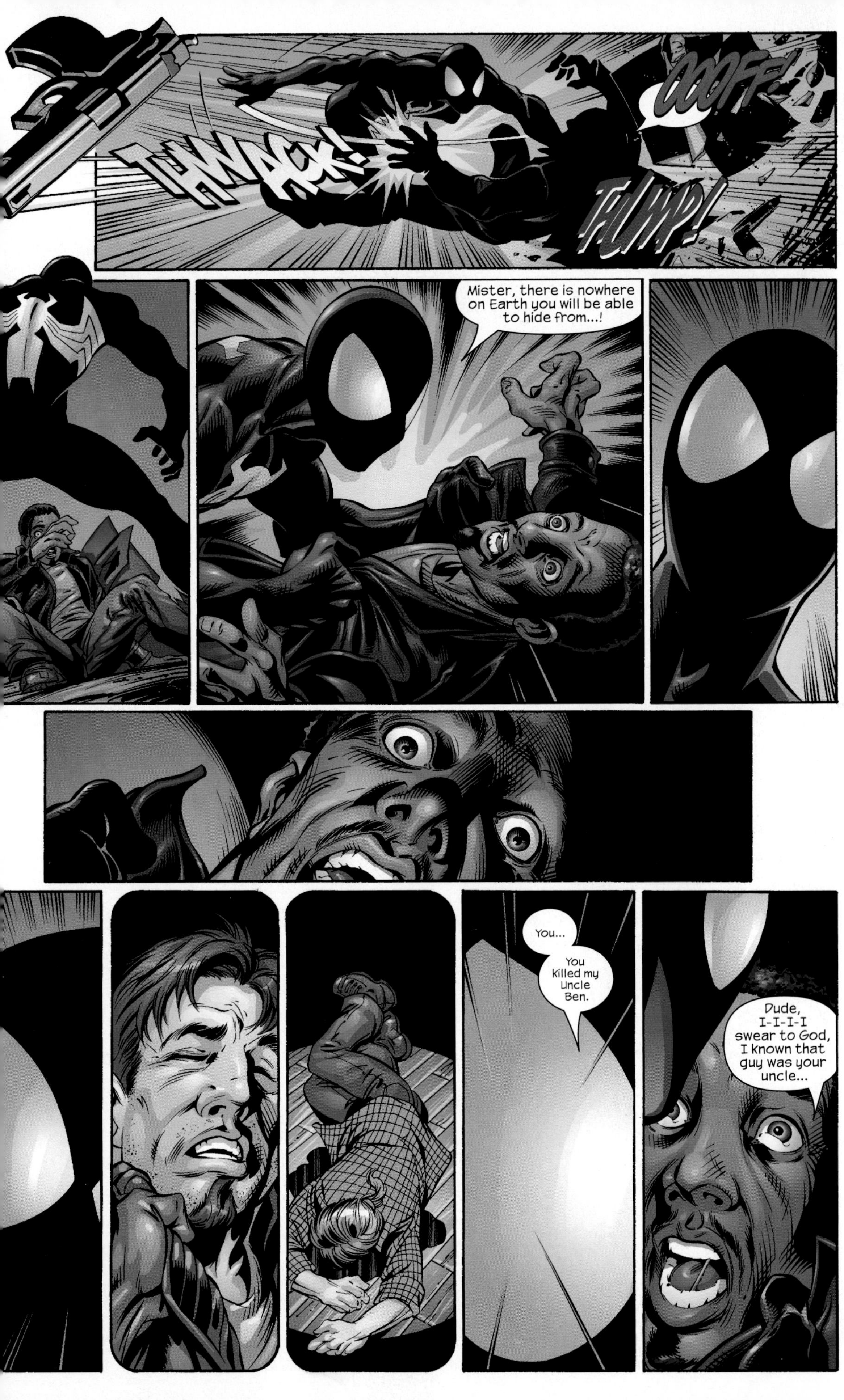
THWACK!
OOOFF!
THUMP!
Mister, there is nowhere on Earth you will be able to hide from...!
You...
You killed my Uncle Ben.
Dude, I-I-I-I swear to God, I known that guy was your uncle...

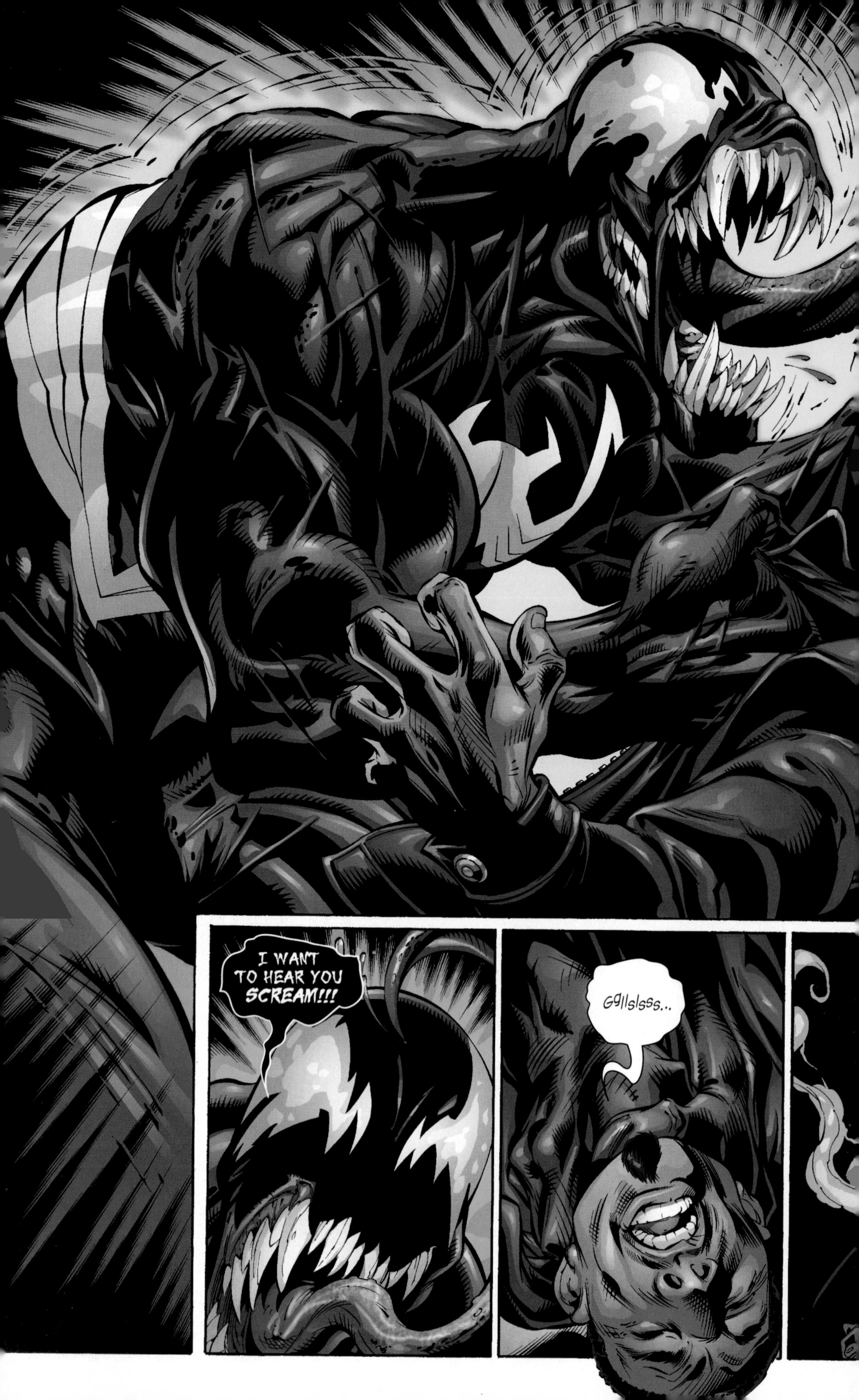
I WANT TO HEAR YOU SCREAM!!!
Ggllslsss...

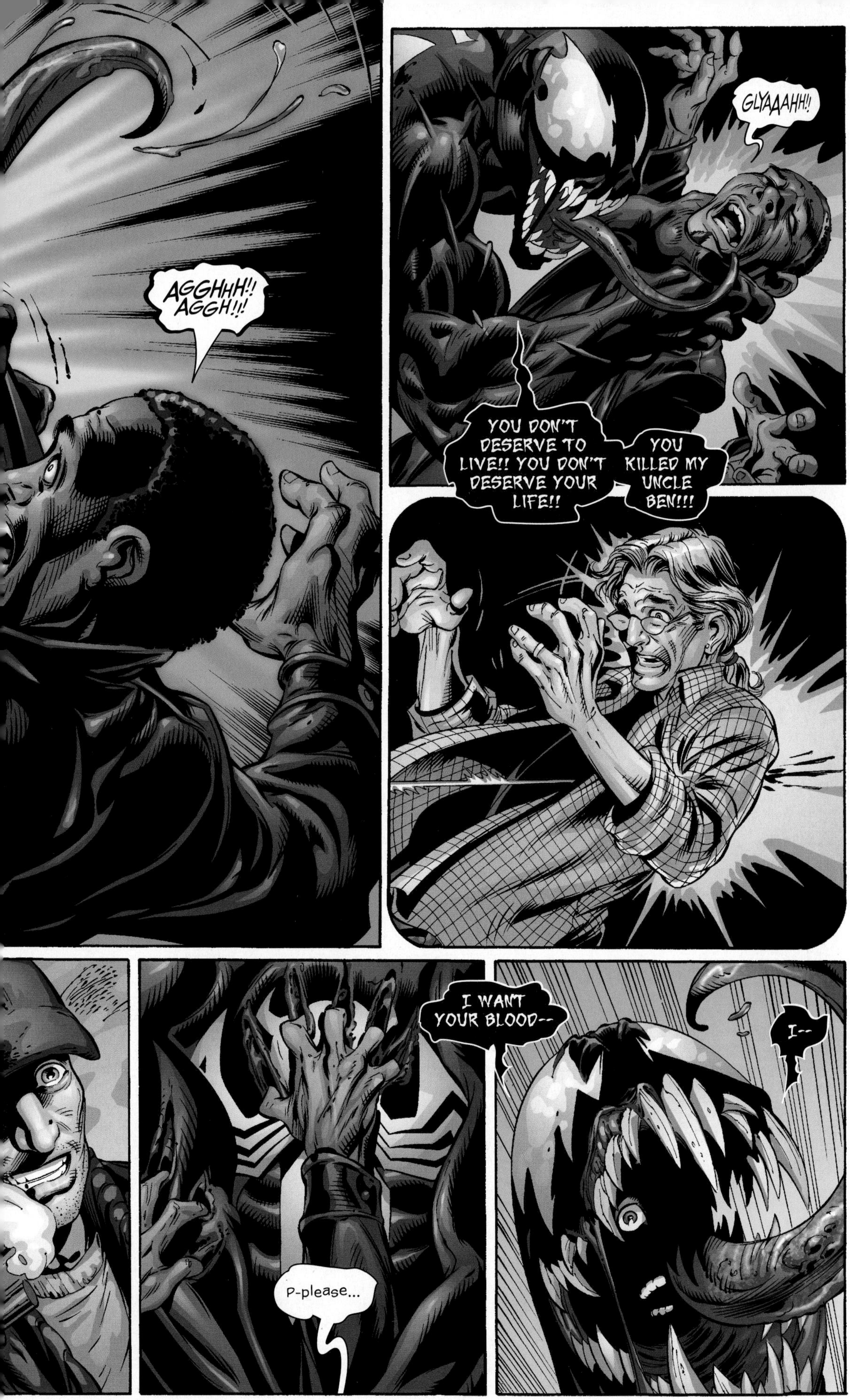
AGGHHH!! AGGH!!!
GLYAAAHH!!
YOU DON'T DESERVE TO LIVE!! YOU DON'T DESERVE YOUR LIFE!!
YOU KILLED MY UNCLE BEN!!!
I WANT YOUR BLOOD--
P-please...
I--

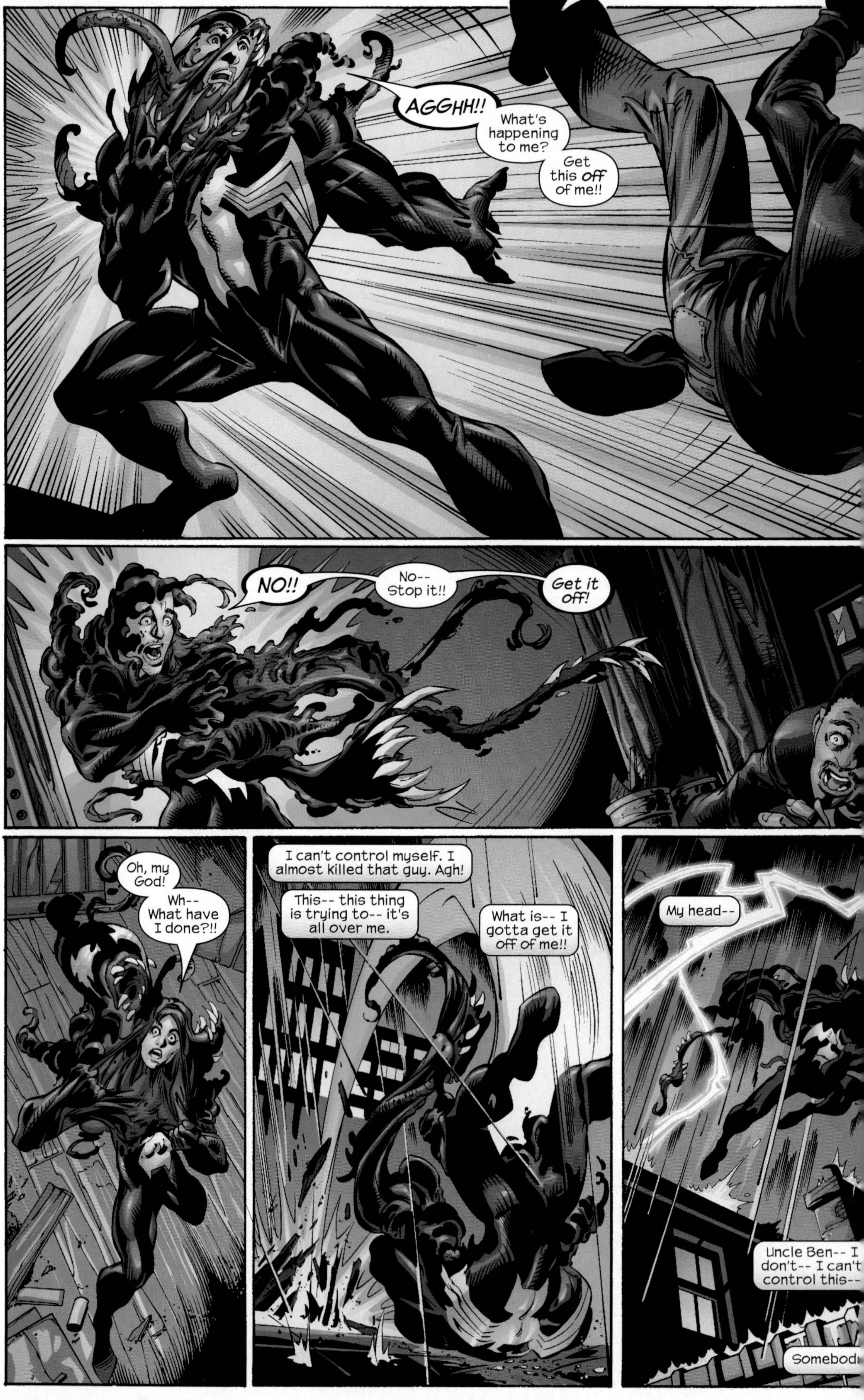
AGGHH!!
What's happening to me?
Get this off of me!!
NO!!
No-- Stop it!!
Get it off!
Oh, my God!
Wh-- What have I done?!!
I can't control myself. I almost killed that guy. Agh!
This-- this thing is trying to-- it's all over me.
What is-- I gotta get it off of me!!
My head--
Uncle Ben-- I don't-- I can't control this--

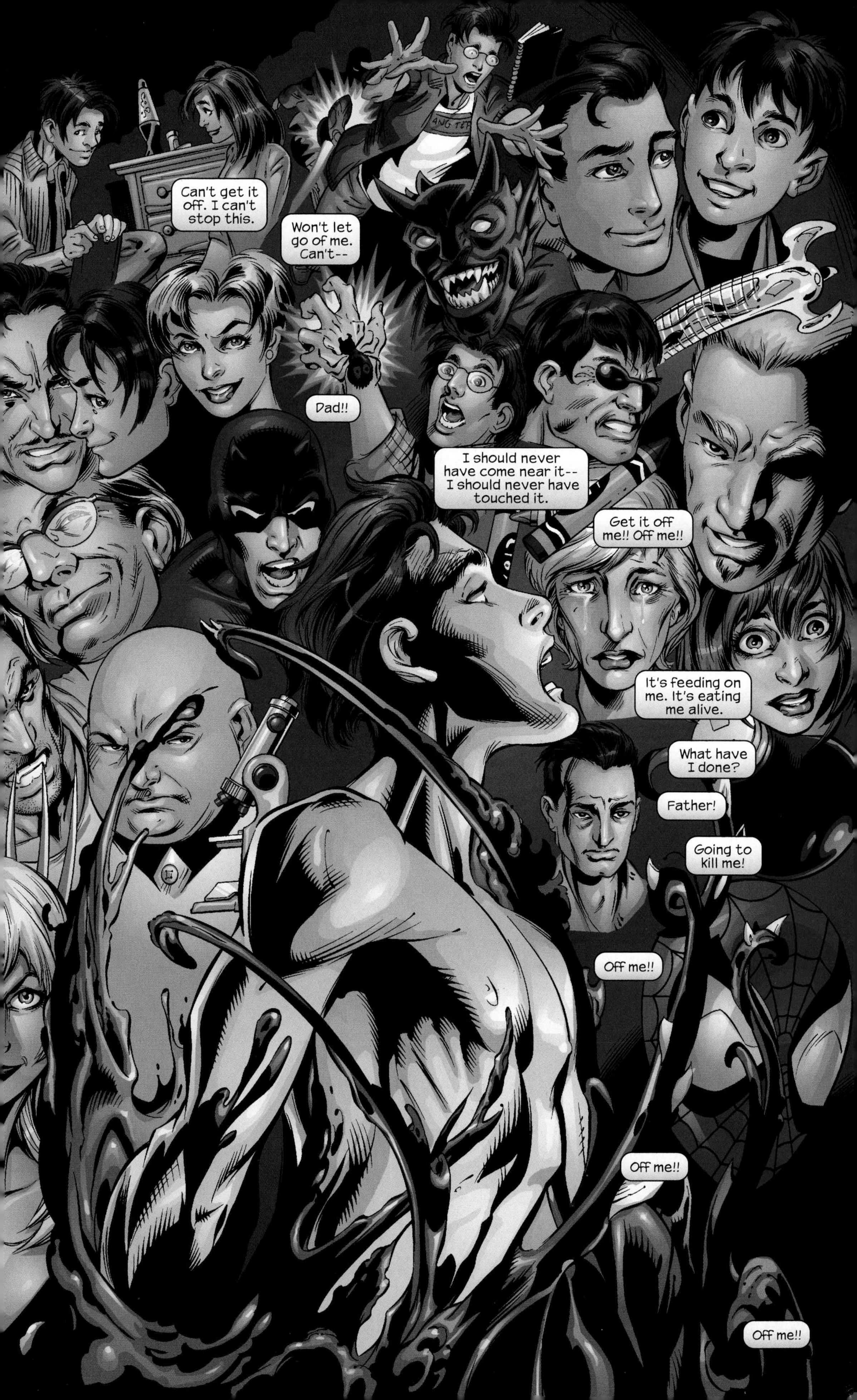

Can't get it off. I can't stop this.
Won't let go of me. Can't--
Dad!!
I should never have come near it-- I should never have touched it.
Get it off me!! Off me!!
It's feeding on me. It's eating me alive.
What have I done?
Father!
Going to kill me!
Off me!!
Off me!!
Off me!!

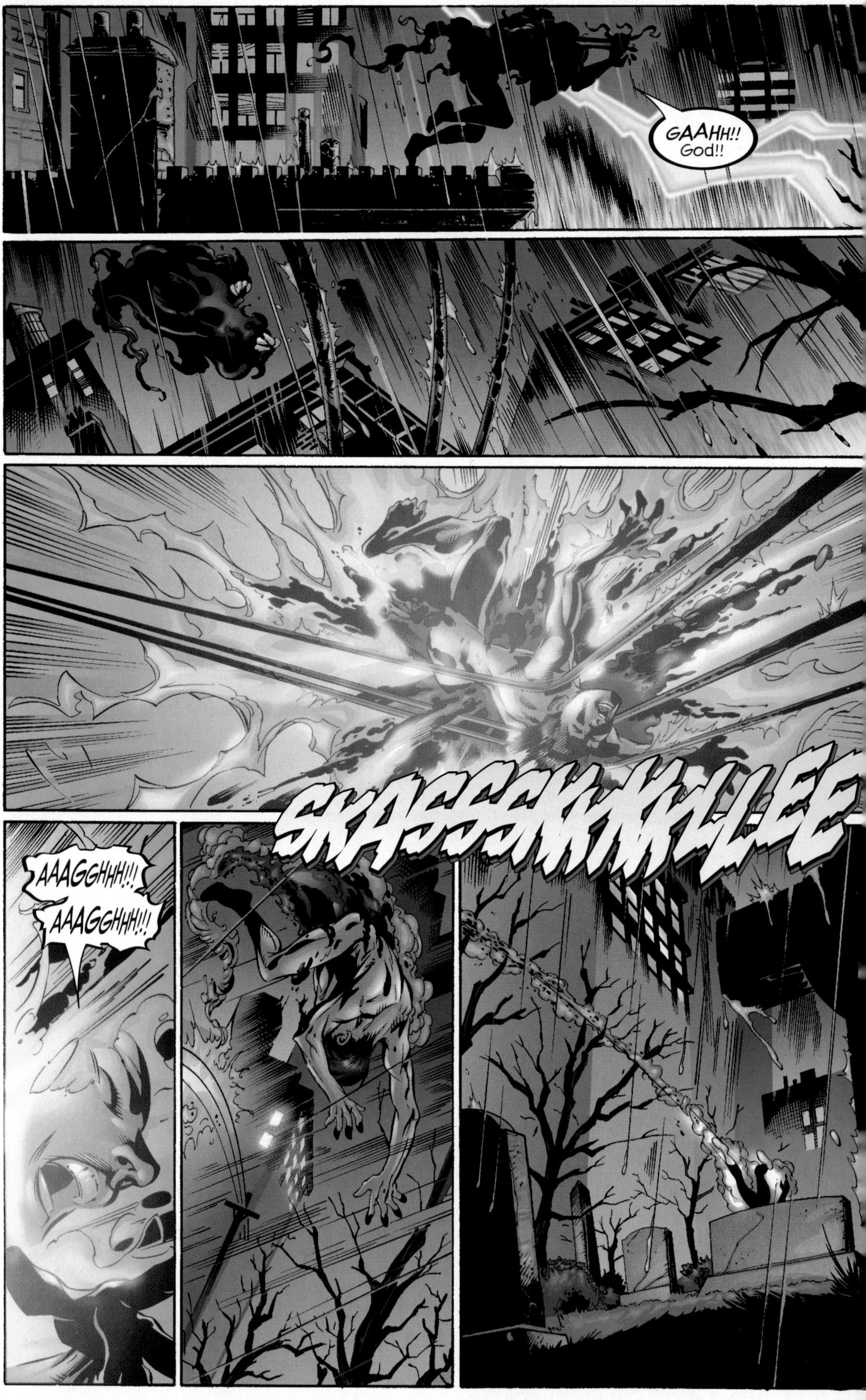
GAAHH!! God!!
SKASSSKKKKLLEE
AAAGGHHH!!!
AAAGGHHH!!!

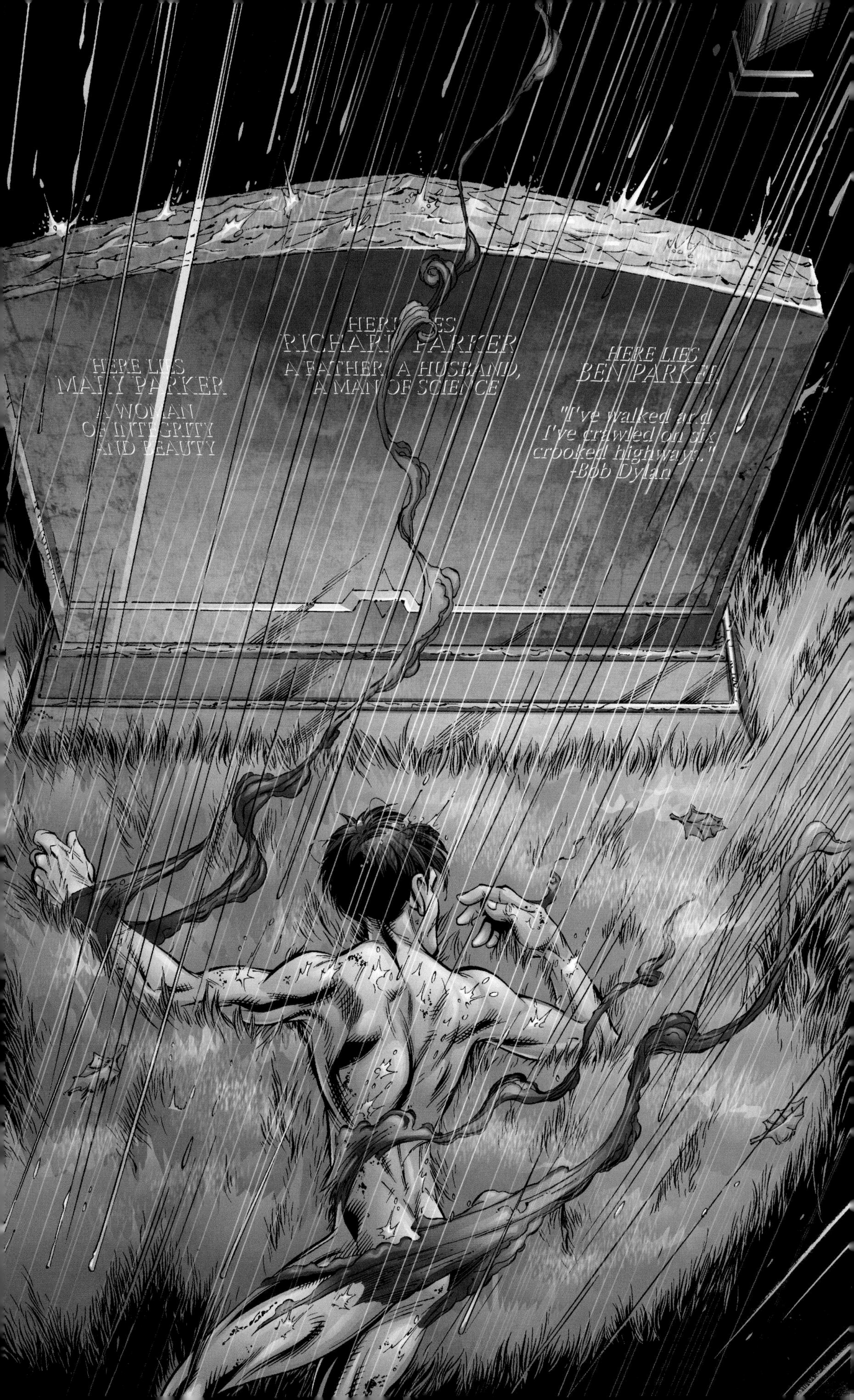
HERE LIES
MARY PARKER
A WOMAN
OF INTEGRITY
AND BEAUTY
RICHARD PARKER
A FATHER, A HUSBAND,
A MAN OF SCIENCE
HERE LIES
BEN PARKER
"I've walked and
I've crawled on six
crooked highways."
-Bob Dylan

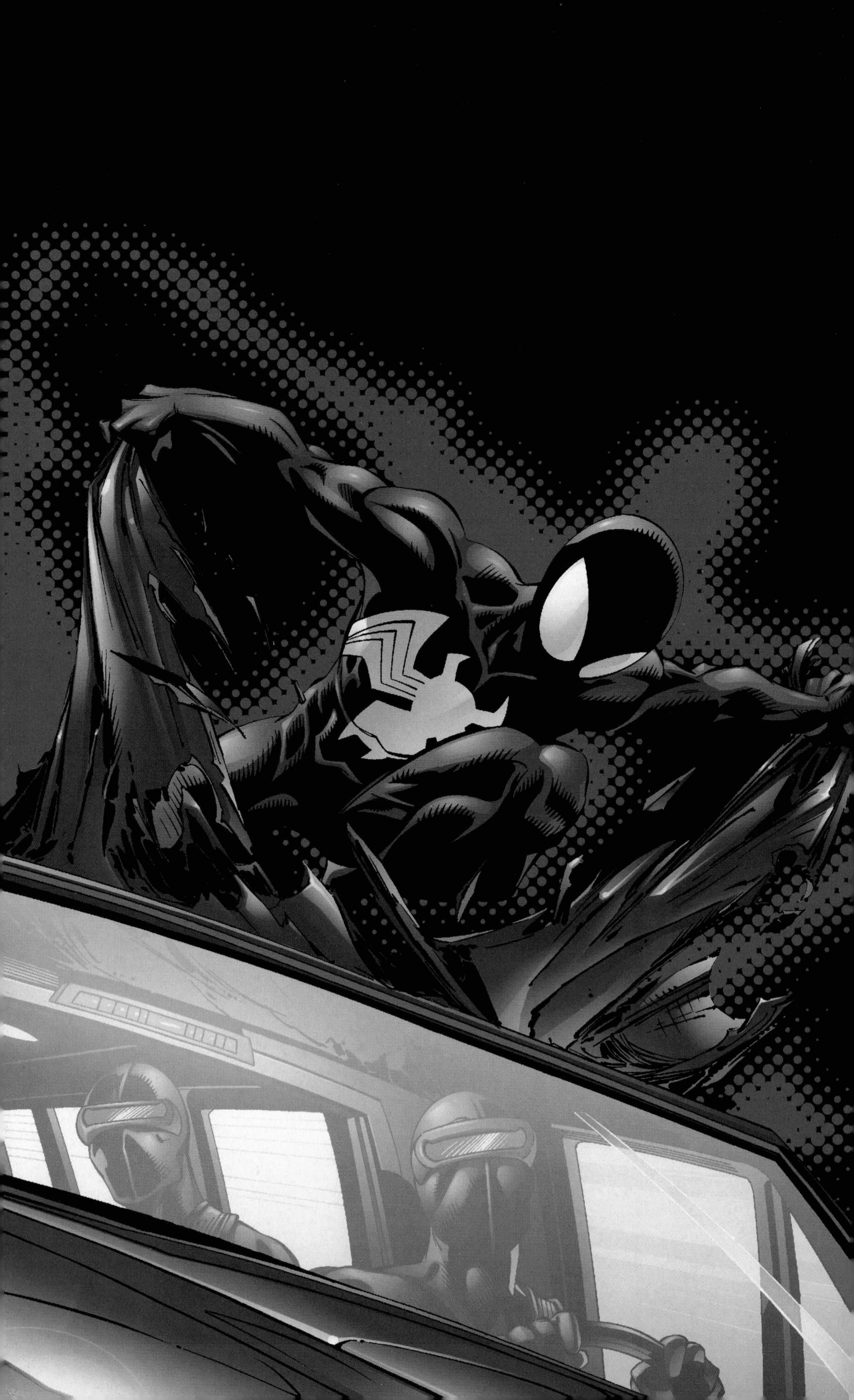

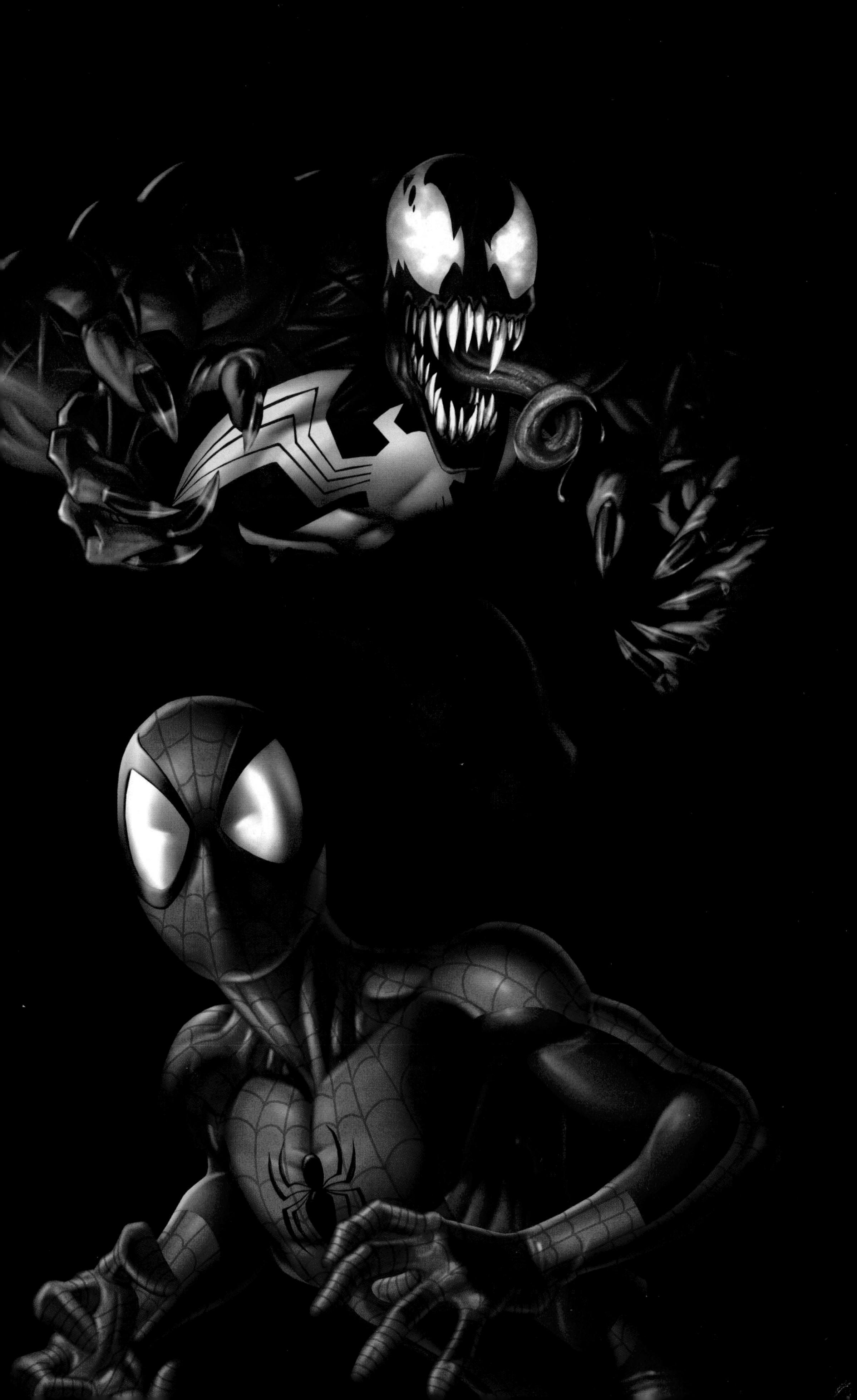

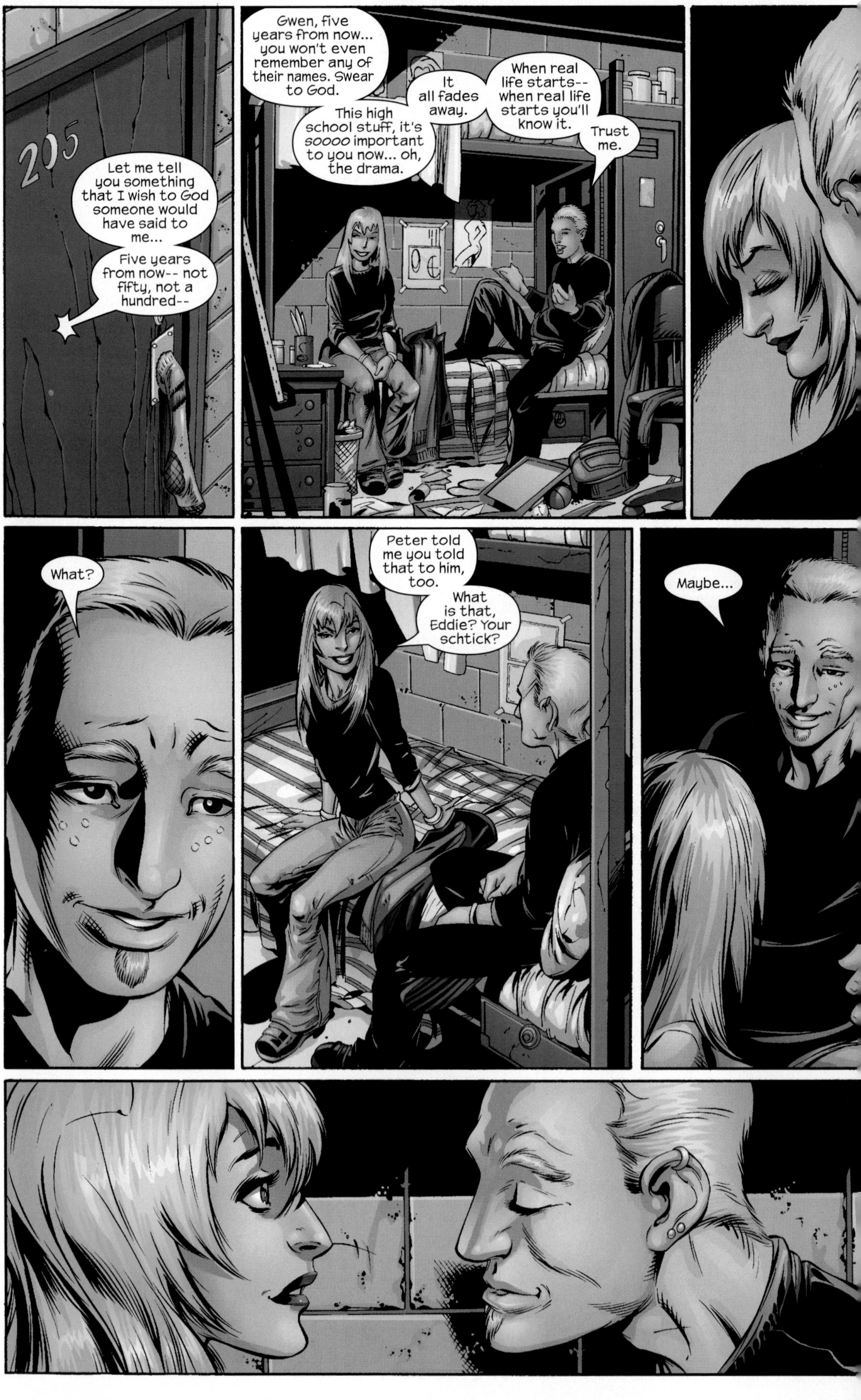
205
Let me tell you something that I wish to God someone would have said to me...
Five years from now-- not fifty, not a hundred--
Gwen, five years from now... you won't even remember any of their names. Swear to God.
This high school stuff, it's *soooo* important to you now... oh, the drama.
It all fades away.
When real life starts-- when real life starts you'll know it.
Trust me.
What?
Peter told me you told that to him, too.
What is that, Eddie? Your schtick?
Maybe...

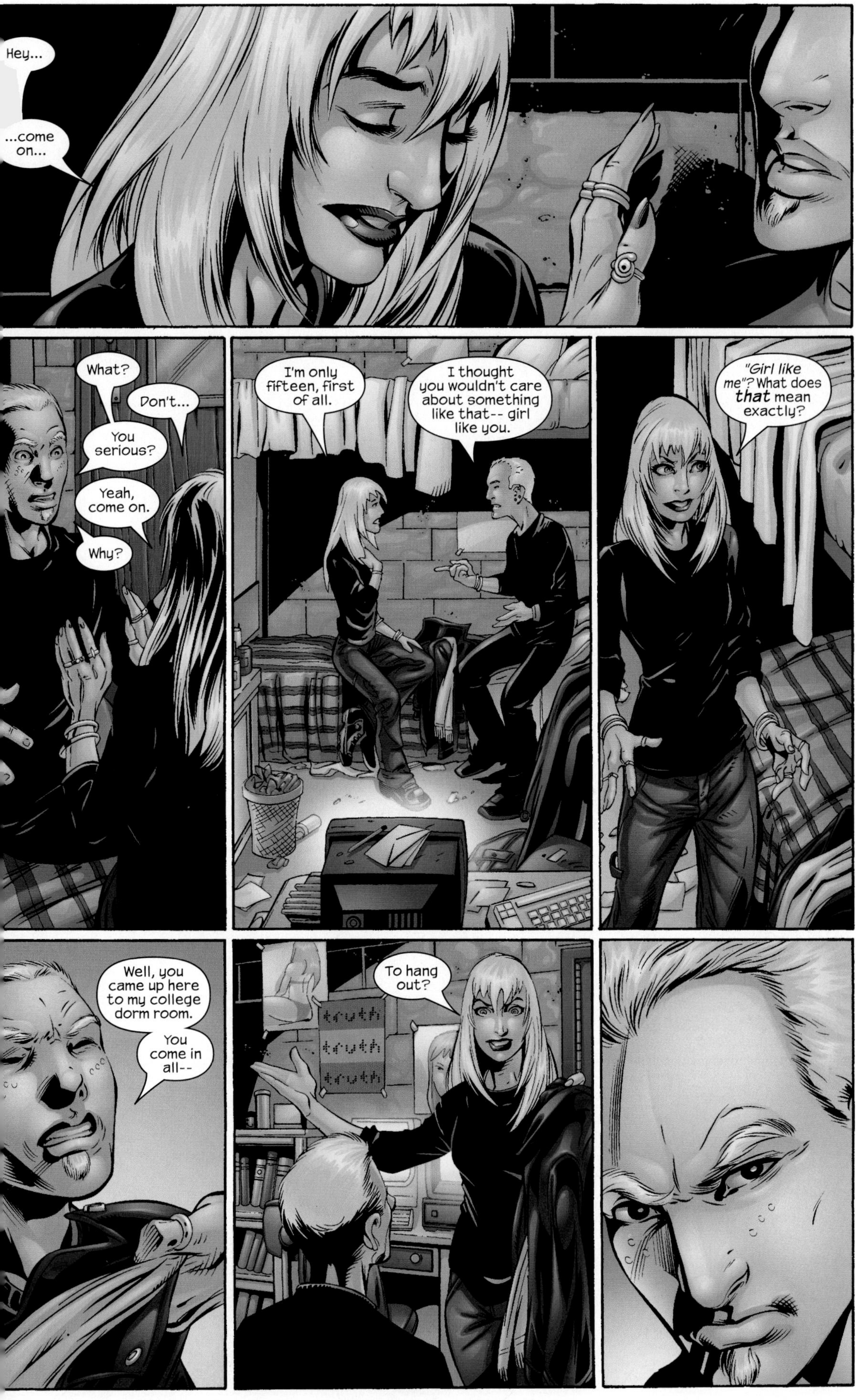
Hey...
...come on...
What?
Don't...
You serious?
Yeah, come on.
Why?
I'm only fifteen, first of all.
I thought you wouldn't care about something like that-- girl like you.
"Girl like me"? What does **that** mean exactly?
Well, you came up here to my college dorm room.
You come in all--
To hang out?
truth
truth
truth

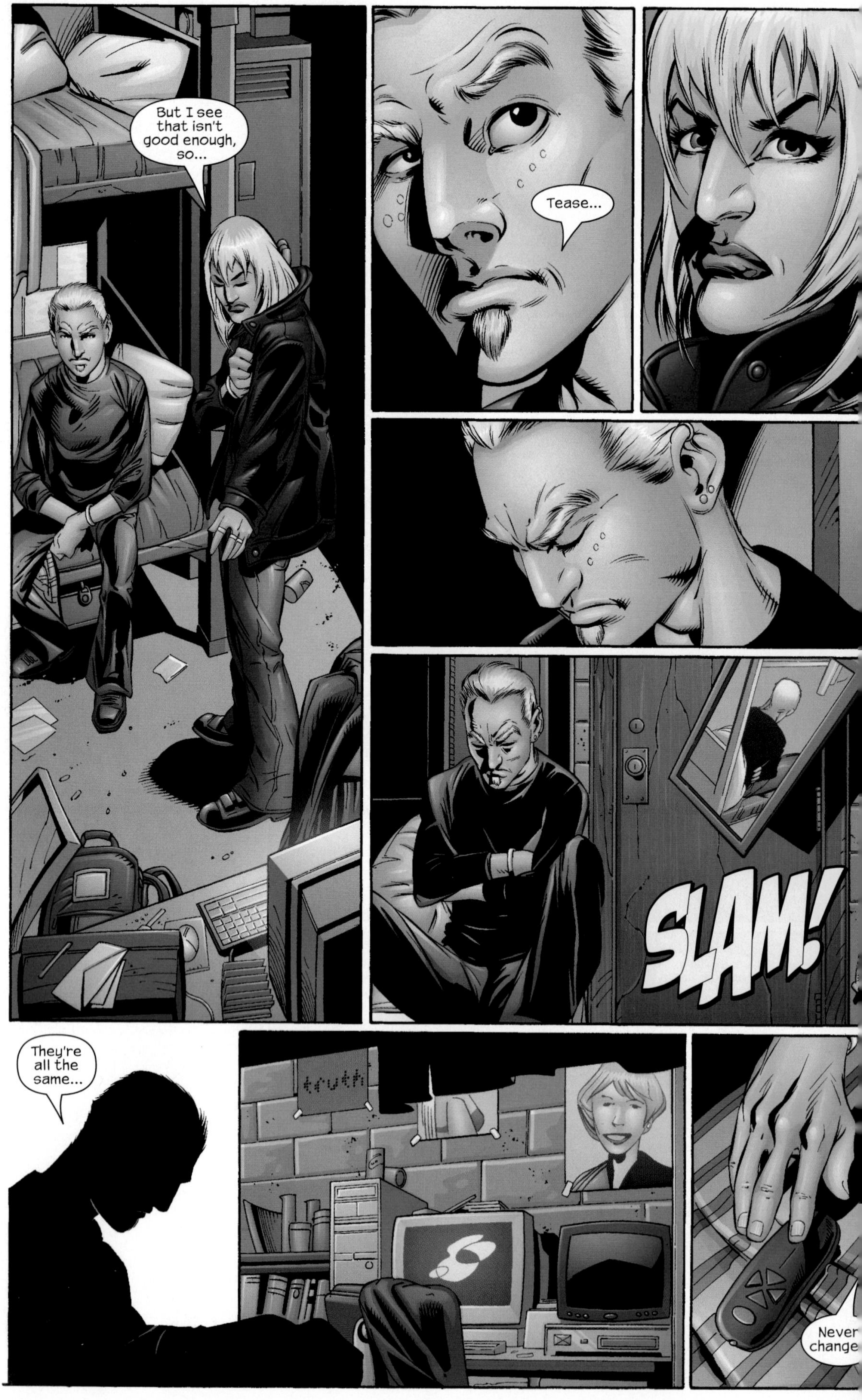
But I see that isn't good enough, so...
Tease...
SLAM!
They're all the same...
truth
Never change

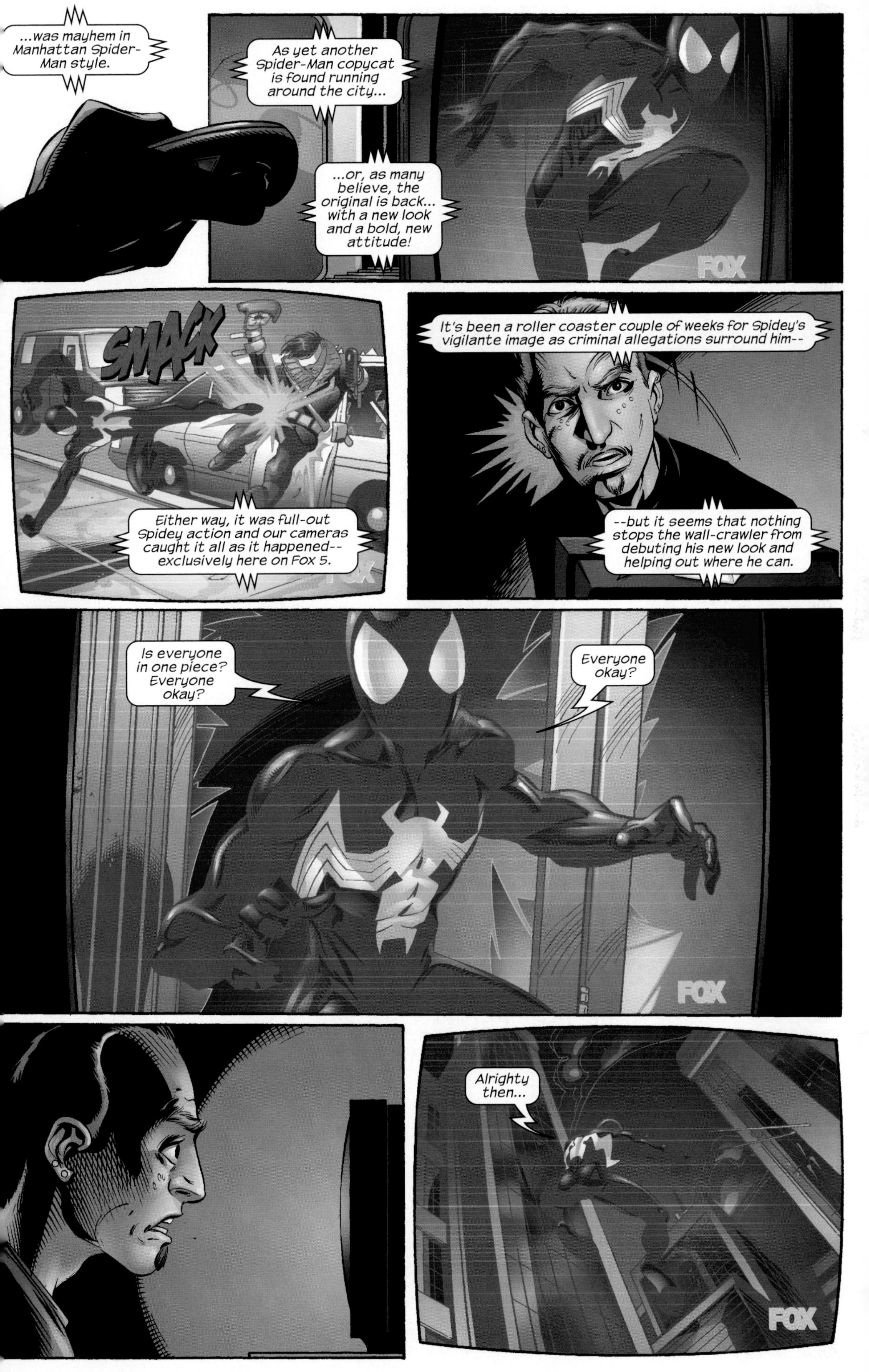
...was mayhem in Manhattan Spider-Man style.
As yet another Spider-Man copycat is found running around the city...
...or, as many believe, the original is back... with a new look and a bold, new attitude!
FOX
SMACK
Either way, it was full-out Spidey action and our cameras caught it all as it happened-- exclusively here on Fox 5.
It's been a roller coaster couple of weeks for Spidey's vigilante image as criminal allegations surround him--
--but it seems that nothing stops the wall-crawler from debuting his new look and helping out where he can.
Is everyone in one piece? Everyone okay?
Everyone okay?
FOX
Alrighty then...
FOX

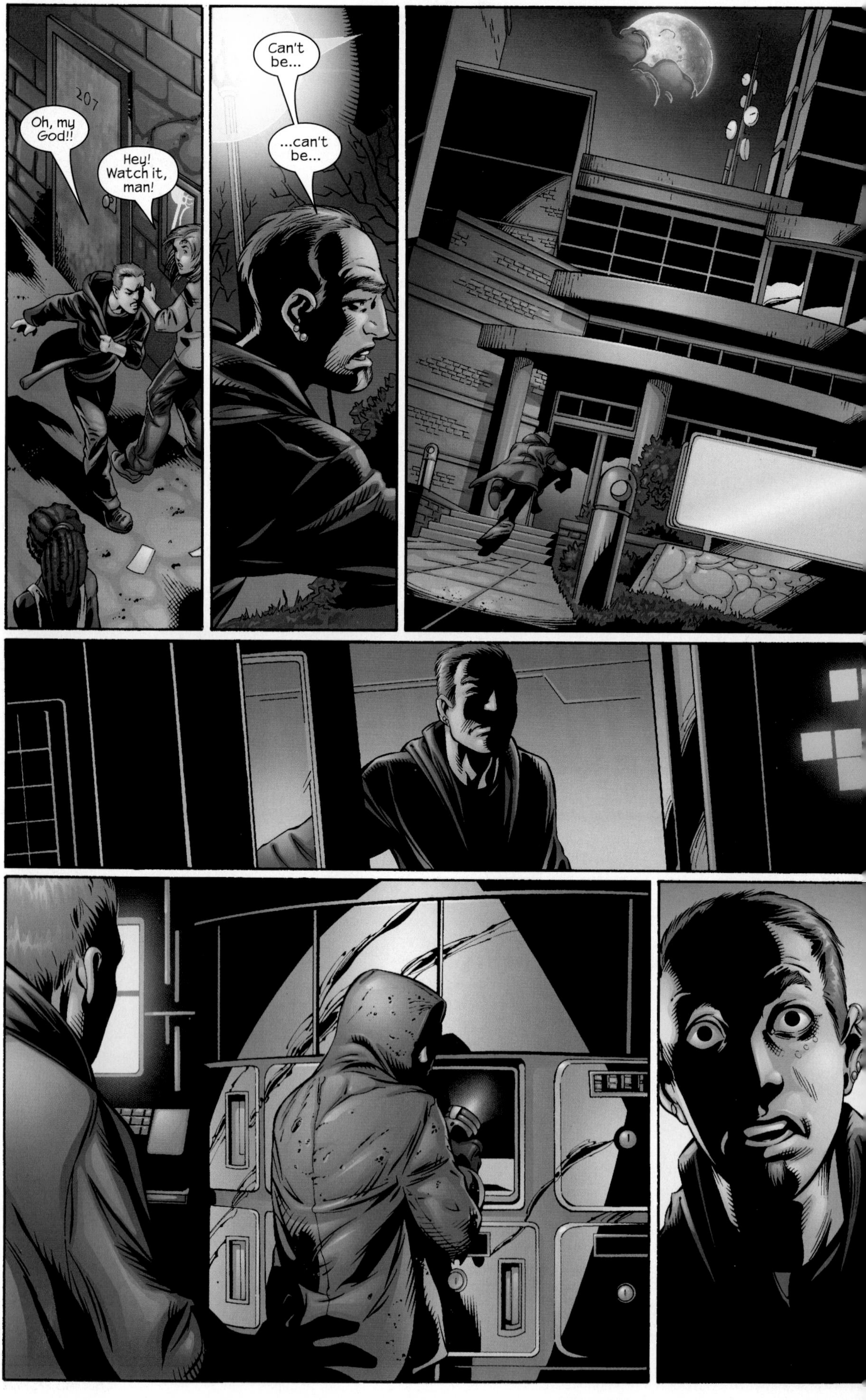
Oh, my God!!
Hey! Watch it, man!
Can't be...
...can't be...

Peter?

Peter Parker?

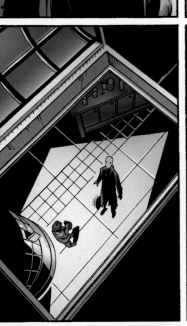

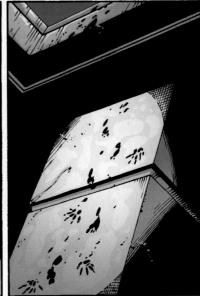

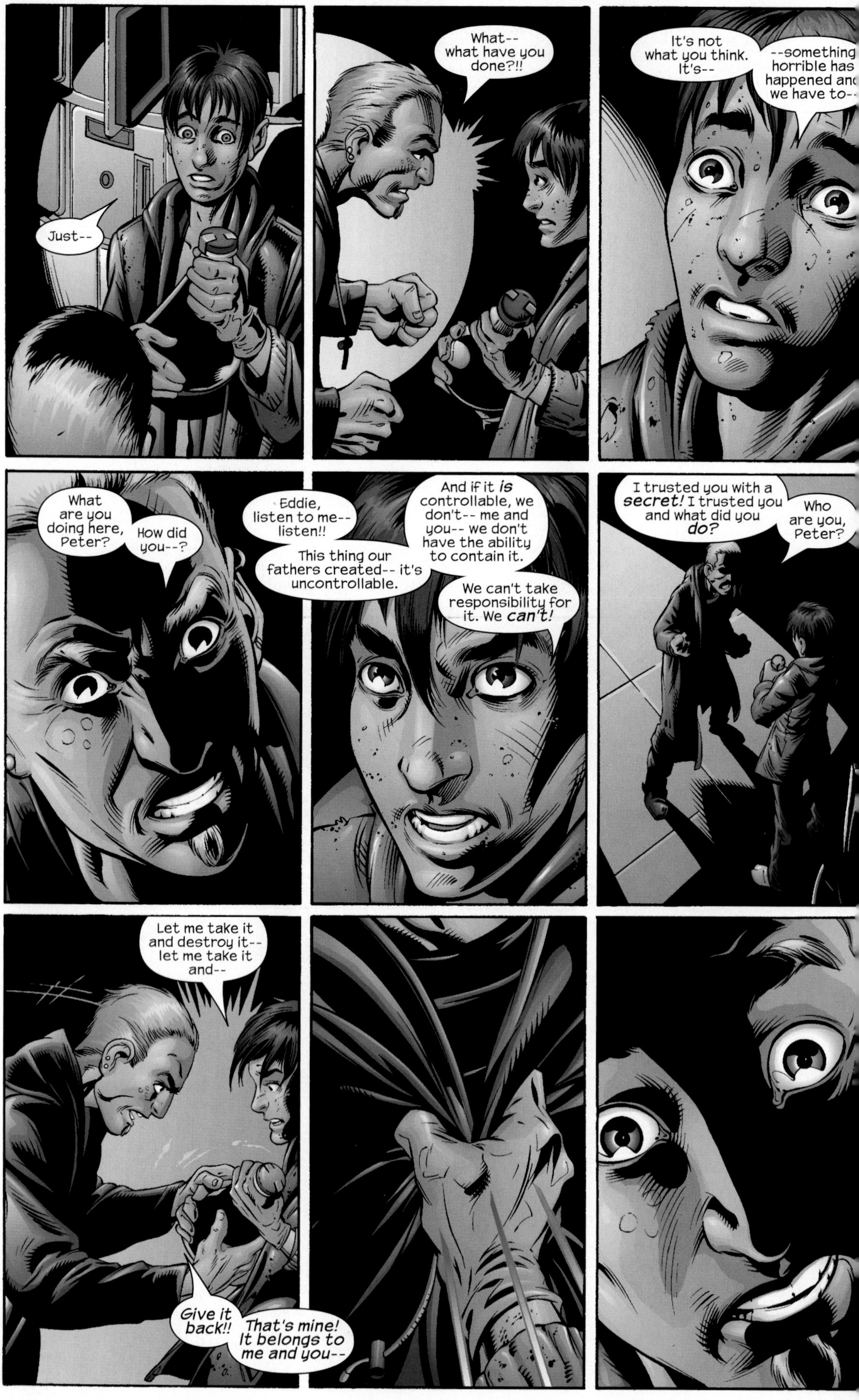
Just--
What-- what have you done?!!
It's not what you think. It's--
--something horrible has happened and we have to--
What are you doing here, Peter?
How did you--?
Eddie, listen to me-- listen!!
This thing our fathers created-- it's uncontrollable.
And if it *is* controllable, we don't-- me and you-- we don't have the ability to contain it.
We can't take responsibility for it. We *can't!*
I trusted you with a *secret!* I trusted you and what did you *do?*
Who are you, Peter?
Let me take it and destroy it-- let me take it and--
Give it back!!
That's mine! It belongs to me and you--

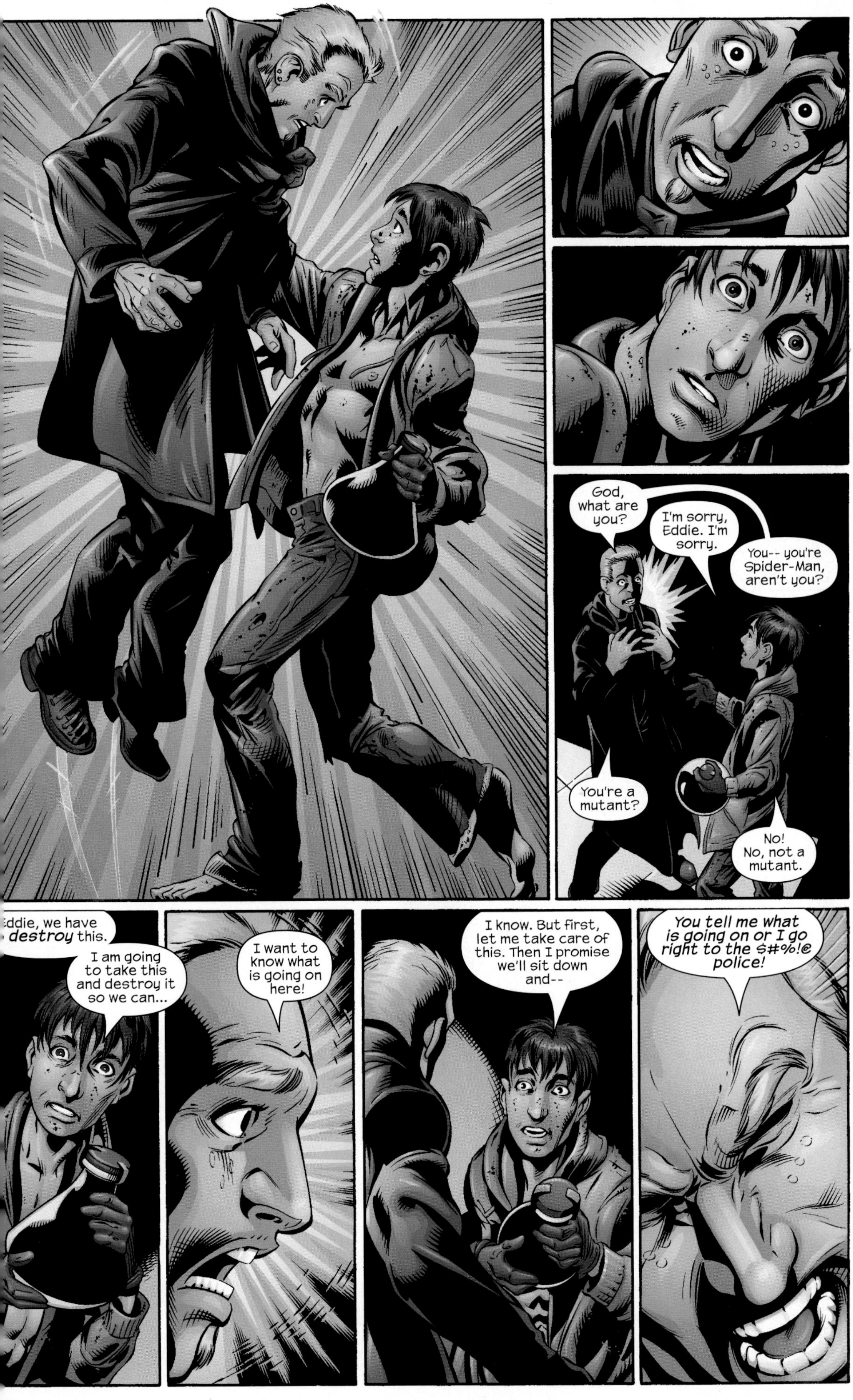

God, what are you?
I'm sorry, Eddie. I'm sorry.
You-- you're Spider-Man, aren't you?
You're a mutant?
No! No, not a mutant.
Eddie, we have destroy this.
I am going to take this and destroy it so we can...
I want to know what is going on here!
I know. But first, let me take care of this. Then I promise we'll sit down and--
You tell me what is going on or I go right to the $#%!© police!

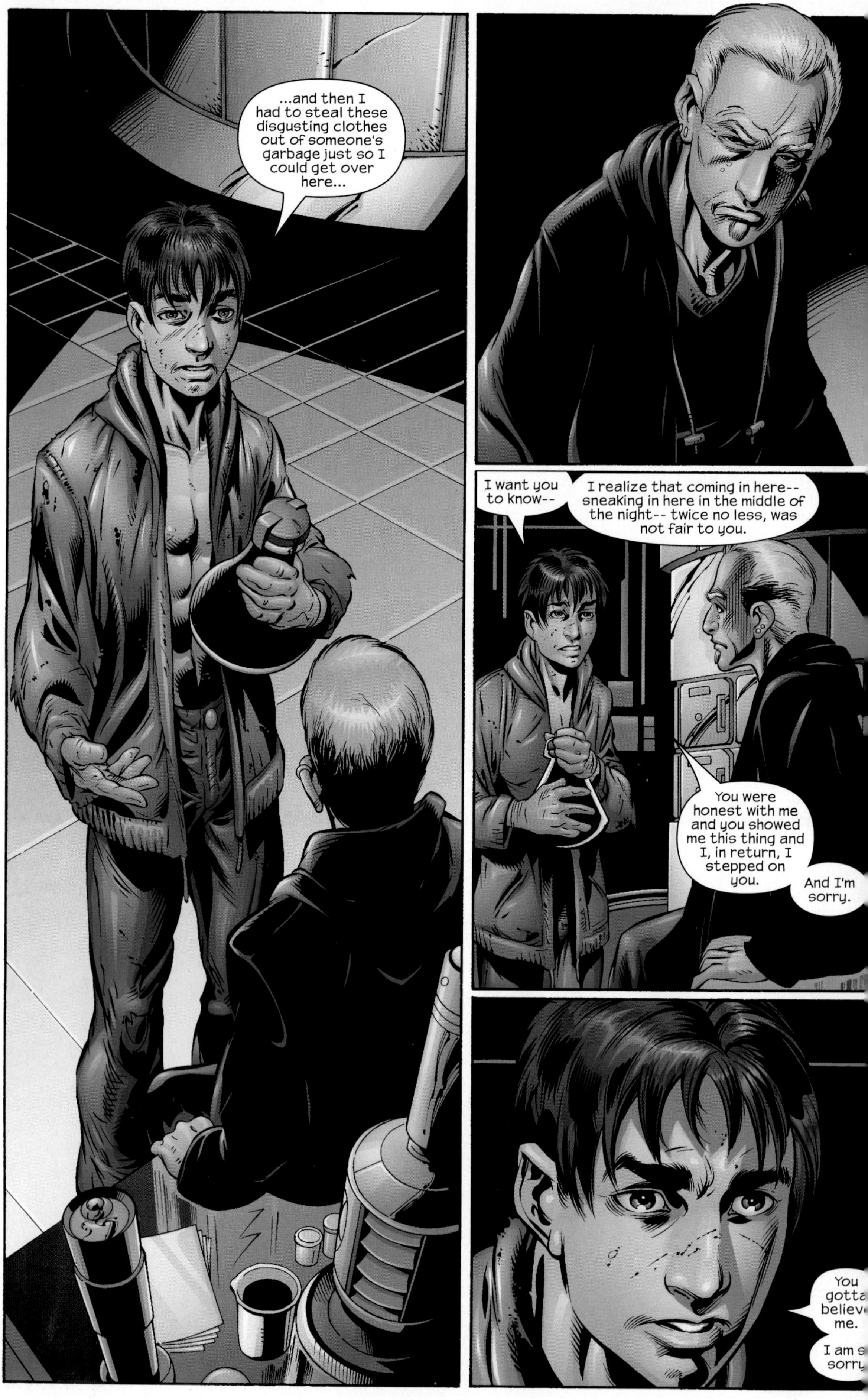
...and then I had to steal these disgusting clothes out of someone's garbage just so I could get over here...
I want you to know--
I realize that coming in here-- sneaking in here in the middle of the night-- twice no less, was not fair to you.
You were honest with me and you showed me this thing and I, in return, I stepped on you.
And I'm sorry.
You gott believ me.
I am s sorr

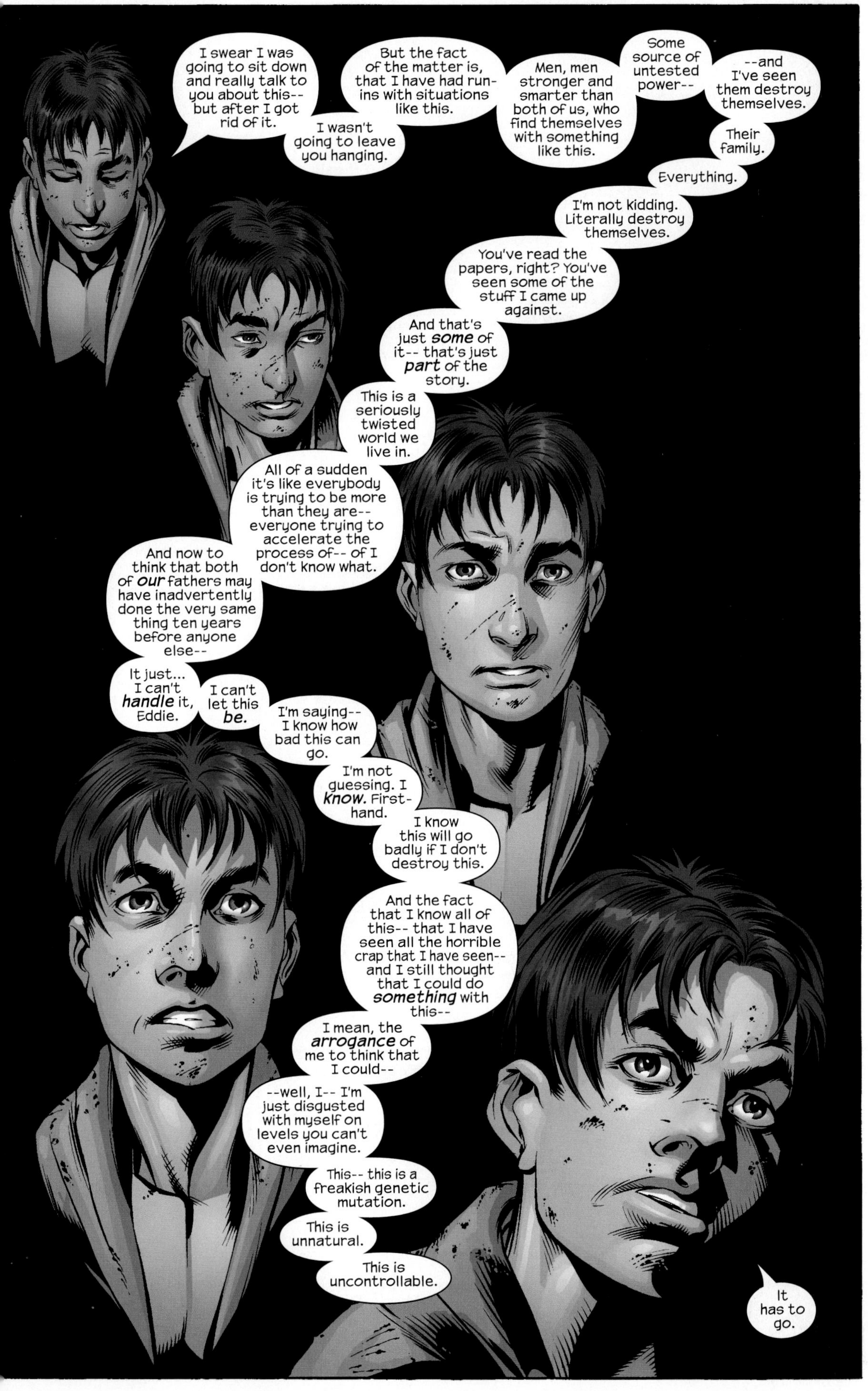
I swear I was going to sit down and really talk to you about this-- but after I got rid of it.
I wasn't going to leave you hanging.
But the fact of the matter is, that I have had run-ins with situations like this.
Men, men stronger and smarter than both of us, who find themselves with something like this.
Some source of untested power--
--and I've seen them destroy themselves.
Their family.
Everything.
I'm not kidding. Literally destroy themselves.
You've read the papers, right? You've seen some of the stuff I came up against.
And that's just *some* of it-- that's just *part* of the story.
This is a seriously twisted world we live in.
All of a sudden it's like everybody is trying to be more than they are-- everyone trying to accelerate the process of-- of I don't know what.
And now to think that both of *our* fathers may have inadvertently done the very same thing ten years before anyone else--
It just... I can't *handle* it, Eddie.
I can't let this *be.*
I'm saying-- I know how bad this can go.
I'm not guessing. I *know.* First-hand.
I know this will go badly if I don't destroy this.
And the fact that I know all of this-- that I have seen all the horrible crap that I have seen-- and I still thought that I could do *something* with this--
I mean, the *arrogance* of me to think that I could--
--well, I-- I'm just disgusted with myself on levels you can't even imagine.
This-- this is a freakish genetic mutation.
This is unnatural.
This is uncontrollable.
It has to go.

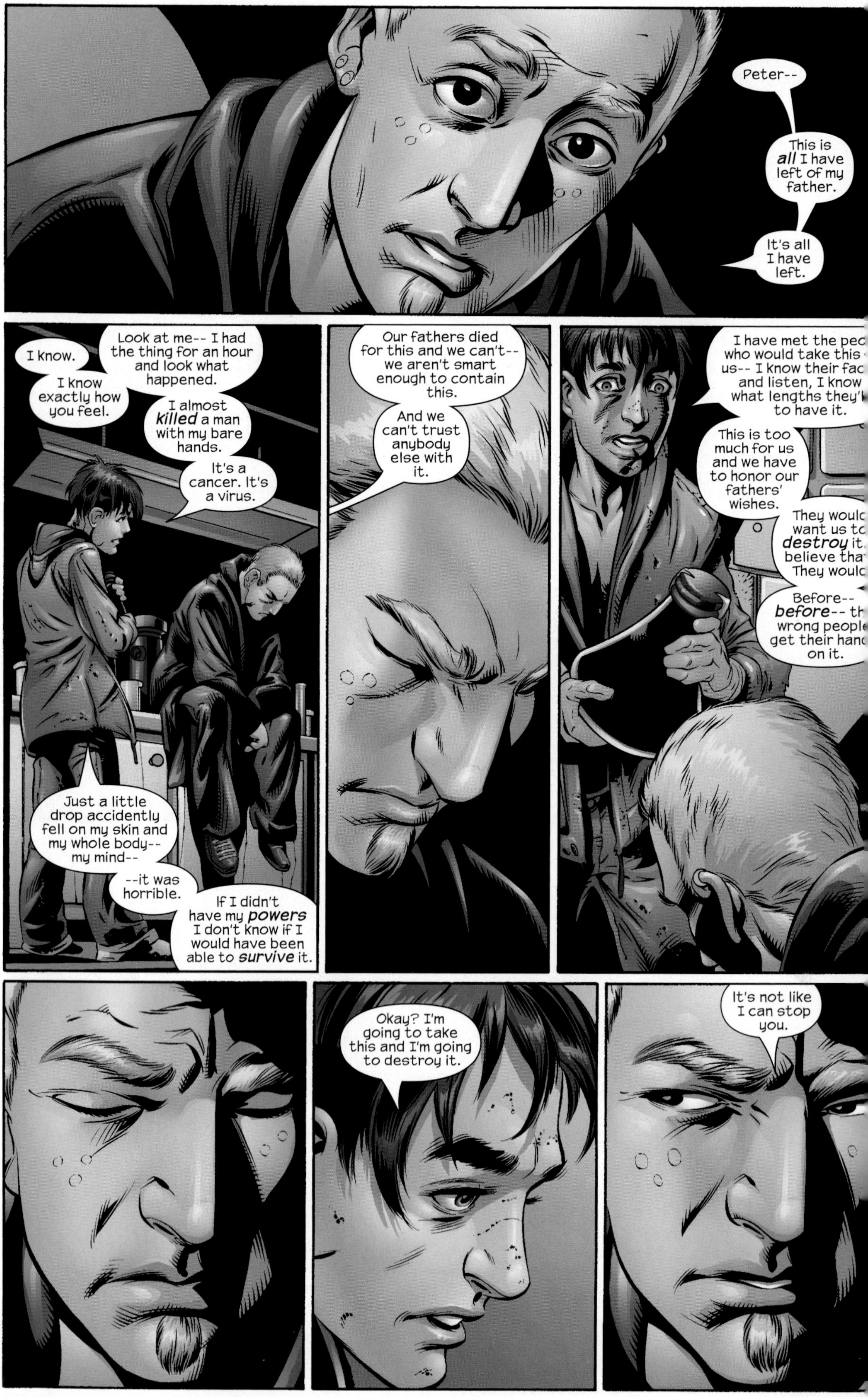
Peter--
This is *all* I have left of my father.
It's all I have left.
I know.
I know exactly how you feel.
Look at me-- I had the thing for an hour and look what happened.
I almost *killed* a man with my bare hands.
It's a cancer. It's a virus.
Just a little drop accidently fell on my skin and my whole body-- my mind--
--it was horrible.
If I didn't have my *powers* I don't know if I would have been able to *survive* it.
Our fathers died for this and we can't-- we aren't smart enough to contain this.
And we can't trust anybody else with it.
This is too much for us and we have to honor our fathers' wishes.
Okay? I'm going to take this and I'm going to destroy it.
It's not like I can stop you.

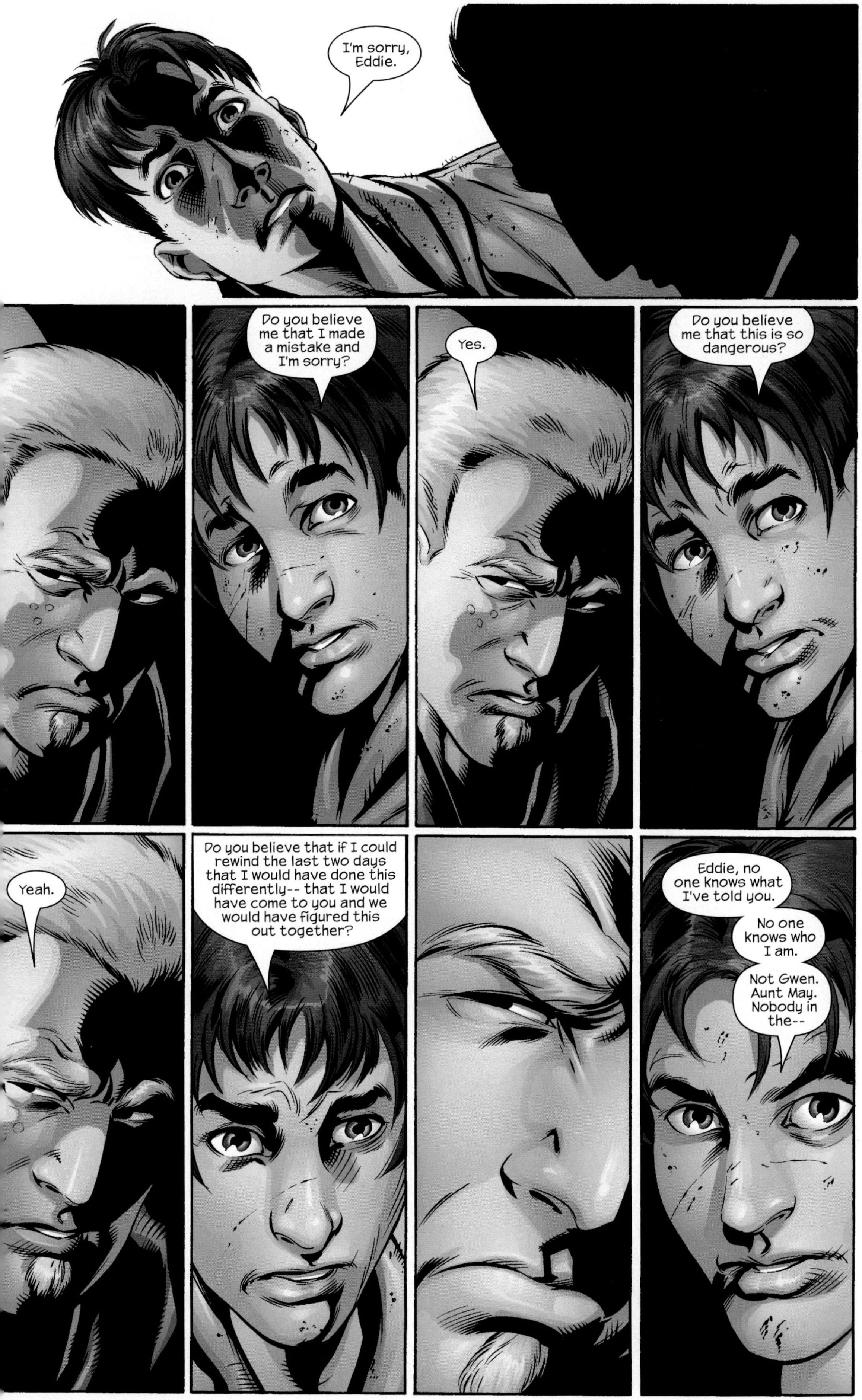
I'm sorry, Eddie.
Do you believe me that I made a mistake and I'm sorry?
Yes.
Do you believe me that this is so dangerous?
Yeah.
Do you believe that if I could rewind the last two days that I would have done this differently-- that I would have come to you and we would have figured this out together?
Eddie, no one knows what I've told you.
No one knows who I am.
Not Gwen. Aunt May. Nobody in the--

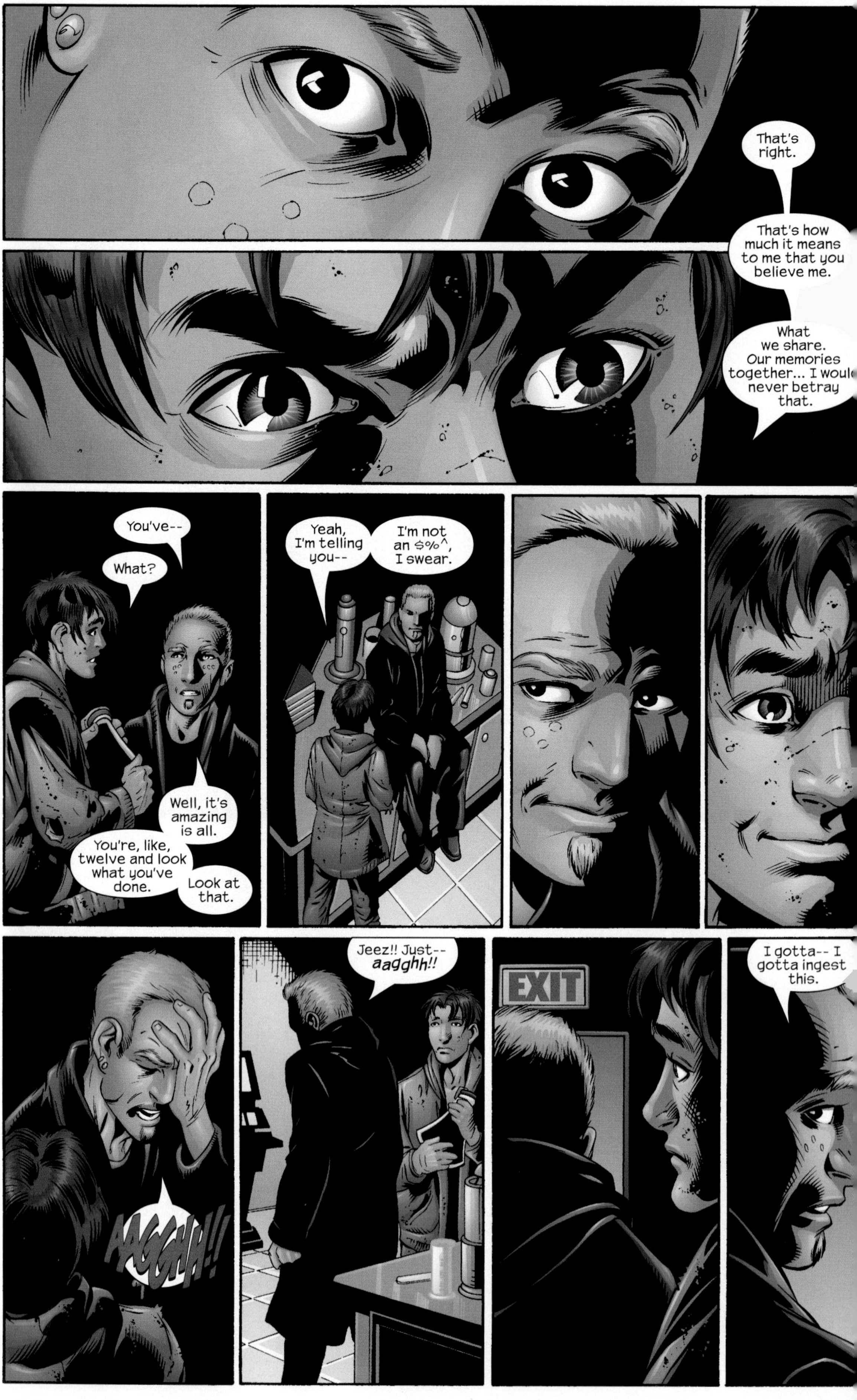
That's right.
That's how much it means to me that you believe me.
What we share. Our memories together... I would never betray that.
You've--
What?
Well, it's amazing is all.
You're, like, twelve and look what you've done.
Look at that.
Yeah, I'm telling you--
I'm not an $%^, I swear.
AAGGHH!!
Jeez!! Just-- aagghh!!
EXIT
I gotta-- I gotta ingest this.

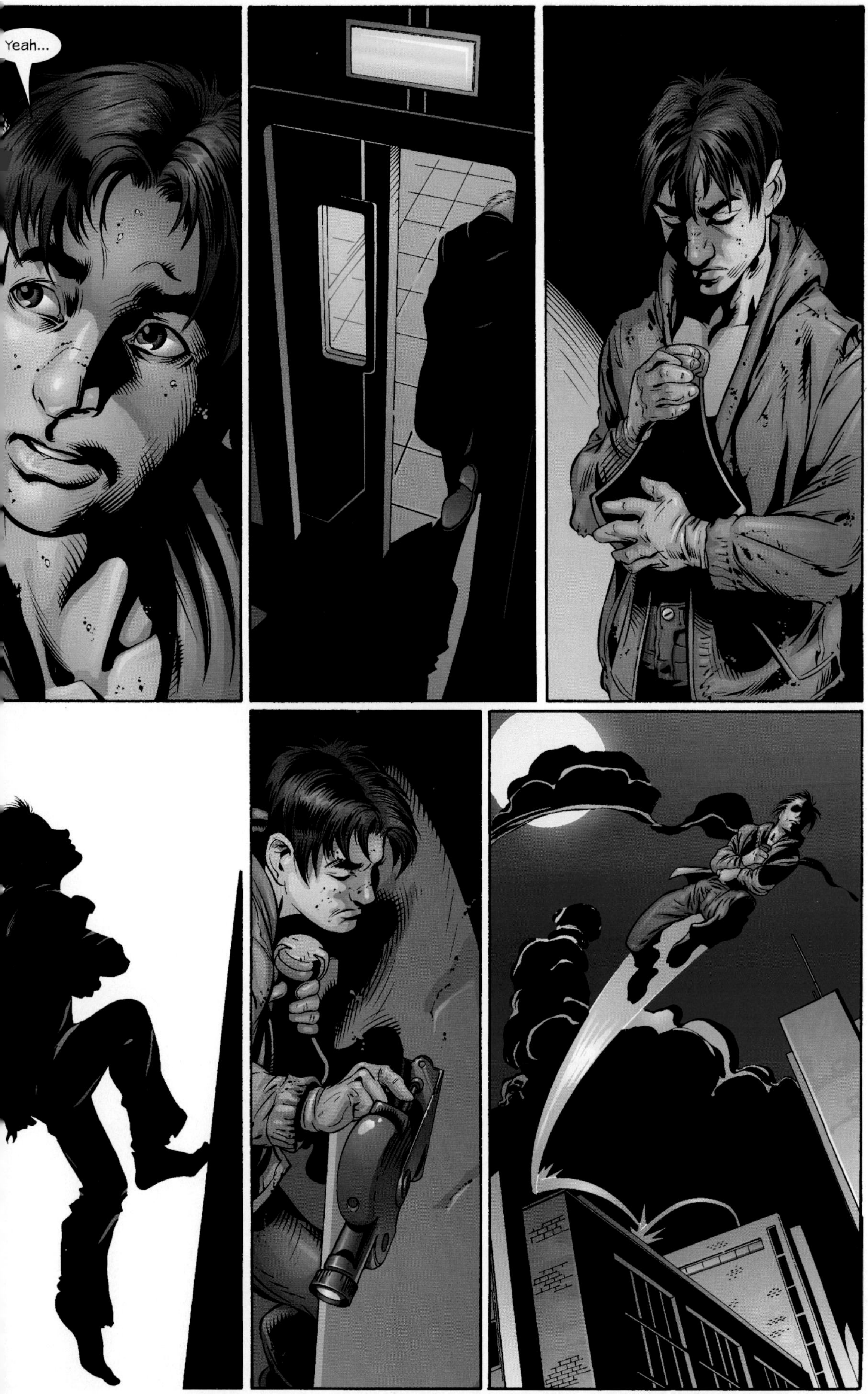
Yeah...

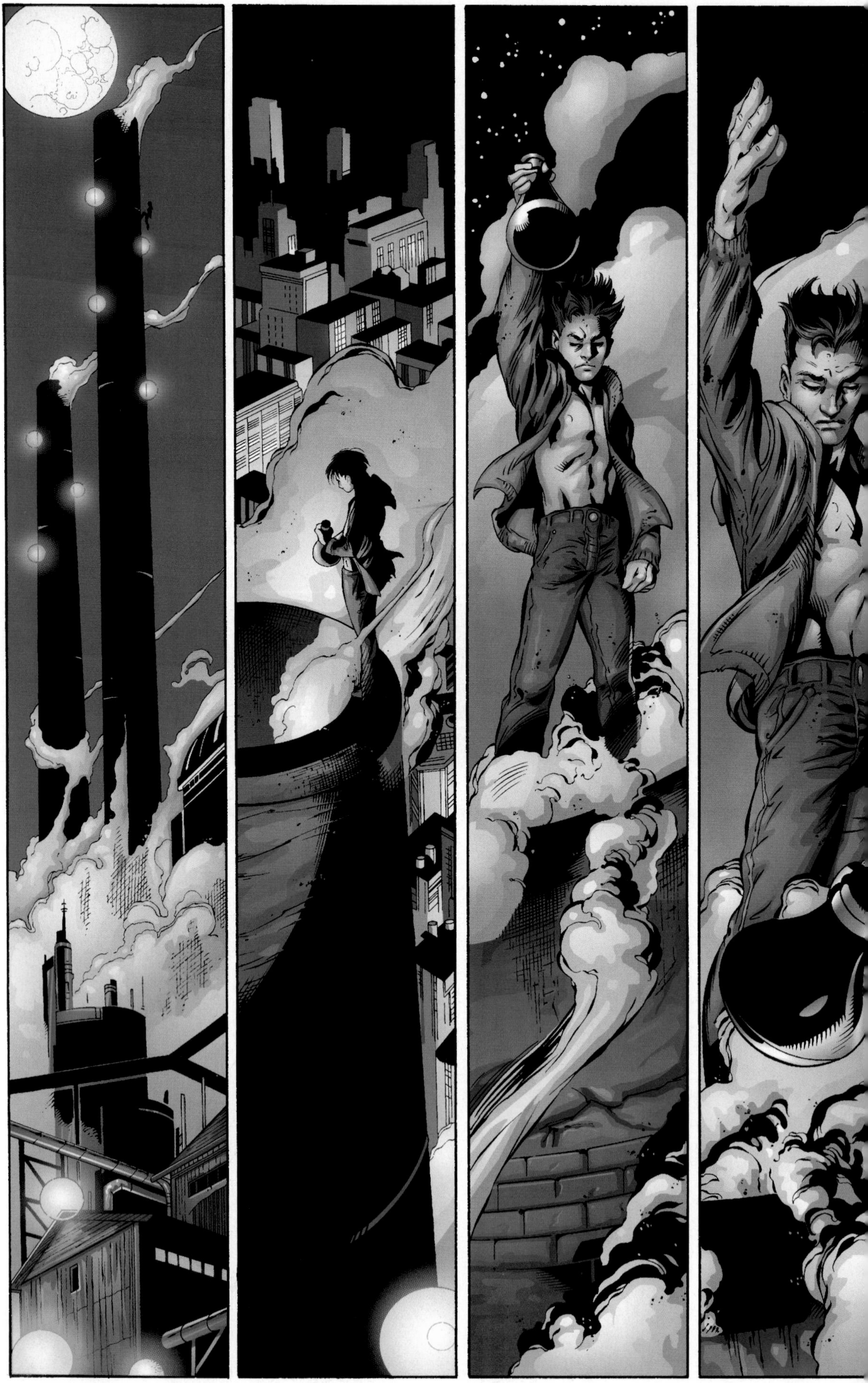

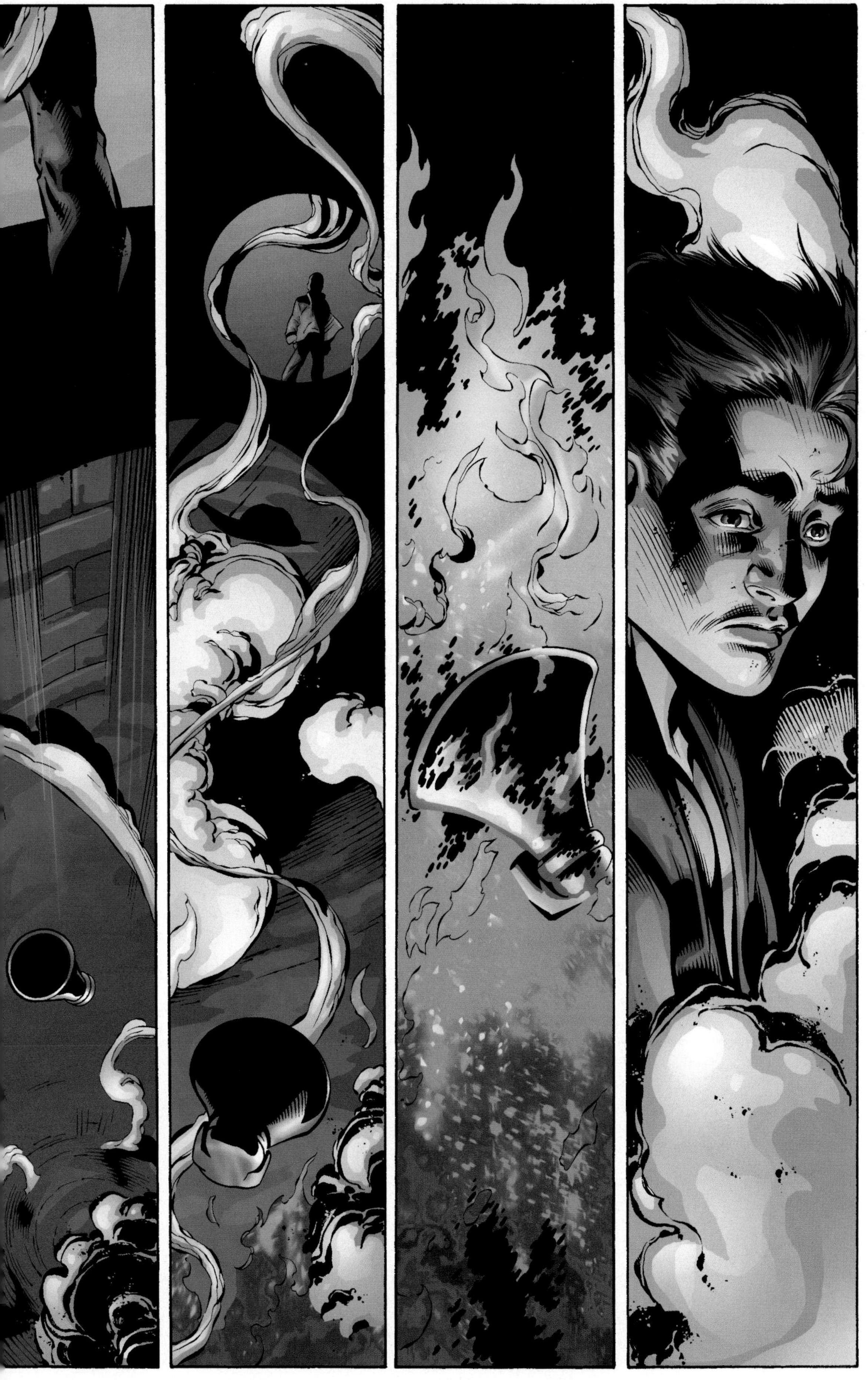

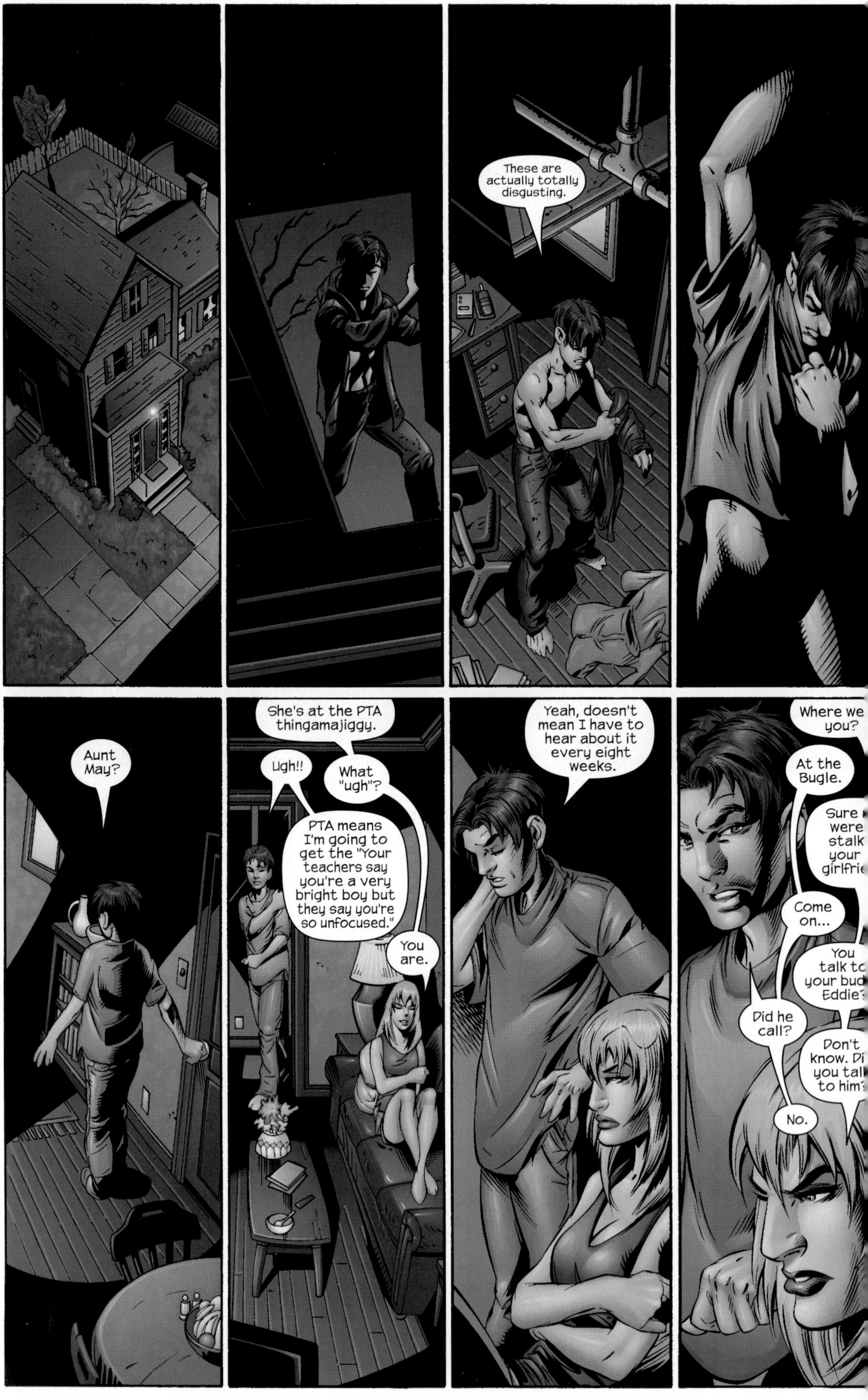
These are actually totally disgusting.
Aunt May?
She's at the PTA thingamajiggy.
Ugh!!
What "ugh"?
PTA means I'm going to get the "Your teachers say you're a very bright boy but they say you're so unfocused."
You are.
Yeah, doesn't mean I have to hear about it every eight weeks.
Where we you?
At the Bugle.
Sure were stalk your girlfrie
Come on...
You talk to your bud Eddie?
Did he call?
Don't know. Di you tal to him?
No.

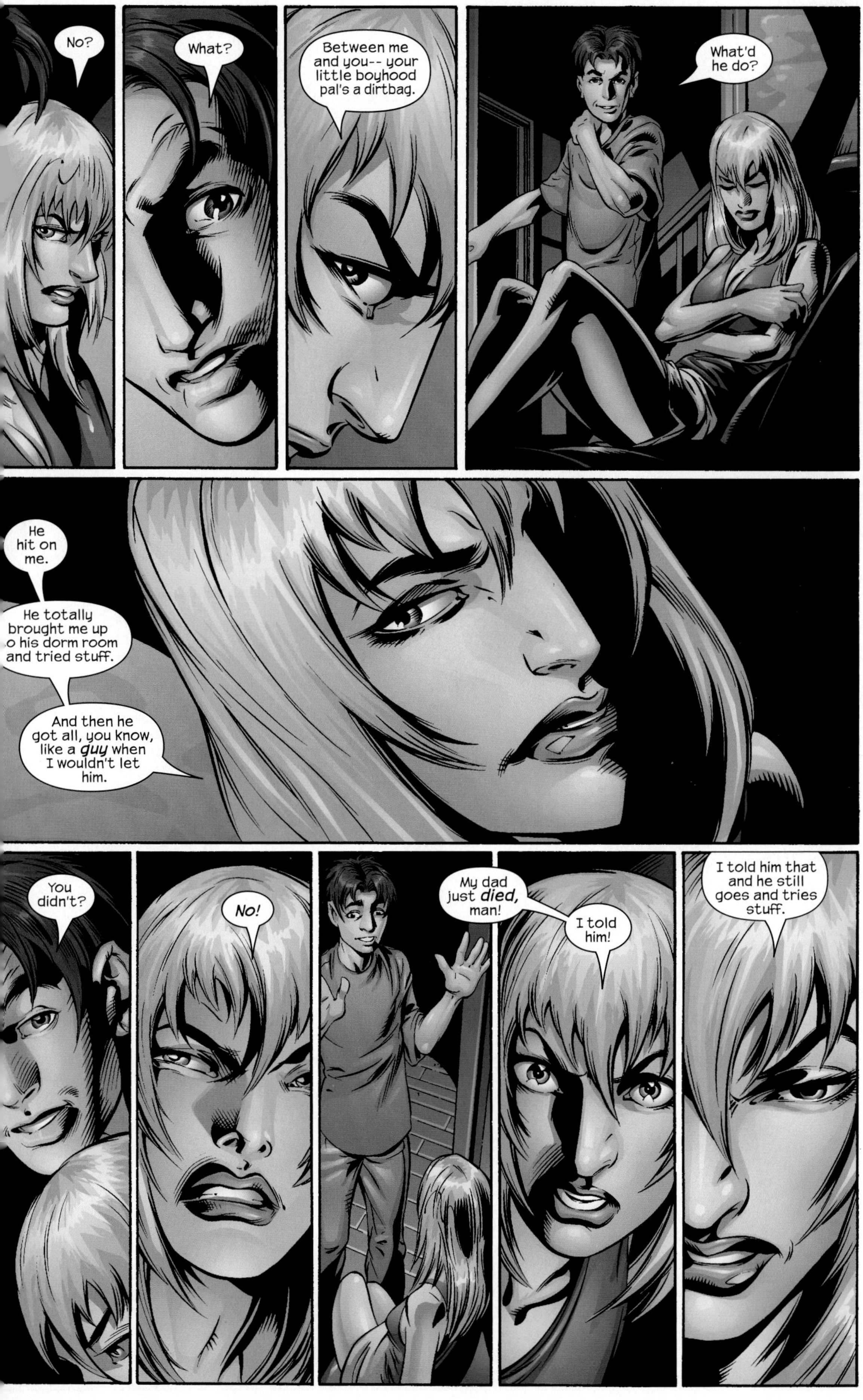

No?
What?
Between me and you-- your little boyhood pal's a dirtbag.
What'd he do?
He hit on me.
He totally brought me up o his dorm room and tried stuff.
And then he got all, you know, like a *guy* when I wouldn't let him.
You didn't?
No!
My dad just *died,* man!
I told him!
I told him that and he still goes and tries stuff.

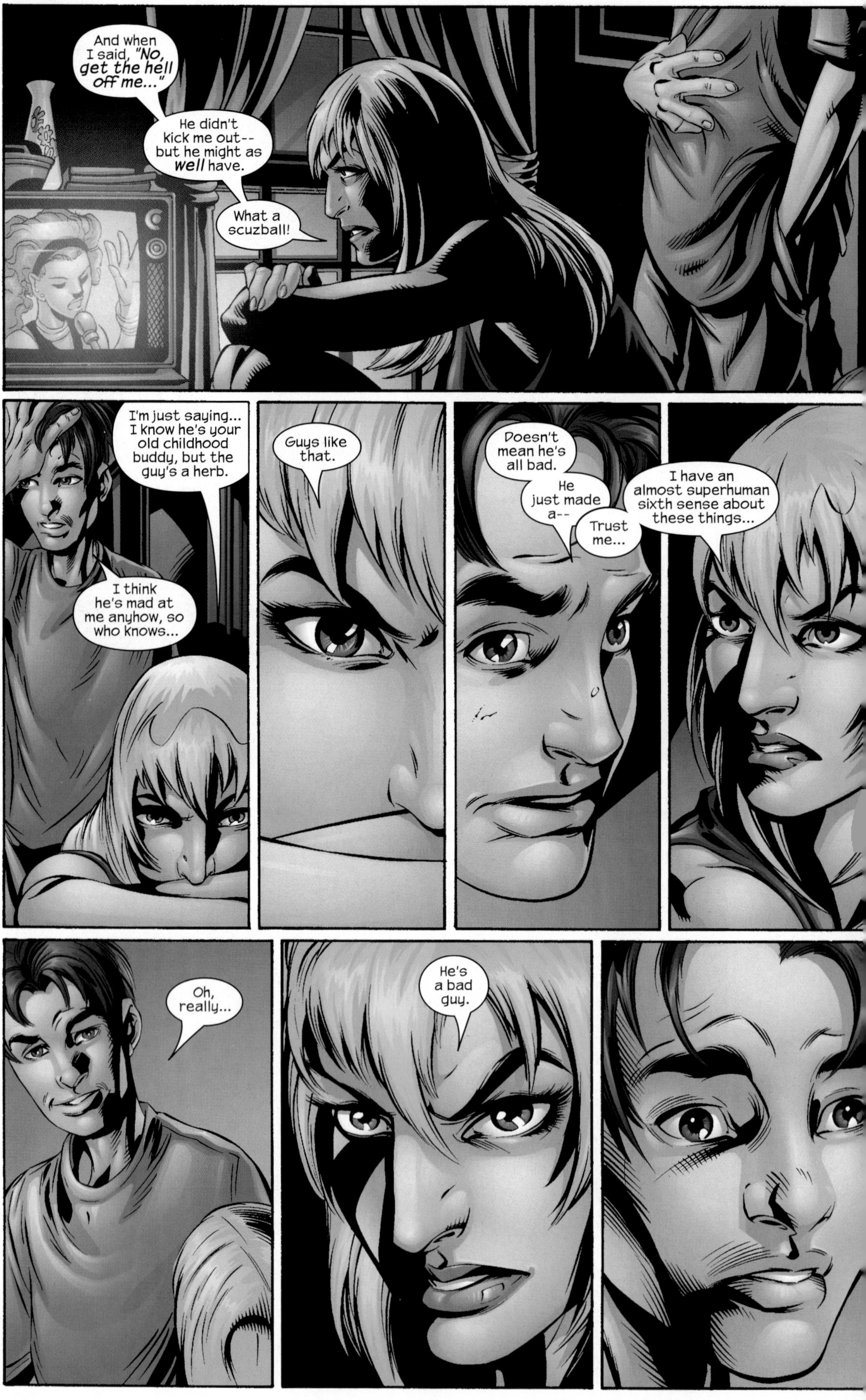

And when I said, "No, get the hell off me..."
He didn't kick me out-- but he might as well have.
What a scuzball!
I'm just saying... I know he's your old childhood buddy, but the guy's a herb.
I think he's mad at me anyhow, so who knows...
Guys like that.
Doesn't mean he's all bad.
He just made a--
Trust me...
I have an almost superhuman sixth sense about these things...
Oh, really...
He's a bad guy.

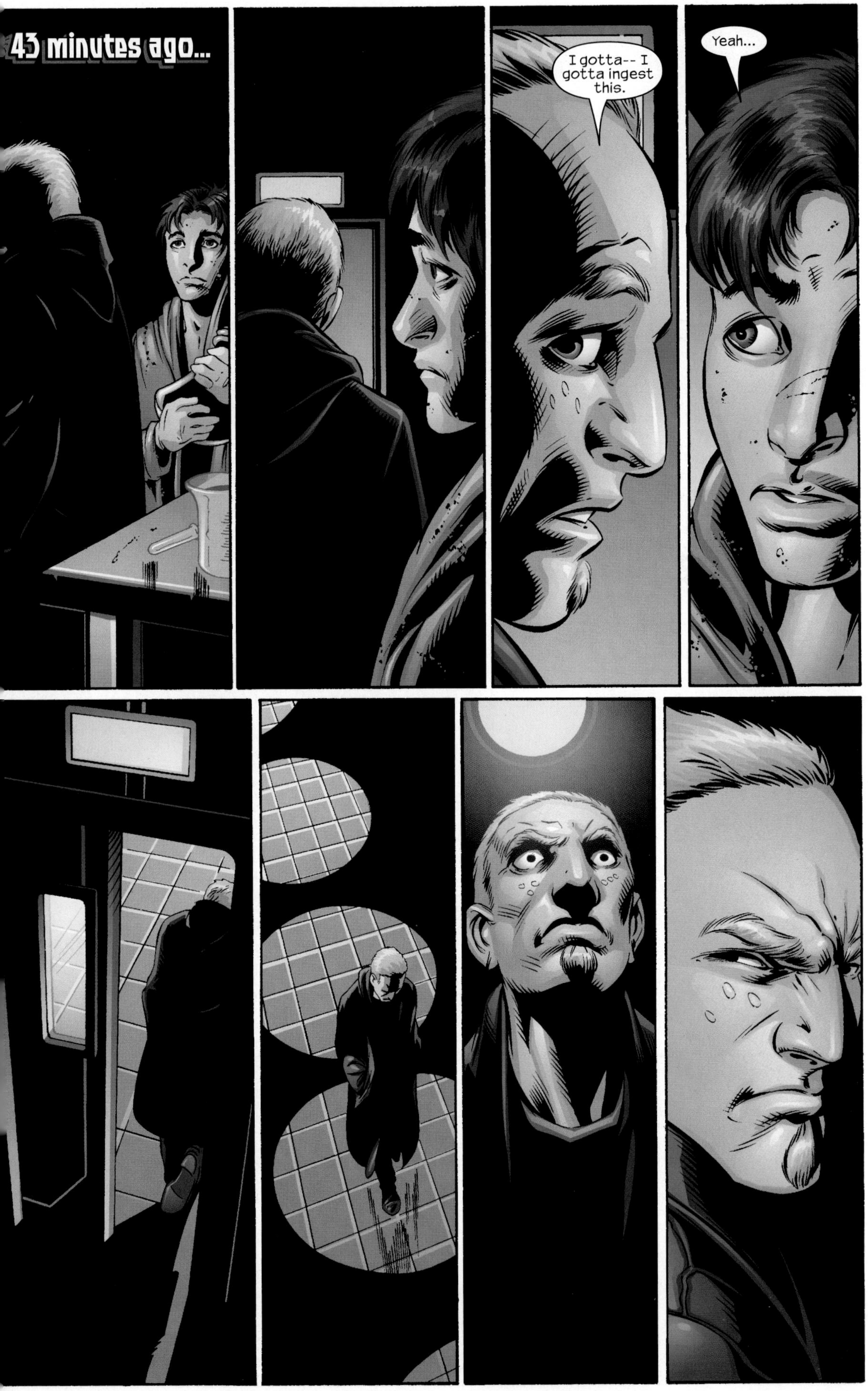

43 minutes ago...
I gotta-- I gotta ingest this.
Yeah...

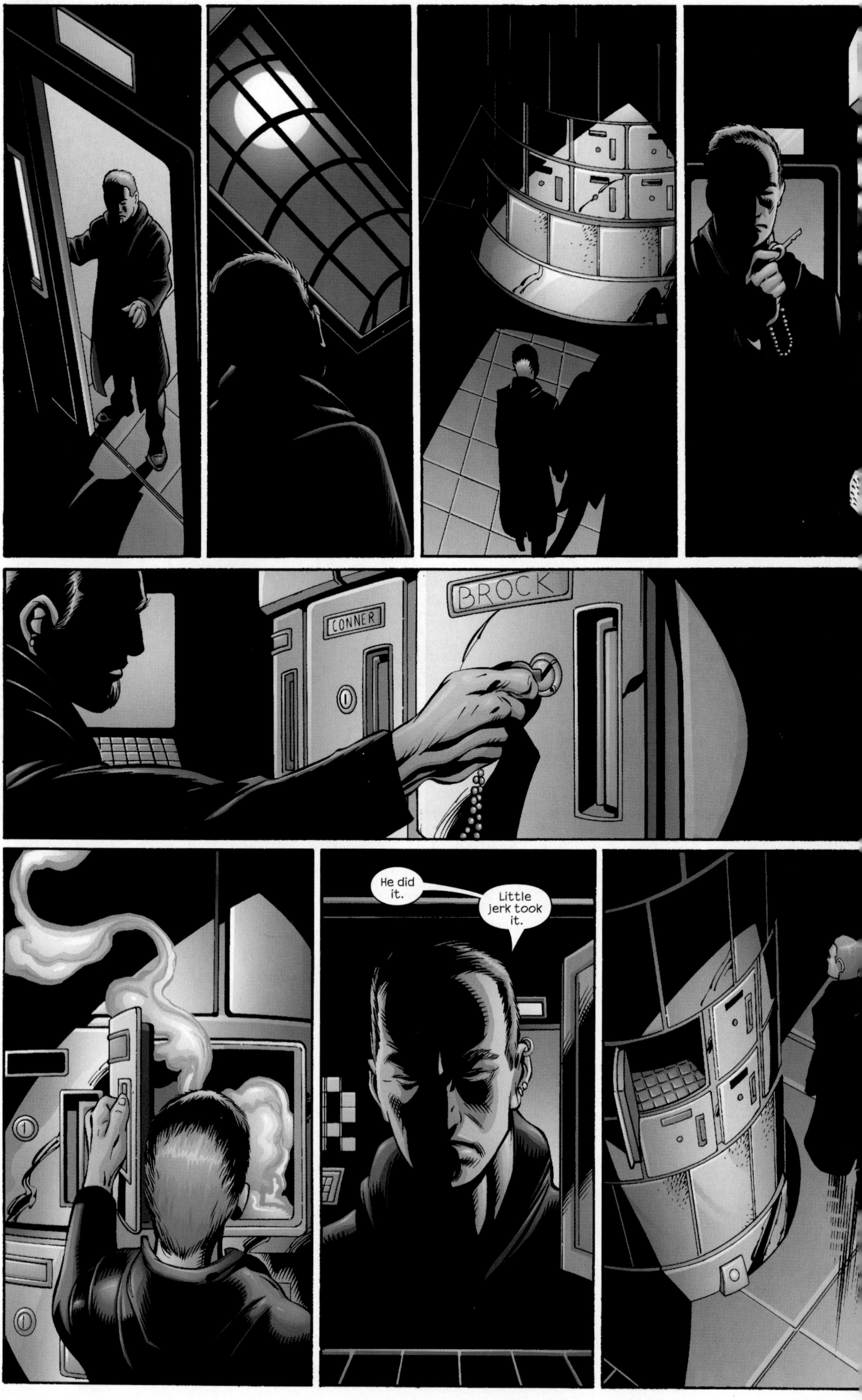

CONNER
BROCK
He did it.
Little jerk took it.

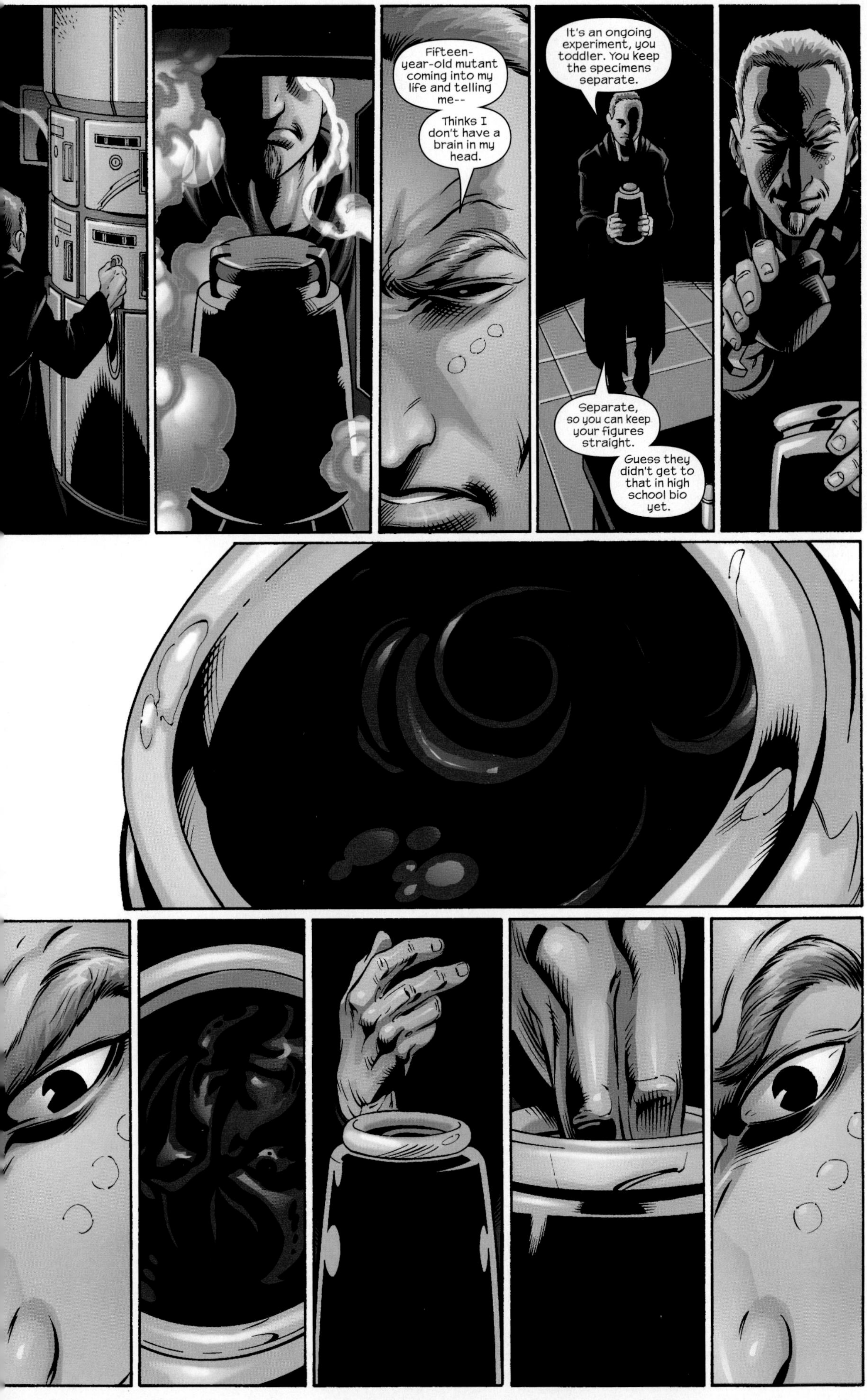
Fifteen-year-old mutant coming into my life and telling me--
Thinks I don't have a brain in my head.
It's an ongoing experiment, you toddler. You keep the specimens separate.
Separate, so you can keep your figures straight.
Guess they didn't get to that in high school bio yet.

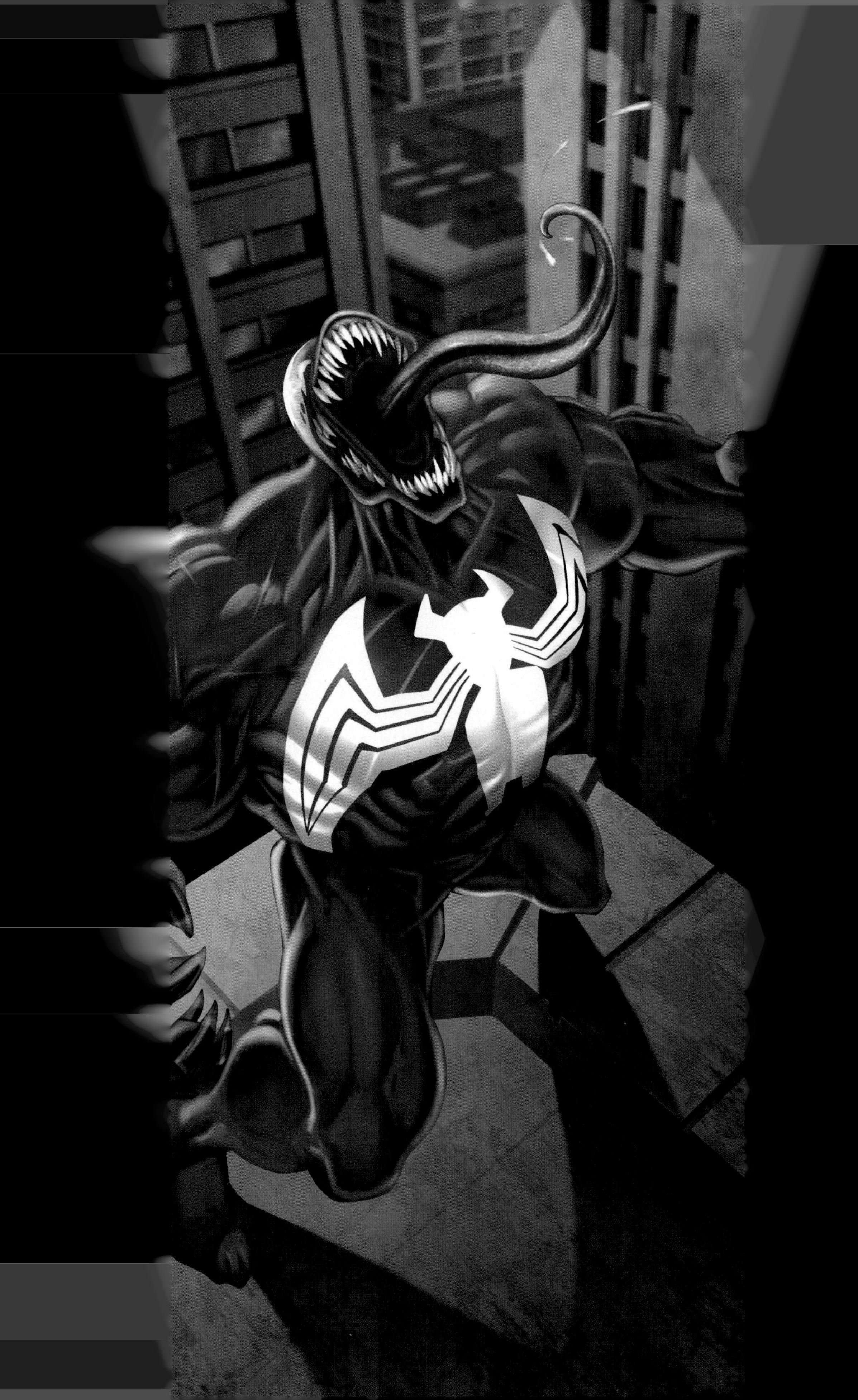

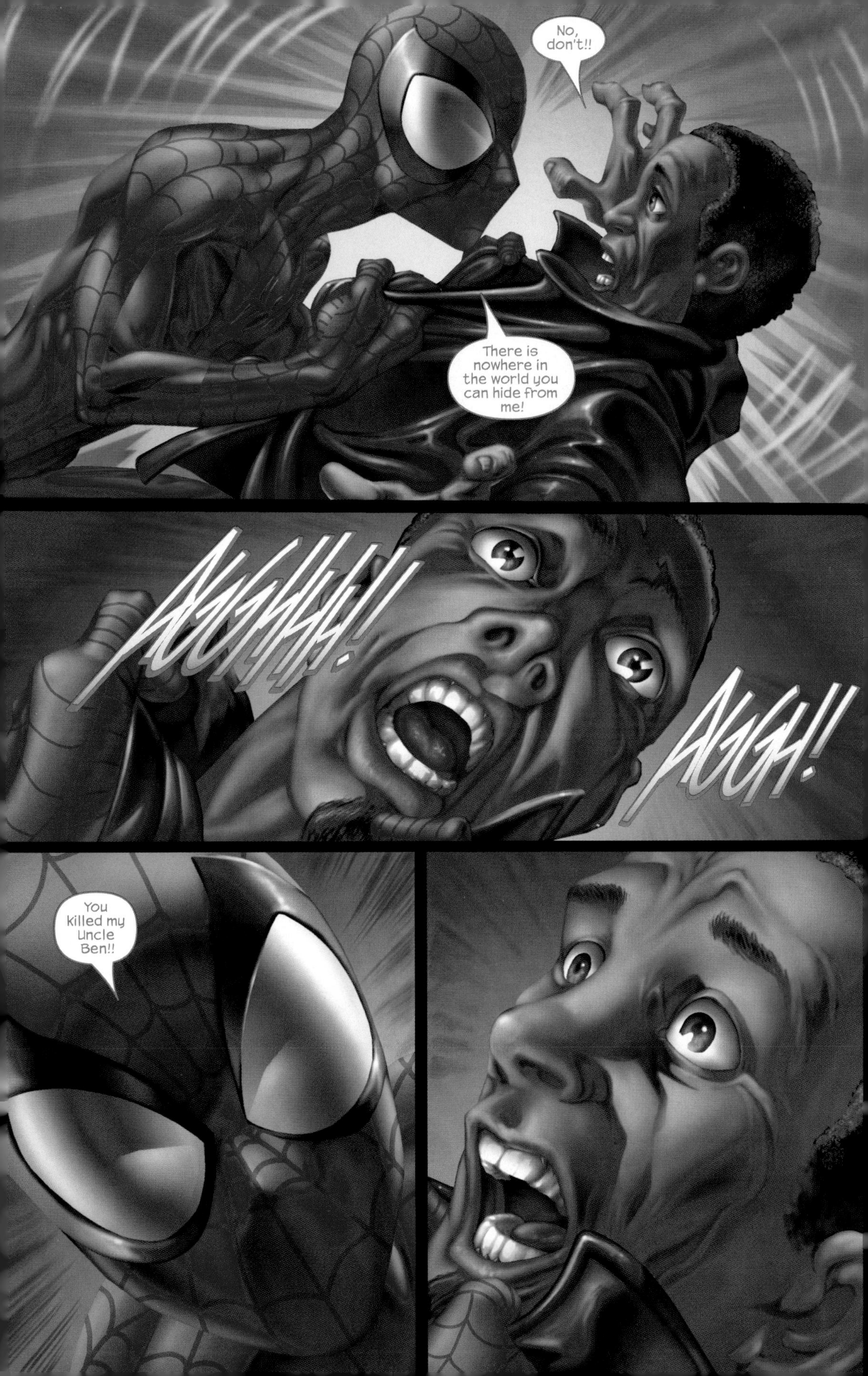
No, don't!!
There is nowhere in the world you can hide from me!
AAGHHH!!
AUGH!
You killed my Uncle Ben!!

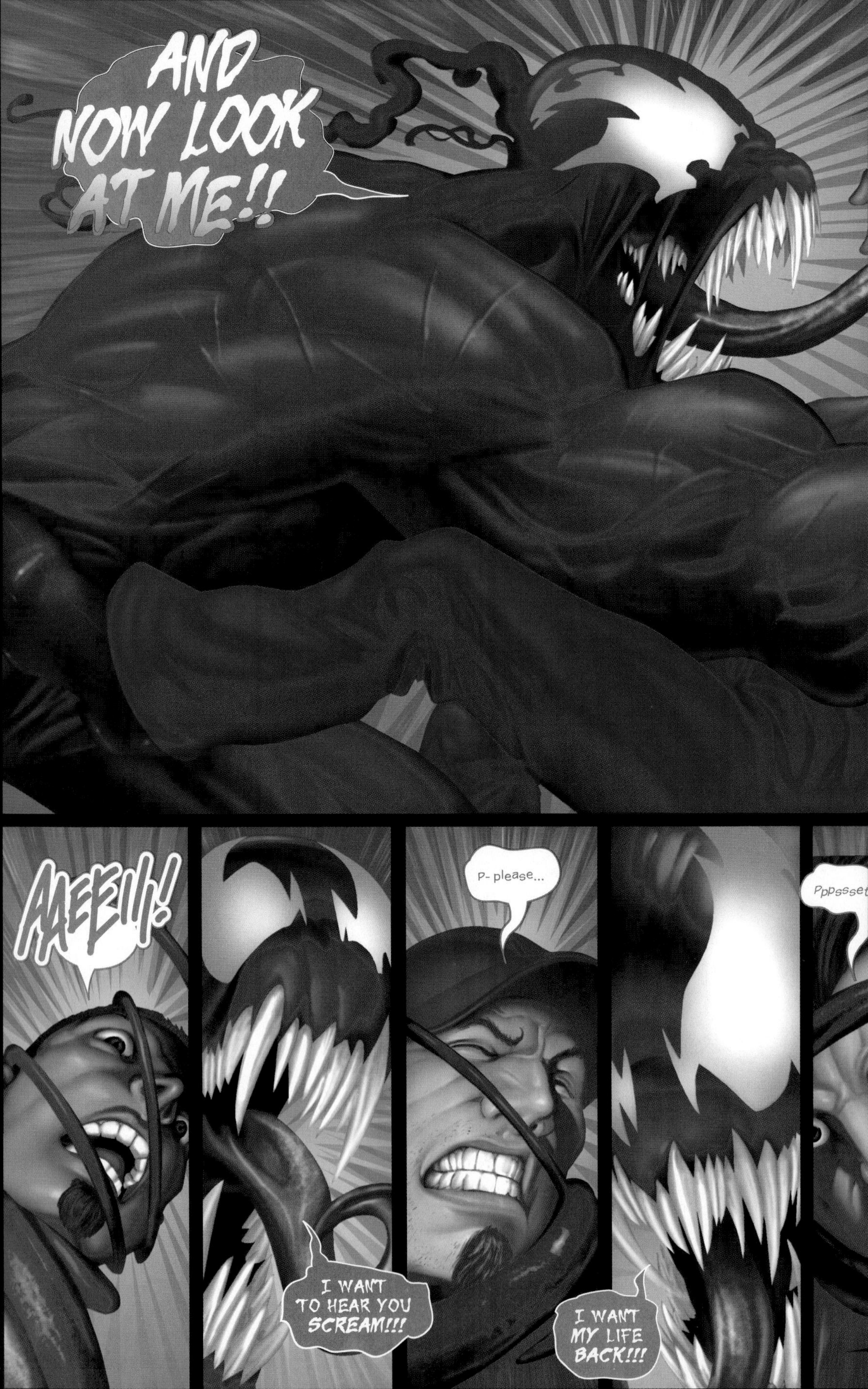
AND NOW LOOK AT ME!!
AAEEIIII!
I WANT TO HEAR YOU SCREAM!!!
P- please...
I WANT MY LIFE BACK!!!
Pppssset

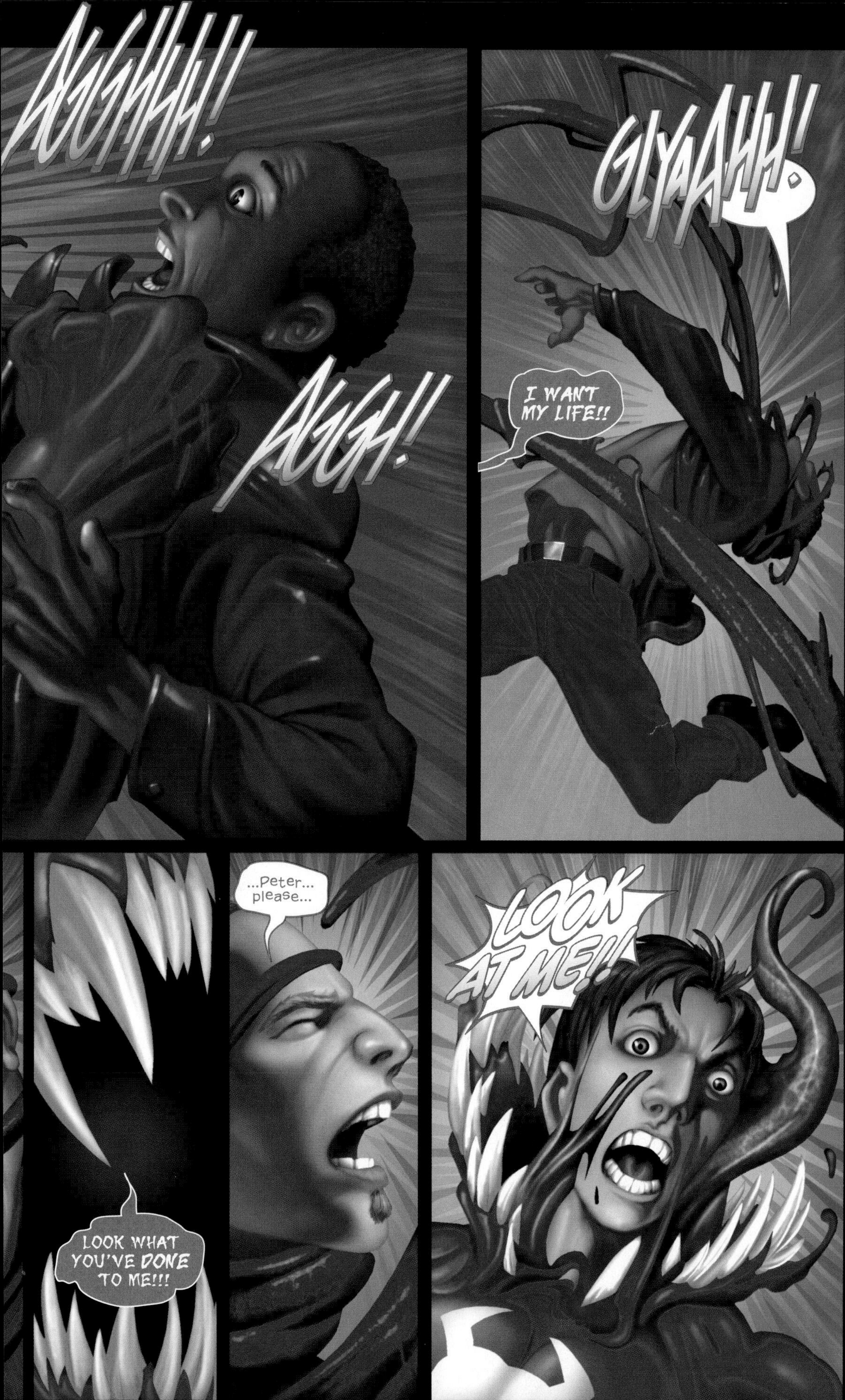
AUGHHH!!
AUGH!
GLYAAHH!
I WANT MY LIFE!!
LOOK WHAT YOU'VE DONE TO ME!!!
...Peter... please...
LOOK AT ME!!!

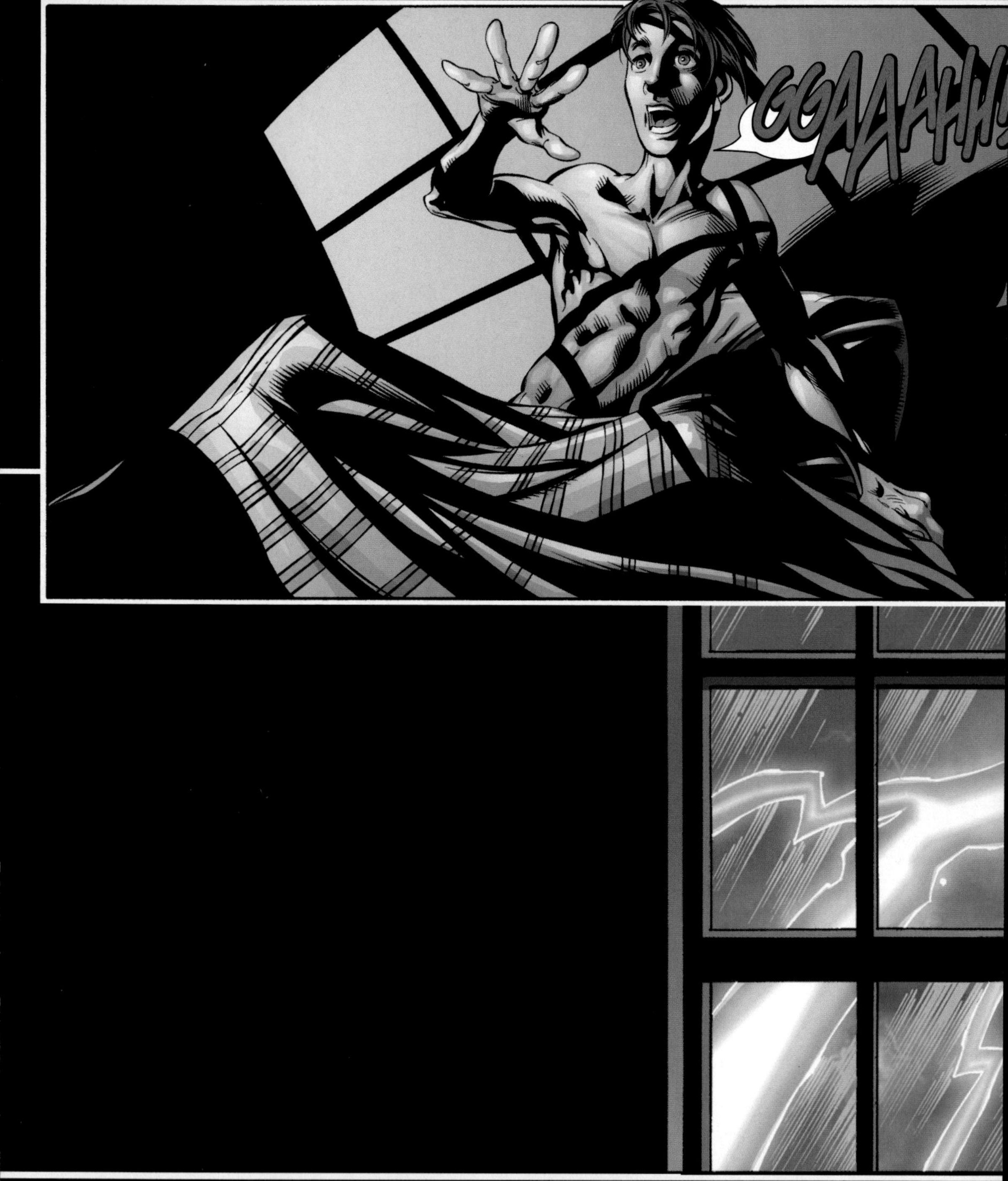
GGAAAHH!

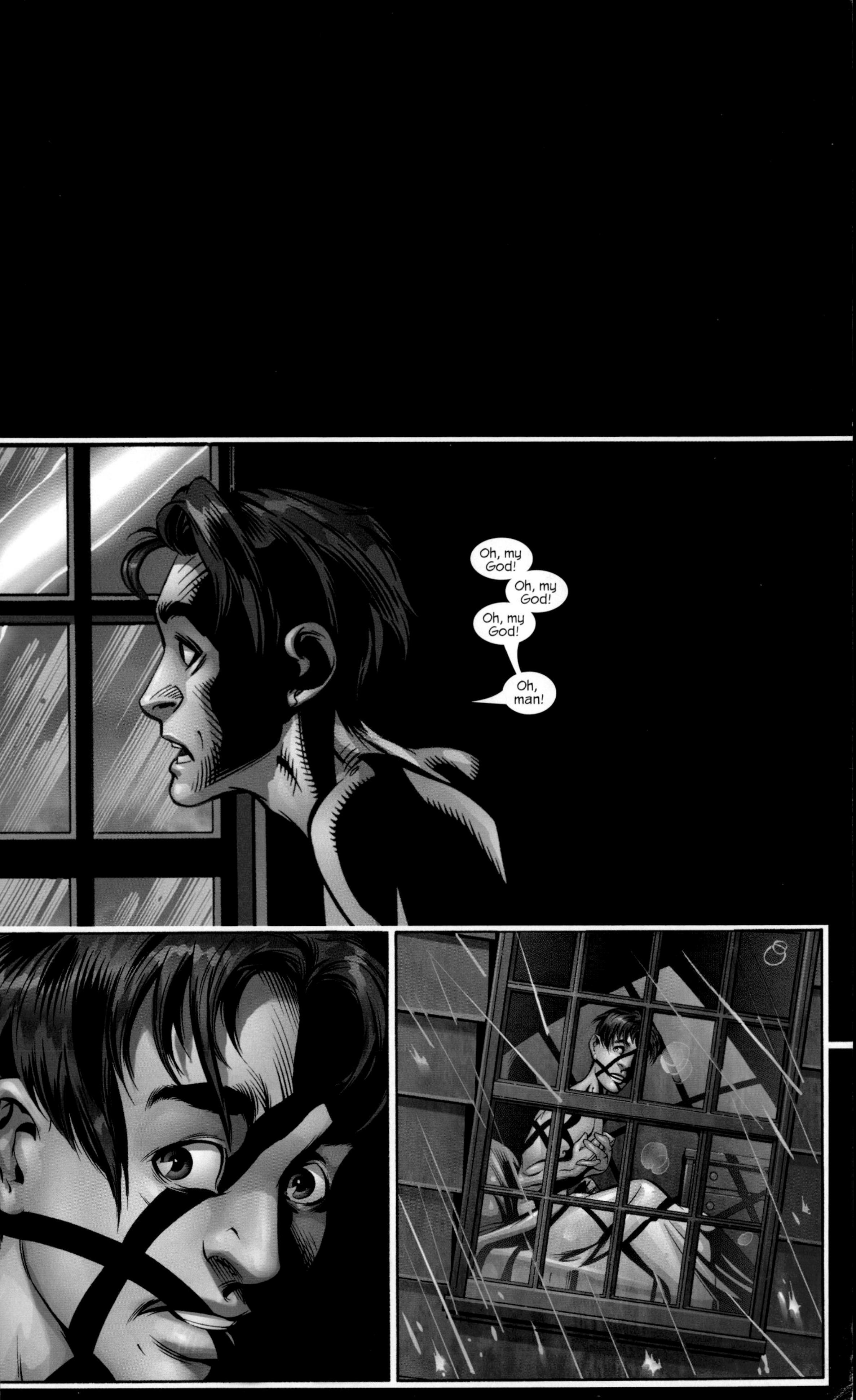

Oh, my God!
Oh, my God!
Oh, my God!
Oh, man!

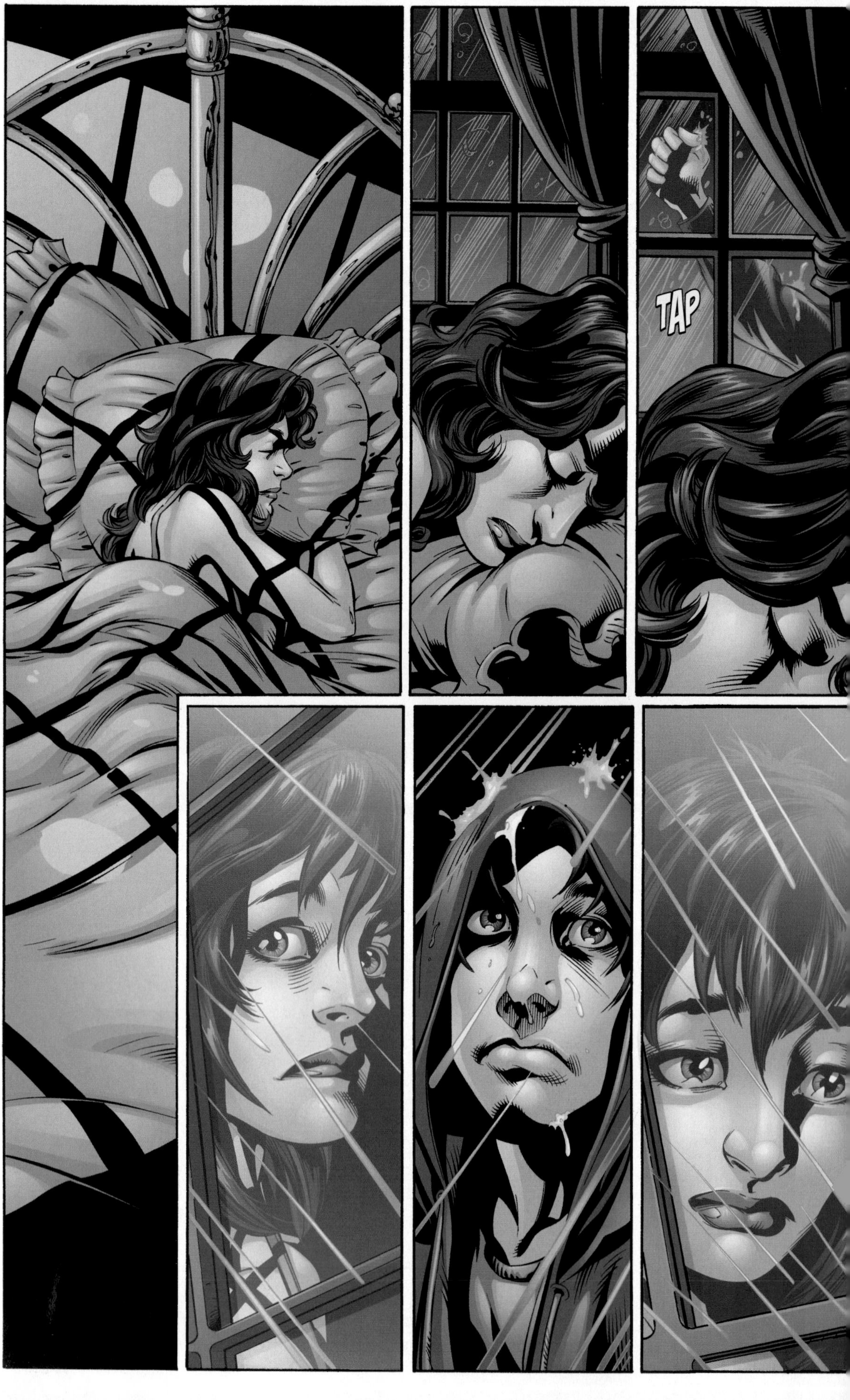
TAP

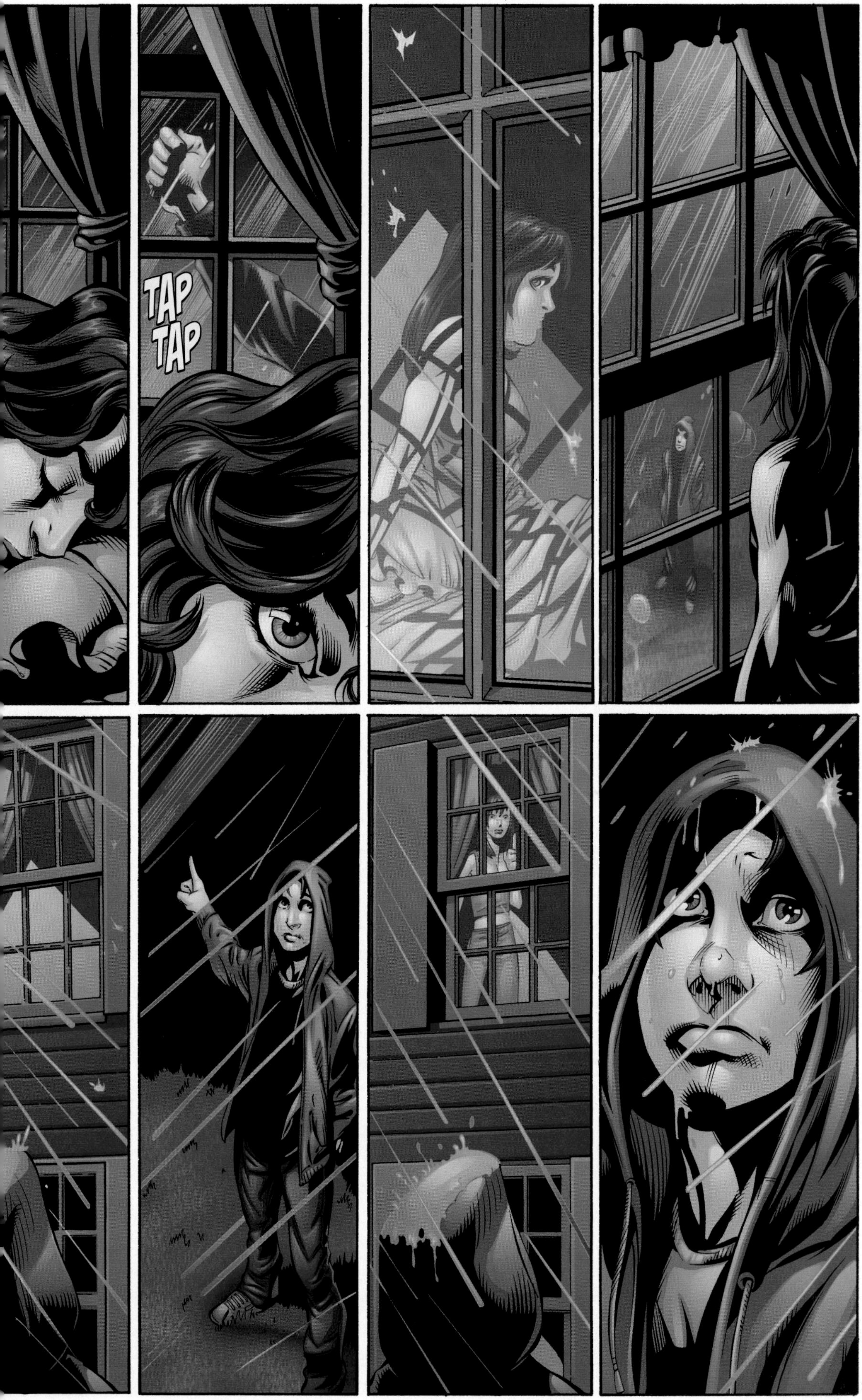
TAP TAP

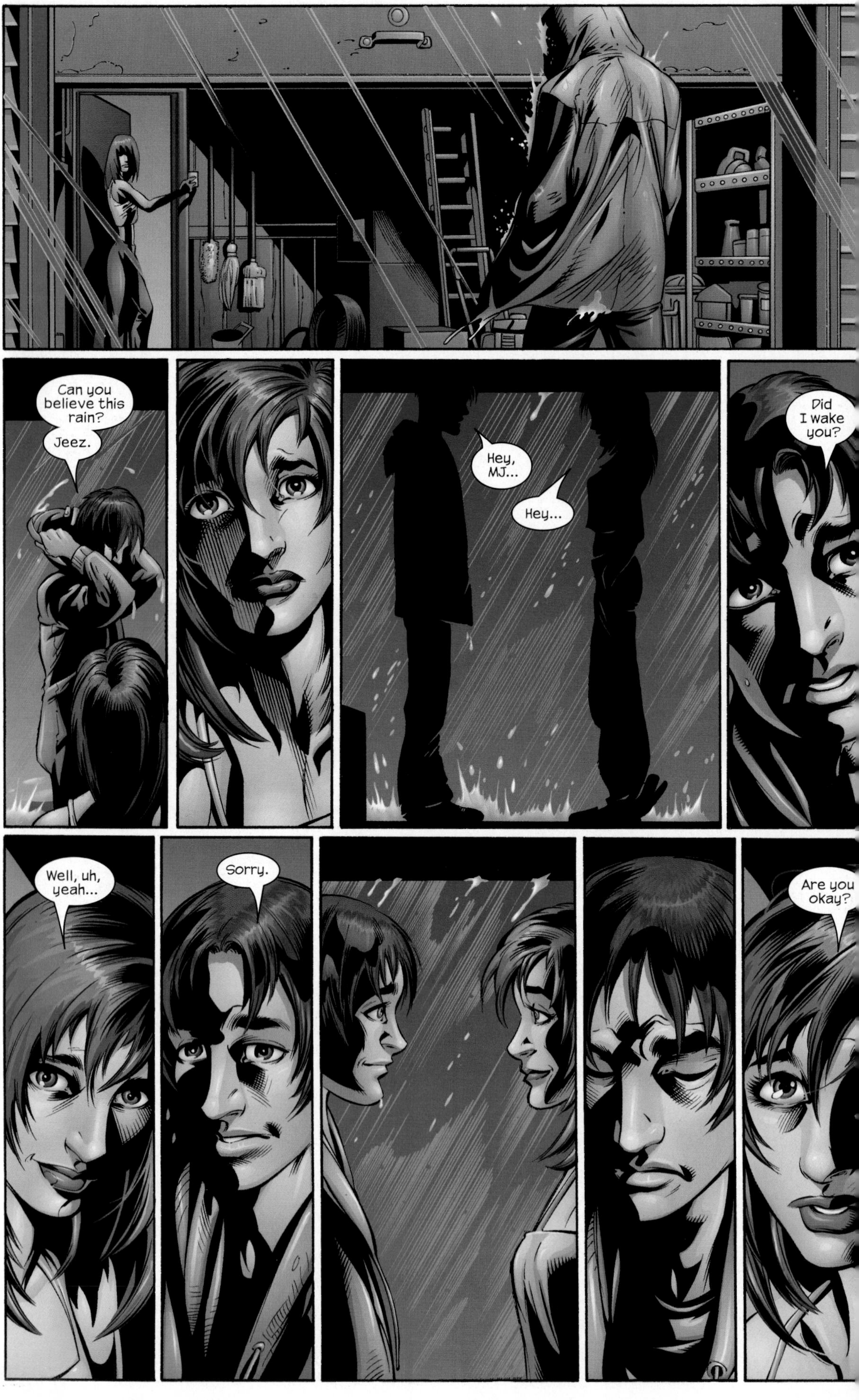
Can you believe this rain?
Jeez.
Hey, MJ...
Hey...
Did I wake you?
Well, uh, yeah...
Sorry.
Are you okay?

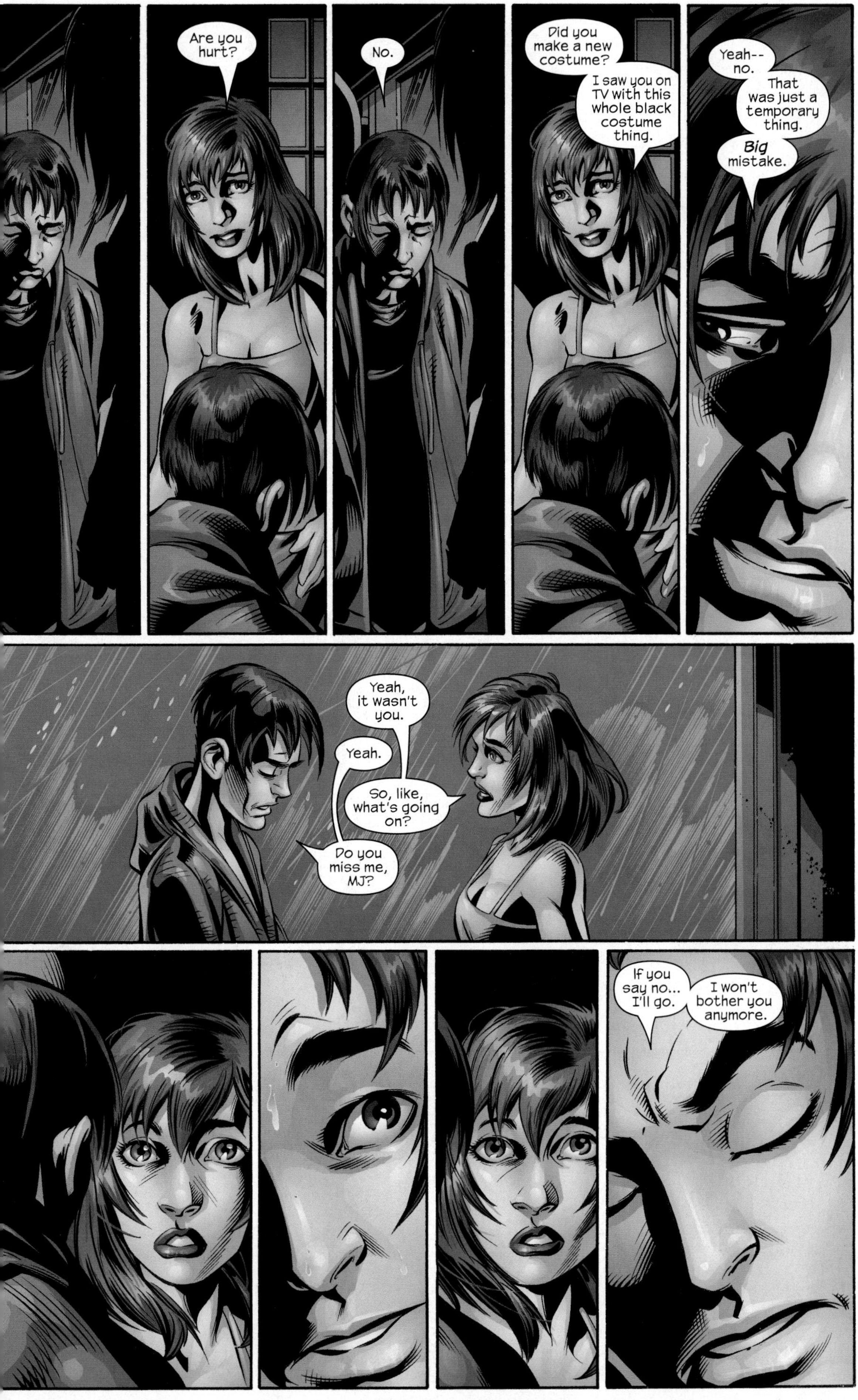

Are you hurt?
No.
Did you make a new costume?
I saw you on TV with this whole black costume thing.
Yeah-- no.
That was just a temporary thing.
Big mistake.
Yeah, it wasn't you.
Yeah.
So, like, what's going on?
Do you miss me, MJ?
If you say no... I'll go.
I won't bother you anymore.

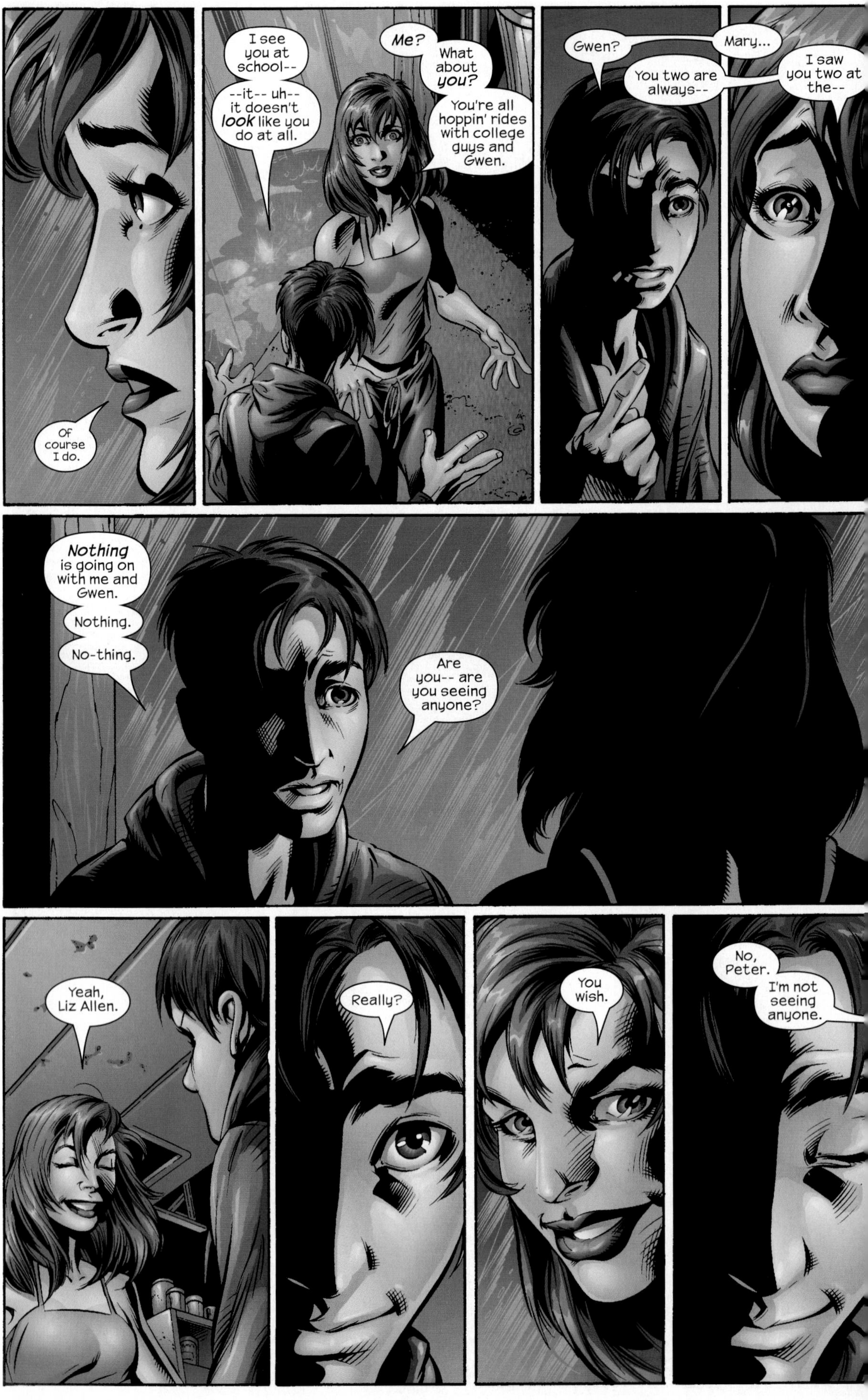
Of course I do.
I see you at school--
--it-- uh-- it doesn't look like you do at all.
Me? What about you?
You're all hoppin' rides with college guys and Gwen.
Gwen?
Mary...
You two are always--
I saw you two at the--
Nothing is going on with me and Gwen.
Nothing.
No-thing.
Are you-- are you seeing anyone?
Yeah, Liz Allen.
Really?
You wish.
No, Peter.
I'm not seeing anyone.

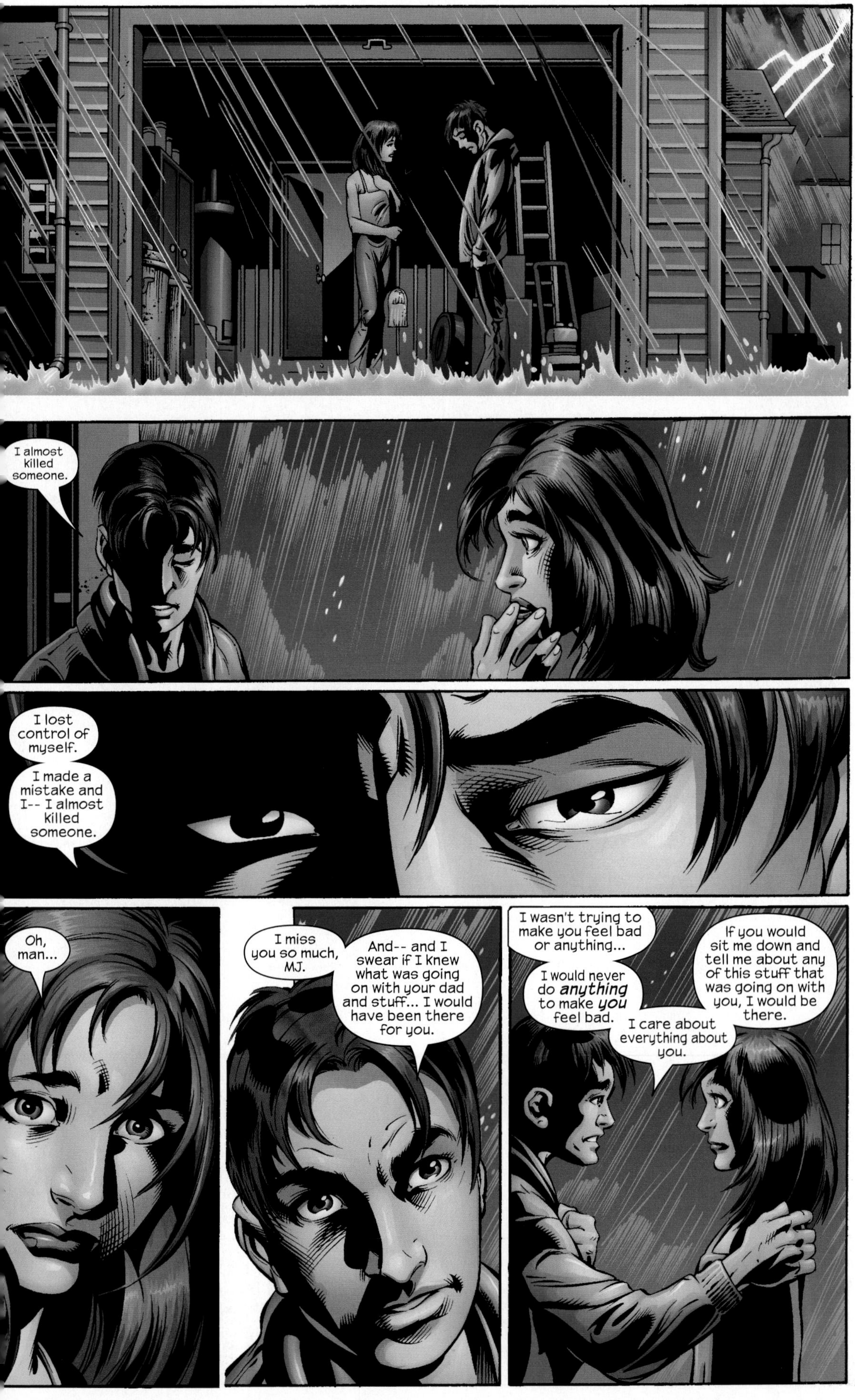
I almost killed someone.
I lost control of myself.
I made a mistake and I-- I almost killed someone.
Oh, man...
I miss you so much, MJ.
And-- and I swear if I knew what was going on with your dad and stuff... I would have been there for you.
I wasn't trying to make you feel bad or anything...
I would never do *anything* to make *you* feel bad.
I care about everything about you.
If you would sit me down and tell me about any of this stuff that was going on with you, I would be there.

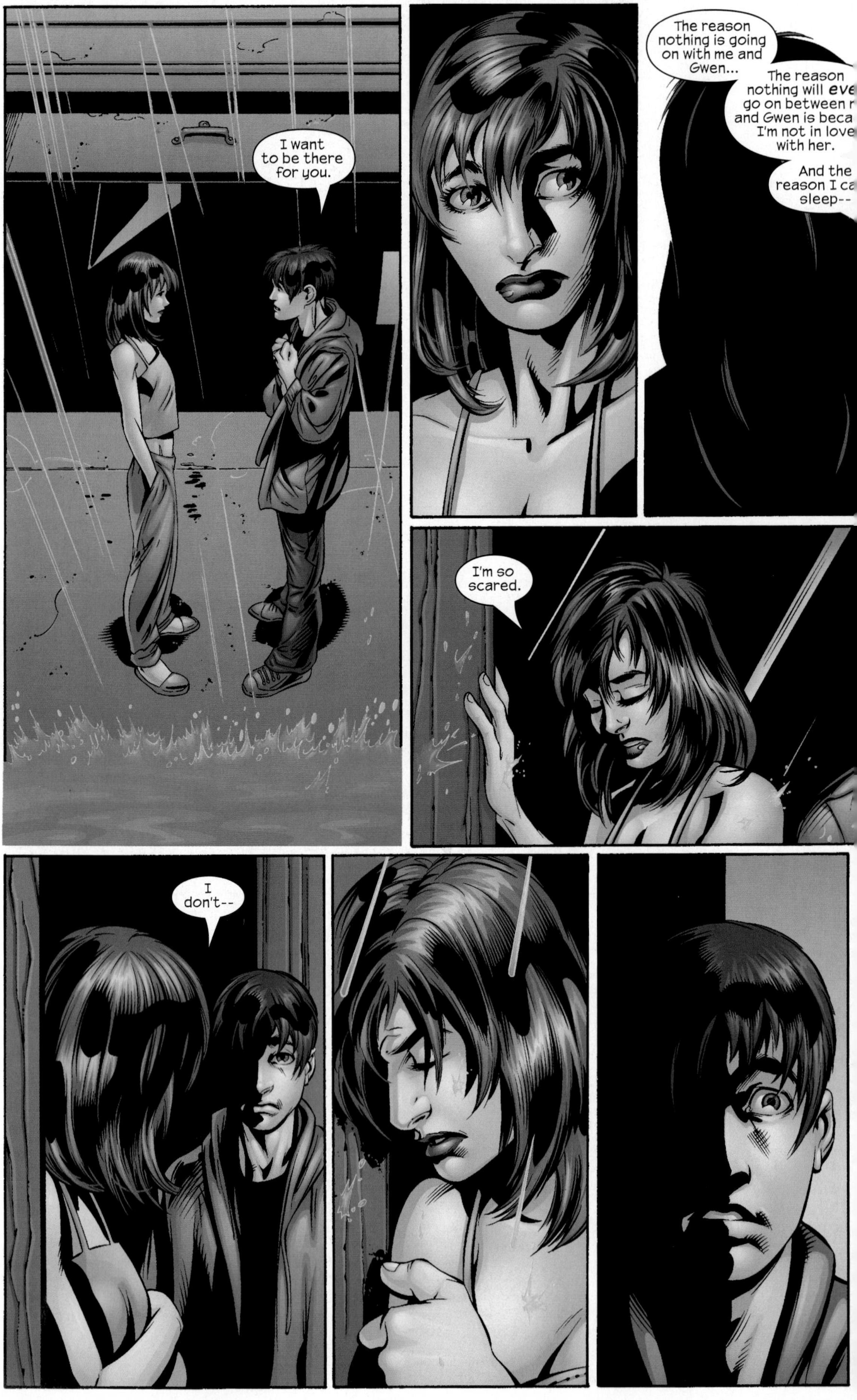
I want to be there for you.
The reason nothing is going on with me and Gwen...
The reason nothing will eve go on between and Gwen is beca I'm not in love with her.
And the reason I ca sleep--
I'm so scared.
I don't--

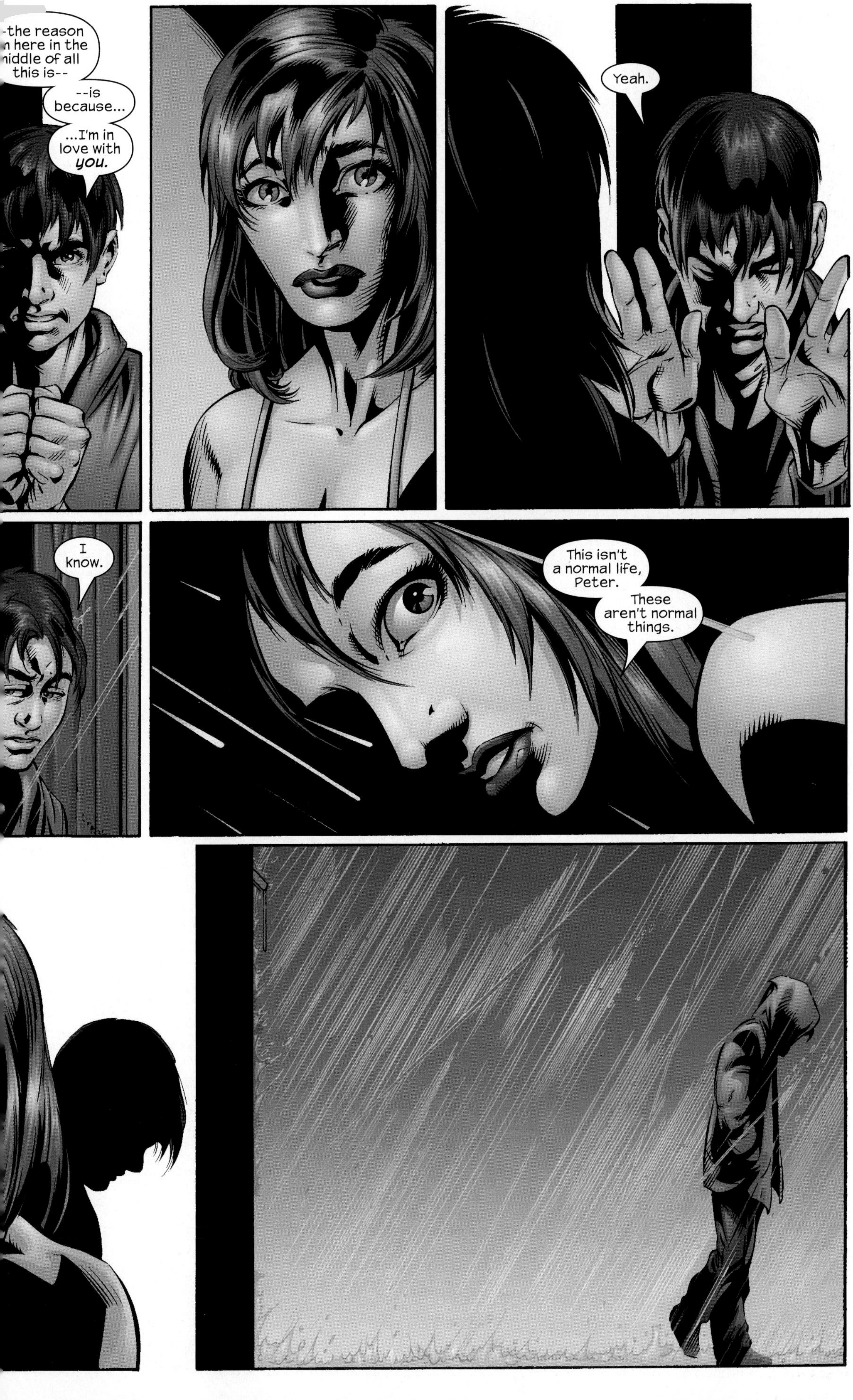
-the reason
n here in the
niddle of all
this is--
--is
because...
...I'm in
love with
you.
Yeah.
I
know.
This isn't
a normal life,
Peter.
These
aren't normal
things.

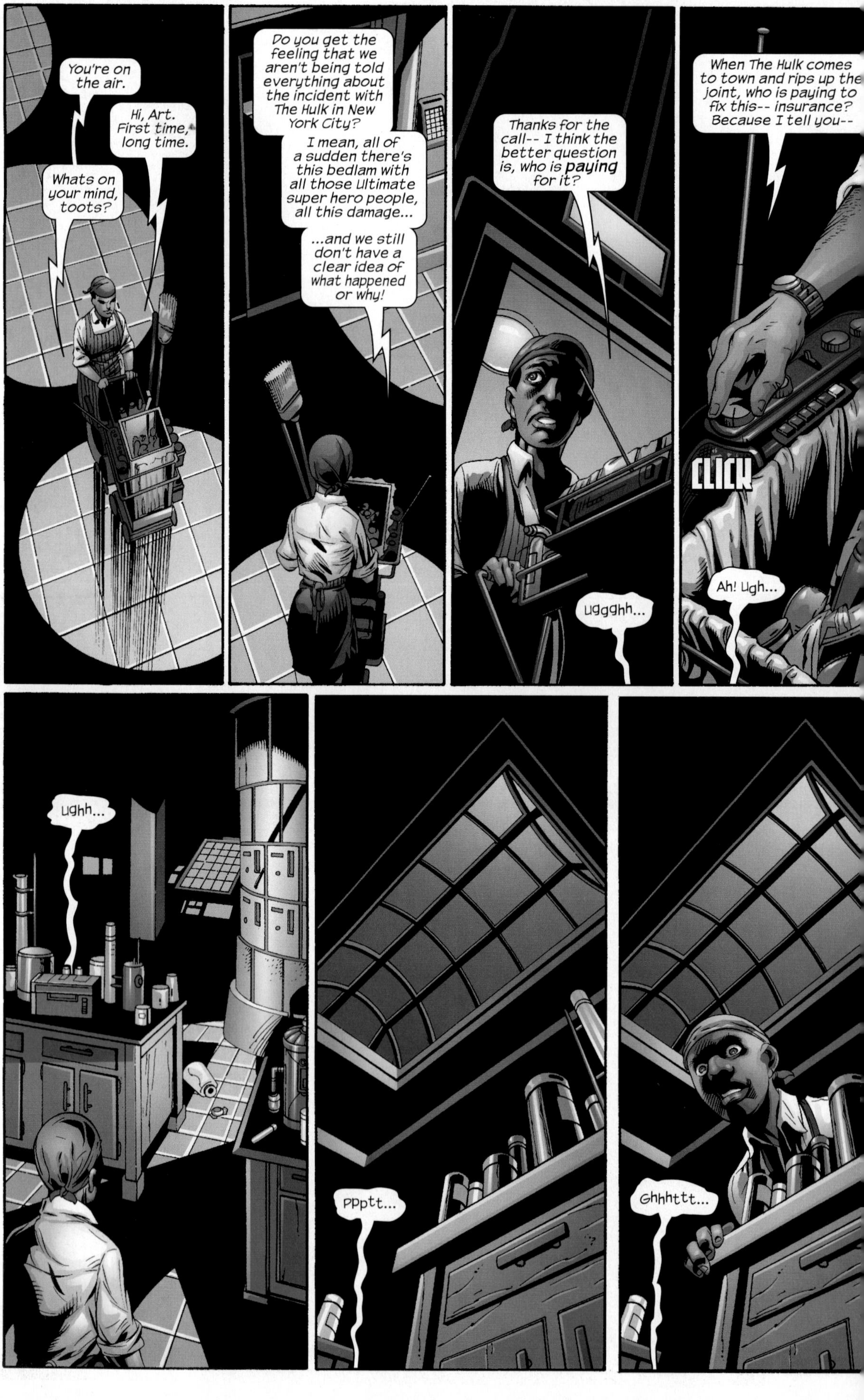

You're on the air.
Hi, Art. First time, long time.
Whats on your mind, toots?
Do you get the feeling that we aren't being told everything about the incident with The Hulk in New York City?
I mean, all of a sudden there's this bedlam with all those Ultimate super hero people, all this damage...
...and we still don't have a clear idea of what happened or why!
Thanks for the call-- I think the better question is, who is paying for it?
uggghh...
When The Hulk comes to town and rips up the joint, who is paying to fix this-- insurance? Because I tell you--
CLICK
Ah! Ugh...
ughh...
Ppptt...
Ghhhttt...

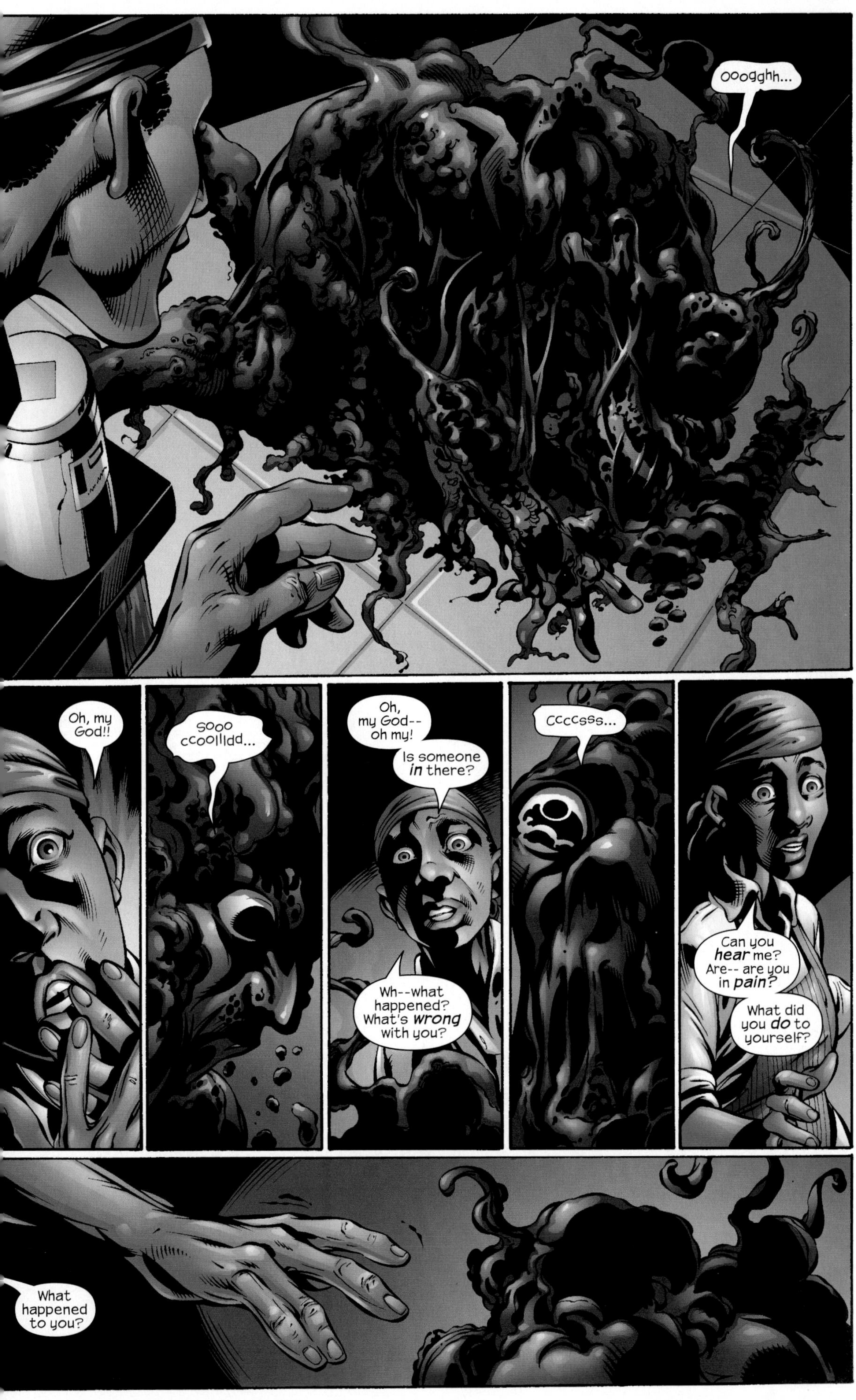
Ooogghh...
Oh, my God!!
Sooo cccoollldd...
Oh, my God-- oh my!
Is someone *in* there?
Wh--what happened? What's *wrong* with you?
Ccccsss...
Can you *hear* me? Are-- are you in *pain?*
What did you *do* to yourself?
What happened to you?

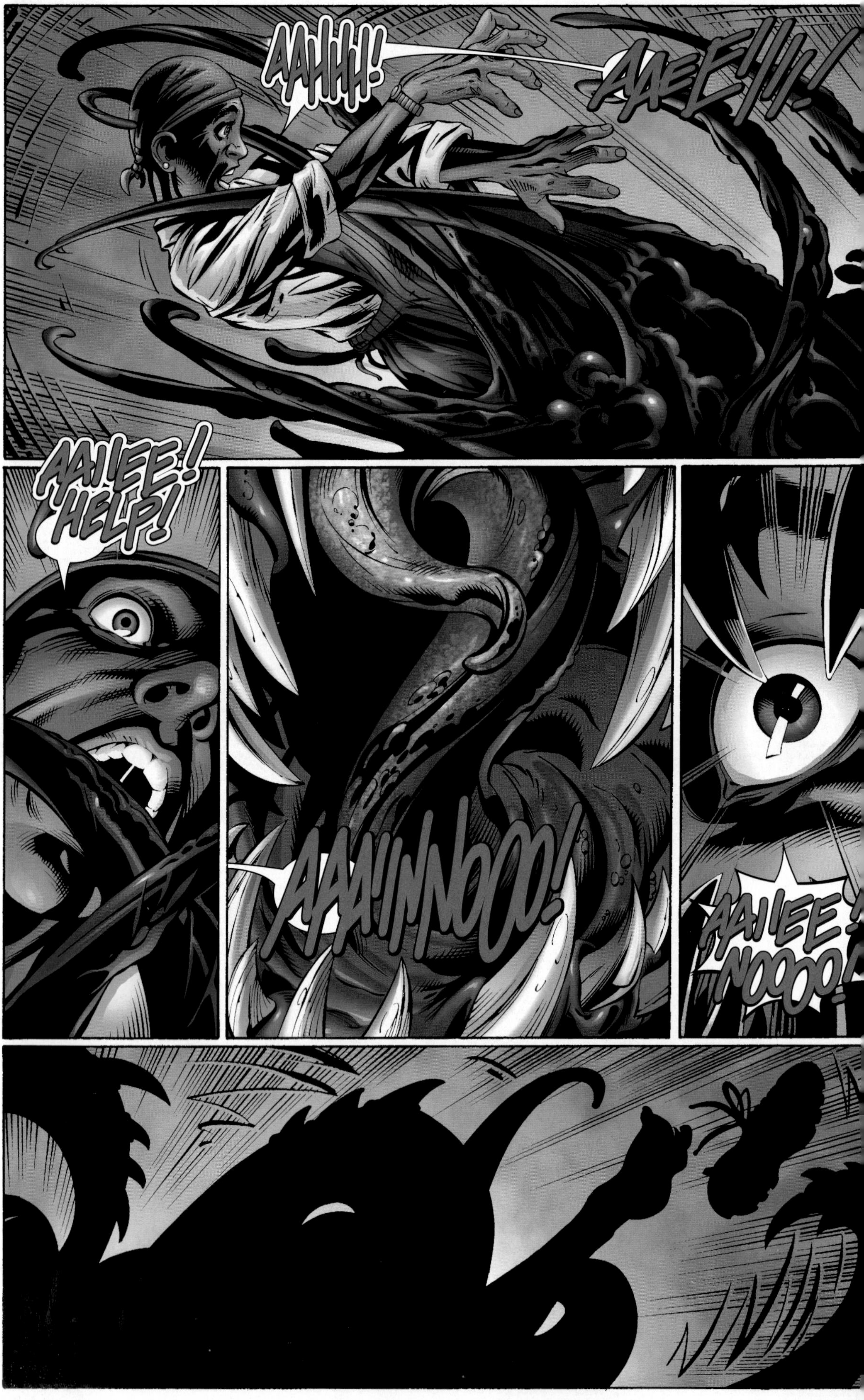
AAHHH!
AAEEE!!!!
AAIIEE! HELP!
AAA!NNOOO!
AAIIEE! NOOOO!

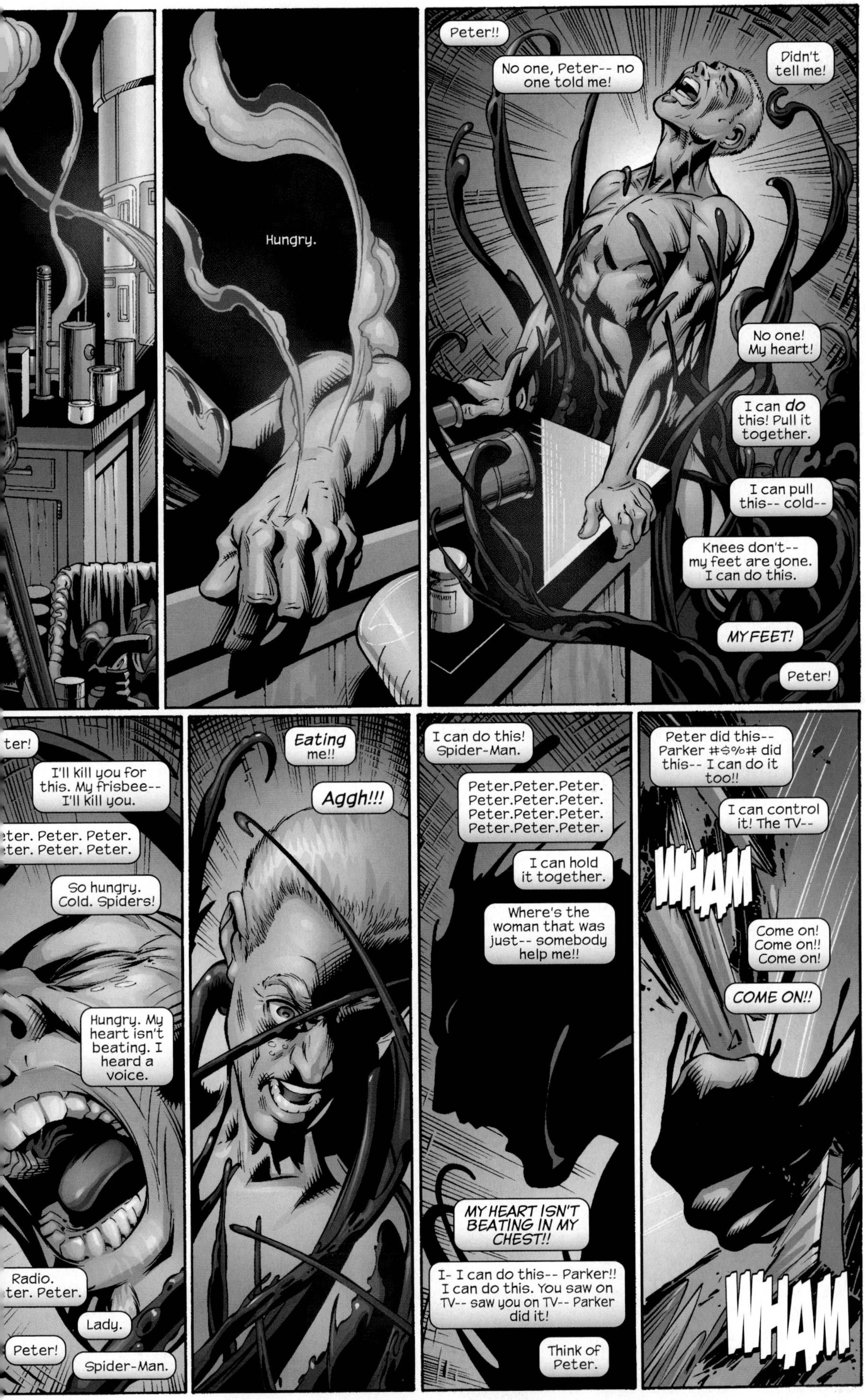

Hungry.
Peter!!
No one, Peter-- no one told me!
Didn't tell me!
No one! My heart!
I can *do* this! Pull it together.
I can pull this-- cold--
Knees don't-- my feet are gone. I can do this.
MY FEET!
Peter!
ter!
I'll kill you for this. My frisbee-- I'll kill you.
eter. Peter. Peter.
eter. Peter. Peter.
So hungry. Cold. Spiders!
Hungry. My heart isn't beating. I heard a voice.
Radio.
ter. Peter.
Lady.
Peter!
Spider-Man.
Eating me!!
Aggh!!!
I can do this! Spider-Man.
Peter.Peter.Peter. Peter.Peter.Peter. Peter.Peter.Peter. Peter.Peter.Peter.
I can hold it together.
Where's the woman that was just-- somebody help me!!
MY HEART ISN'T BEATING IN MY CHEST!!
I- I can do this-- Parker!! I can do this. You saw on TV-- saw you on TV-- Parker did it!
Think of Peter.
Peter did this-- Parker #$%# did this-- I can do it too!!
I can control it! The TV--
WHAM
Come on! Come on!! Come on!
COME ON!!
WHAM

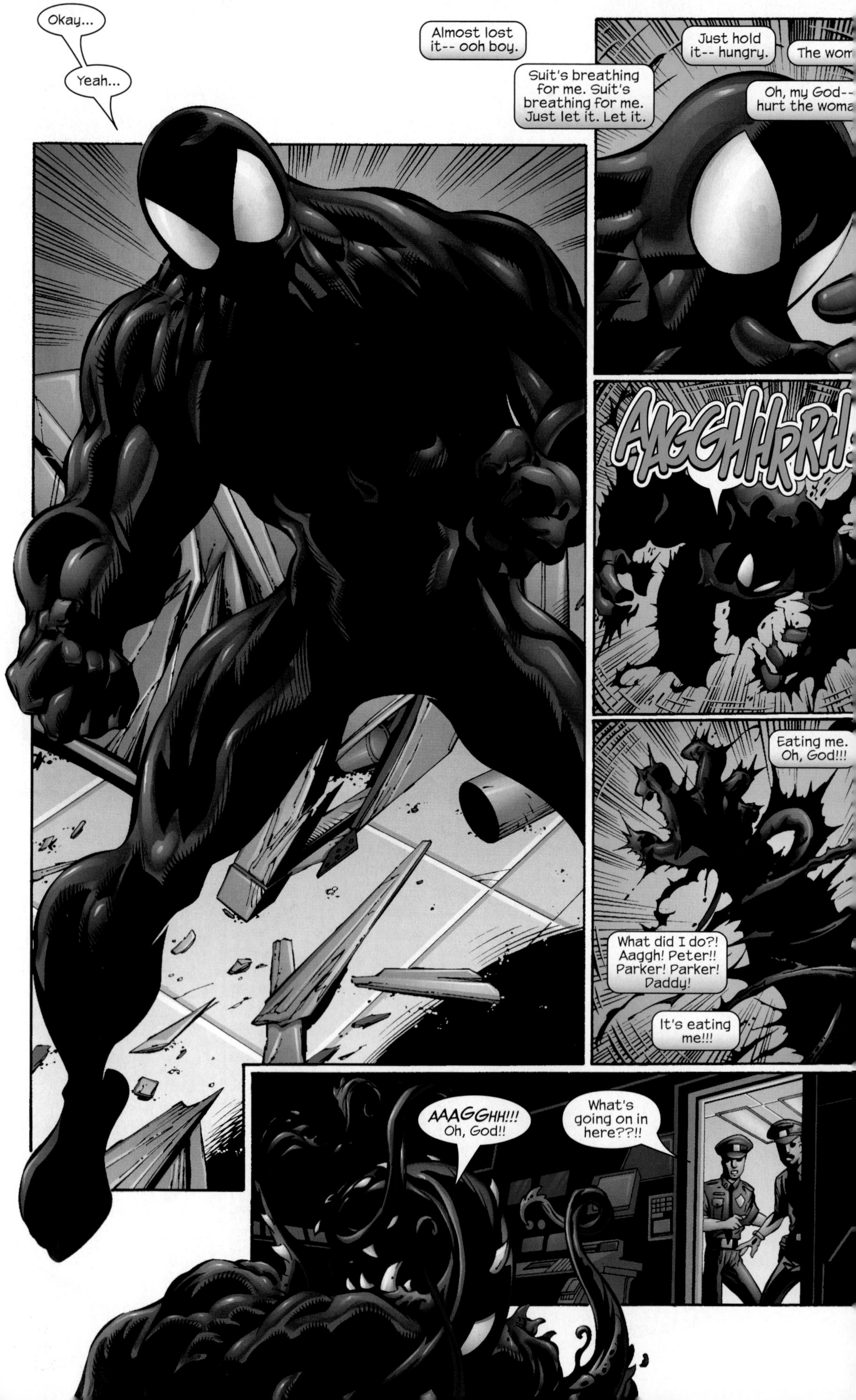
Okay...
Yeah...
Almost lost it-- ooh boy.
Suit's breathing for me. Suit's breathing for me. Just let it. Let it.
Just hold it-- hungry.
The wom
Oh, my God--
hurt the woma
AAGGHHRRH!
Eating me. Oh, God!!!
What did I do?! Aagh! Peter!! Parker! Parker! Daddy!
It's eating me!!!
AAAGGHH!!! Oh, God!!
What's going on in here??!!

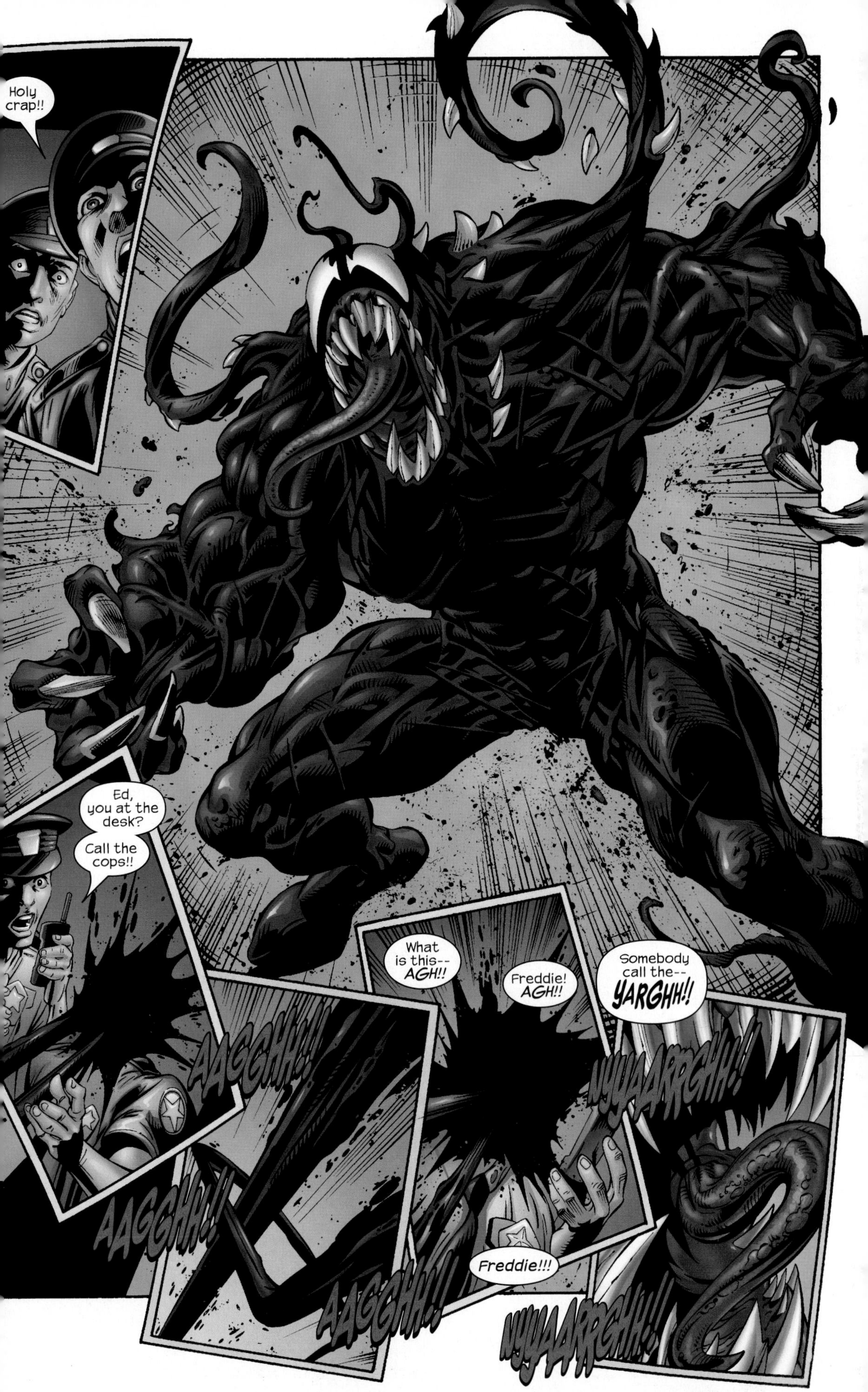

Holy crap!!
Ed, you at the desk?
Call the cops!!
AAGGHH!!
AAGGHH!!
What is this-- AGH!!
Freddie! AGH!!
AAGGHH!!
Freddie!!!
Somebody call the-- YARGHH!!
NYYAARRGHH!!
NYYAARRGHH!!

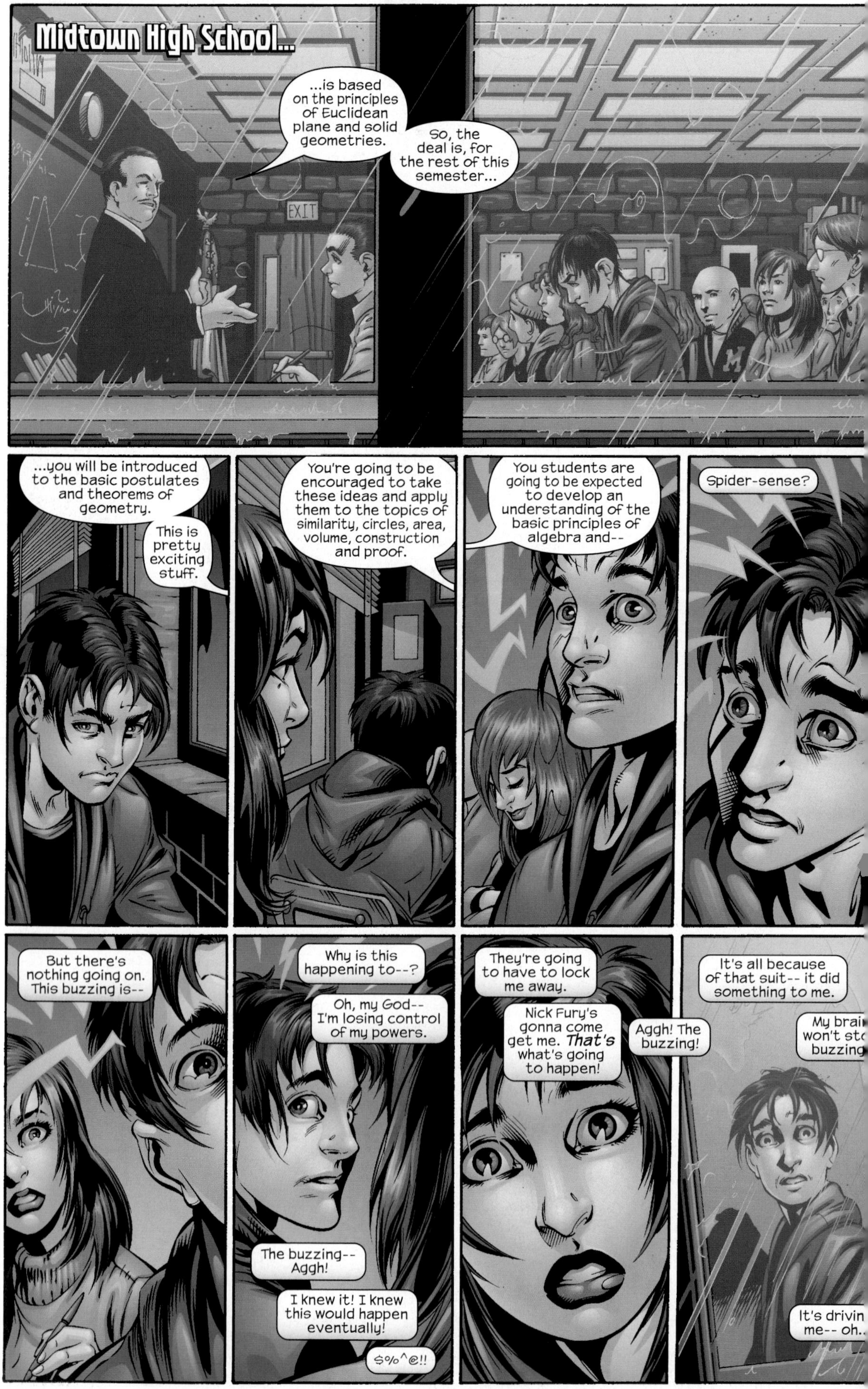
Midtown High School...
...is based on the principles of Euclidean plane and solid geometries.
So, the deal is, for the rest of this semester...
...you will be introduced to the basic postulates and theorems of geometry.
This is pretty exciting stuff.
You're going to be encouraged to take these ideas and apply them to the topics of similarity, circles, area, volume, construction and proof.
You students are going to be expected to develop an understanding of the basic principles of algebra and--
Spider-sense?
But there's nothing going on. This buzzing is--
Why is this happening to--?
Oh, my God-- I'm losing control of my powers.
The buzzing-- Agqh!
I knew it! I knew this would happen eventually!
$%^@!!
They're going to have to lock me away.
Nick Fury's gonna come get me. *That's* what's going to happen!
Aggh! The buzzing!
It's all because of that suit-- it did something to me.
My brai won't st buzzing
It's drivin me-- oh..

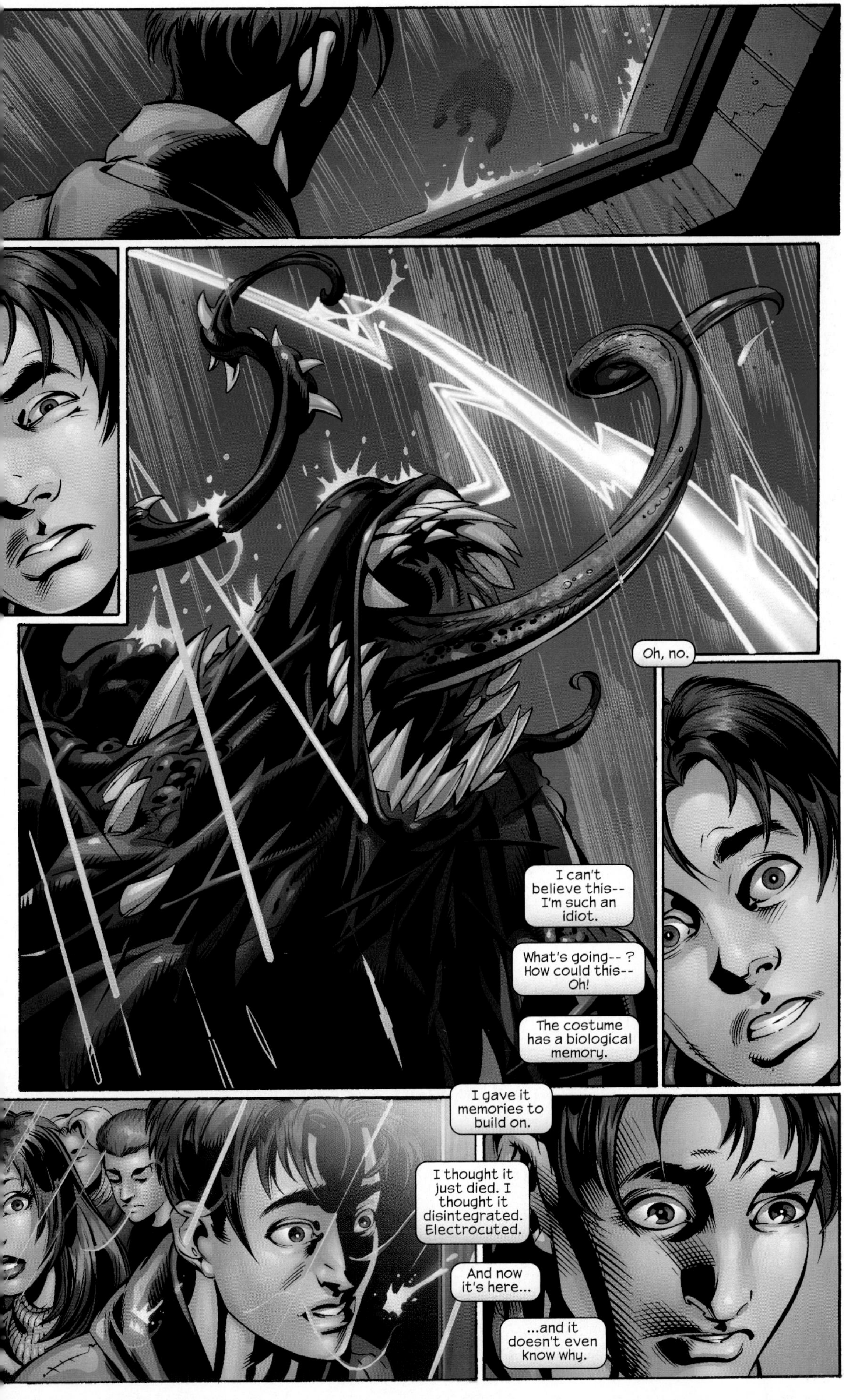
Oh, no.
I can't believe this-- I'm such an idiot.
What's going-- ? How could this-- Oh!
The costume has a biological memory.
I gave it memories to build on.
I thought it just died. I thought it disintegrated. Electrocuted.
And now it's here...
...and it doesn't even know why.

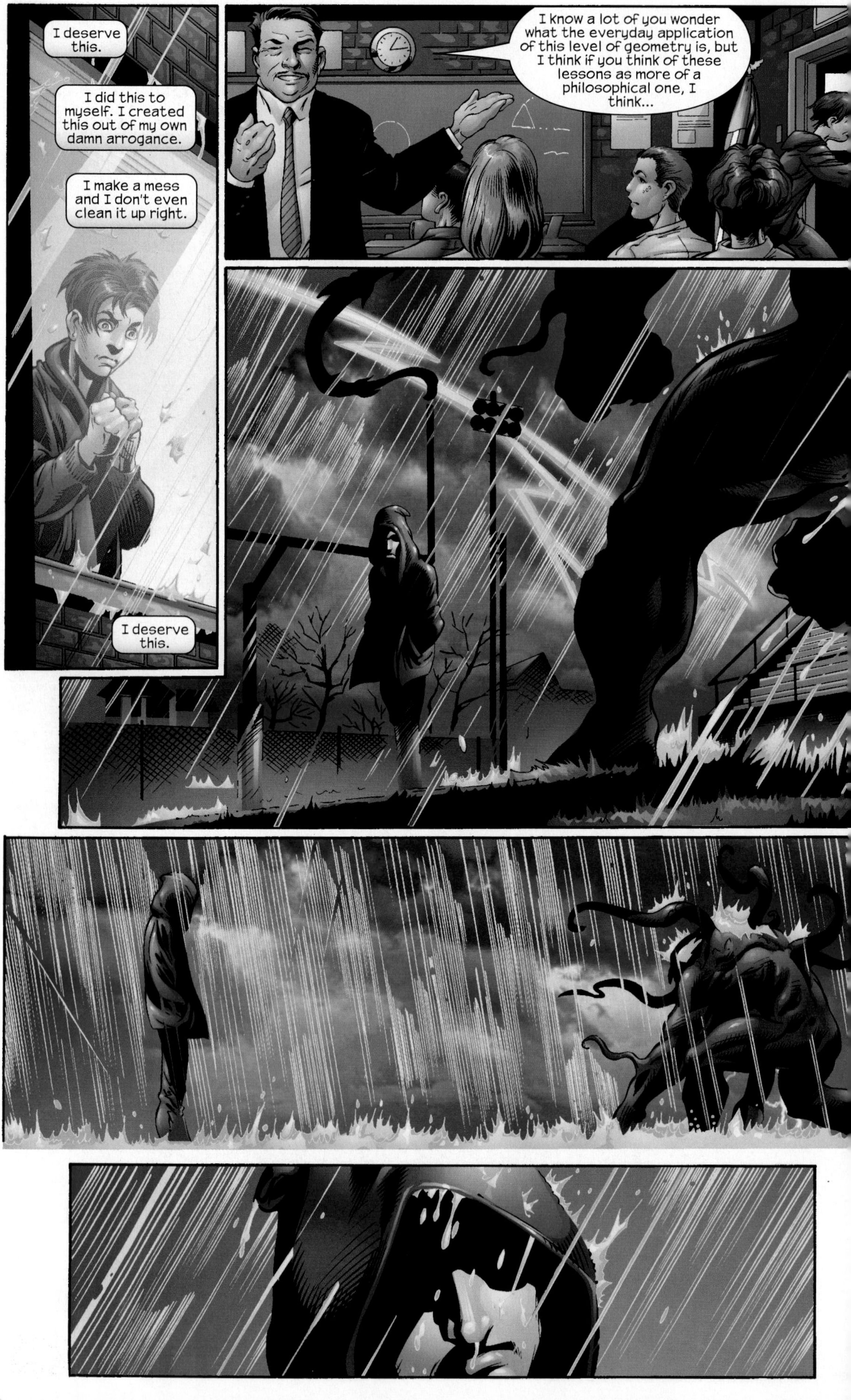
I deserve this.
I did this to myself. I created this out of my own damn arrogance.
I make a mess and I don't even clean it up right.
I deserve this.
I know a lot of you wonder what the everyday application of this level of geometry is, but I think if you think of these lessons as more of a philosophical one, I think...

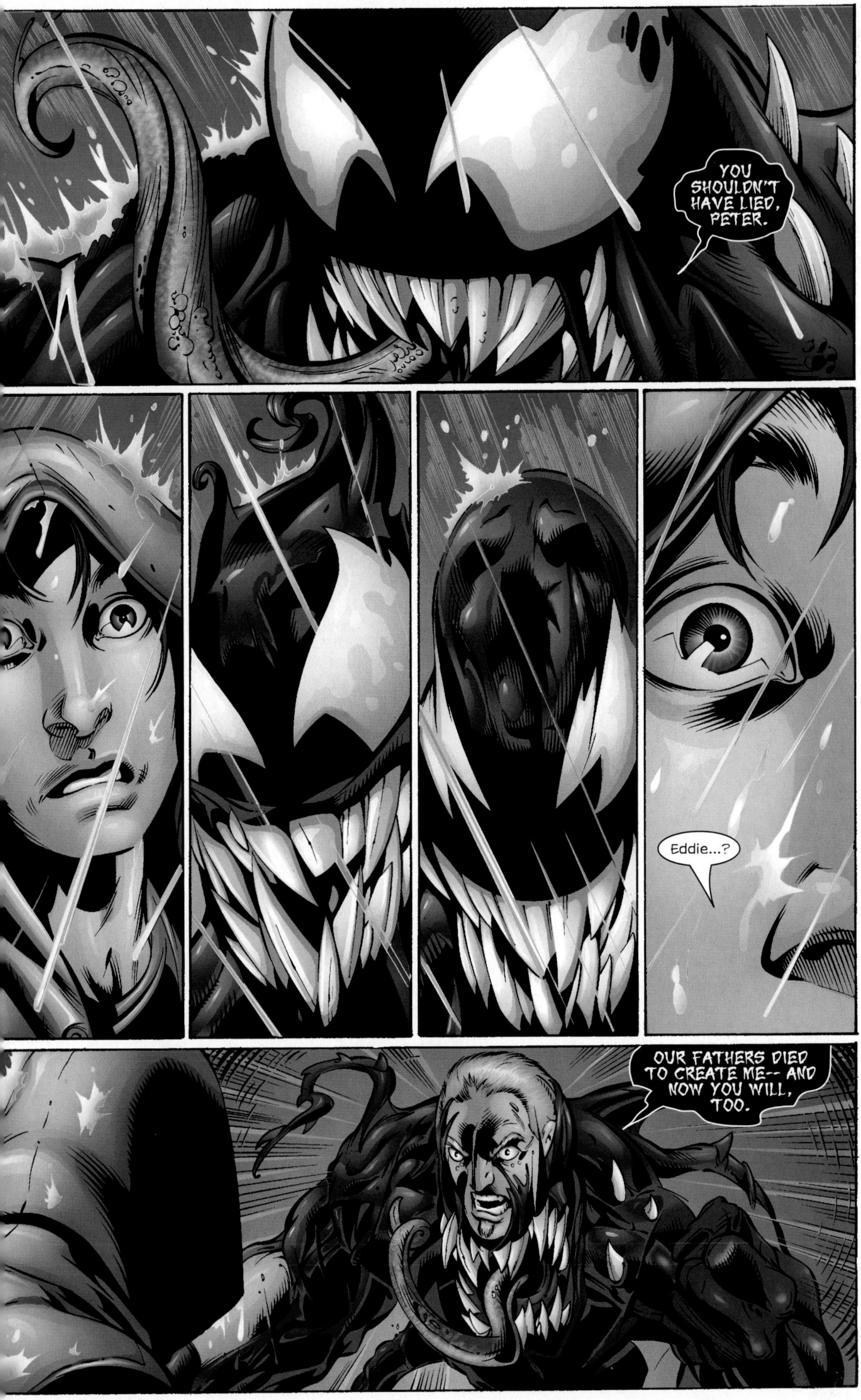
YOU SHOULDN'T HAVE LIED, PETER.
Eddie...?
OUR FATHERS DIED TO CREATE ME-- AND NOW YOU WILL, TOO.

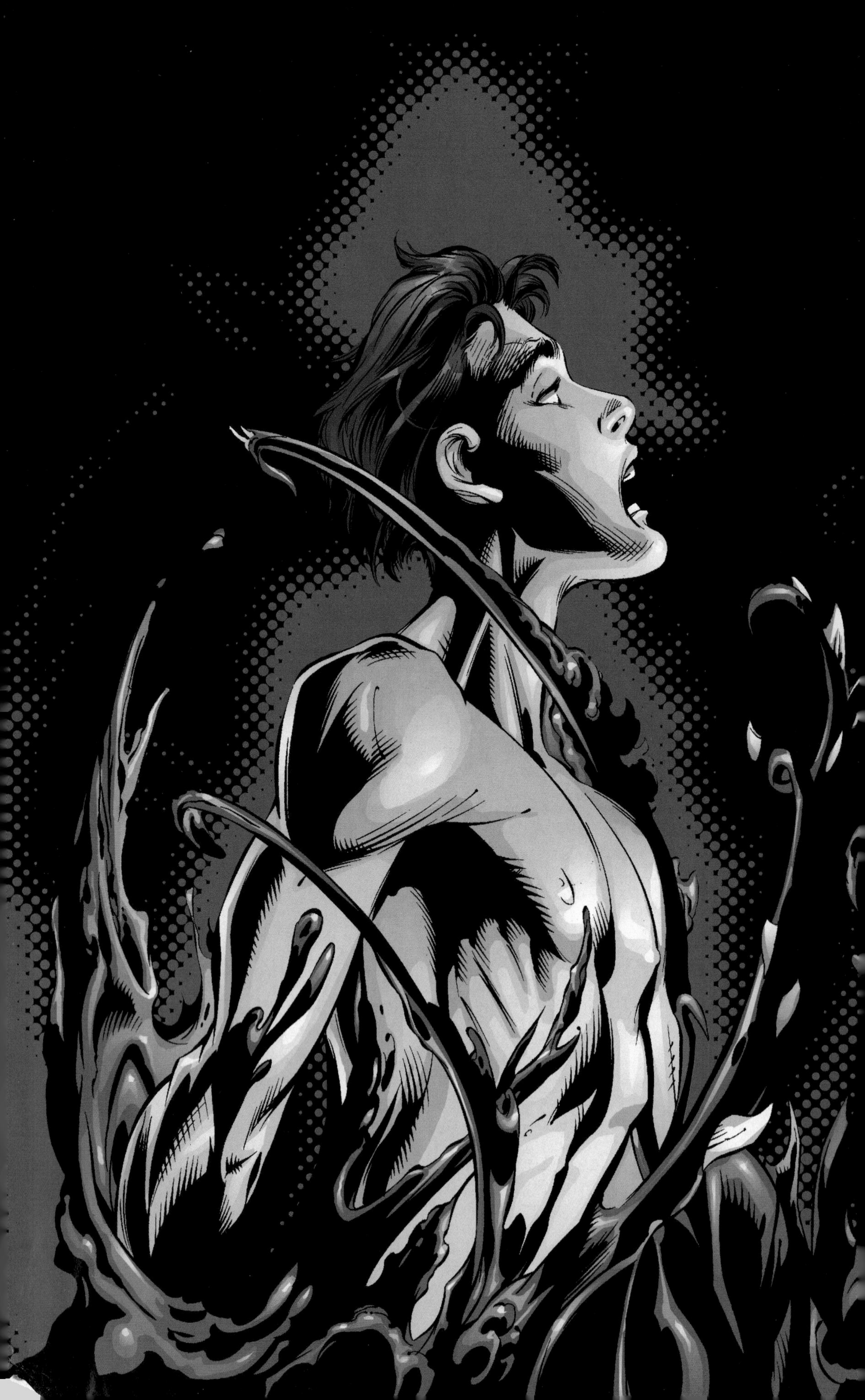

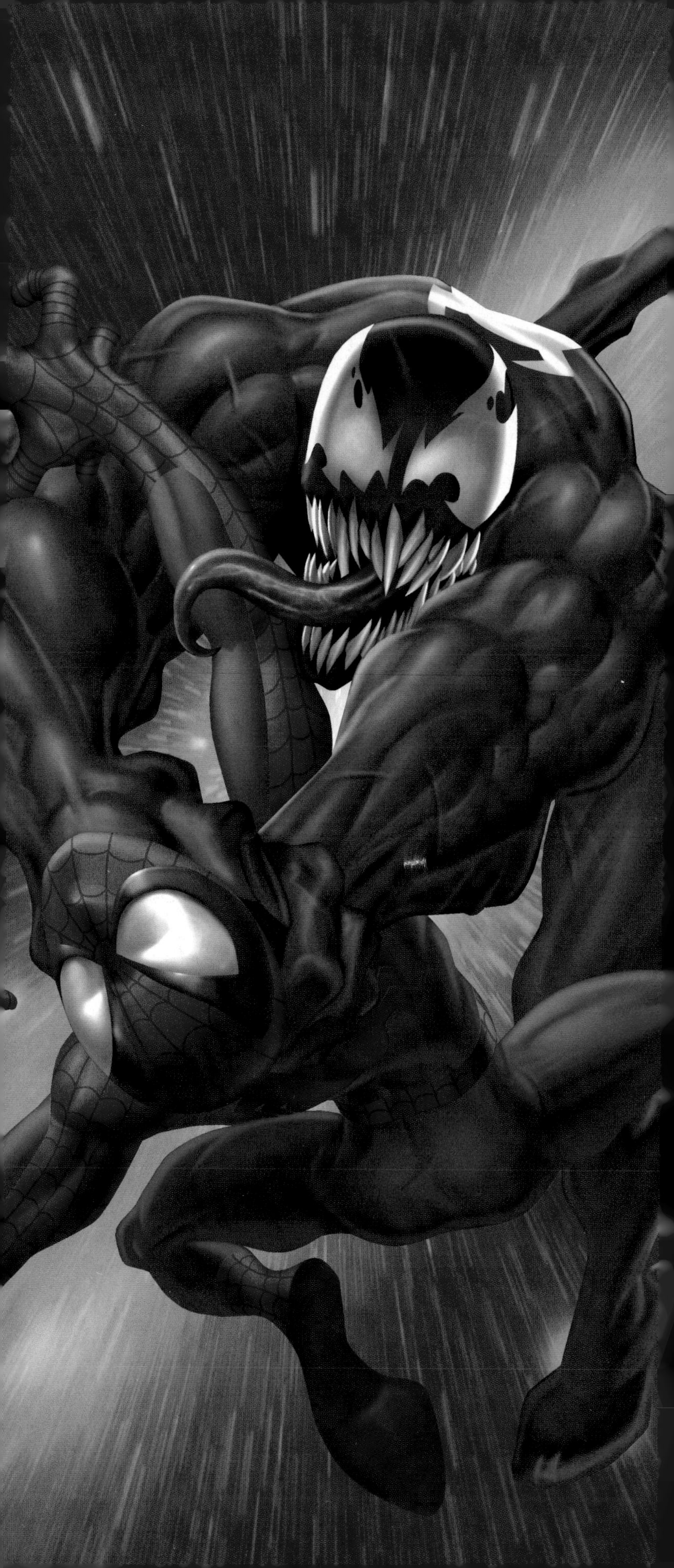

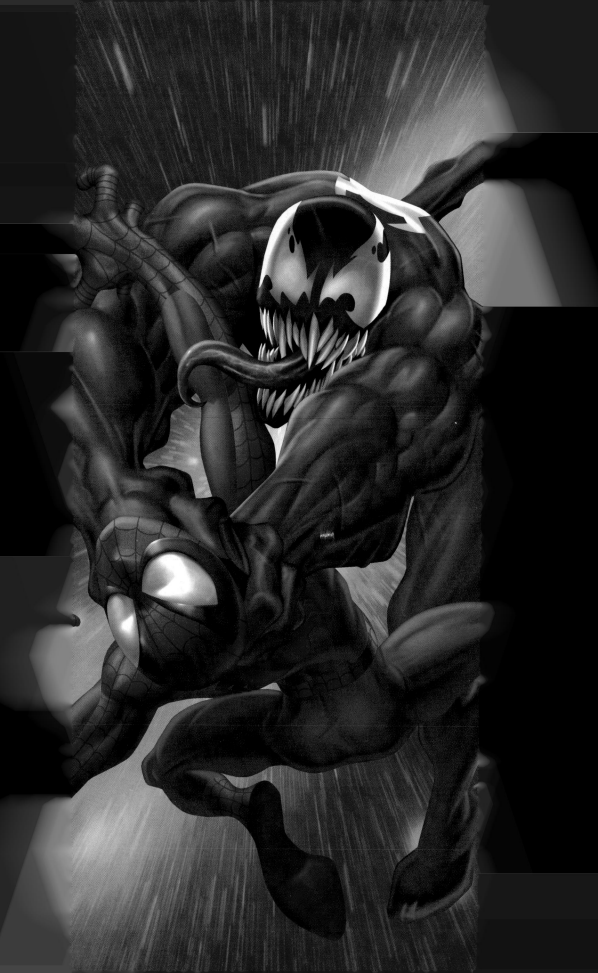

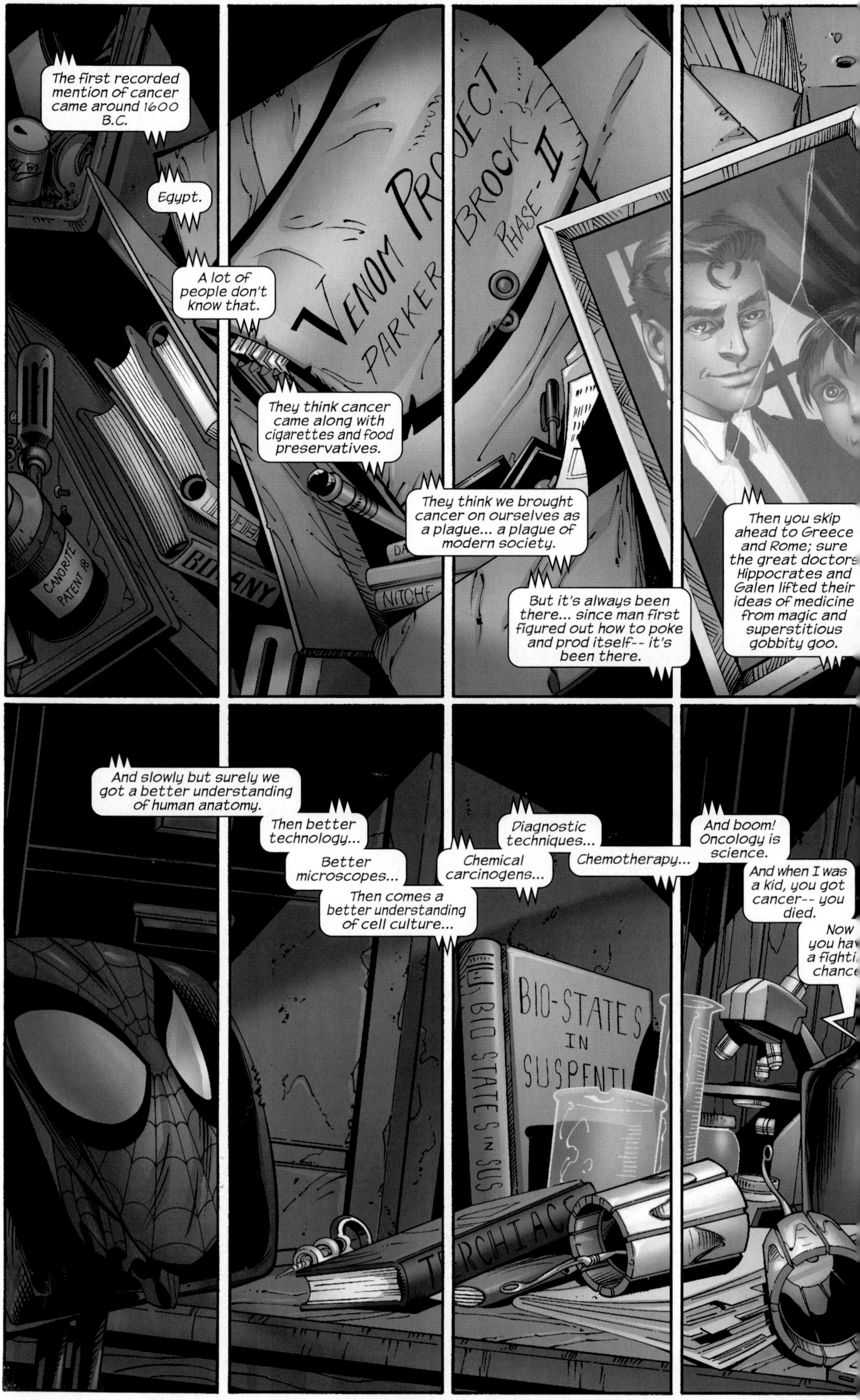

The first recorded mention of cancer came around 1600 B.C.
Egypt.
A lot of people don't know that.
VENOM PROJECT
PARKER
BROCK
PHASE - II
They think cancer came along with cigarettes and food preservatives.
They think we brought cancer on ourselves as a plague... a plague of modern society.
But it's always been there... since man first figured out how to poke and prod itself-- it's been there.
Then you skip ahead to Greece and Rome; sure the great doctors Hippocrates and Galen lifted their ideas of medicine from magic and superstitious gobbity goo.
CANORITE PATENT 18
BOTANY
NITCHE
And slowly but surely we got a better understanding of human anatomy.
Then better technology...
Better microscopes...
Then comes a better understanding of cell culture...
Chemical carcinogens...
Diagnostic techniques...
Chemotherapy...
And boom! Oncology is science.
And when I was a kid, you got cancer-- you died.
BIO-STATES IN SUSPENTI
BIO STATES IN SUS

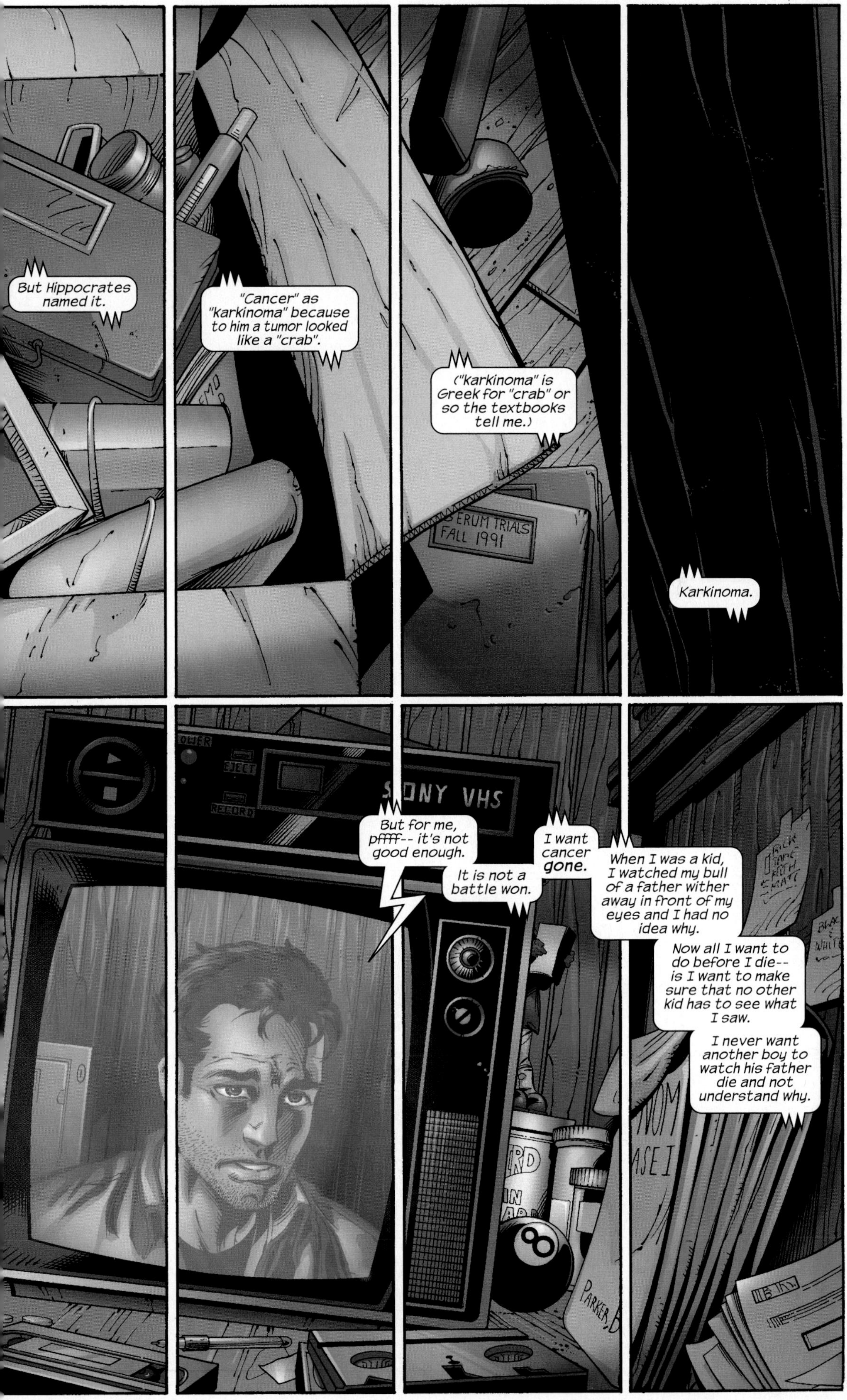

But Hippocrates named it.
"Cancer" as "karkinoma" because to him a tumor looked like a "crab".
("karkinoma" is Greek for "crab" or so the textbooks tell me.)
SERUM TRIALS FALL 1991
Karkinoma.
EJECT
RECORD
SONY VHS
But for me, pffff-- it's not good enough.
It is not a battle won.
I want cancer **gone.**
When I was a kid, I watched my bull of a father wither away in front of my eyes and I had no idea why.
Now all I want to do before I die-- is I want to make sure that no other kid has to see what I saw.
I never want another boy to watch his father die and not understand why.
PARKER, B

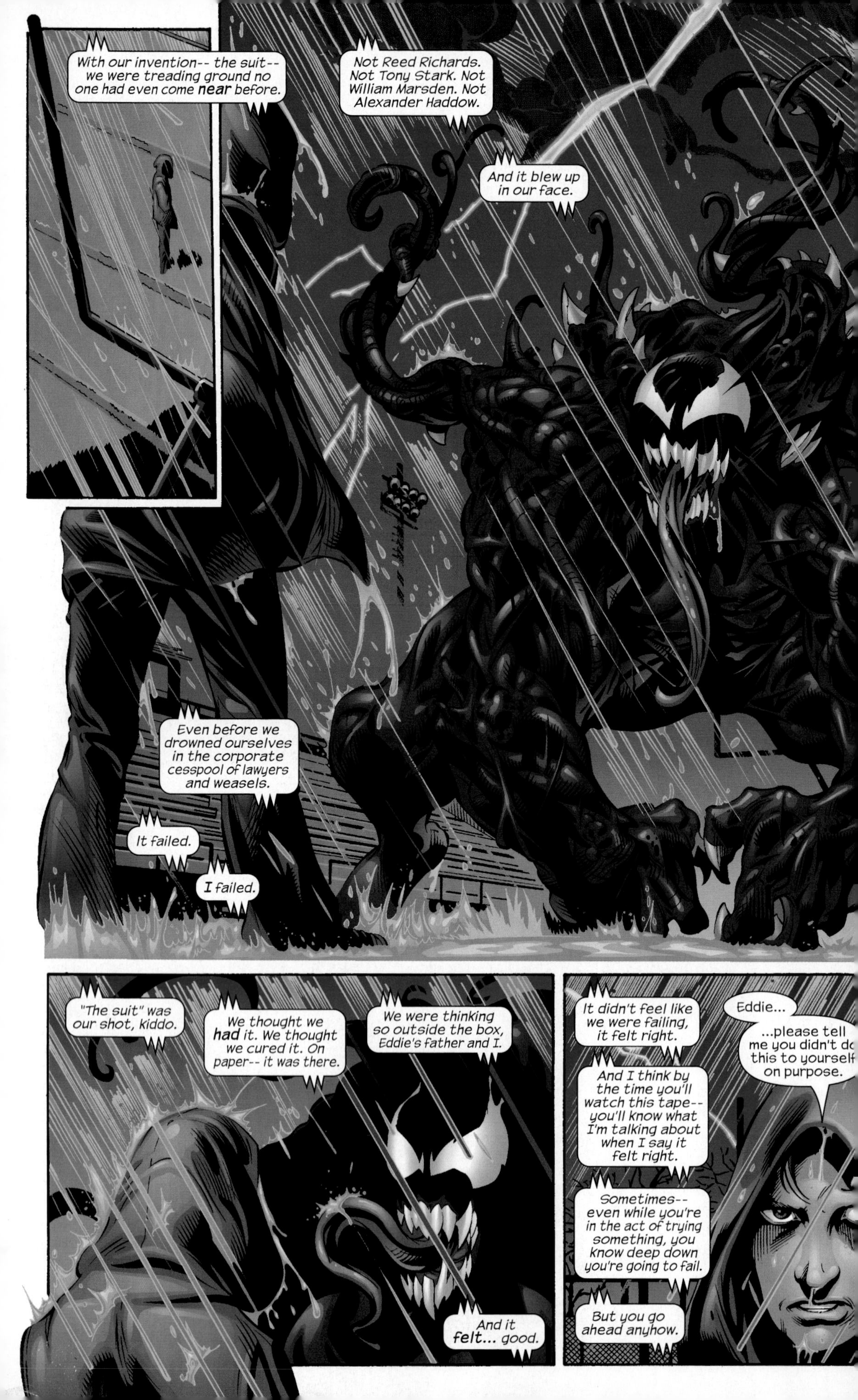
With our invention-- the suit-- we were treading ground no one had even come near before.
Not Reed Richards. Not Tony Stark. Not William Marsden. Not Alexander Haddow.
And it blew up in our face.
Even before we drowned ourselves in the corporate cesspool of lawyers and weasels.
It failed.
I failed.
"The suit" was our shot, kiddo.
We thought we had it. We thought we cured it. On paper-- it was there.
We were thinking so outside the box, Eddie's father and I.
And it felt... good.
It didn't feel like we were failing, it felt right.
And I think by the time you'll watch this tape-- you'll know what I'm talking about when I say it felt right.
Sometimes-- even while you're in the act of trying something, you know deep down you're going to fail.
But you go ahead anyhow.
Eddie...
...please tell me you didn't do this to yourself on purpose.

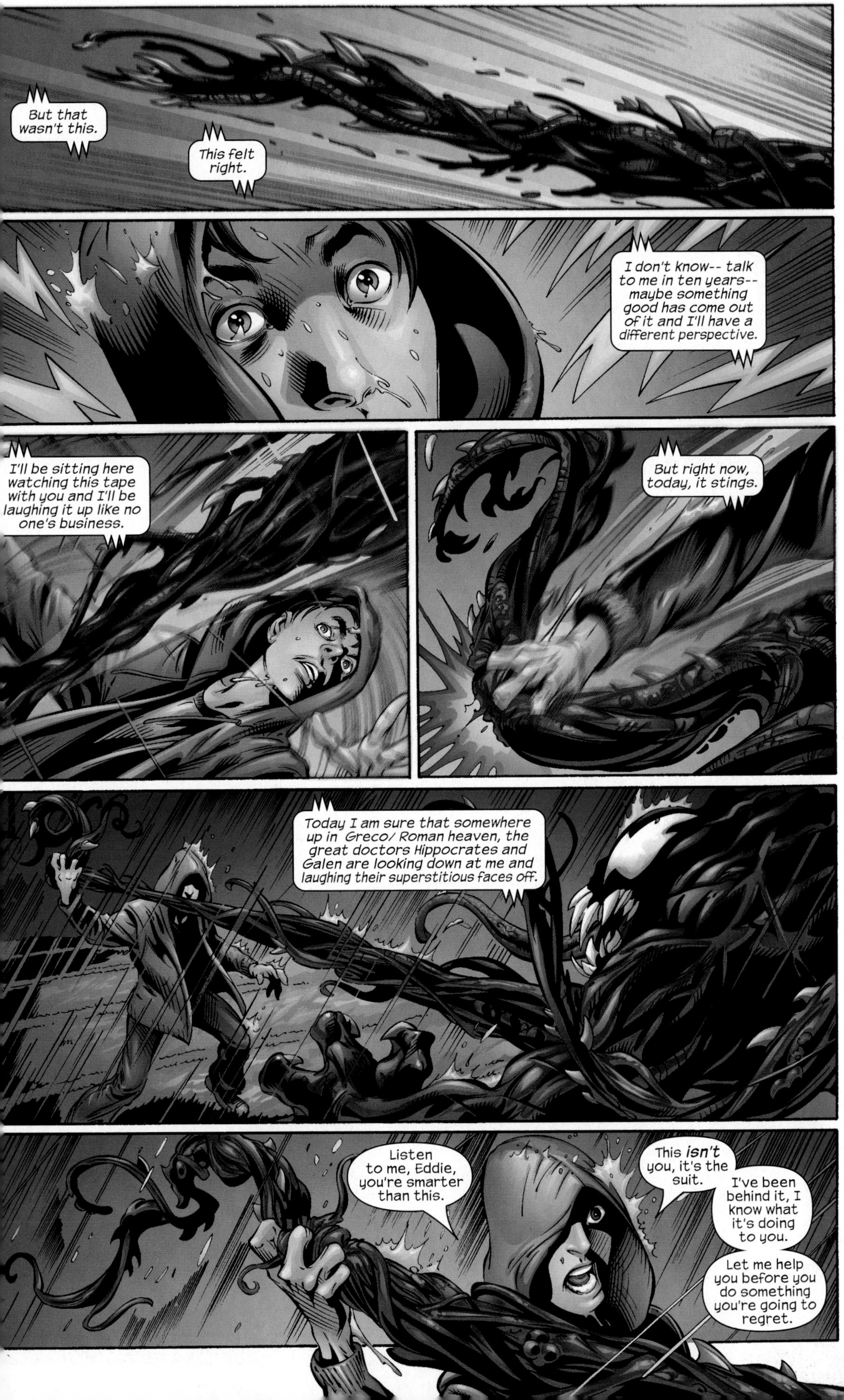
But that wasn't this.
This felt right.
I don't know-- talk to me in ten years-- maybe something good has come out of it and I'll have a different perspective.
I'll be sitting here watching this tape with you and I'll be laughing it up like no one's business.
But right now, today, it stings.
Today I am sure that somewhere up in Greco/ Roman heaven, the great doctors Hippocrates and Galen are looking down at me and laughing their superstitious faces off.
Listen to me, Eddie, you're smarter than this.
This isn't you, it's the suit.
I've been behind it, I know what it's doing to you.
Let me help you before you do something you're going to regret.

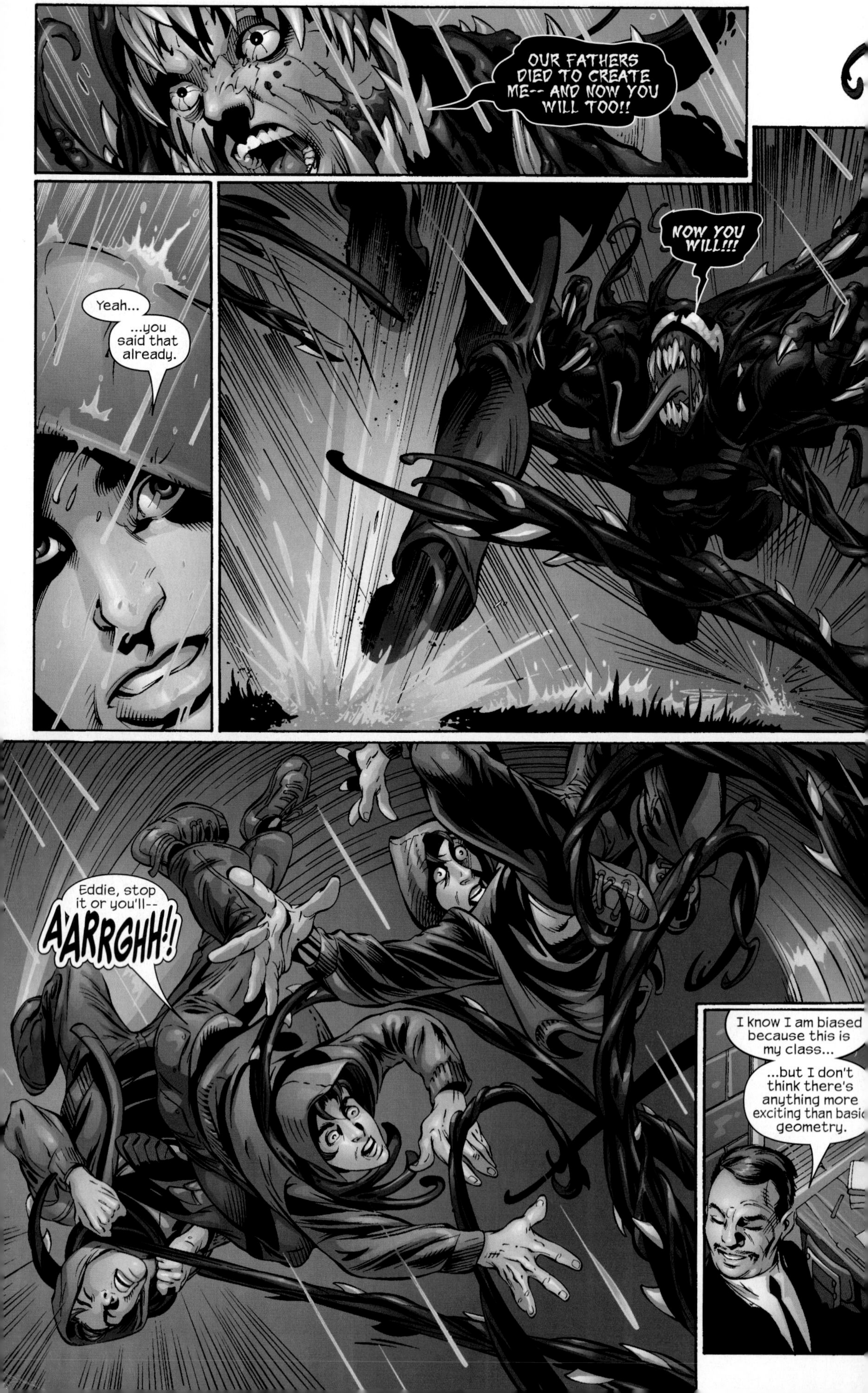
OUR FATHERS DIED TO CREATE ME-- AND NOW YOU WILL TOO!!
Yeah... ...you said that already.
NOW YOU WILL!!!
Eddie, stop it or you'll--
AARRGHH!!
I know I am biased because this is my class...
...but I don't think there's anything more exciting than basic geometry.

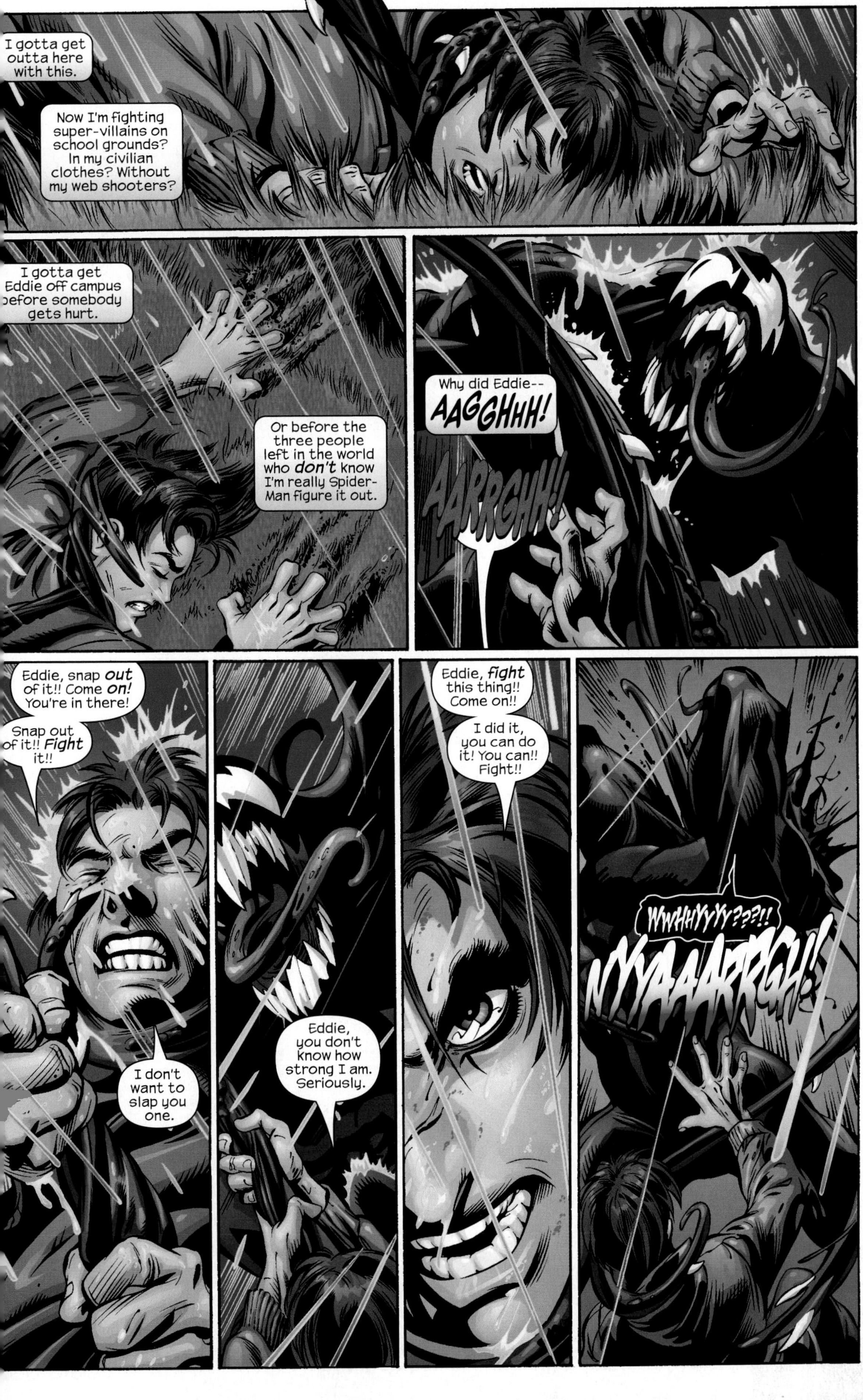

I gotta get outta here with this.
Now I'm fighting super-villains on school grounds? In my civilian clothes? Without my web shooters?
I gotta get Eddie off campus before somebody gets hurt.
Or before the three people left in the world who don't know I'm really Spider-Man figure it out.
Why did Eddie-- AAGGHHH!
AARRGHH!!
Eddie, snap out of it!! Come on! You're in there!
Snap out of it!! Fight it!!
I don't want to slap you one.
Eddie, you don't know how strong I am. Seriously.
Eddie, fight this thing!! Come on!!
I did it, you can do it! You can!! Fight!!
WWHHYYYY???!!
NYYAAARRGH!!

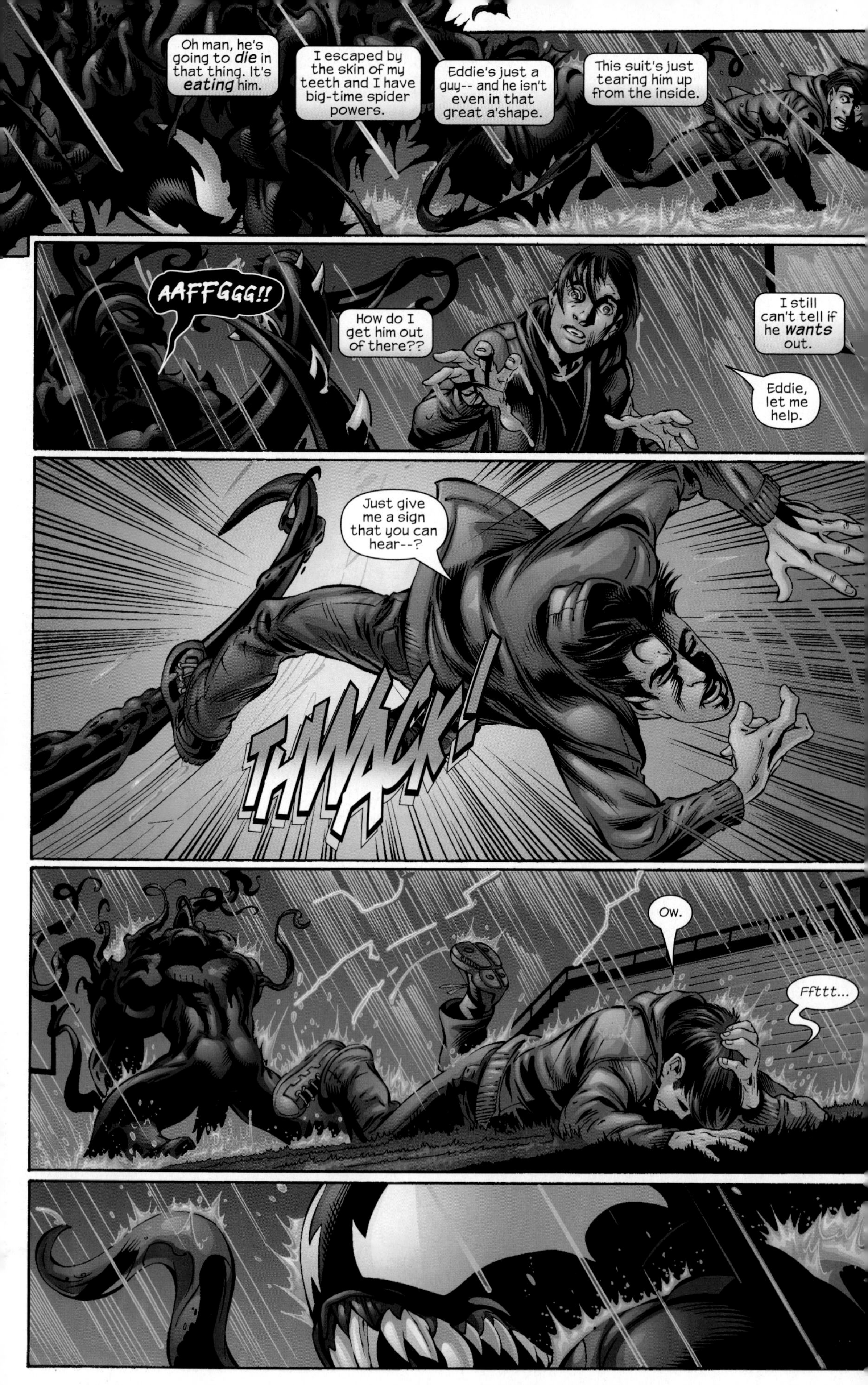
Oh man, he's going to die in that thing. It's eating him.
I escaped by the skin of my teeth and I have big-time spider powers.
Eddie's just a guy-- and he isn't even in that great a'shape.
This suit's just tearing him up from the inside.
AAFFGGG!!
How do I get him out of there??
I still can't tell if he wants out.
Eddie, let me help.
Just give me a sign that you can hear--?
THWACK!
Ow.
Fftt...

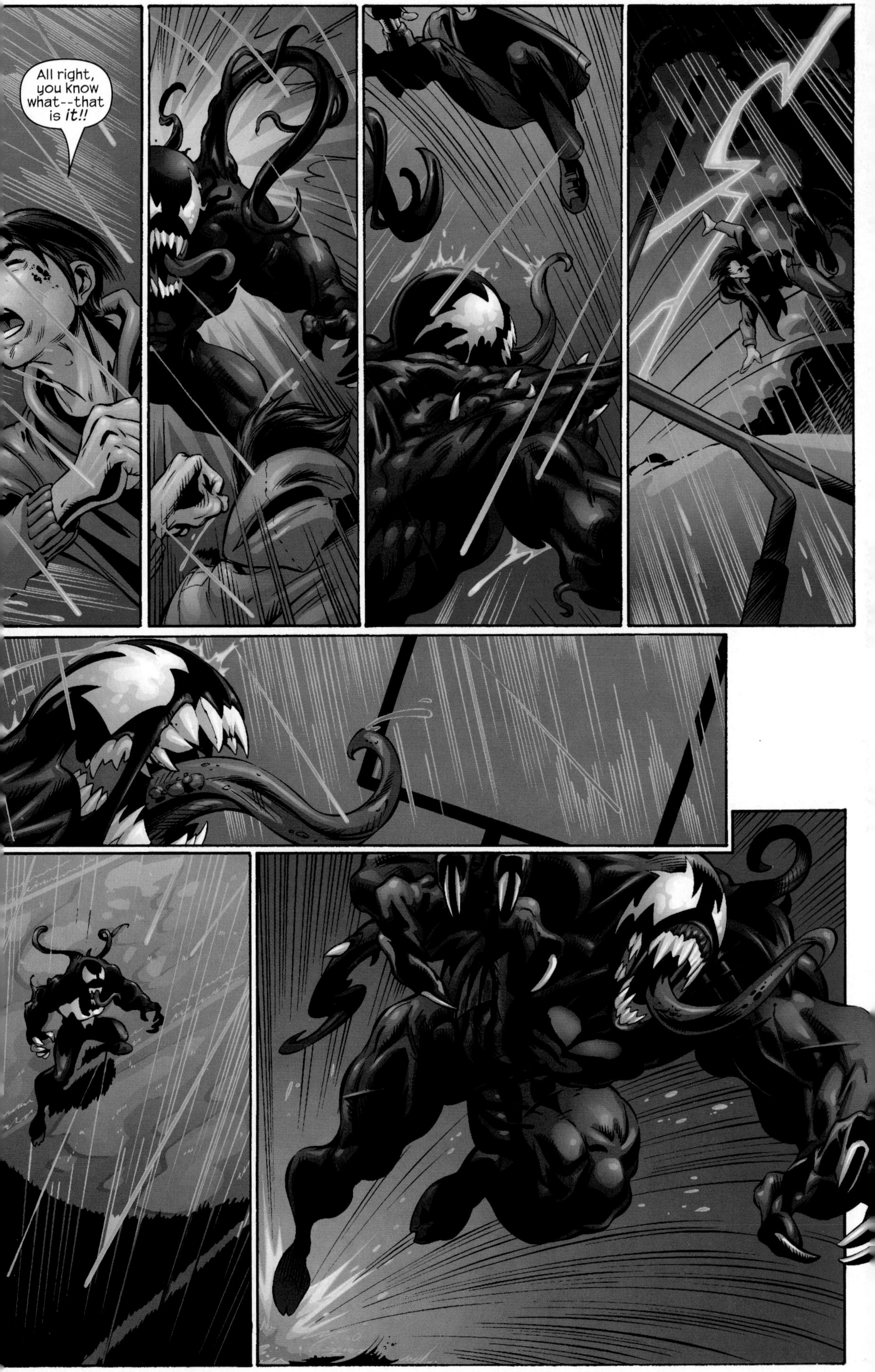
All right, you know what--that is *it!!*

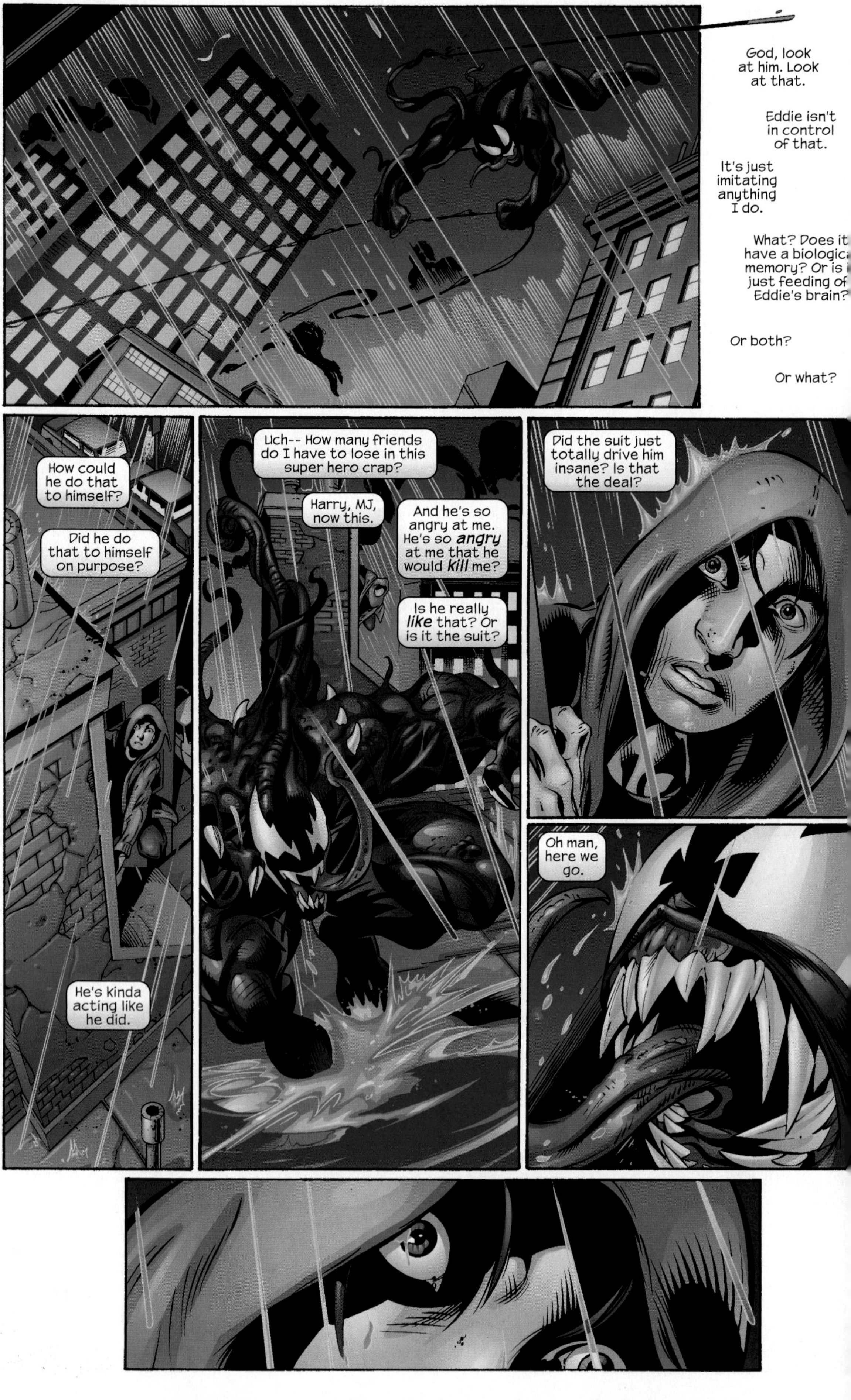
God, look at him. Look at that.
Eddie isn't in control of that.
It's just imitating anything I do.
What? Does it have a biologic memory? Or is just feeding of Eddie's brain?
Or both?
Or what?
How could he do that to himself?
Did he do that to himself on purpose?
He's kinda acting like he did.
Uch-- How many friends do I have to lose in this super hero crap?
Harry, MJ, now this.
And he's so angry at me. He's so *angry* at me that he would *kill* me?
Is he really *like* that? Or is it the suit?
Did the suit just totally drive him insane? Is that the deal?
Oh man, here we go.

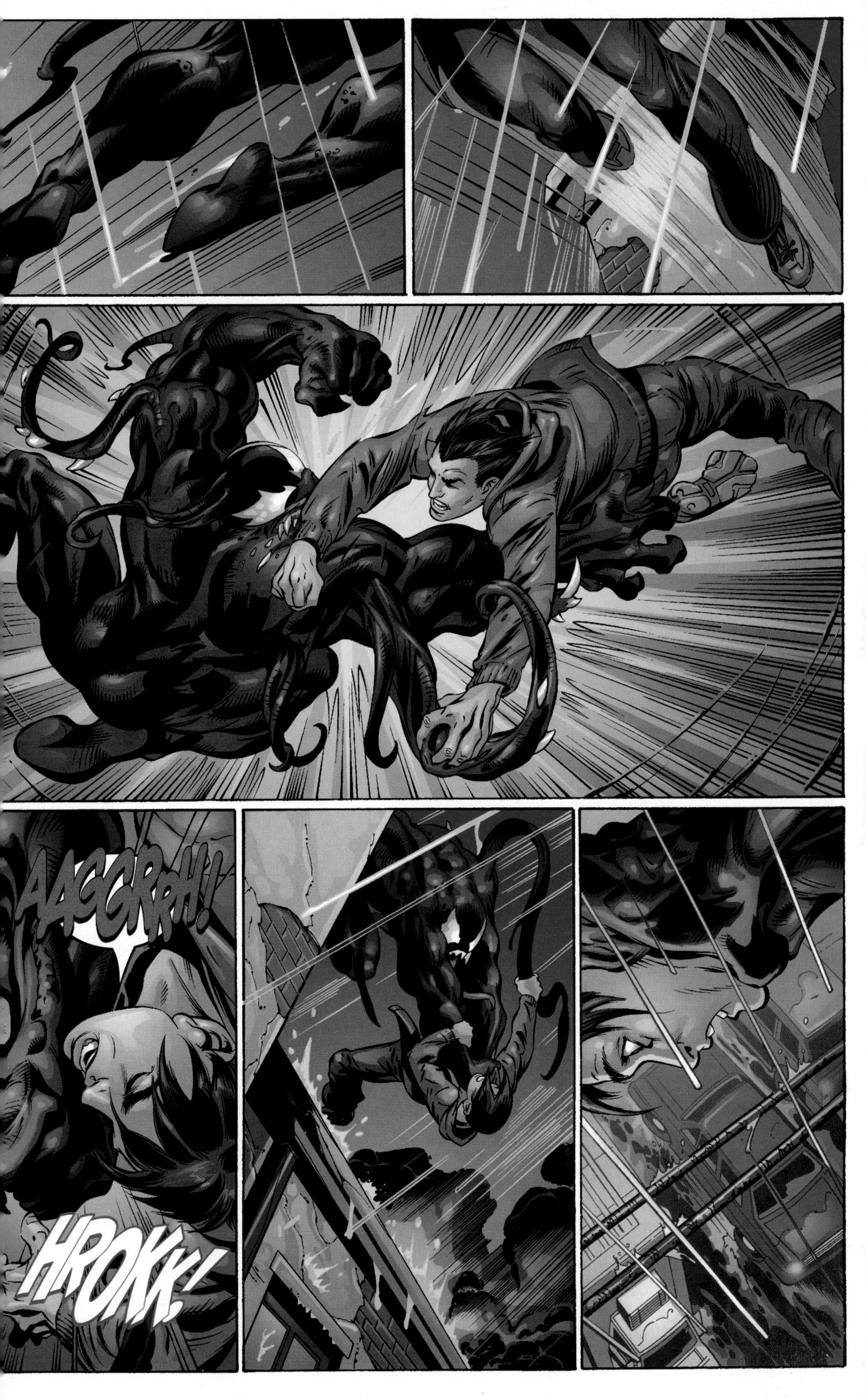
AAGGRRH!
HROKK!

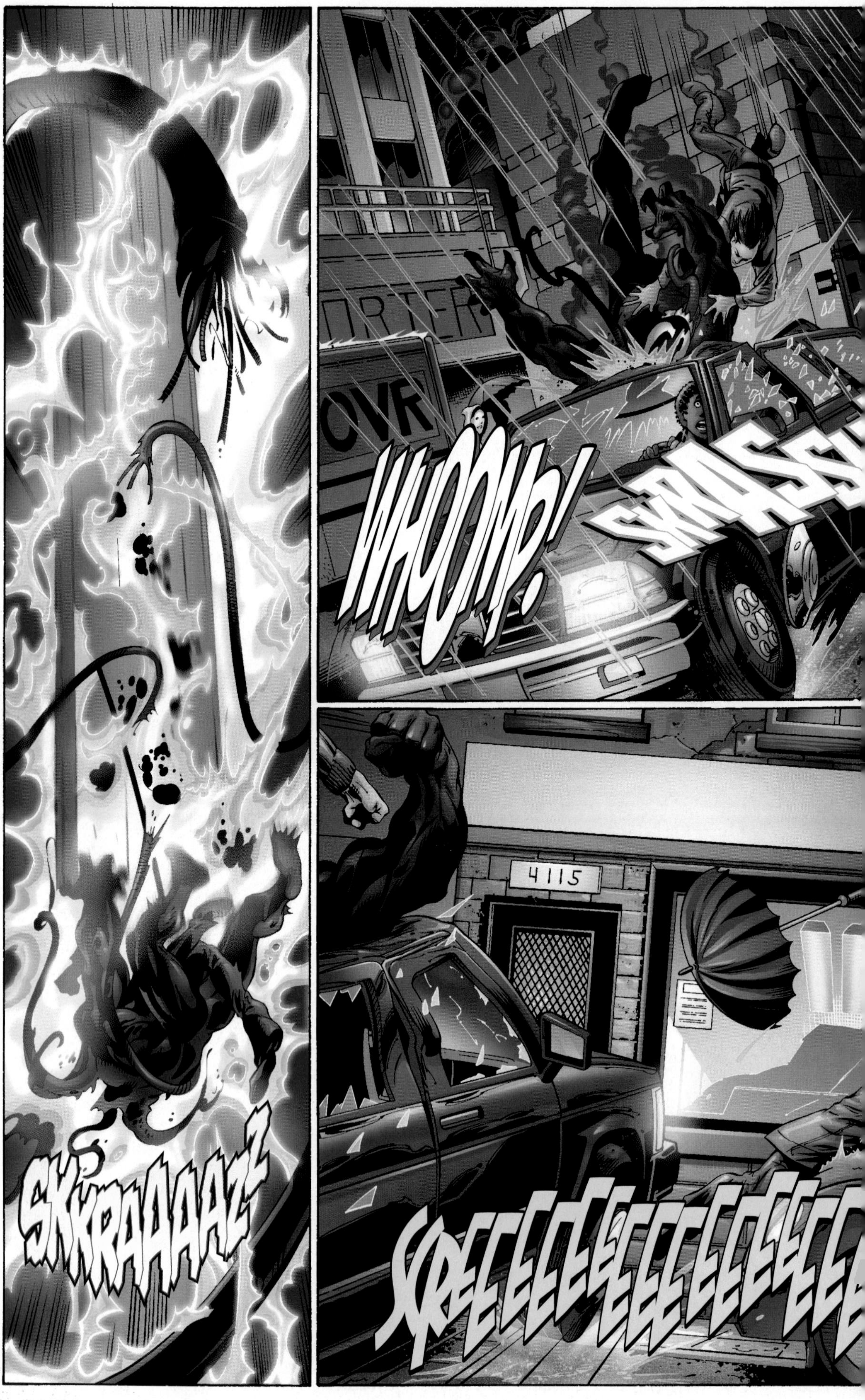
SKRAAAAZ
WHOOMP!
4115
SKREEEEEEEEEEEEEE

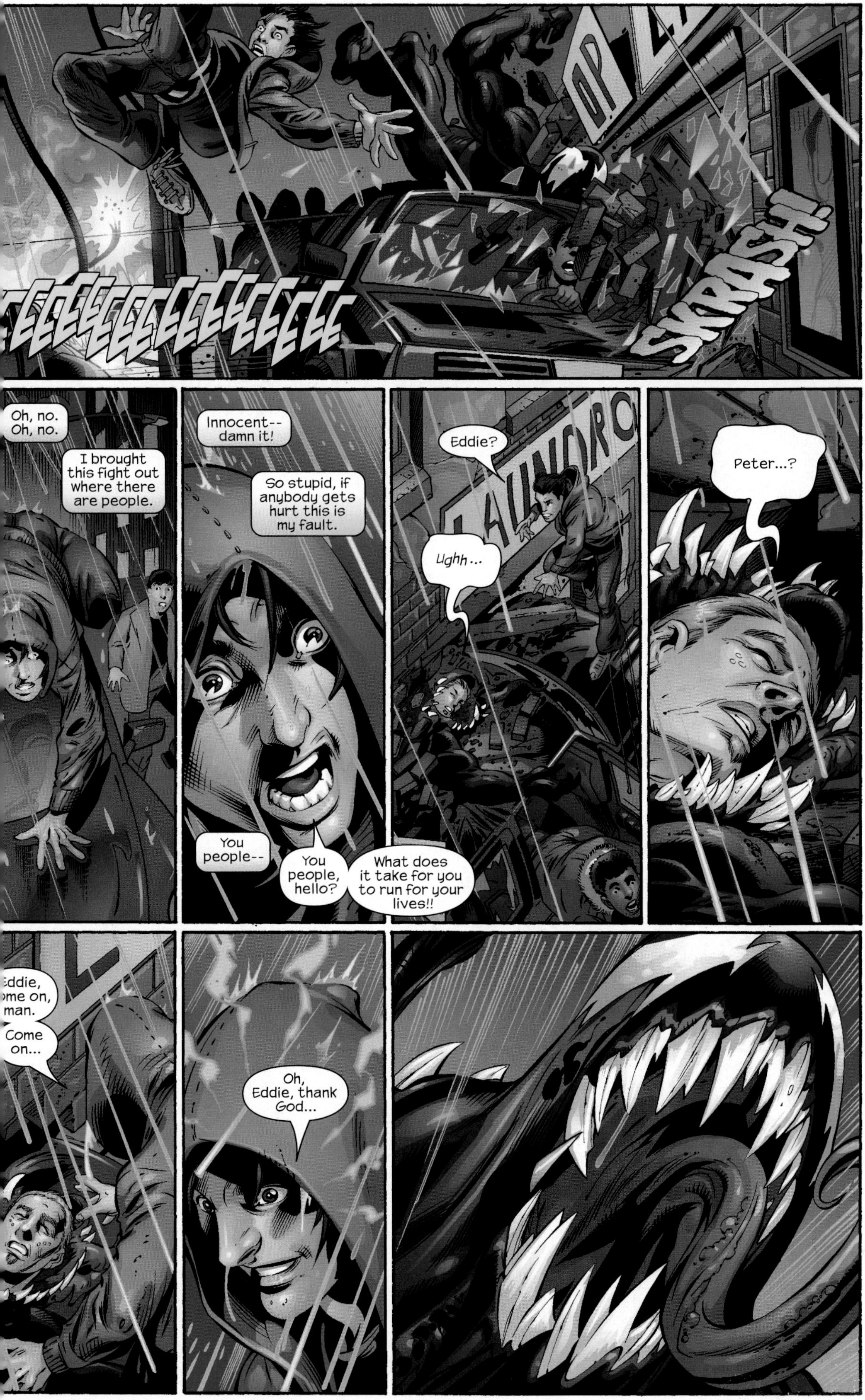
EEEEEEEEEEEEEEEEEEE
SMASH
Oh, no. Oh, no.
I brought this fight out where there are people.
Innocent-- damn it!
So stupid, if anybody gets hurt this is my fault.
You people--
You people, hello?
What does it take for you to run for your lives!!
Eddie?
Ughh...
Peter...?
Come on...
Oh, Eddie, thank God...

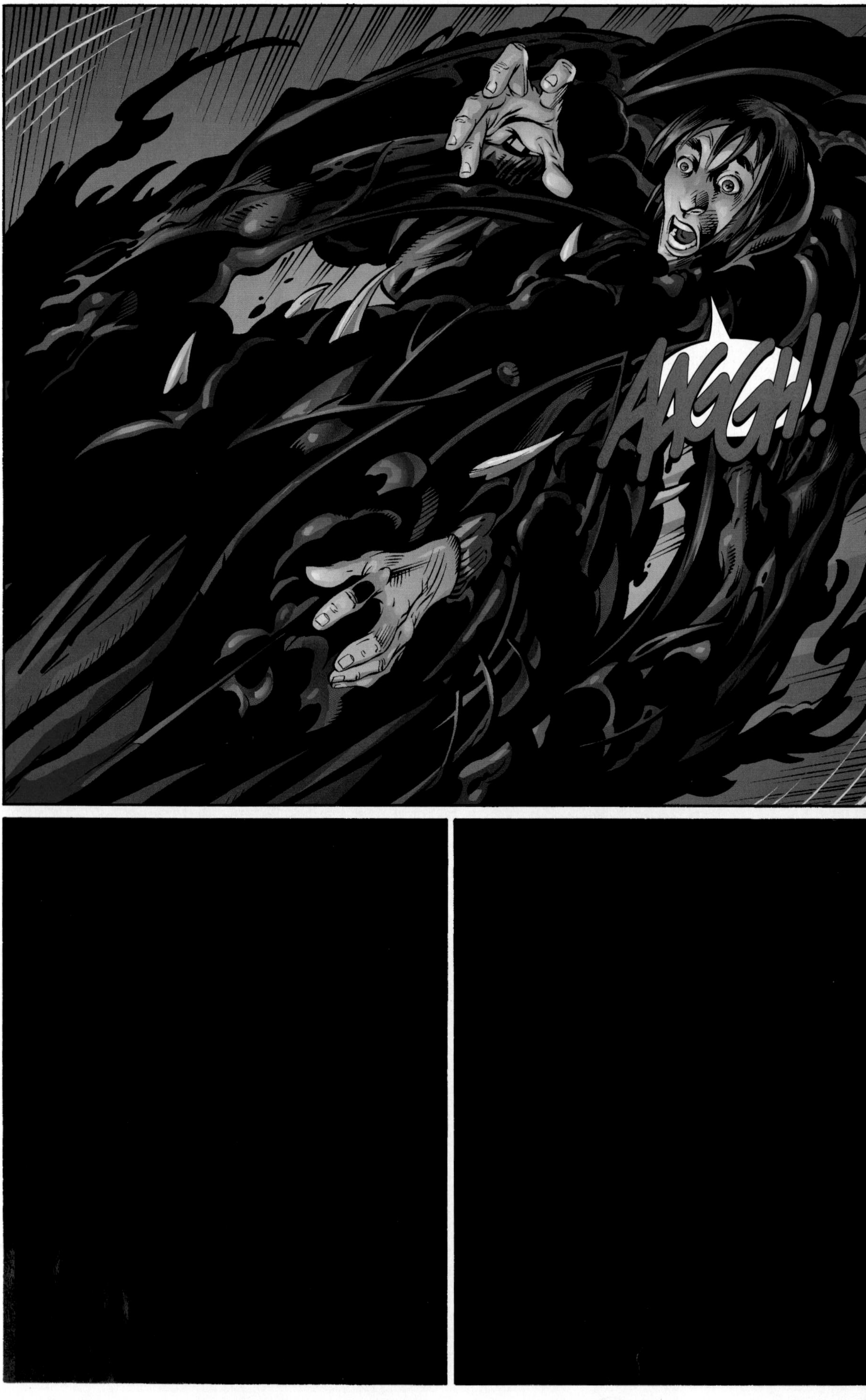
AAGGH!

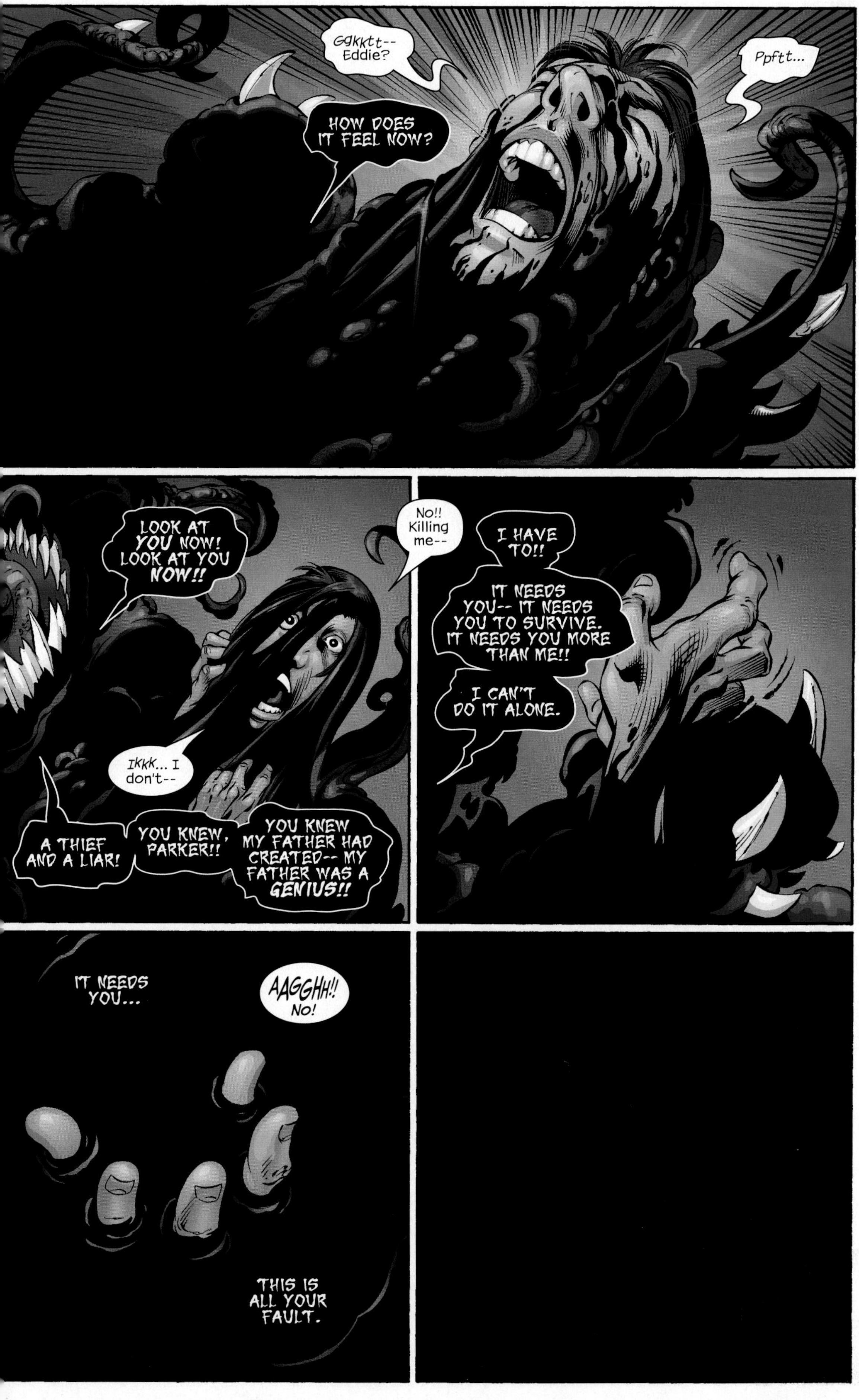

Ggkktt--
Eddie?
HOW DOES IT FEEL NOW?
Ppftt...
LOOK AT YOU NOW! LOOK AT YOU NOW!!
Ikkk... I don't--
A THIEF AND A LIAR!
YOU KNEW, PARKER!!
YOU KNEW MY FATHER HAD CREATED-- MY FATHER WAS A GENIUS!!
No!! Killing me--
I HAVE TO!!
IT NEEDS YOU-- IT NEEDS YOU TO SURVIVE. IT NEEDS YOU MORE THAN ME!!
I CAN'T DO IT ALONE.
IT NEEDS YOU...
AAGGHH!! No!
THIS IS ALL YOUR FAULT.

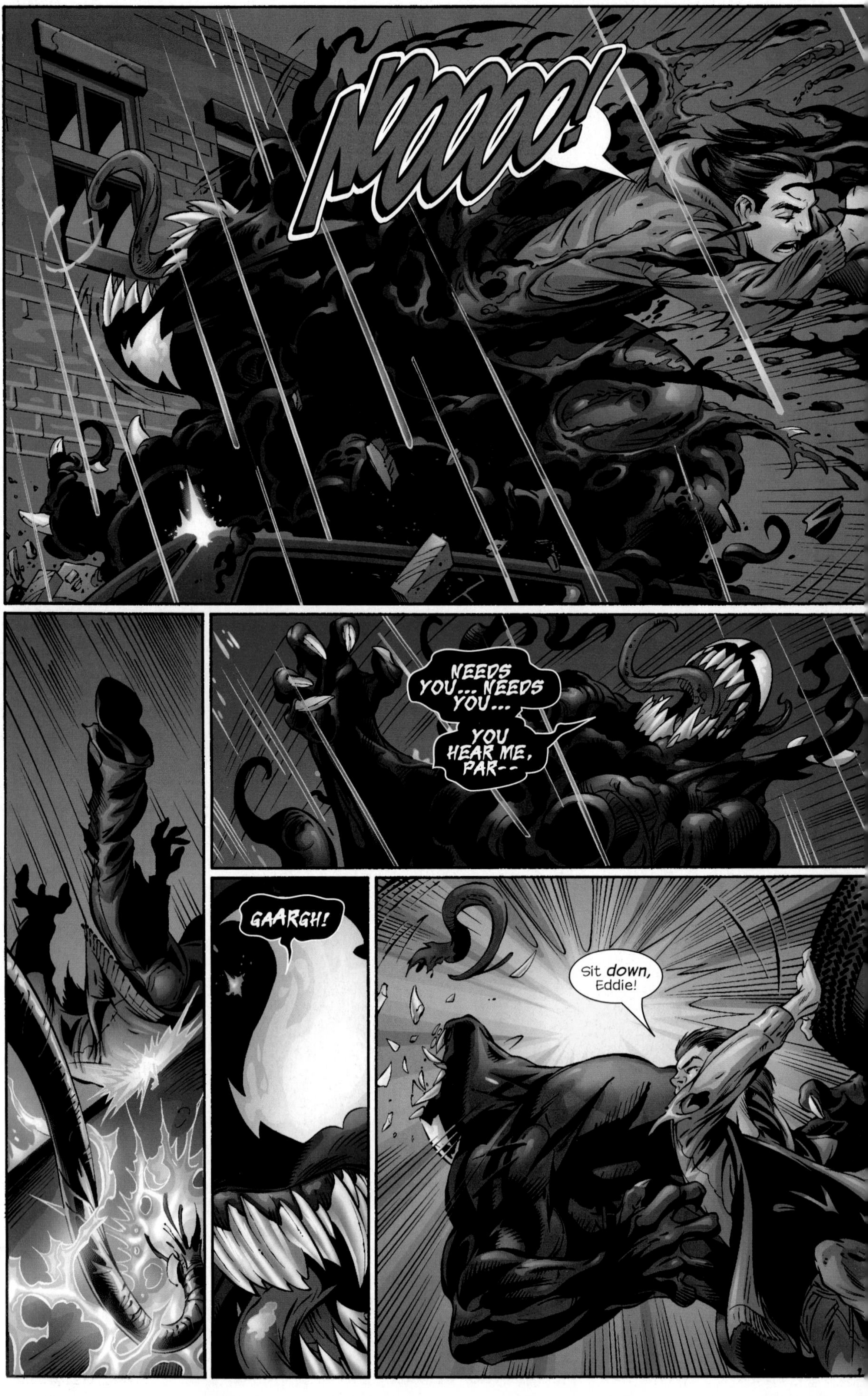
NOOOO!
NEEDS YOU... NEEDS YOU...
YOU HEAR ME, PAR--
GAARGH!
Sit down, Eddie!

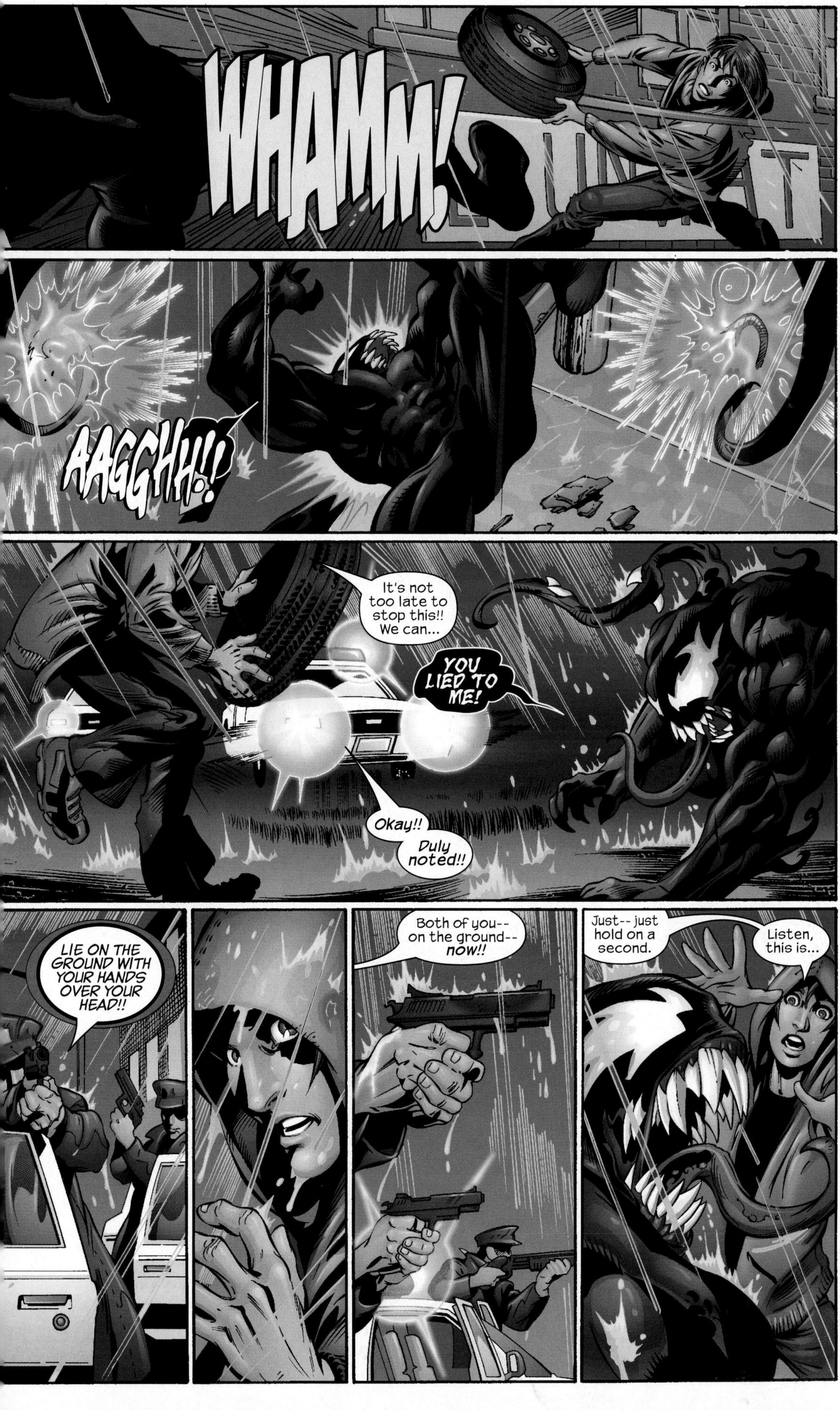
WHAMM!
AAGGHH!!
It's not too late to stop this!! We can...
YOU LIED TO ME!
Okay!! Duly noted!!
LIE ON THE GROUND WITH YOUR HANDS OVER YOUR HEAD!!
Both of you-- on the ground-- now!!
Just-- just hold on a second.
Listen, this is...

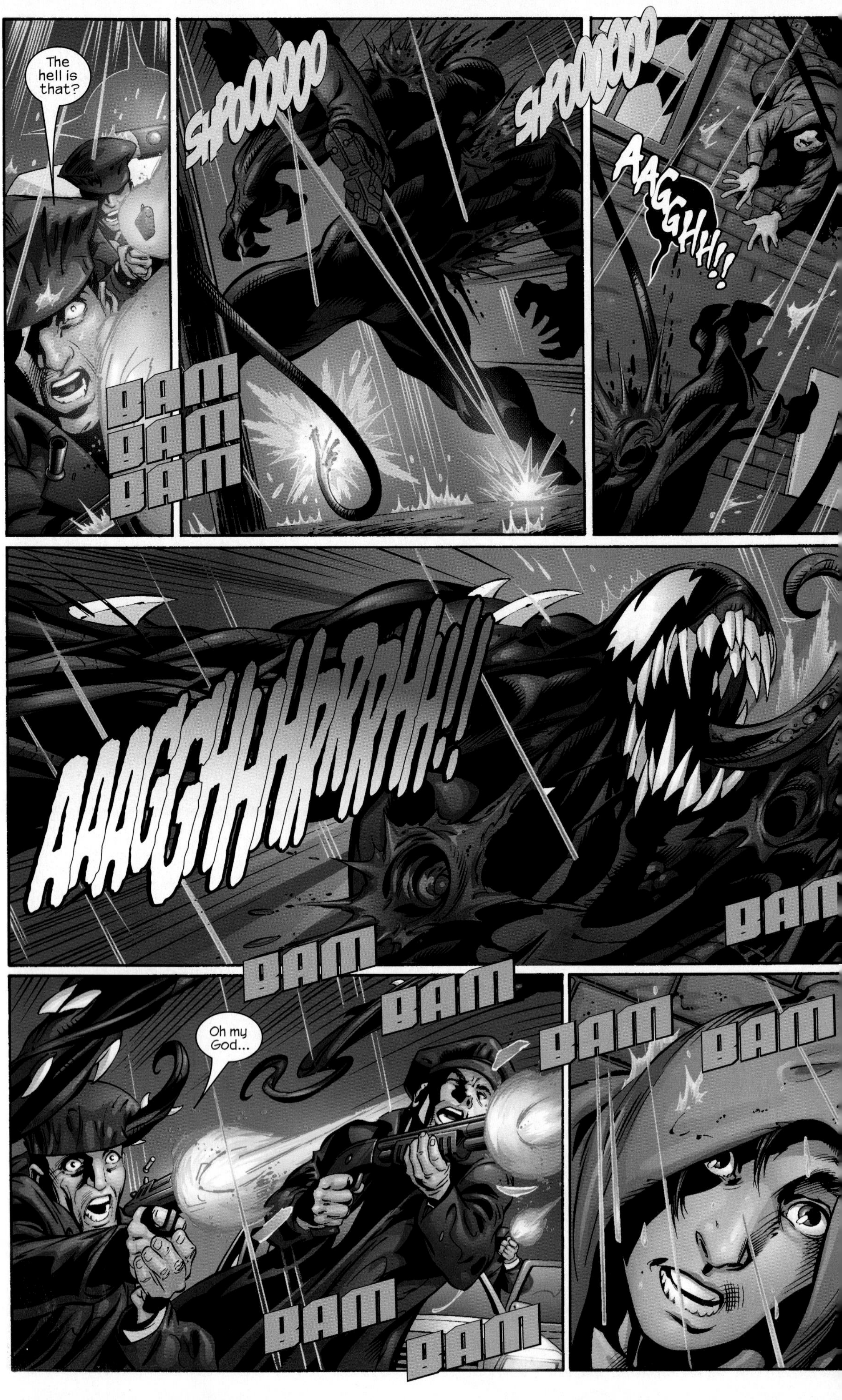
The hell is that?
BAM BAM BAM
SHPOOOOOO
SHPOOOOOO
AAGGHH!!
AAAGHHRRRHH!!
BAM
BAM
BAM
Oh my God...
BAM
BAM
BAM
BAM

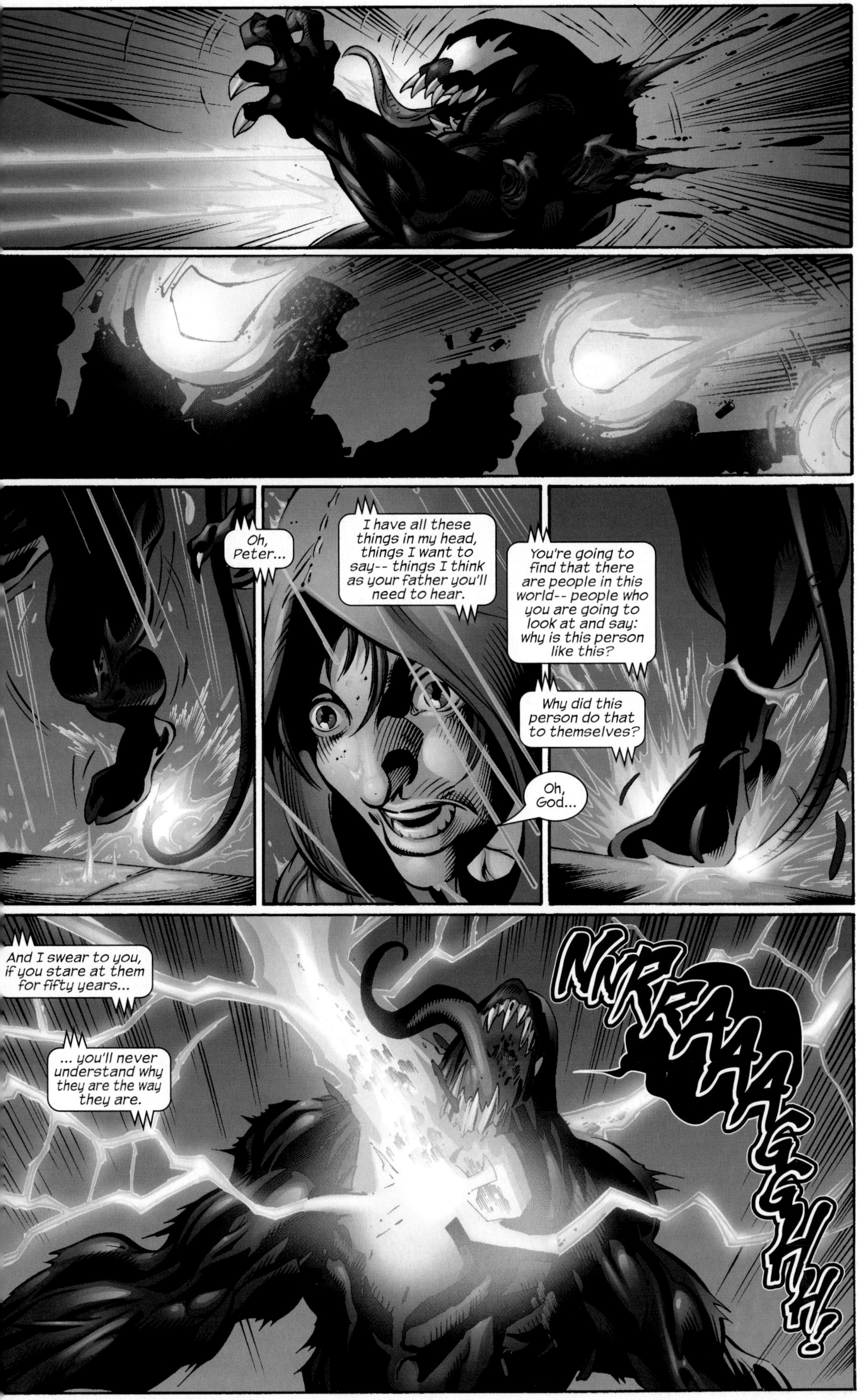

Oh, Peter...
I have all these things in my head, things I want to say-- things I think as your father you'll need to hear.
You're going to find that there are people in this world-- people who you are going to look at and say: why is this person like this?
Why did this person do that to themselves?
Oh, God...
And I swear to you, if you stare at them for fifty years...
... you'll never understand why they are the way they are.
NNRRAAAGGHH!

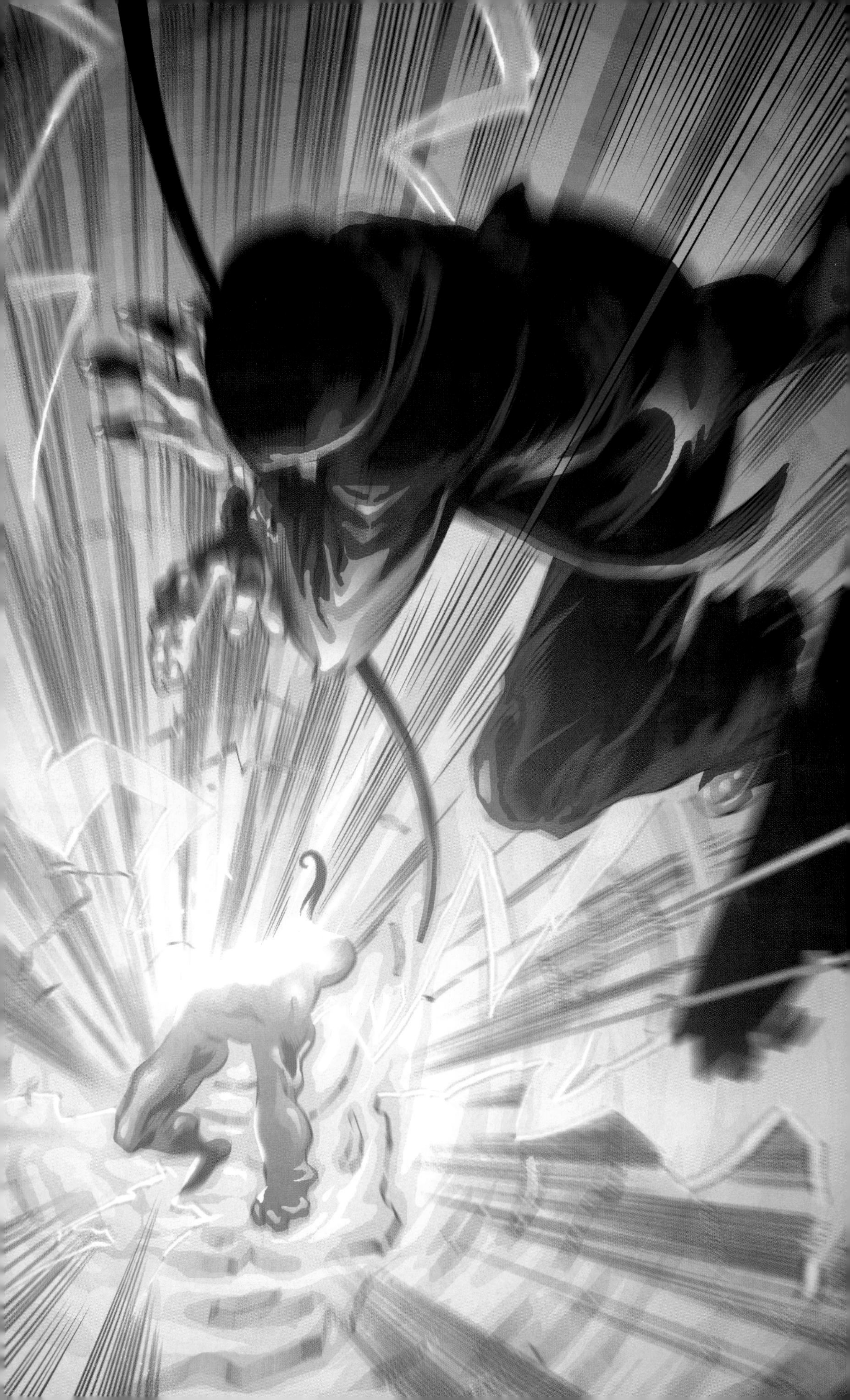

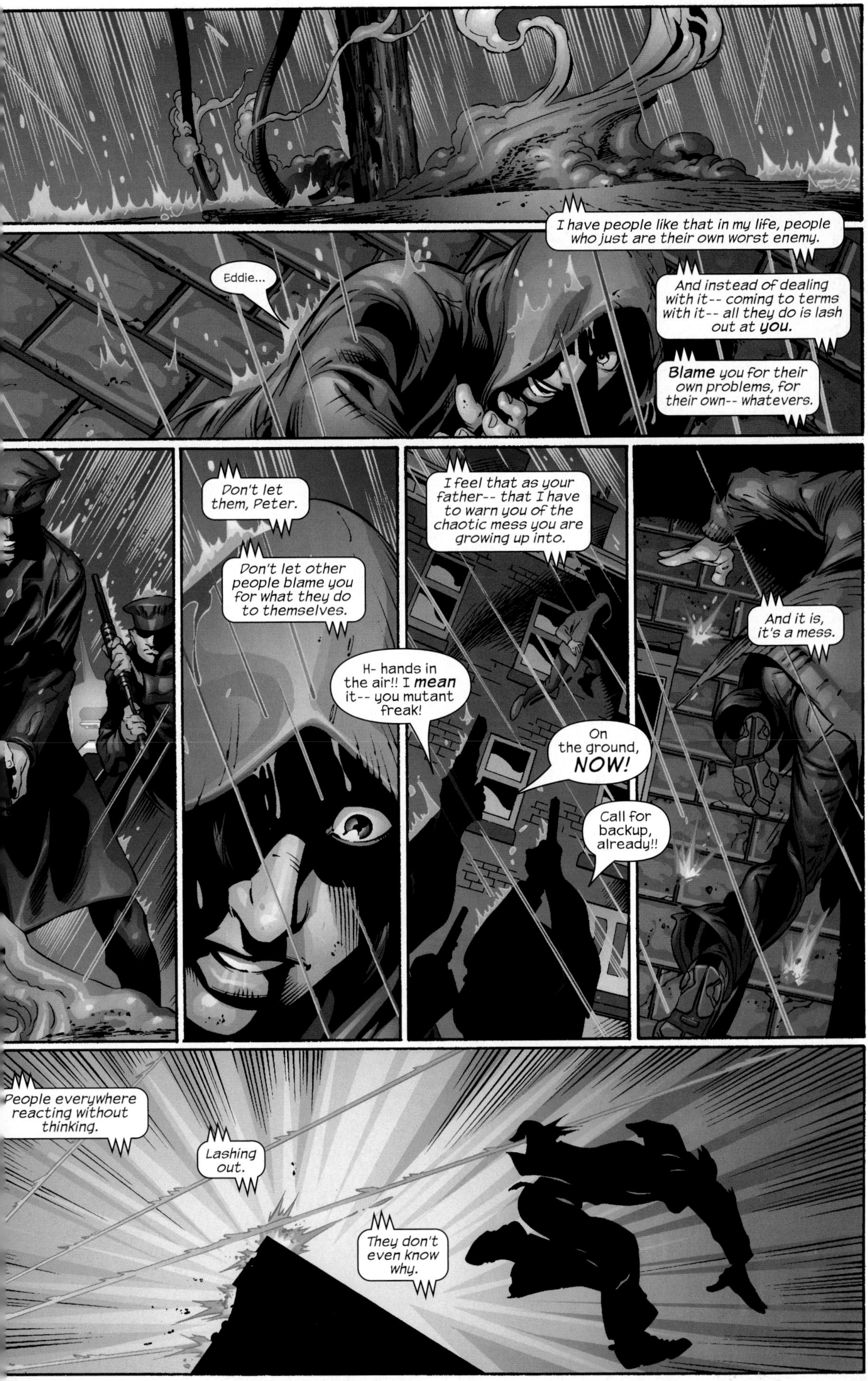
I have people like that in my life, people who just are their own worst enemy.
Eddie...
And instead of dealing with it-- coming to terms with it-- all they do is lash out at **you.**
Blame you for their own problems, for their own-- whatevers.
Don't let them, Peter.
Don't let other people blame you for what they do to themselves.
I feel that as your father-- that I have to warn you of the chaotic mess you are growing up into.
H- hands in the air!! I **mean** it-- you mutant freak!
On the ground, **NOW!**
Call for backup, already!!
And it is, it's a mess.
People everywhere reacting without thinking.
Lashing out.
They don't even know why.

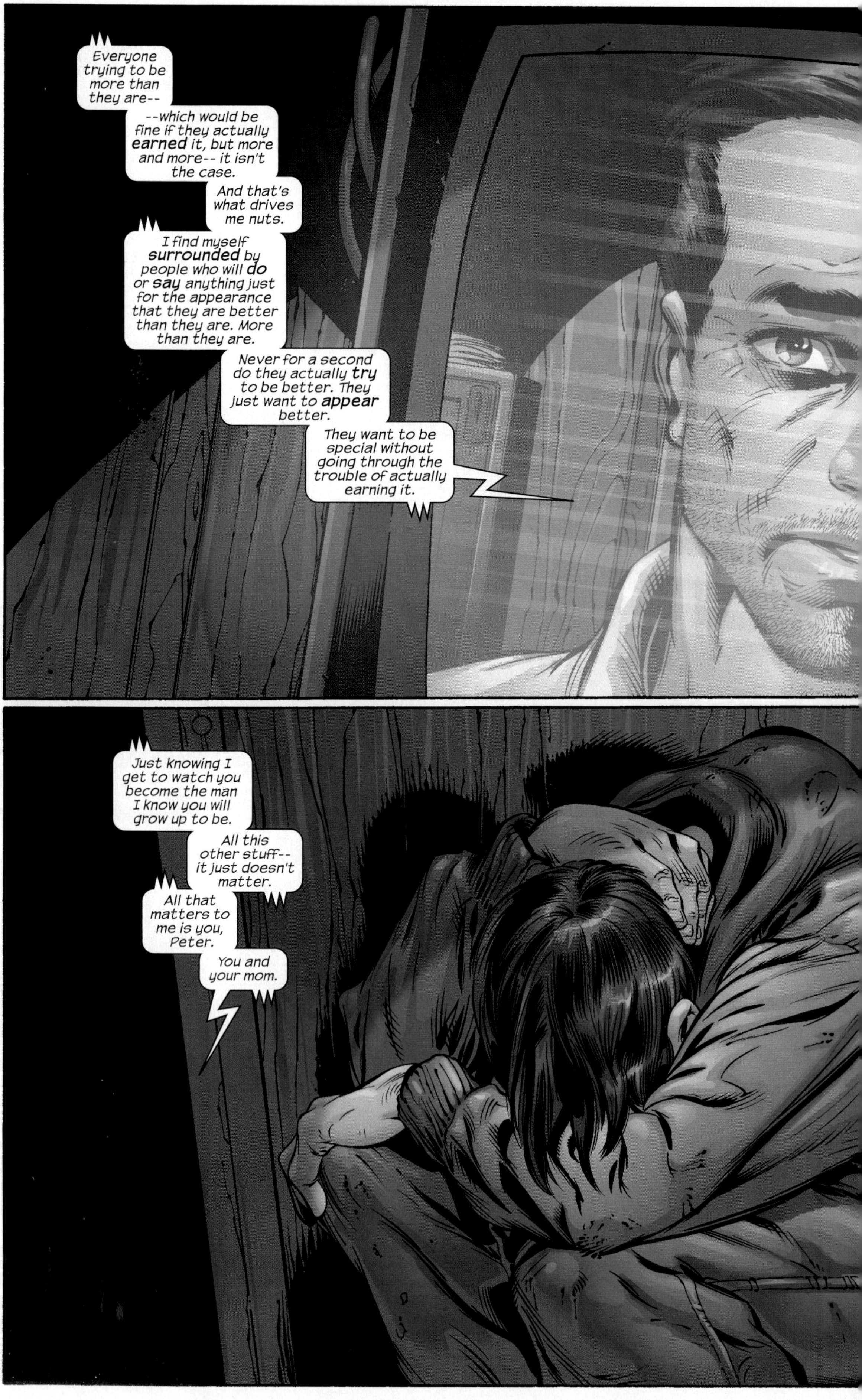
Everyone trying to be more than they are--
--which would be fine if they actually **earned** it, but more and more-- it isn't the case.
And that's what drives me nuts.
I find myself **surrounded** by people who will **do** or **say** anything just for the appearance that they are better than they are. More than they are.
Never for a second do they actually **try** to be better. They just want to **appear** better.
They want to be special without going through the trouble of actually earning it.
Just knowing I get to watch you become the man I know you will grow up to be.
All this other stuff-- it just doesn't matter.
All that matters to me is you, Peter.
You and your mom.

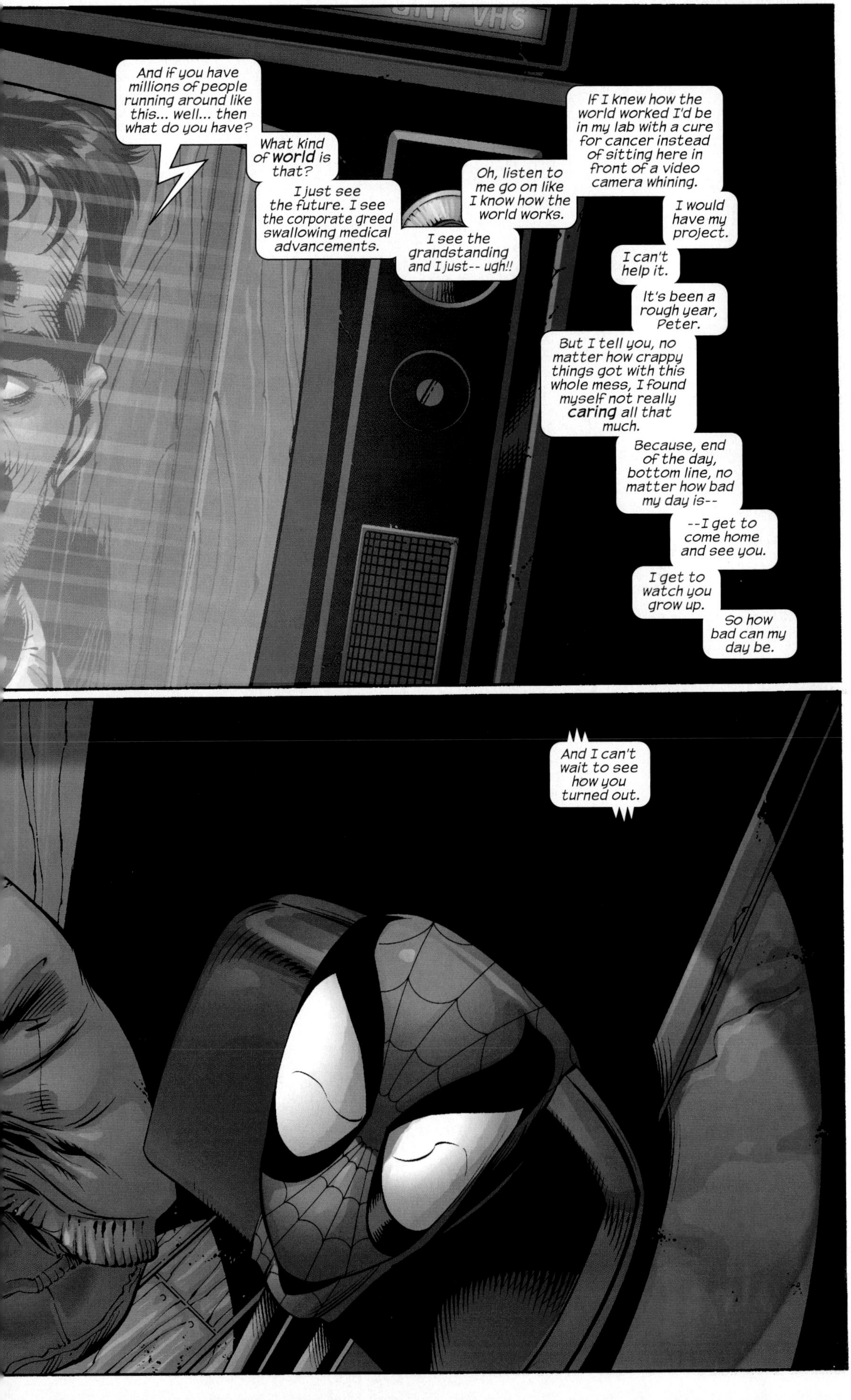
And if you have millions of people running around like this... well... then what do you have?
What kind of **world** is that?
I just see the future. I see the corporate greed swallowing medical advancements.
I see the grandstanding and I just-- ugh!!
Oh, listen to me go on like I know how the world works.
If I knew how the world worked I'd be in my lab with a cure for cancer instead of sitting here in front of a video camera whining.
I would have my project.
I can't help it.
It's been a rough year, Peter.
But I tell you, no matter how crappy things got with this whole mess, I found myself not really **caring** all that much.
Because, end of the day, bottom line, no matter how bad my day is--
--I get to come home and see you.
I get to watch you grow up.
So how bad can my day be.
And I can't wait to see how you turned out.

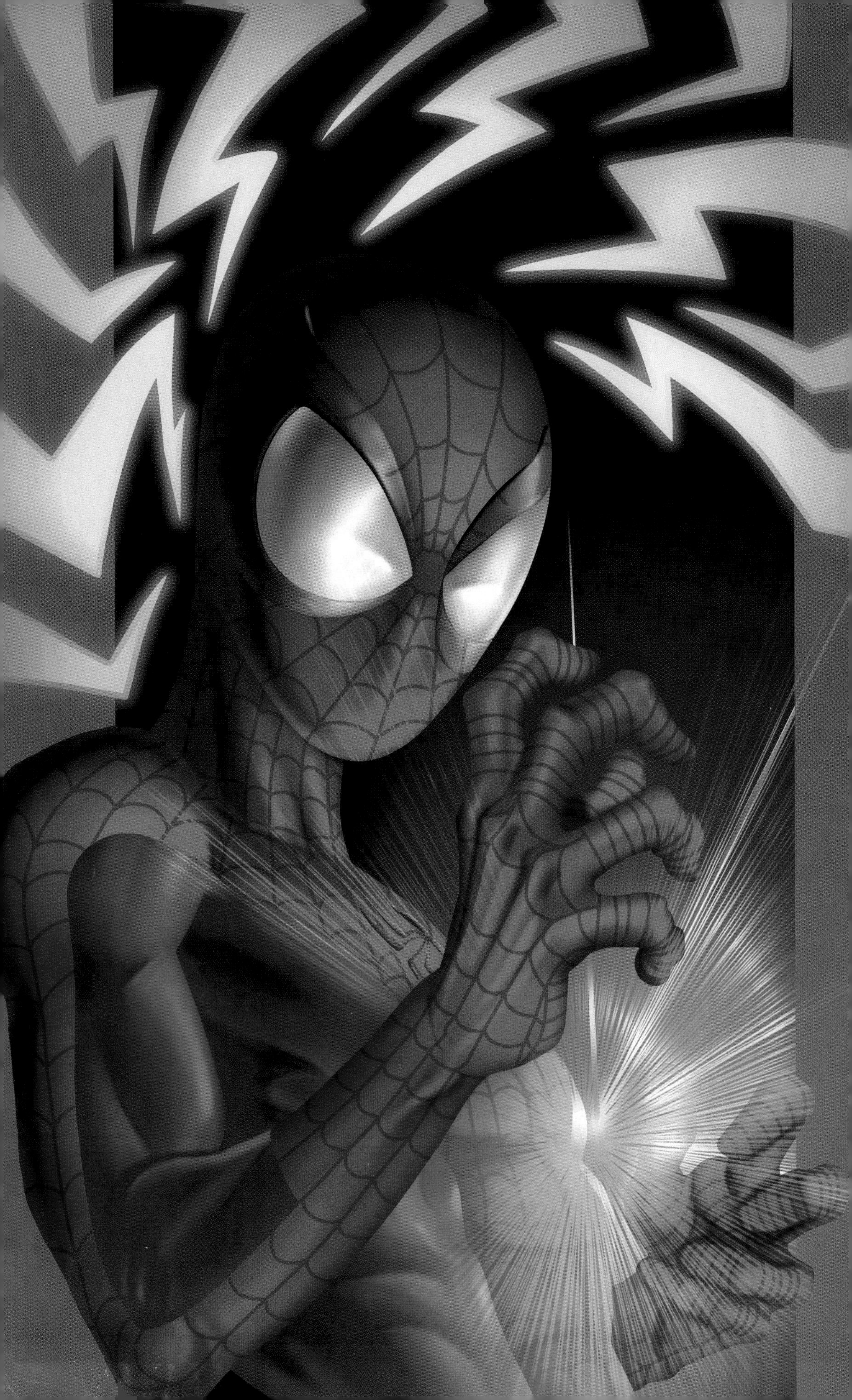

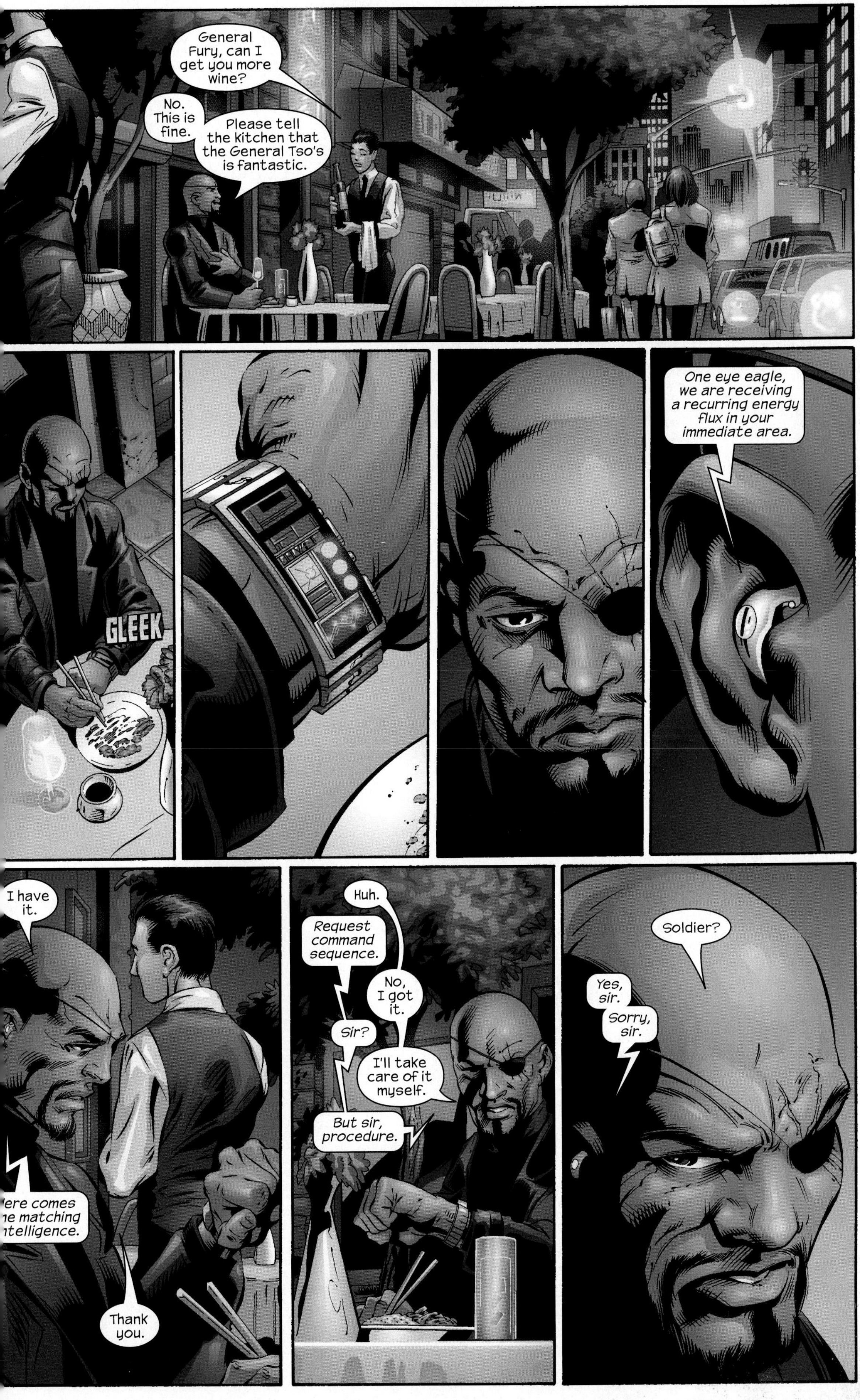
General Fury, can I get you more wine?
No. This is fine.
Please tell the kitchen that the General Tso's is fantastic.
GLEEK
One eye eagle, we are receiving a recurring energy flux in your immediate area.
I have it.
ere comes e matching telligence.
Thank you.
Huh.
Request command sequence.
No, I got it.
Sir?
I'll take care of it myself.
But sir, procedure.
Soldier?
Yes, sir.
Sorry, sir.

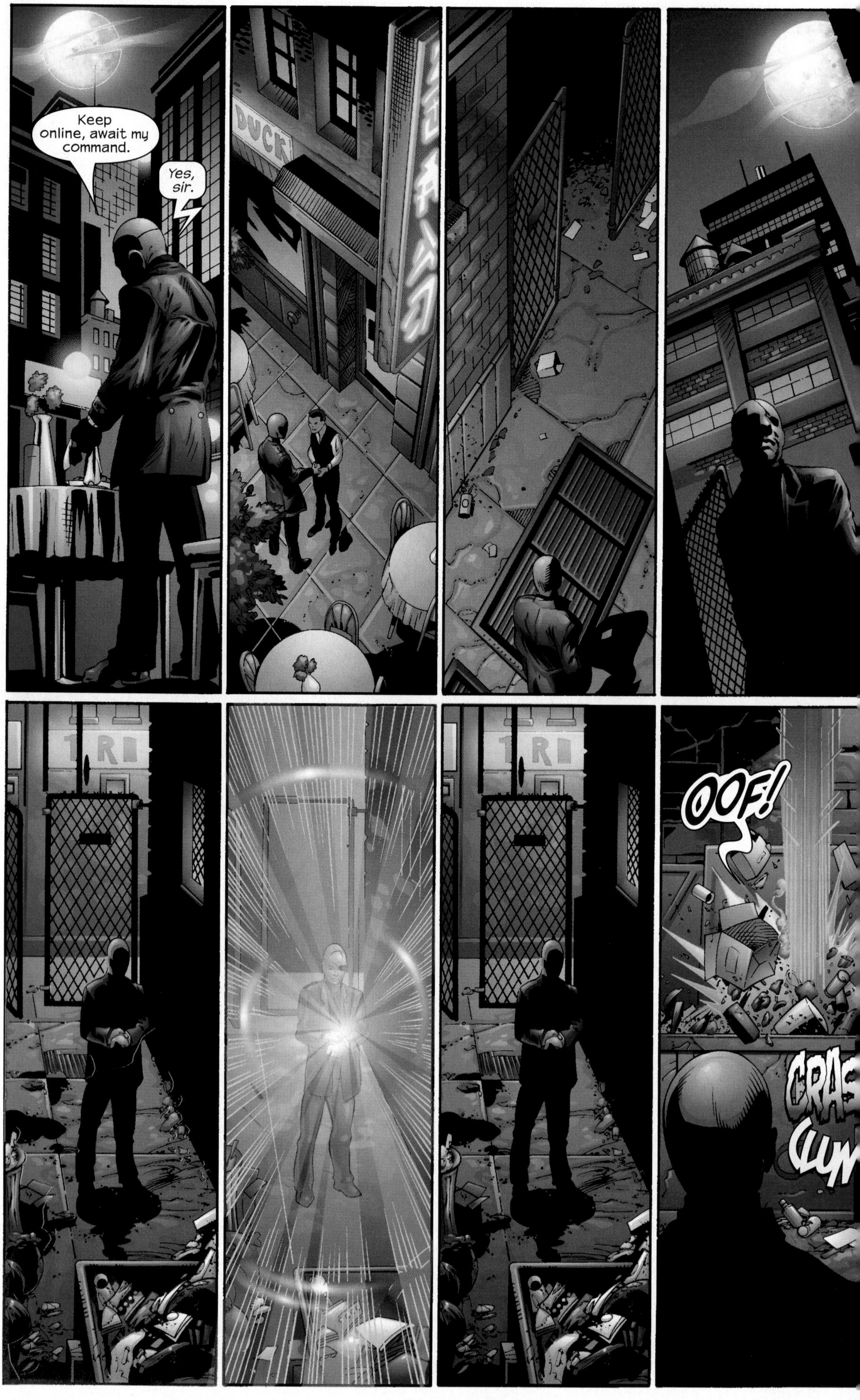
Keep online, await my command.
Yes, sir.
DUCK
OOF!
CRAS
CLUN

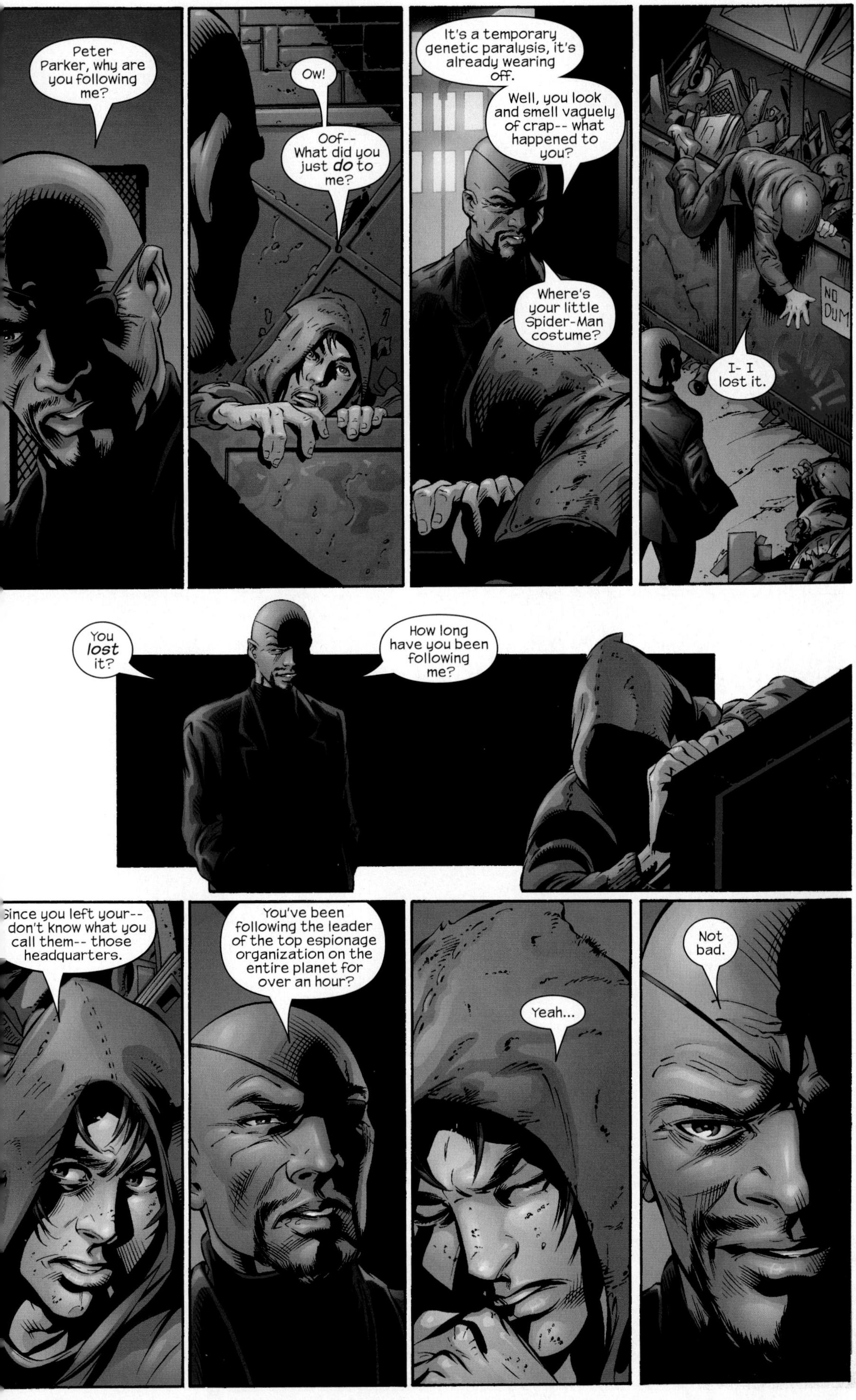
Peter Parker, why are you following me?
Ow!
Oof-- What did you just *do* to me?
It's a temporary genetic paralysis, it's already wearing off.
Well, you look and smell vaguely of crap-- what happened to you?
Where's your little Spider-Man costume?
I- I lost it.
You *lost* it?
How long have you been following me?
Since you left your-- don't know what you call them-- those headquarters.
You've been following the leader of the top espionage organization on the entire planet for over an hour?
Yeah...
Not bad.

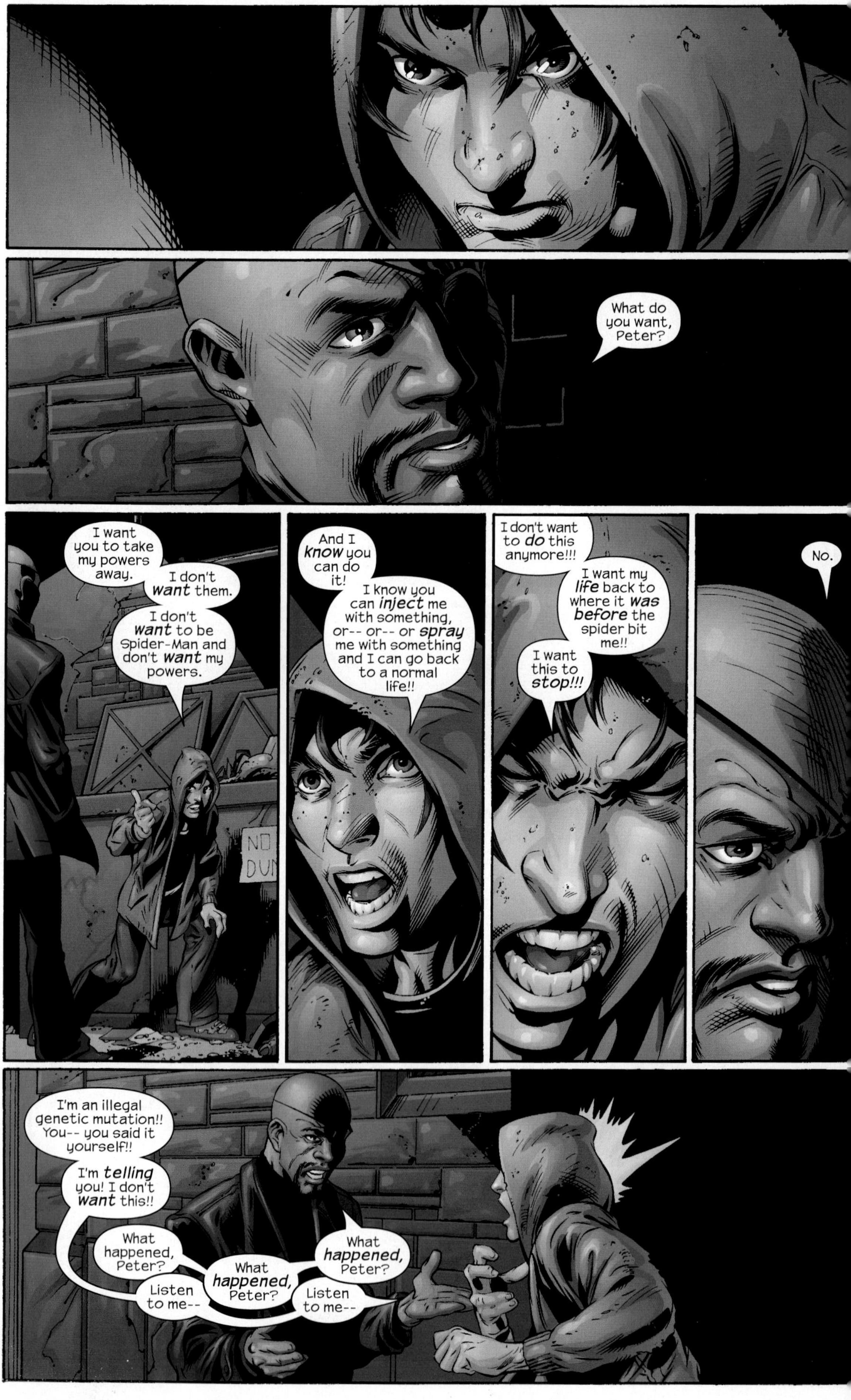

What do you want, Peter?
I want you to take my powers away.
I don't want them.
I don't want to be Spider-Man and don't want my powers.
NO
DUM
And I know you can do it!
I know you can inject me with something, or-- or-- or spray me with something and I can go back to a normal life!!
I don't want to do this anymore!!!
I want my life back to where it was before the spider bit me!!
I want this to stop!!!
No.
I'm an illegal genetic mutation!! You-- you said it yourself!!
I'm telling you! I don't want this!!
What happened, Peter?
Listen to me--
What happened, Peter?
What happened, Peter?
Listen to me--

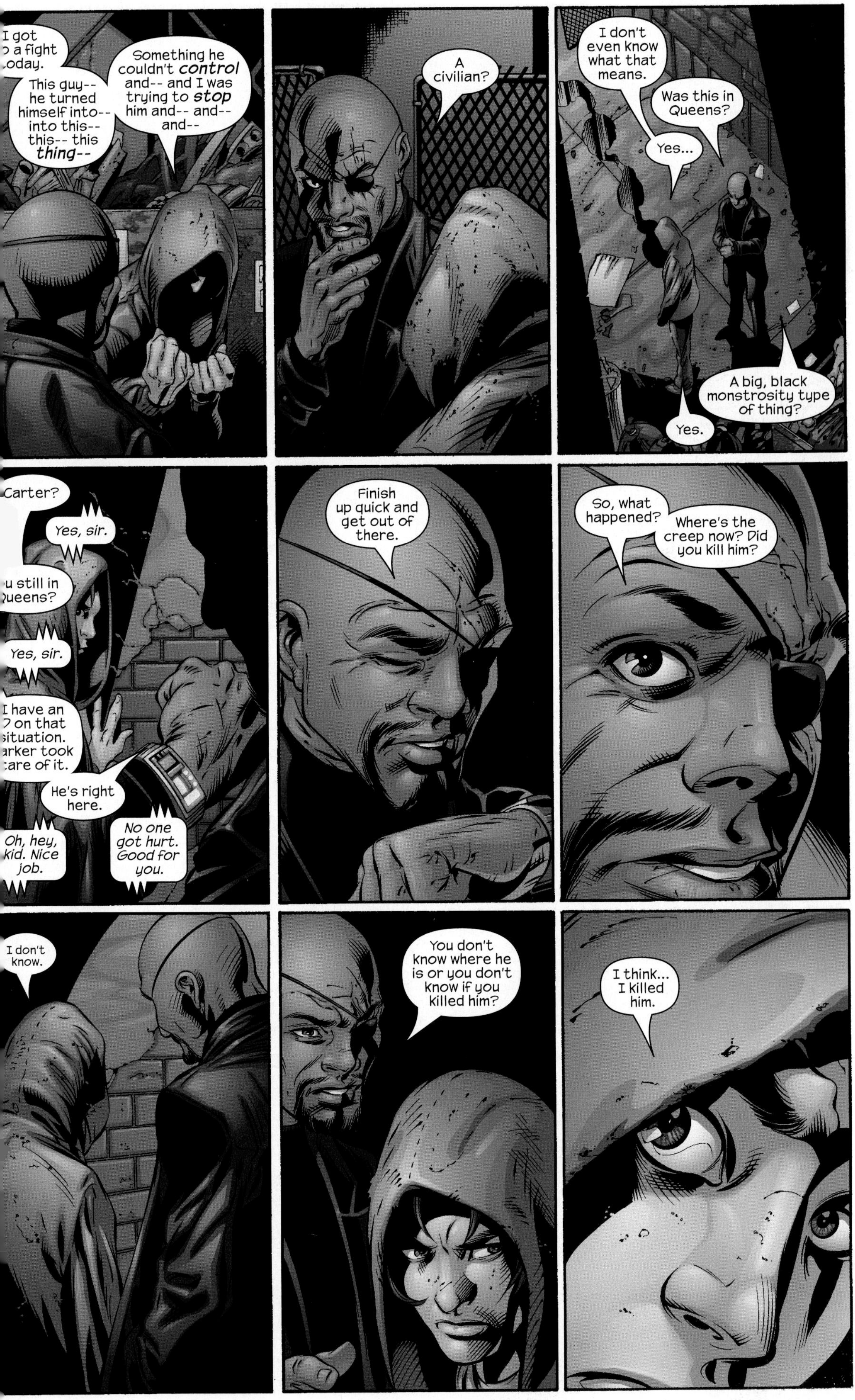

I got
o a fight
oday.
This guy--
he turned
himself into--
into this--
this-- this
thing--
Something he
couldn't control
and-- and I was
trying to stop
him and-- and--
and--
A
civilian?
I don't
even know
what that
means.
Was this in
Queens?
Yes...
A big, black
monstrosity type
of thing?
Yes.
Carter?
Yes, sir.
u still in
Queens?
Yes, sir.
I have an
? on that
situation.
arker took
care of it.
He's right
here.
Oh, hey,
kid. Nice
job.
No one
got hurt.
Good for
you.
Finish
up quick and
get out of
there.
So, what
happened?
Where's the
creep now? Did
you kill him?
I don't
know.
You don't
know where he
is or you don't
know if you
killed him?
I think...
I killed
him.

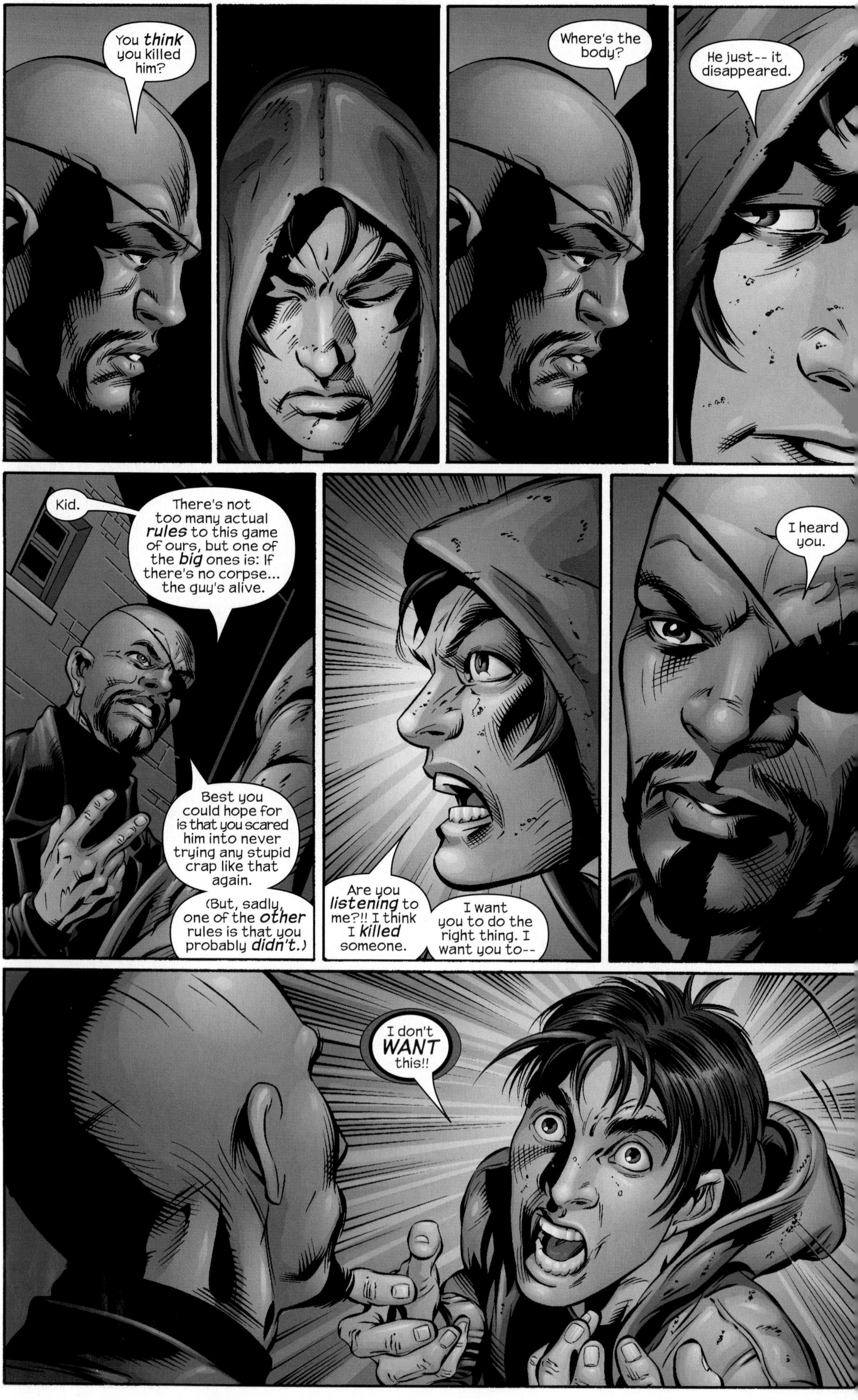

You think you killed him?
Where's the body?
He just-- it disappeared.
Kid.
There's not too many actual rules to this game of ours, but one of the big ones is: If there's no corpse... the guy's alive.
Best you could hope for is that you scared him into never trying any stupid crap like that again.
(But, sadly, one of the other rules is that you probably didn't.)
Are you listening to me?!! I think I killed someone.
I want you to do the right thing. I want you to--
I heard you.
I don't WANT this!!

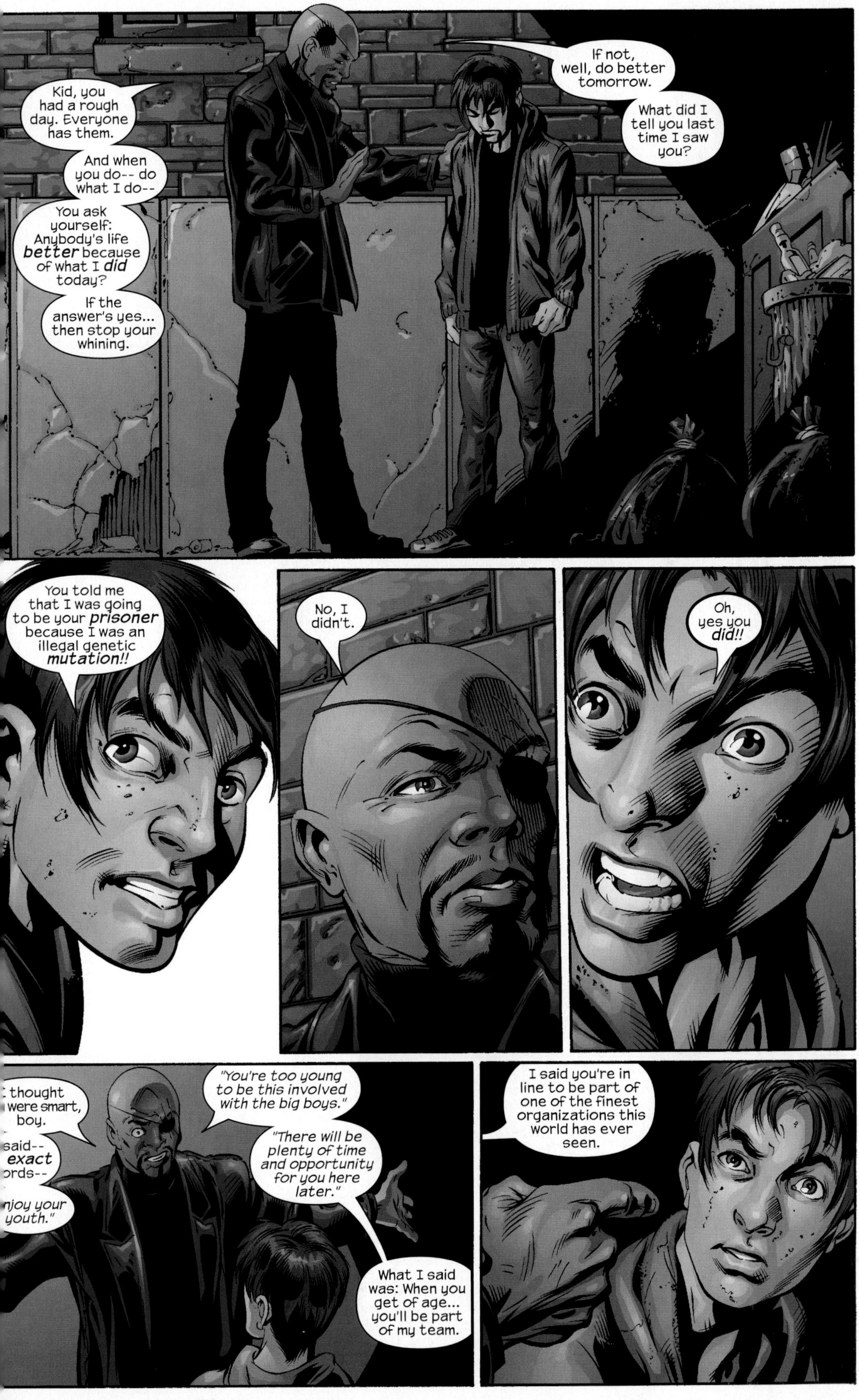
Kid, you had a rough day. Everyone has them.
And when you do-- do what I do--
You ask yourself: Anybody's life *better* because of what I *did* today?
If the answer's yes... then stop your whining.
If not, well, do better tomorrow.
What did I tell you last time I saw you?
You told me that I was going to be your *prisoner* because I was an illegal genetic *mutation!!*
No, I didn't.
Oh, yes you *did!!*
thought
were smart,
boy.
said--
exact
ords--
njoy your
youth."
"You're too young to be this involved with the big boys."
"There will be plenty of time and opportunity for you here later."
What I said was: When you get of age... you'll be part of my team.
I said you're in line to be part of one of the finest organizations this world has ever seen.

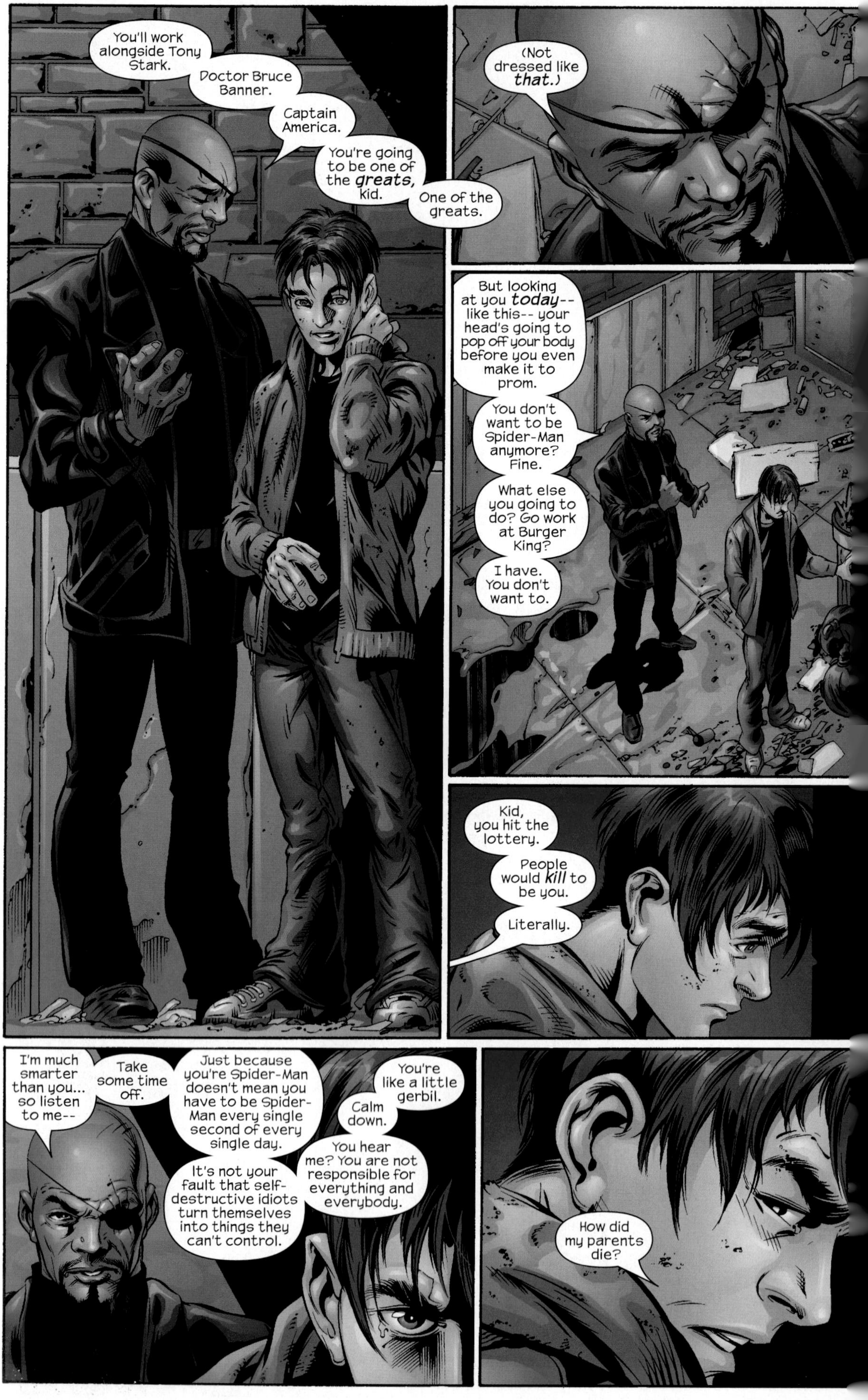
You'll work alongside Tony Stark.
Doctor Bruce Banner.
Captain America.
You're going to be one of the *greats,* kid.
One of the greats.
(Not dressed like *that.*)
But looking at you *today*-- like this-- your head's going to pop off your body before you even make it to prom.
You don't want to be Spider-Man anymore? Fine.
What else you going to do? Go work at Burger King?
I have. You don't want to.
Kid, you hit the lottery.
People would *kill* to be you.
Literally.
I'm much smarter than you... so listen to me--
Take some time off.
Just because you're Spider-Man doesn't mean you have to be Spider-Man every single second of every single day.
It's not your fault that self-destructive idiots turn themselves into things they can't control.
You're like a little gerbil.
Calm down.
You hear me? You are not responsible for everything and everybody.
How did my parents die?

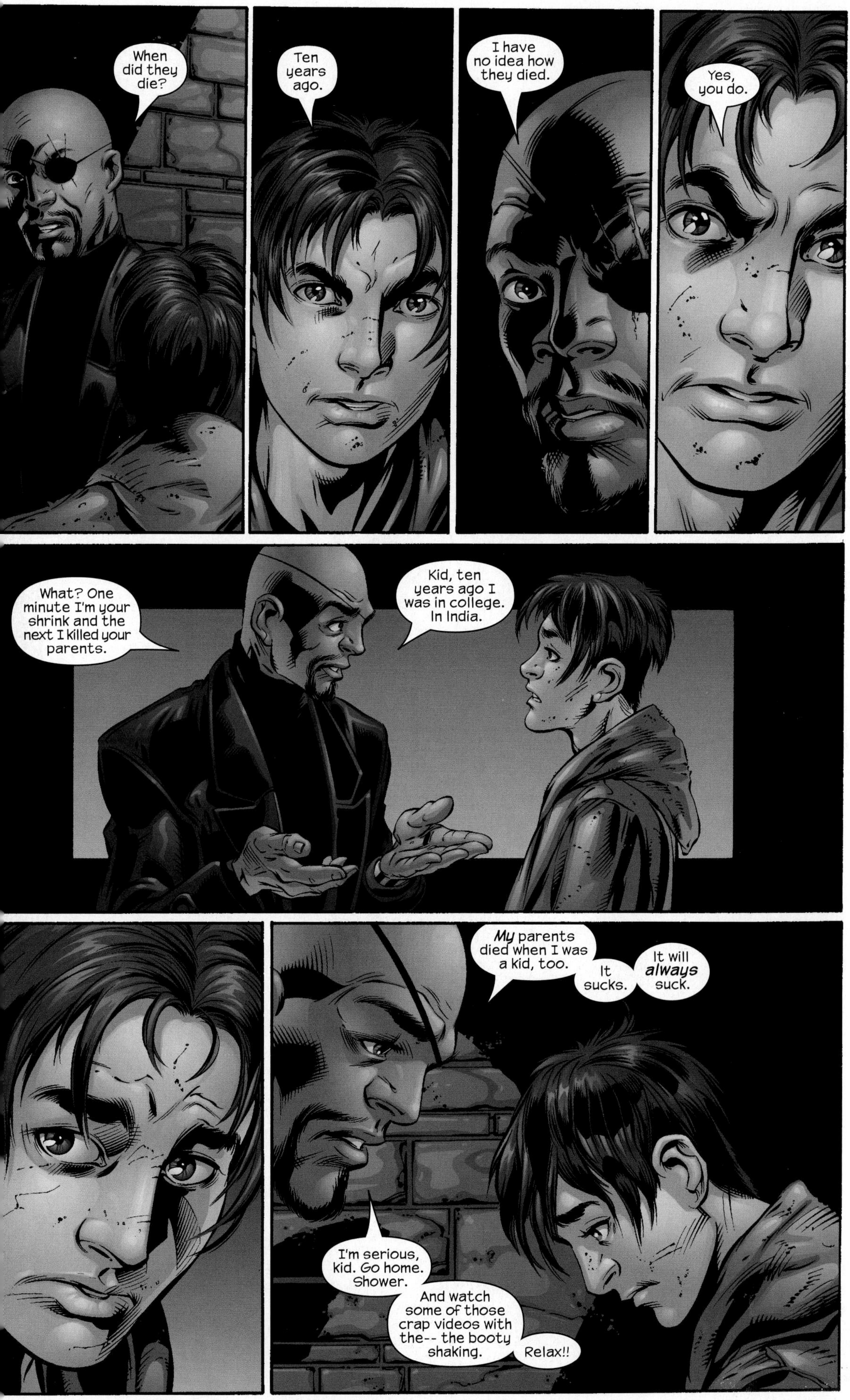

When did they die?
Ten years ago.
I have no idea how they died.
Yes, you do.
What? One minute I'm your shrink and the next I killed your parents.
Kid, ten years ago I was in college. In India.
My parents died when I was a kid, too.
It sucks.
It will *always* suck.
I'm serious, kid. Go home. Shower.
And watch some of those crap videos with the-- the booty shaking.
Relax!!

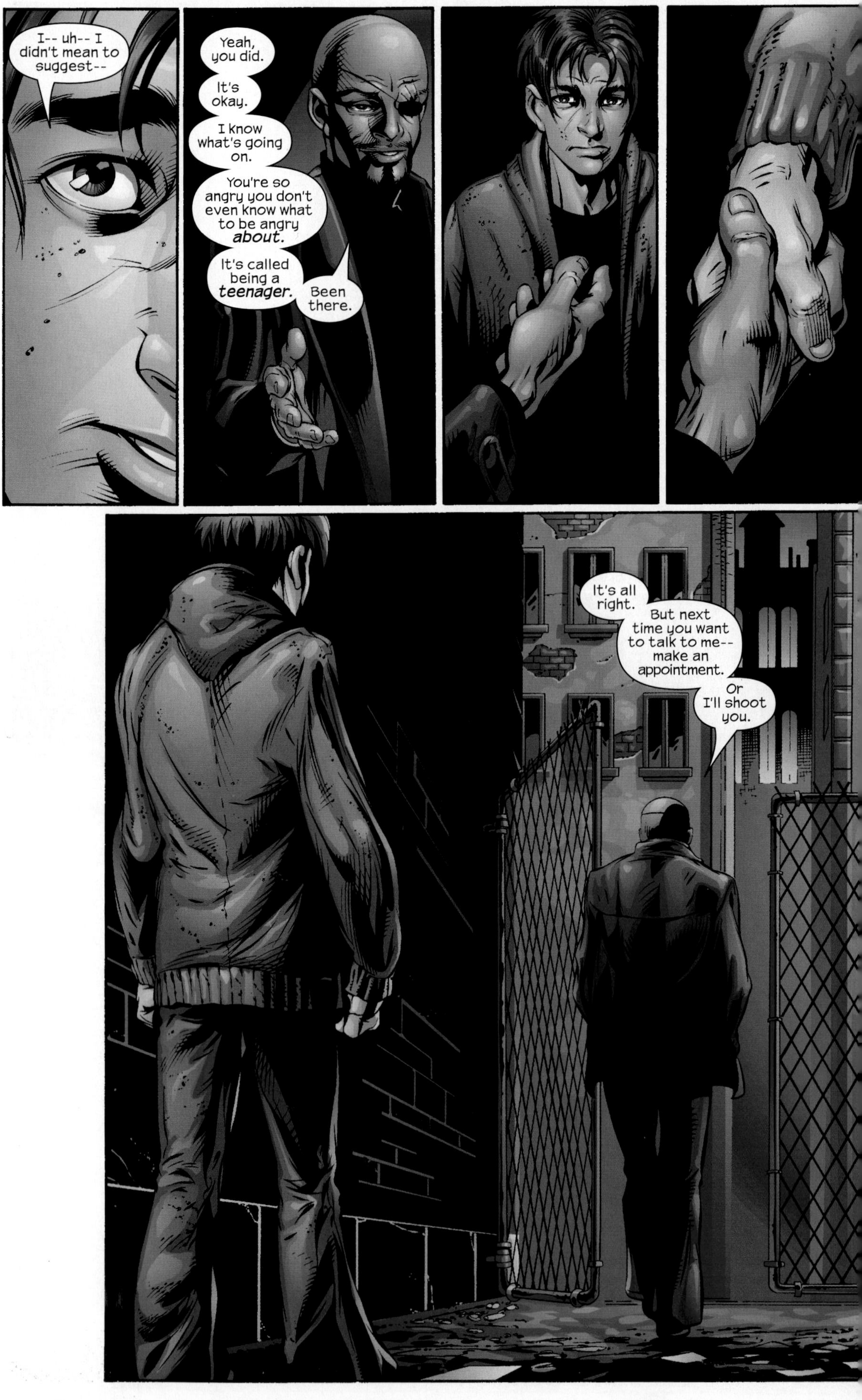

I-- uh-- I didn't mean to suggest--
Yeah, you did.
It's okay.
I know what's going on.
You're so angry you don't even know what to be angry *about.*
It's called being a *teenager.*
Been there.
It's all right.
But next time you want to talk to me-- make an appointment.
Or I'll shoot you.

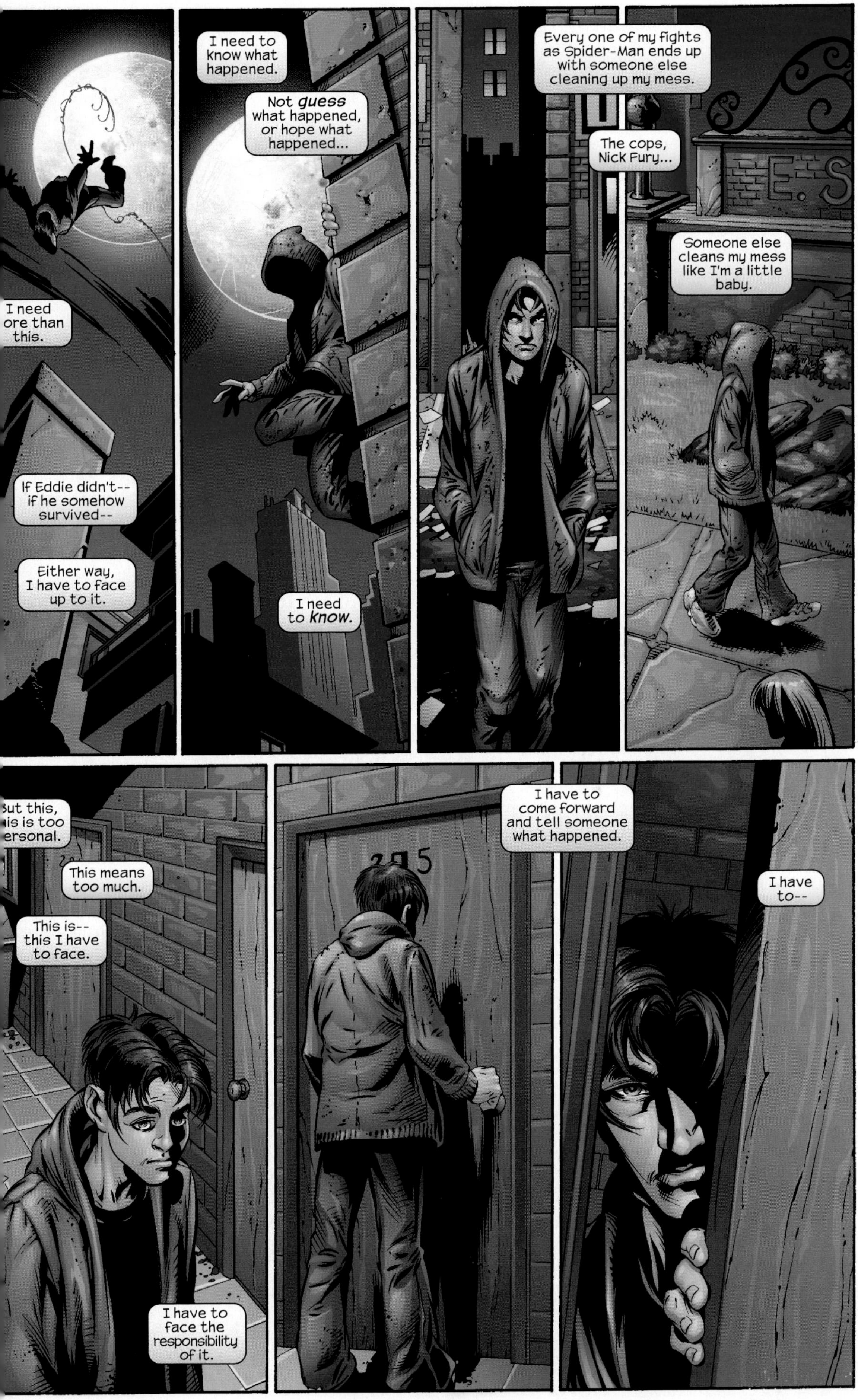
I need
ore than
this.
If Eddie didn't--
if he somehow
survived--
Either way,
I have to face
up to it.
I need to
know what
happened.
Not *guess*
what happened,
or hope what
happened...
I need
to *know.*
Every one of my fights
as Spider-Man ends up
with someone else
cleaning up my mess.
The cops,
Nick Fury...
Someone else
cleans my mess
like I'm a little
baby.
ut this,
is is too
ersonal.
This means
too much.
This is--
this I have
to face.
I have to
face the
responsibility
of it.
I have to
come forward
and tell someone
what happened.
I have
to--

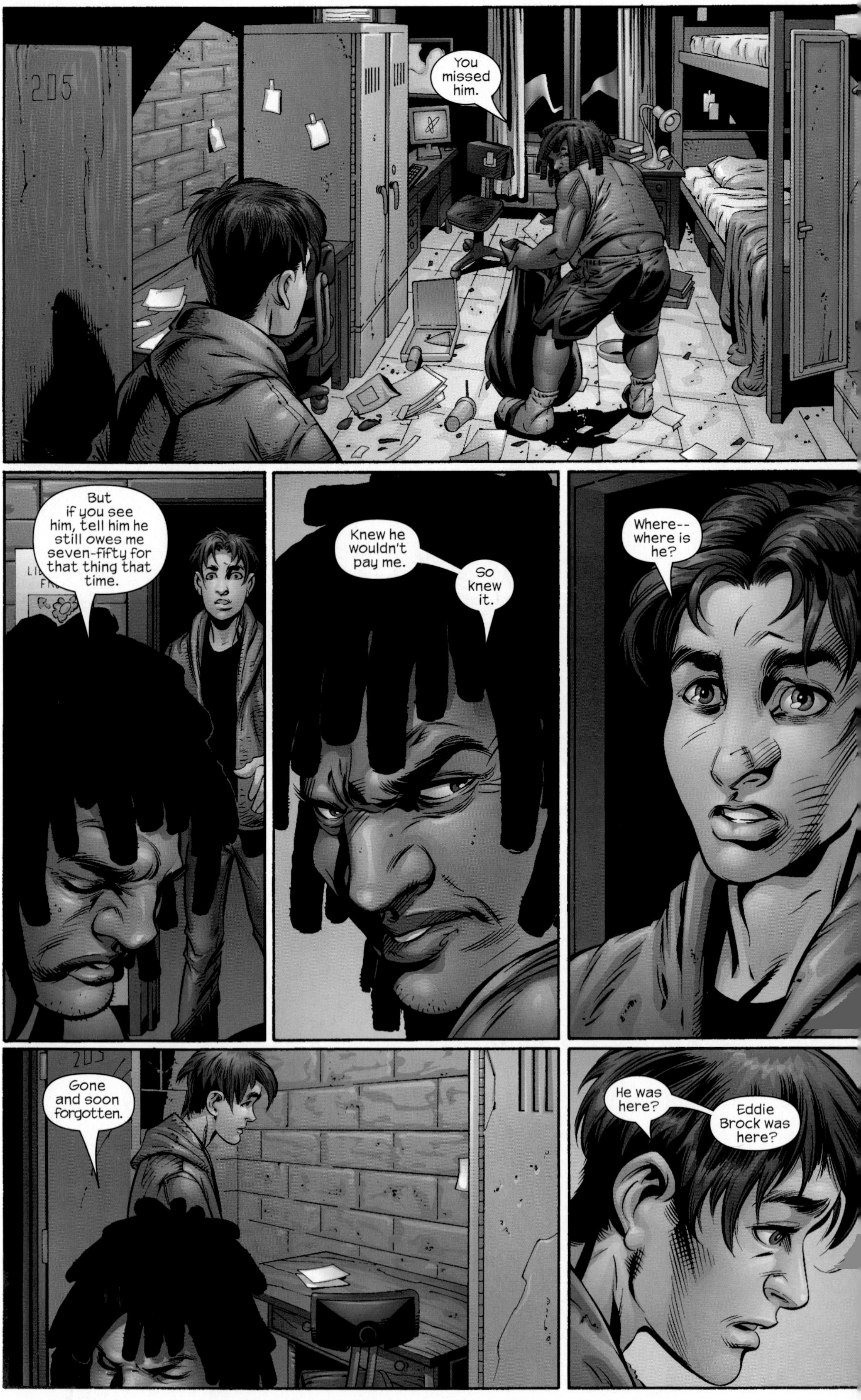

205
You missed him.
But if you see him, tell him he still owes me seven-fifty for that thing that time.
Knew he wouldn't pay me.
So knew it.
Where-- where is he?
Gone and soon forgotten.
He was here?
Eddie Brock was here?

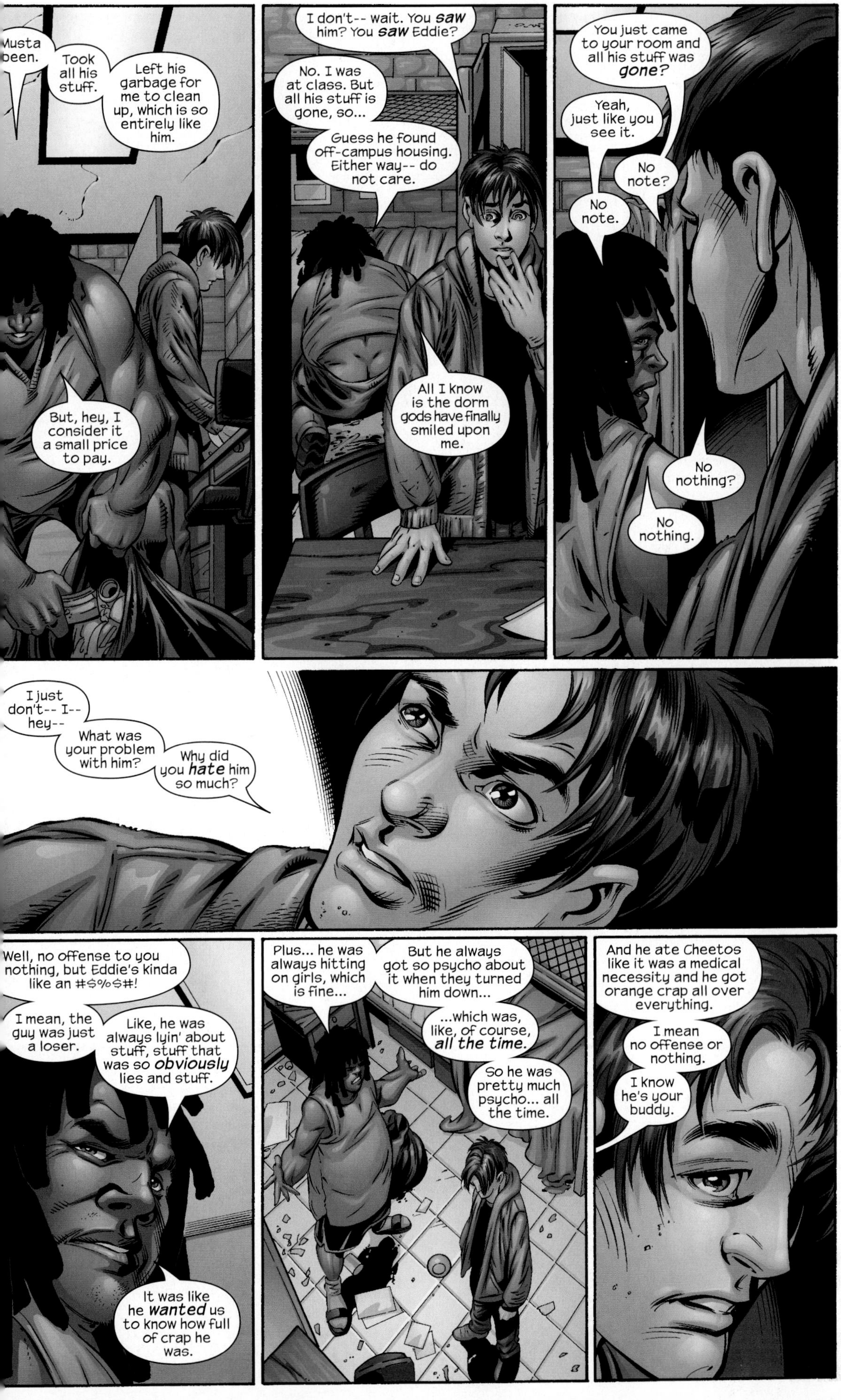
Musta been.
Took all his stuff.
Left his garbage for me to clean up, which is so entirely like him.
But, hey, I consider it a small price to pay.
I don't-- wait. You *saw* him? You *saw* Eddie?
No. I was at class. But all his stuff is gone, so...
Guess he found off-campus housing. Either way-- do not care.
All I know is the dorm gods have finally smiled upon me.
You just came to your room and all his stuff was *gone?*
Yeah, just like you see it.
No note?
No note.
No nothing?
No nothing.
I just don't-- I-- hey--
What was your problem with him?
Why did you *hate* him so much?
Well, no offense to you nothing, but Eddie's kinda like an #$%$#!
I mean, the guy was just a loser.
Like, he was always lyin' about stuff, stuff that was so *obviously* lies and stuff.
It was like he *wanted* us to know how full of crap he was.
Plus... he was always hitting on girls, which is fine...
But he always got so psycho about it when they turned him down...
...which was, like, of course, *all the time.*
So he was pretty much psycho... all the time.
And he ate Cheetos like it was a medical necessity and he got orange crap all over everything.
I mean no offense or nothing.
I know he's your buddy.

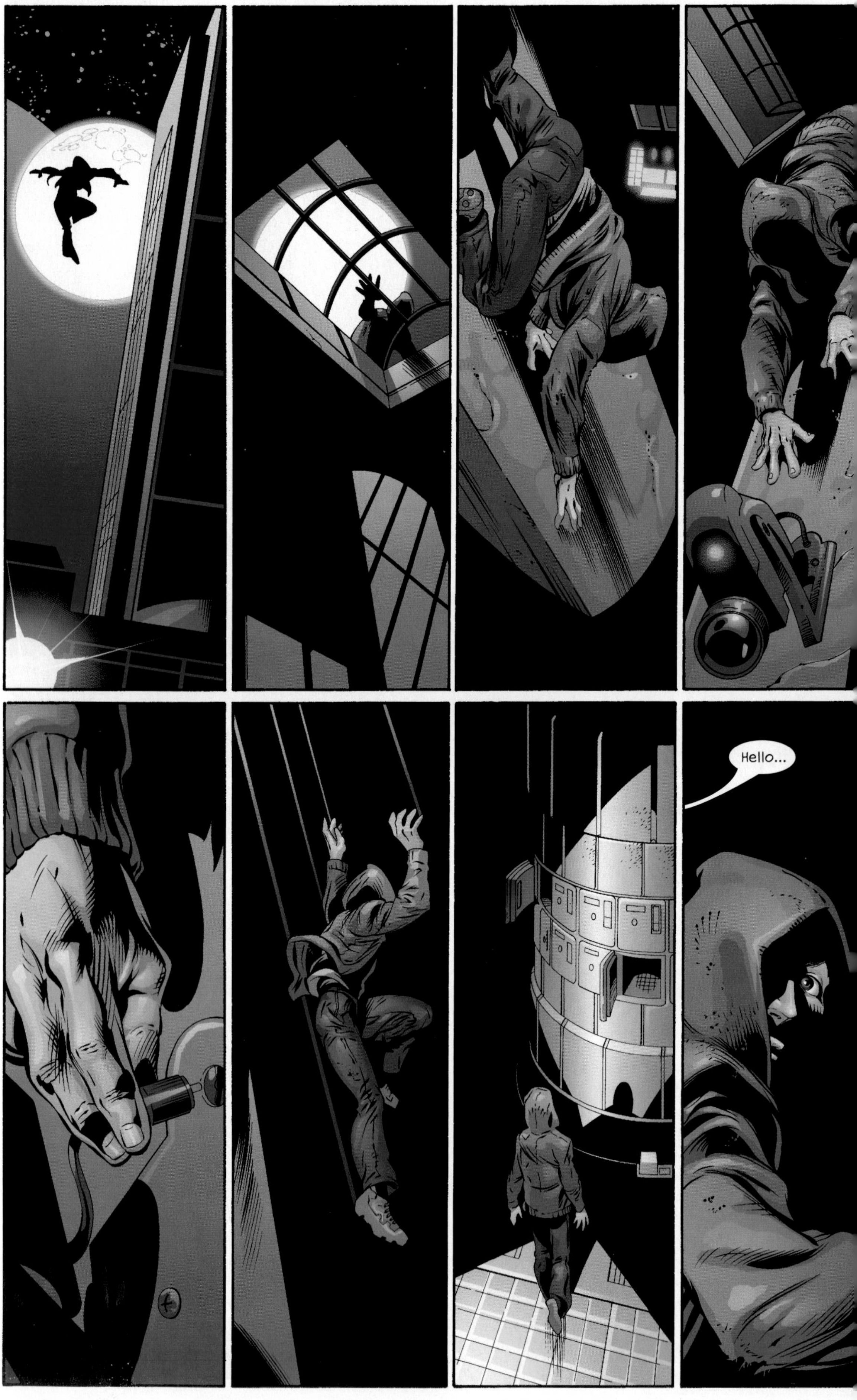
Hello...

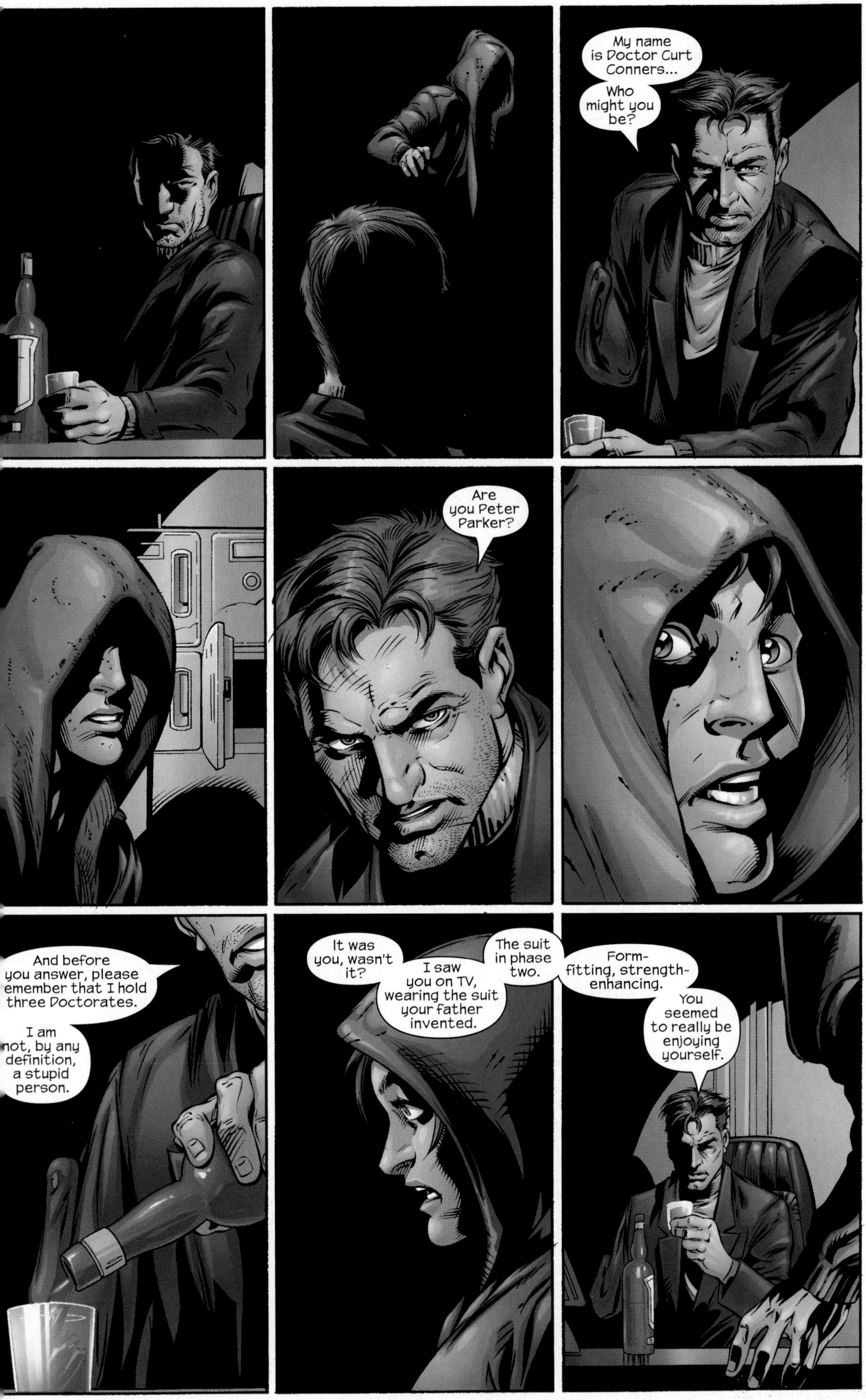
My name is Doctor Curt Conners...
Who might you be?
Are you Peter Parker?
And before you answer, please emember that I hold three Doctorates.
I am not, by any definition, a stupid person.
It was you, wasn't it?
I saw you on TV, wearing the suit your father invented.
The suit in phase two.
Form-fitting, strength-enhancing.
You seemed to really be enjoying yourself.

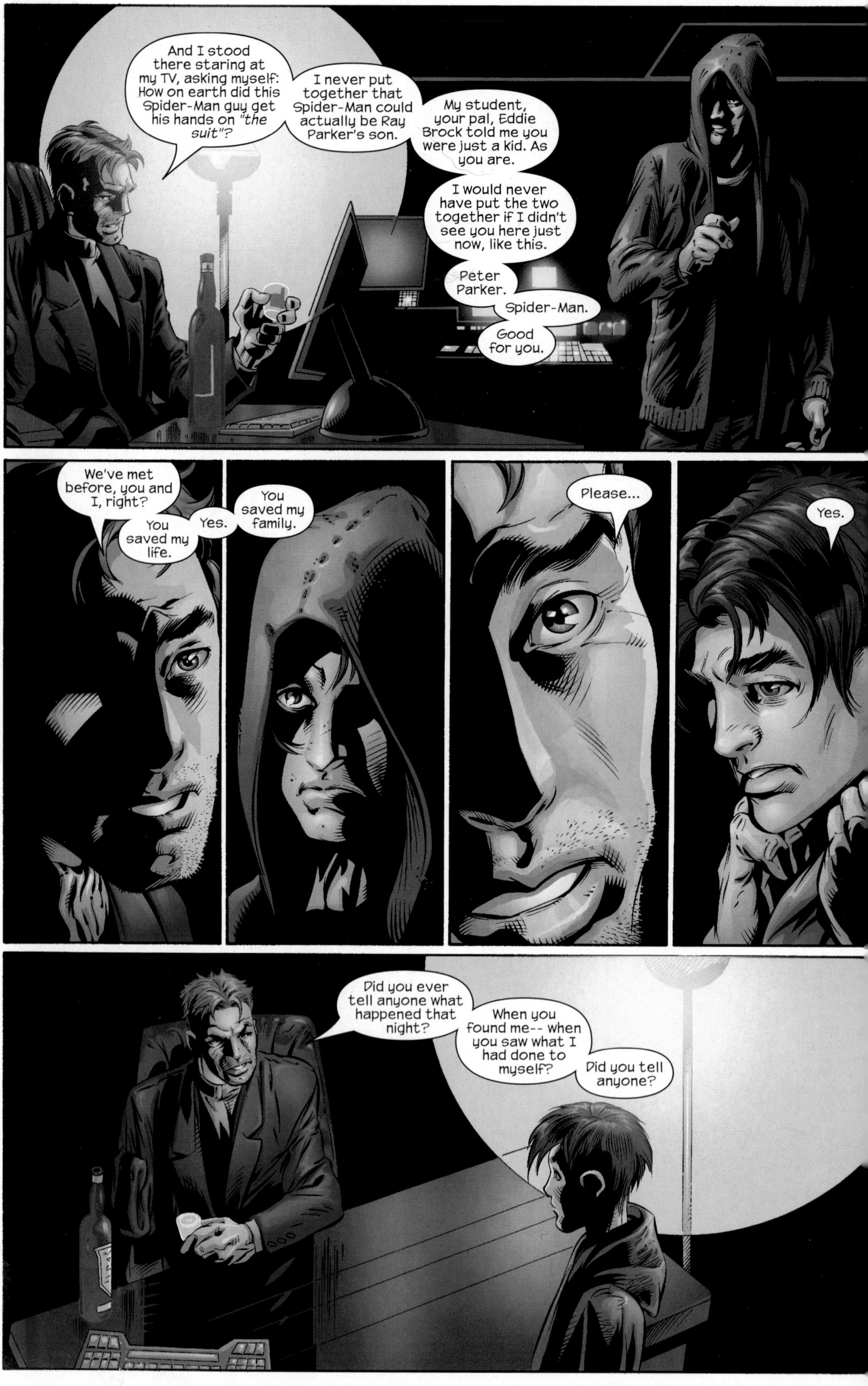
And I stood there staring at my TV, asking myself: How on earth did this Spider-Man guy get his hands on "the suit"?
I never put together that Spider-Man could actually be Ray Parker's son.
My student, your pal, Eddie Brock told me you were just a kid. As you are.
I would never have put the two together if I didn't see you here just now, like this.
Peter Parker.
Spider-Man.
Good for you.
We've met before, you and I, right?
You saved my life.
Yes.
You saved my family.
Please...
Yes.
Did you ever tell anyone what happened that night?
When you found me-- when you saw what I had done to myself?
Did you tell anyone?

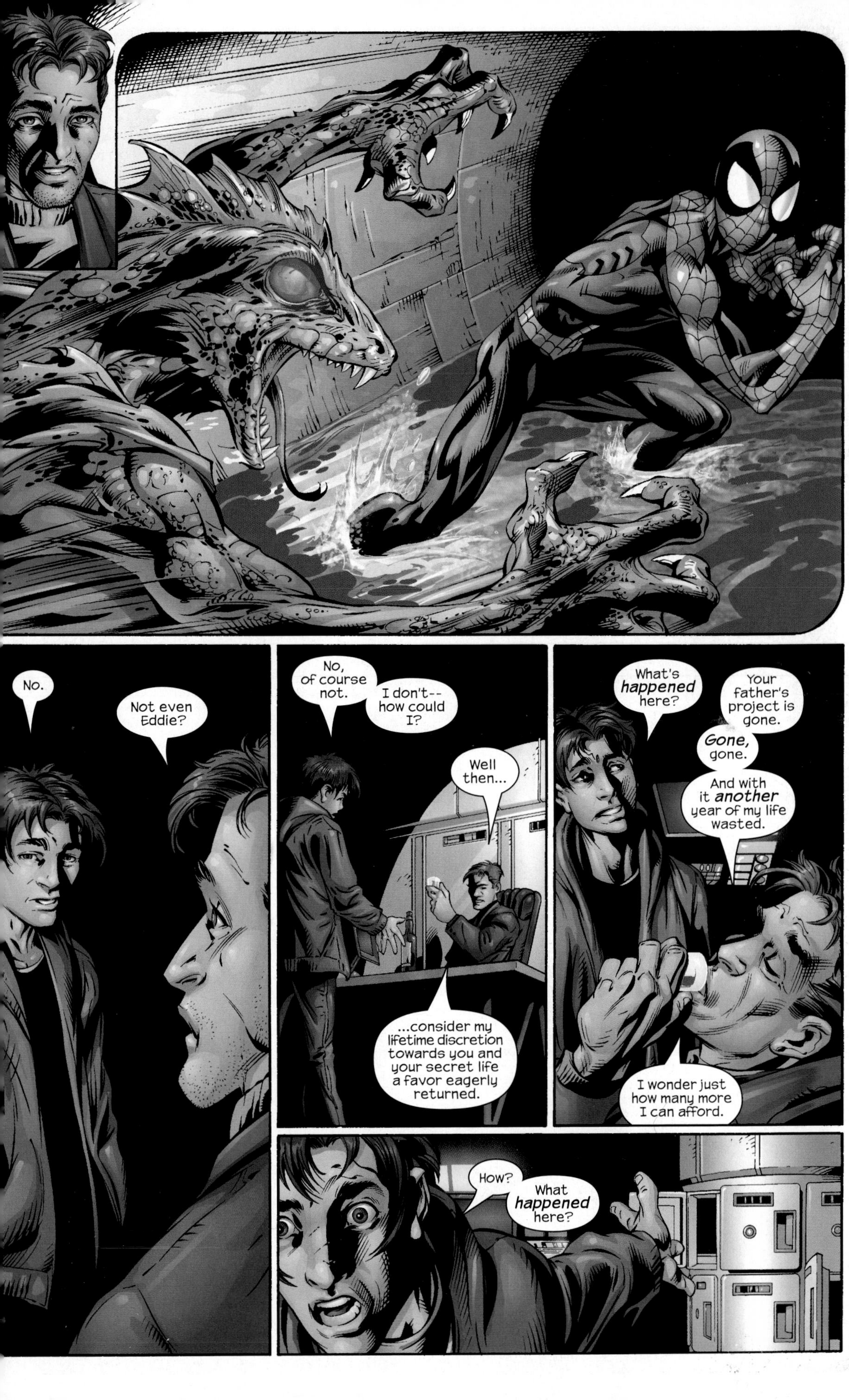

No.
Not even Eddie?
No, of course not.
I don't-- how could I?
Well then...
...consider my lifetime discretion towards you and your secret life a favor eagerly returned.
What's *happened* here?
Your father's project is gone.
Gone, gone.
And with it *another* year of my life wasted.
I wonder just how many more I can afford.
How?
What *happened* here?

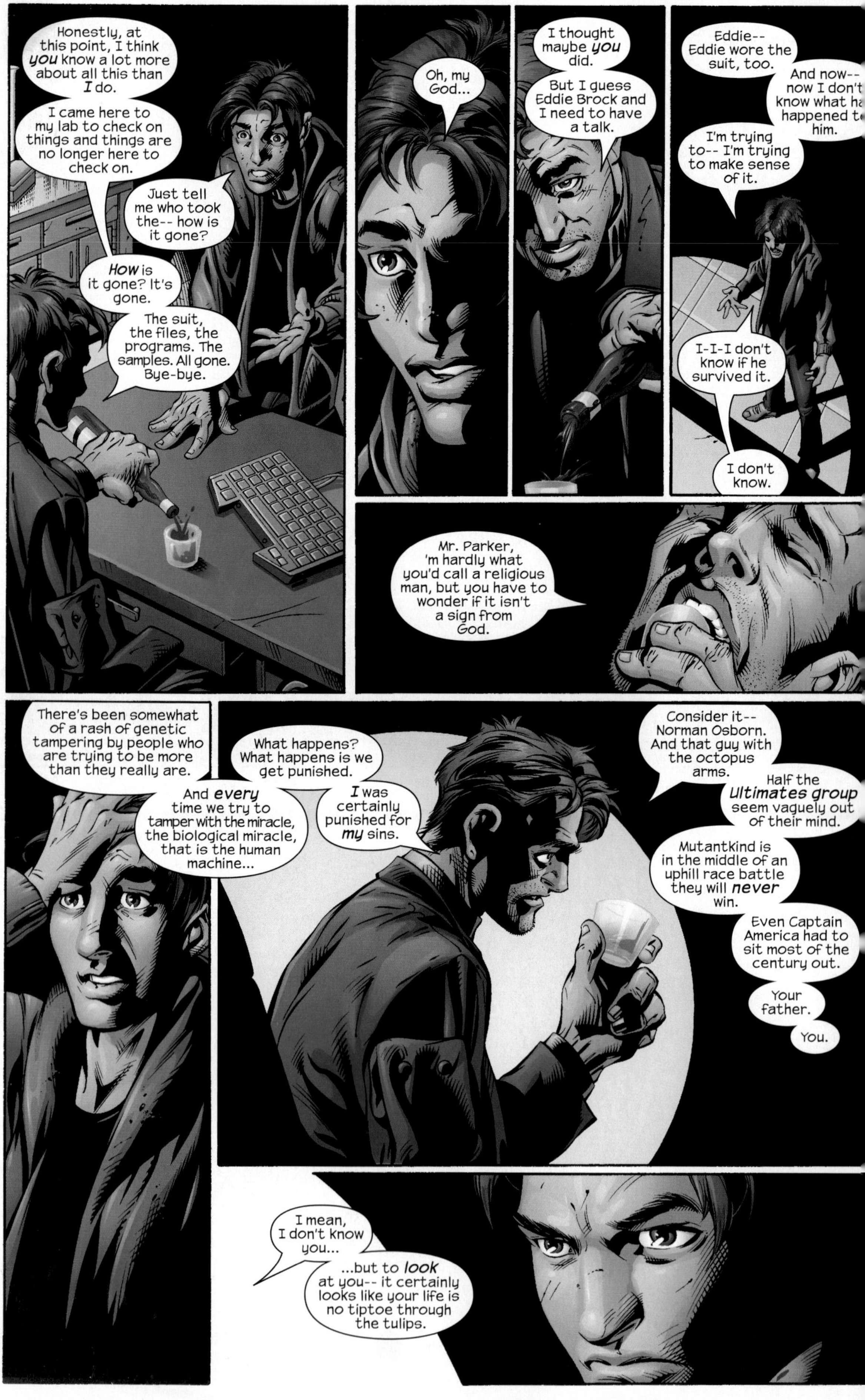
Honestly, at this point, I think you know a lot more about all this than I do.
I came here to my lab to check on things and things are no longer here to check on.
Just tell me who took the-- how is it gone?
HOW is it gone? It's gone.
The suit, the files, the programs. The samples. All gone. Bye-bye.
Oh, my God...
I thought maybe you did.
But I guess Eddie Brock and I need to have a talk.
Eddie-- Eddie wore the suit, too.
And now-- now I don't know what ha happened to him.
I'm trying to-- I'm trying to make sense of it.
I-I-I don't know if he survived it.
I don't know.
Mr. Parker, 'm hardly what you'd call a religious man, but you have to wonder if it isn't a sign from God.
There's been somewhat of a rash of genetic tampering by people who are trying to be more than they really are.
And every time we try to tamper with the miracle, the biological miracle, that is the human machine...
What happens? What happens is we get punished.
I was certainly punished for my sins.
Consider it-- Norman Osborn. And that guy with the octopus arms.
Half the Ultimates group seem vaguely out of their mind.
Mutantkind is in the middle of an uphill race battle they will never win.
Even Captain America had to sit most of the century out.
Your father.
You.
I mean, I don't know you...
...but to look at you-- it certainly looks like your life is no tiptoe through the tulips.

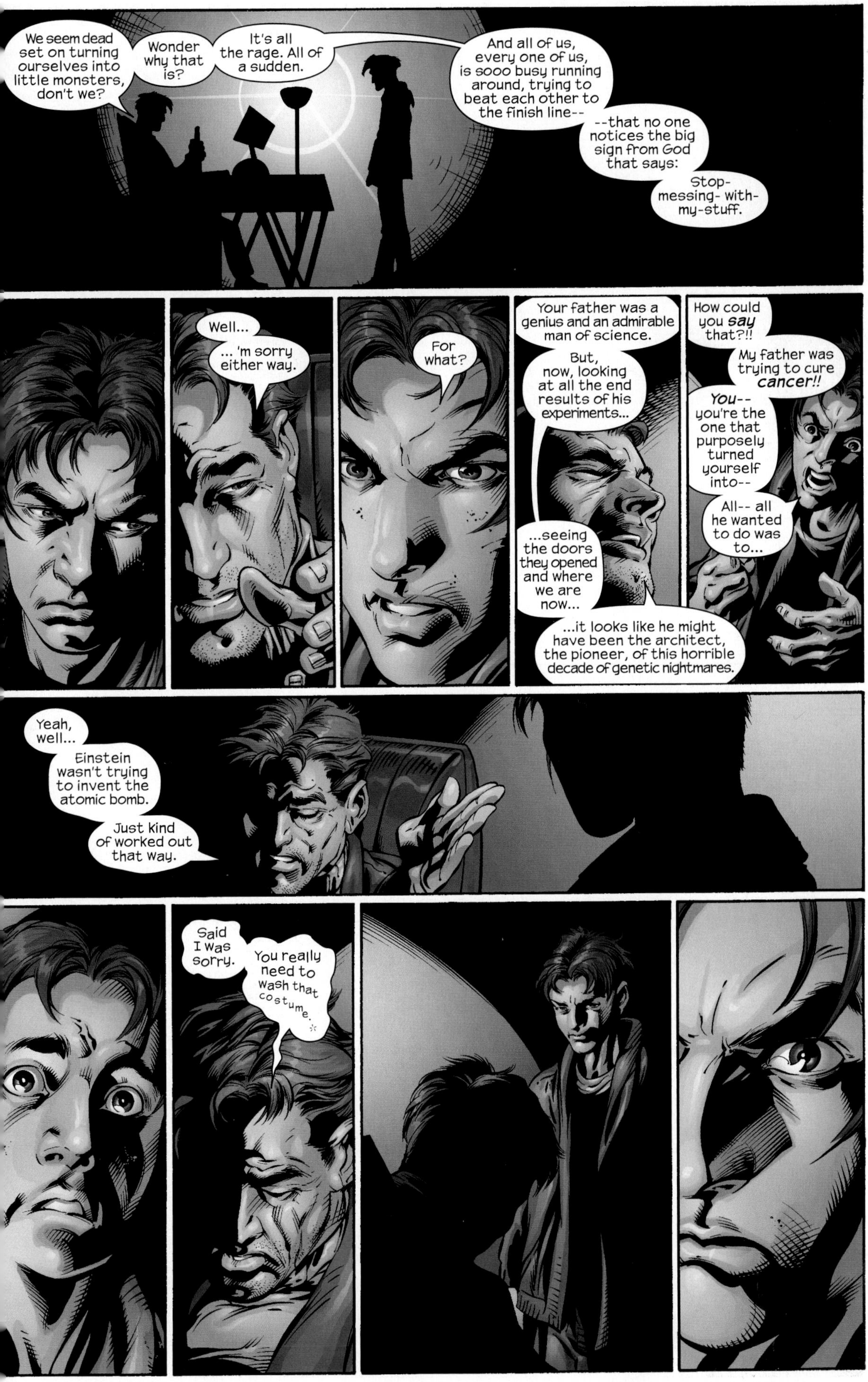
We seem dead set on turning ourselves into little monsters, don't we?
Wonder why that is?
It's all the rage. All of a sudden.
And all of us, every one of us, is sooo busy running around, trying to beat each other to the finish line--
--that no one notices the big sign from God that says:
Stop-messing- with-my-stuff.
Well...
... 'm sorry either way.
For what?
Your father was a genius and an admirable man of science.
But, now, looking at all the end results of his experiments...
...seeing the doors they opened and where we are now...
...it looks like he might have been the architect, the pioneer, of this horrible decade of genetic nightmares.
How could you say that?!!
My father was trying to cure cancer!!
You-- you're the one that purposely turned yourself into--
All-- all he wanted to do was to...
Yeah, well...
Einstein wasn't trying to invent the atomic bomb.
Just kind of worked out that way.
Said I was sorry.
You really need to wash that costume.

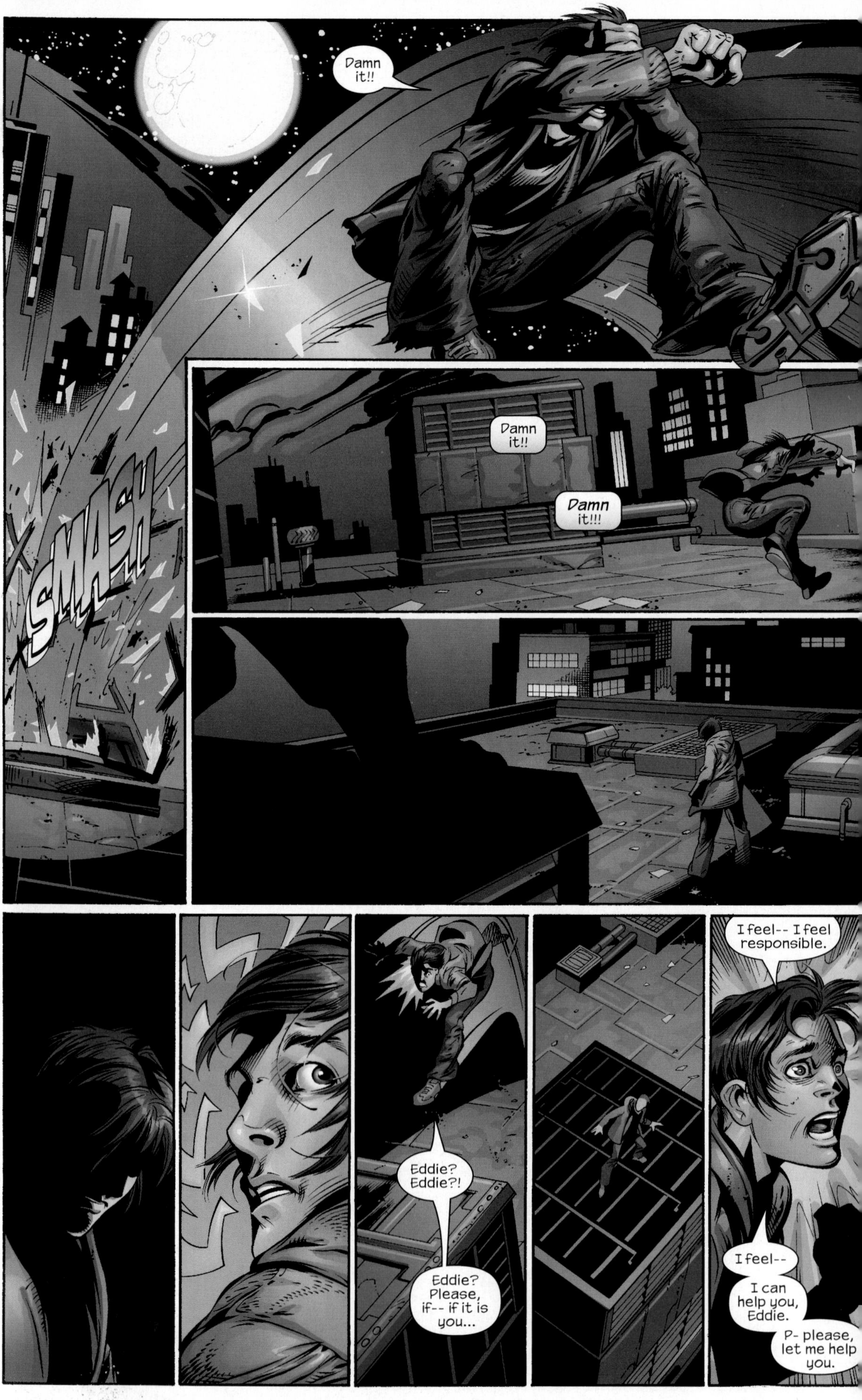
Damn it!!
SMASH
Damn it!!
Damn it!!!
Eddie? Eddie?!
Eddie? Please, if-- if it is you...
I feel-- I feel responsible.
I feel--
I can help you, Eddie.
P- please, let me help you.

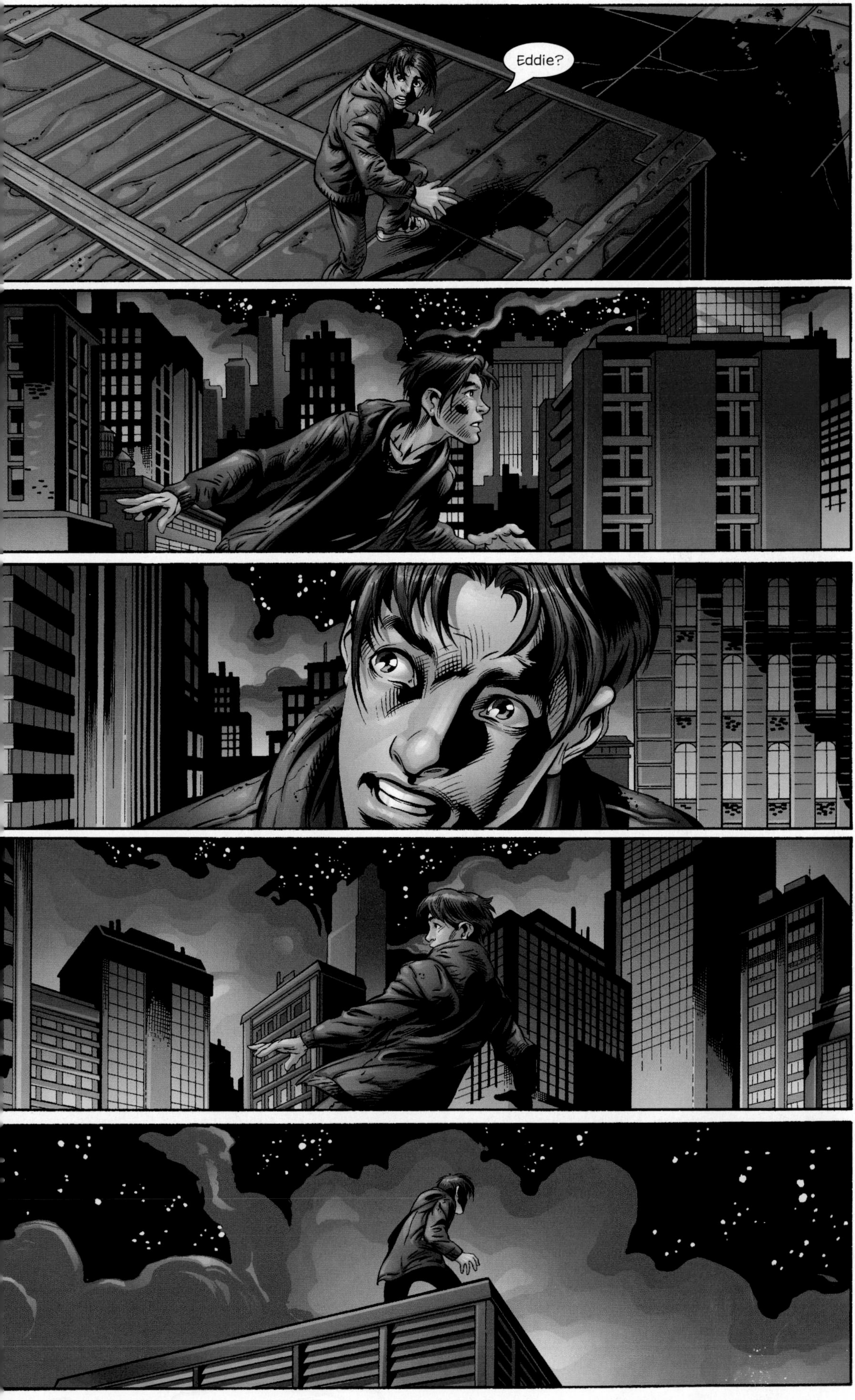
Eddie?

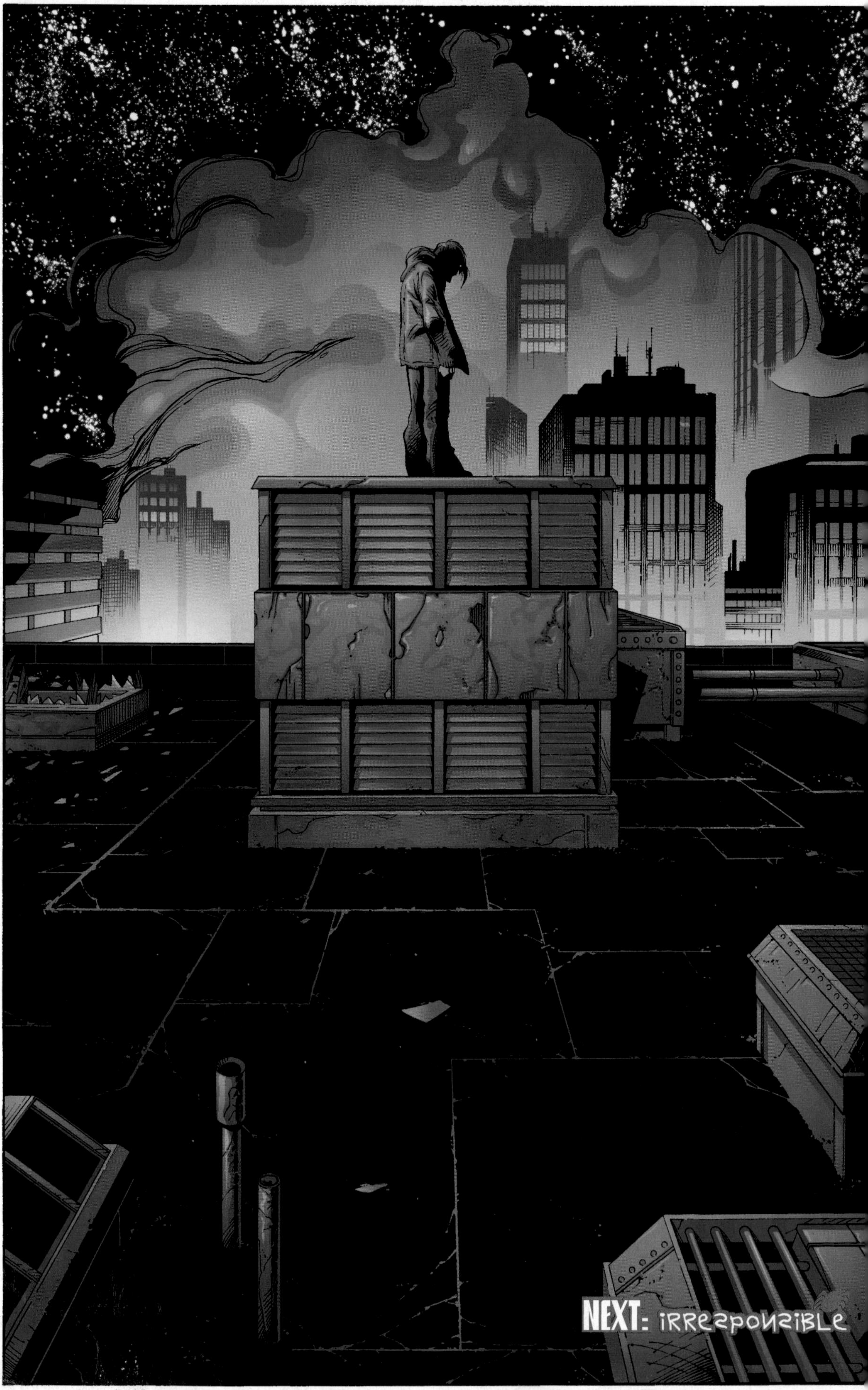
NEXT: IRRESPONSIBLE